BISHOP CURTIS
OF WILMINGTON

Love + blessing to all
Ys faithfully in xt
A. A. Curtis.
Bp. Titr. of Echinus

BISHOP CURTIS OF WILMINGTON

THE LIFE AND WRITINGS OF
RT. REV. ALFRED ALLEN CURTIS, D.D. (1831-1908)
SECOND BISHOP OF WILMINGTON, DELAWARE
AND FORMER EPISCOPALIAN PASTOR

Compiled by

The Sisters of the Visitation
WILMINGTON, DELAWARE

Prefaces by

James Cardinal Gibbons of Baltimore
and
Bishop Robert E. Mulvee of Wilmington

TAN BOOKS AND PUBLISHERS, INC.
Rockford, Illinois 61105

Nihil Obstat: Remigius Lafort, S.T.L.
                Censor

Imprimatur: ✠ John Cardinal Farley
                Archbishop of New York
                October 12, 1913

Republished in 1991 by TAN Books and Publishers, Inc. The 1991 printing of this book was made possible by the generosity of M. Catherine Long.

Library of Congress Catalog Card No.: 91-67821

ISBN: 0-89555-456-9

Printed and bound in the United States of America.

TAN BOOKS AND PUBLISHERS, INC.
P.O. Box 424
Rockford, Illinois 61105

1991

DECLARATION

According to the decree of Urban VIII, we declare that if we have made use of any terms of veneration in this book, they are meant solely in the sense authorized by Holy Church, to whose judgment we submit with filial affection.

PREFACE

By Cardinal Gibbons

FOR many reasons I am glad to introduce and recommend the "Life" of the Right Reverend Alfred A. Curtis, D.D.

Although he was a self-educated — in contradistinction to a college-bred — man, yet he early attained to real scholarship in ecclesiastical learning. His knowledge of the Sacred Scriptures, which he read in their original Hebrew and Greek, and of the Fathers of the Church, also read in their Greek and Latin texts, was deep and accurate. From these pure sources of Christian truth he drew rich material for his unique preaching, his sermons portraying an originality of thought, a precision of language and an earnestness of delivery peculiarly his own. Moreover, his character of sterling honesty, his hatred of sham, his practices of mortification, sense of duty and many other virtues are even stronger motives for writing his biography.

Then there was that test, proof of religious faith and love, next to martyrdom: that uprooting of himself from dear lifelong surroundings, that tearing of tendrils and breaking asunder of interlacing branches of personal friends and religious bonds, suffered by every man who is transplanted into a higher place of spiritual obedience in the vineyard of the Lord.

While for these reasons I commend the subject of this book, I congratulate the writers, the Sisters of the Visitation of Wilmington, who have surprised me by bringing to light letters of keenest interest. This is all the more delightful, as I had fancied that the

Preface

good Bishop's hatred of notoriety had made it quite impossible to gather any such documentary evidence of his life-story.

From what I have already perused of the manuscript copy of " The Life," I feel sure that it will not only charm and edify the many personal friends of Bishop Curtis in Maryland and Delaware, but I also hope that as the Life of Newman in England, so that of Bishop Curtis in America, may become a signboard, pointing out to many a religious traveller " the way and the truth and the life." John xiv. 6.

J. CARD. GIBBONS.

THE CATHEDRAL, BALTIMORE,
    Feast of Saint Mark, 1913.

PREFACE TO THE 1991 PRINTING

By Bishop Mulvee of Wilmington

RT. REV. ALFRED ALLEN CURTIS, D.D., PRIEST AND BISHOP

THE Sisters of the Visitation showed great wisdom and care when some eighty years ago, shortly after the death of Alfred Allen Curtis, second Bishop of Wilmington, they compiled and published in one volume his life, sermons and writings. For the greater part of this century that study volume has memorialized the far-reaching accomplishments of his saintly and productive life, and has documented the living legend that grew up about him from eyewitnesses.

Stories have circulated from time to time about a Bishop who rode his bicycle up and down the highways of the peninsula or who regularly boarded a train on weekends to go to the outposts of the diocese to minister in place of a pastor who had become ill. There are more stories about a bishop who was as comfortable with Hebrew, Greek and the classics as he was with sharp business tactics, who was as eloquent in public address as he was devout in prayer, who was austere in his own self-discipline, and who revelled in sailing and fishing on the Eastern Shore.

This bishop was especially beloved to the Sisters of the Visitation because of the significant role he played in their transformation from a teaching to a contemplative community in Wilmington. As a priest in Baltimore, he had become a close friend of the Abell family, then publishers of *The Baltimore Sun.*

ix

Rt. Rev. A. A. Curtis, D.D.

As spiritual director to Sister Mary Joseph Abell, Bishop Curtis was instrumental in bringing her to Wilmington, where her inheritance was invested to endow a new monastery. He served as spiritual director to the Visitation Sisters until he died.

Baltimore's Cardinal James Gibbons showed great confidence in sending his secretary, Alfred Curtis, to shepherd the relatively undeveloped Delmarva Peninsula [consisting of portions of Delaware, Maryland and Virginia], and in charging him to free the young diocese of a million-dollar debt incurred by his predecessor, who had built eighteen churches in eighteen years. Bishop Curtis agreed to undertake both tasks and within ten years to return to Baltimore. That he did. In his decade of service to the Wilmington Diocese he showed particular solicitude for the rural missions, preaching in many country towns from a horse-drawn wagon, and taking pride in the establishment of a parish and school at the southernmost tip of the Diocese at Cape Charles, Virginia.

With the passing of time, the living legend has faded a bit, and a new look at Bishop Curtis' excellent qualities as priest, scholar and leader is appropriate. The story of his journey of faith as a convert is as inspiring to those searching for religious truth now as it was in his own day.

Bishop Curtis was indeed our own. His boyhood days, early ministry, ten years of episcopate, last Mass and burial all took place within the confines of the Diocese of Wilmington. I am delighted with the prospect of a second printing of the "life and characteristics" of this noteworthy predecessor.

—MOST REVEREND ROBERT E. MULVEE
Bishop of Wilmington
July 11, 1991

x

AUTHOR'S INTRODUCTION

THIS humble sketch, as simple and unpretending as the life of the noble soul whose characteristics it endeavors so inadequately to portray, is the fruit of obedience. Furnished with this passport in which we are told "all is safe," we have every hope that our labors will be blessed, and should the perusal of this biography make our readers better acquainted with the holy Bishop, or inspire a deeper love of the spiritual life, our mission will be accomplished.

Should any be tempted to think the Bishop's fasting and penance too austere, his long hours of prayer extreme, his love of poverty and simple living eccentric, and his views incompatible with modern ideas, let them for a moment consider the lives of other men eminent for holiness, and note the presence of these characteristics in a marked degree. The Bishop was in the world, but conspicuously out of it, while his wonderful knowledge was veiled by a modest simplicity. He was always hard on himself, but his tenderness and leniency for others could scarcely be exceeded.

Afflicted with the true homesickness of the saints he lived on a plane elevated above the low and perishable things of earth, and his occupation with the invisible world caused him to soar to the Infinite, where in the extremity of his anguish he exclaimed, "I long to be dissolved and to be with Christ."

CONVENT OF THE VISITATION, WILMINGTON, DELAWARE,
Feast of Our Lady of Good Counsel, April 26, 1913.

Letter of Right Reverend John J. Monaghan, Bishop of Wilmington, to the Sisters of the Visitation of Wilmington.

MY DEAR DAUGHTERS:

I have learned with genuine pleasure and satisfaction of your purpose of writing and publishing the " Life and Characteristics " of my predecessor of holy memory, the late Rt. Rev. Alfred A. Curtis, D.D., the second Bishop of Wilmington.

Knowing well as I do the intimate relations of your community with him, not only whilst Bishop of this Diocese, but also in the eleven years that followed his resignation of the See of Wilmington, during which time he came to you, week after week, to discharge for you the office of Confessor and Spiritual Director, I cannot but consider you eminently fitted for the work of writing his life. At the same time your grateful devotion to your saintly Father must make it for you a labor of love to gather from every possible source the details of his edifying life, and to interpret to others, who knew him, not as you knew him, the admirable character of this chosen servant of God.

May your undertaking be blessed with success, and may it help to keep alive amongst us the sweet memories of his virtues and apostolic zeal. May it serve also to perpetuate the holy influences which Bishop Curtis exercised over our beloved Diocese of Wilmington.

Yours faithfully in Christ,

✠JOHN J. MONAGHAN,
Bishop of Wilmington

Feast of St. Francis de Sales, January 29, 1913.

CONTENTS

CHAPTER I
1831–1862

CHAPTER II
1862–1872

CHAPTER III
1872

CHAPTER IV
1872 (continued)

CHAPTER V
1872–1875

Contents

xiv

Contents

Contents

PART SECOND

ILLUSTRATIONS

THE LIFE OF
RT. REV. ALFRED ALLEN CURTIS, D.D.

RT. REV. A. A. CURTIS, D.D.

CHAPTER I

1831 – 1862

ALFRED ALLEN CURTIS was born on July the fourth, 1831, near Rehobeth in Somerset County, Maryland, of an old and very estimable family, whose ancestors had lived on the eastern shore of that State as early as the Colonial times. Shortly after his birth, his life being in danger, his parents called in a Methodist preacher to baptize him, although they attended the Episcopal church in the village.[1] Little is known of his early life, aside from the fact that he was devoted to reading and study, having inherited this taste from his father, who, besides being a farmer and county surveyor of the district, followed his attraction for teaching, and opened a small country school near Rehobeth.[2] It was here young Alfred had all the class instruction he ever received, which he put to such good use, that at the age of fourteen he had learned by heart the Latin grammar, and with the assistance of a dictionary he so completely mastered a Virgil which he bought at the time, that he never afterwards, as he himself admitted, had any difficulty in reading Latin. Taking the book as his only companion in his long walks through the forests, he at first read it from cover to cover three times; analyzing the words, noting

[1] The walls of the little brick Episcopal church at Rehobeth are all that remain to mark the place of worship, which the Bishop so faithfully attended in his boyhood and youth. His Father is buried in the church yard, but the place is so overgrown as to render it difficult to distinguish his grave. The bishop has been seen kneeling there in prayer, when making the rounds of his diocese.

[2] The village of Rehobeth on the Pocomoke River is of little importance to-day, having rather decreased in size since the year 1831; it now counts but two stores, and a few inhabitants. The Episcopal church has been replaced by one of the Presbyterian denomination.

3

closely the construction of sentences and even parsing them; he managed with his logical mind to grasp the whole of its contents. This encouraged him to pursue the study of Greek which he also accomplished by himself, and succeeded in learning this language so perfectly, that it is said by his contemporaries in the priesthood, he had hardly a superior in the United States. "He also acquired a complete mastery of Blackstone's Commentaries which added to his felicity of language, and the natural acumen of his logic, the rare power of legal exactitude," says one of his most devoted friends and admirers. He took pleasure in discussing the classics with the rustic lads at the grocery store, and it is needless to say, that this custom fell into disuse when our bright scholar left them to follow a higher vocation in life. But his most delightful pastime was reading and memorizing the English poets, and it was this recreation which served to store his mind with the wonderful vocabulary that he possessed in so eminent a degree, giving him at the same time an immense command of English. He learned by heart many of Shakespeare's plays, also Byron's Childe Harold, which he could recite with ease. It was at this early period of his life that the great strength and power of his character began to manifest itself. With the wisest of kings he might have said, "God has given me a good soul," and this soul he determined to cultivate; for the earnest youth was an obedient son, a conscientious worker and student; and last, but not least, faithful to God and his religion, according to the light he had received. He could be seen regularly assisting at the Sunday services, in the little church at Rehobeth. Alfred endeared himself to all by his remarkable candor, for his unswerving fidelity to truth made him detest the least duplicity in word or deed, so that he was often heard to reproach himself for having deceived his father, when following his attraction for reading, he would steal to the garret

Rt. Rev. A. A. Curtis, D.D.

where forbidden books were stored, and there spend hours devouring light and romantic literature. He was ardent and impulsive in whatever he undertook, whether work or play, and although of a quick and fiery nature, he possessed a most loving and forgiving disposition, which led him to be always the first to make satisfaction, in the little contentions he encountered with his young companions. This quickness of temper was to be his battlefield in after life, and those who witnessed the sublimity of his virtue can attest that he became one of the meekest and humblest of men, by his magnanimous courage in conquering himself, thus realizing that " He who ruleth his spirit is better than he who taketh cities." Prov. xvi. 32.

In his eighteenth year his father died, leaving a widow and six children: two sons and four daughters. The elder son having left home to seek his fortune on the frontiers of the far west, young Alfred determined to turn his talents to use, for the support of his mother and sisters. He secured a position as assistant teacher at an academy in the town of Princess Anne, Maryland, where he taught for four years.[1] His mother having decided to remove to Pocomoke City, it was there the gifted scholar had the inspiration to study for the ministry. He prepared himself with great care, and after considerable reading and study went to Berlin, Maryland, where he passed a very successful examination before a convention of Episcopal ministers, who immediately began to agitate the question as to the validity of his baptism. It was decided that the young Levite should be re-baptized before receiving orders. This was accordingly done, and the following copy of a license from his bishop, to perform church service in several parishes of the district in which he lived, shows

---

[1] The house in which the Bishop boarded, while teaching at the Academy in Princess Anne, is in use at present. He spent Saturday and Sunday with his mother at Pocomoke City, returning to teach at Princess Anne during the week, and it was in his walks between these two towns, a distance of several miles, that he learned his Greek verbs.

5

Rt. Rev. A. A. Curtis, D.D.

in what esteem the young aspirant was held by his superiors.

In the Name of God. Amen.

I do hereby license Alfred Allen Curtis of the Parish of Pocomoke, Worcester County, of whose soundness in the faith, and godly, righteous and sober life, I am well assured, to perform the service of the Church in the Parishes of Pocomoke, and St. John, Worcester County and Somerset, Somerset County, agreeably to the provisions, and under the limitations of Canon the Eleventh of General Convention of 1832; he being subject in all things pertaining to such performance of public religious service, to the advice and direction of the Reverend the Rectors of said Parishes. In testimony whereof, I have hereunto set my episcopal seal and signature, this first day of October in the year of our Lord, one thousand eight hundred and fifty-five, and of my episcopate the sixteenth.

WILLIAM ROLLINSON WHITTINGHAM,
(Seal) *Bishop of Maryland.*

The next year he was made a deacon and sent "to preach the Gospel, and perform all other functions appertaining to his office," — as the following lines show: "I hereby License the Reverend Alfred Allen Curtis by me ordained a Deacon, to Preach the Gospel, and perform all other functions appertaining to his office, in St. John's and Pocomoke Parishes, in Worcester County, as long as he shall continue a Deacon of the Diocese of Maryland, unless this License be previously withdrawn."

"In Testimony whereof, I have hereunto affixed my seal and signature, at Cambridge, this twenty-first day of September, in the year of our Lord one thousand eight hundred and fifty-six, and in the seventeenth year of my consecration."

WILLIAM ROLLINSON WHITTINGHAM,
(Seal) *Bishop of Maryland.*

6

Rt. Rev. A. A. Curtis, D.D.

If the veil of futurity could have been lifted, what an astounding revelation the ardent young deacon would have received. Laboring now under obedience to a bishop of the Anglican church, with that uprightness and singleness of purpose which was ever to distinguish him, he would have beheld himself after years of painful, anxious waiting, entering the true fold, constituted bishop and pastor of souls in this same vineyard of the Lord. Could his thoughts have been revealed, doubtless, he himself would have marvelled at the providence of God, bringing him into these same fields of his previous labors, to spend himself in seeking and finding the lost sheep of Israel, after the heroic example of so many missionary bishops of America. But all this was as yet the secret of God.

In the year 1859 he received orders according to the ritual of the Protestant Episcopal church, and was immediately sent to Baltimore, to assist Doctor Rankin of St. Luke's Church, which was beginning to adopt ritualistic practices. From thence he was transferred to a small congregation in Frederick, Maryland, and thence to Chestertown, Kent County, Maryland.

This happy return to his rural missions filled his soul with joy, and increased if possible those irresistible longings for solitude, which attracting him from his youth, now pursued him everywhere. It was his chief delight when not engaged with work, to walk alone, through trackless lands and unfrequented woods. This must have been God's way of revealing Himself to this pure soul, which learned the art of communing with God through His creatures; for he comprehended the language of all, and each in its way spoke to him of its Creator.

He loved in after years to recall the scenes of his early life, and held in tender remembrance objects and places associated with his childhood and youth. He often spoke of the profusion of blackberries and cherries, of the peaches "large as saucers," produced

7

on the eastern shore of Maryland, and became quite aroused when his hearers doubted these wonderful stories.

When making the visitation of his diocese as Bishop of Wilmington, he willingly went out of his way to visit these hallowed spots, and could be seen in the churchyard at Pocomoke City, kneeling respectfully at the graves of his mother and sisters. He was heard to say: "If I have a special affection for any part of my diocese it is for the pines, the creeks, the marshes and even the mosquitoes of the eastern shore," where:

> "Each hazel copse, each greenly-tangled bower
> Is sacred to some well-remembered hour."

It was during the three years which preceded his entrance into a wider field of action, that he began to lead a life of deeper study and reflection. He understood the claims God had upon his heart, and conceived a higher idea of sacrifice, such as the priesthood demands, for he was always at heart a priest. This caused him a little later to sever a cherished tie which he now began to look upon as an obstacle, to that perfect consecration and dedication of his life to the salvation of souls. He was then only in his twenty-eighth year, in the vigor of life, and of a robust constitution, possessing a strength of mind and body above the common, of which his brilliant florid complexion was the index. His clear, honest blue eye revealed a depth of religious sincerity, while a certain seriousness pervading his whole exterior gave him an ascendency over others, and portrayed the self-discipline he had already acquired over the impetuosity of his strong irascible nature. He was above medium height, of a light build and graceful mien, with a modest droop of the head to one side, which all the efforts of a loving mother had not succeeded in correcting, while his amiable manner and winning smile gained all — even the unruly boys of his catechetical class. On one occasion, whether by thoughtlessness or wanton mischief, one of the boys sat upon his new silk beaver, which he had carefully placed in a corner of the first pew. When at the close of the lesson the young minister took up his hat to leave, the preceptor of the boys perceiving the mishap was covered with shame and confusion, and hastening towards his pastor, with profuse apologies, begged him to wait until another hat could be procured; whereupon with a smile, Mr. Curtis replied, " It is good enough for me," and thrusting his fist into the crushed crown, smoothed it out, and continued afterwards to wear the hat, as if nothing had happened.

If as the Holy Scripture says, heaven is borne away by the violent *only,* is it not evident that this young Levite was already like the just man, preparing in his heart admirable ascensions of virtue, which were but the dawning of those heroic acts that characterized his after life?

CHAPTER II

1862 – 1872

IT was in the year 1862 that the young minister was elected to the Rectorship of Mt. Calvary Episcopal Church in Baltimore. Here a very devout and select congregation awaited him, — who, like another Baptist, would become to them a burning and a shining light, — burning by his zeal for the glory of God's House, and shining by the practice of the most admirable virtues. His long retreat in the rural missions had prepared him for this contact with the world, and his whole bearing had the stamp of a man of prayer.

For the next nine years he could be seen laboring indefatigably for the salvation of souls, and endearing himself to the white and colored congregations committed to his care. He had a little study adjoining the vestibule of the church where he spent most of his time reading, studying and living a very ascetic life. He fasted whole days at a time, sleeping on the bare floor at night, and praying much. He took up a most scrupulous and faithful study of the Bible, and to enable himself to make more thorough researches he went to a learned Jewish rabbi, living in Baltimore, with whom he studied Hebrew. This brought him in close contact with the Fathers of the Church, in whom he felt an intense interest, especially the old Greek Fathers — Origen, Saints Basil, Gregory Nazianzen and Clement of Alexandria. Thus in a short time he became more and more imbued with the truth, and while drinking refreshing draughts of Catholic doctrine at its source, he found he believed everything our holy Mother the Church teaches. Now he must buy a Roman Breviary,

The Bishop when Rector of
Mt. Calvary Protestant Episcopal Church,
Baltimore.
–1862–

and although he had never heard of an Ordo, he learned how to say the Office from the instructions given in the beginning of this book, but, as these instructions are for choirs, and not for individuals or for the Office in private, the young minister charged himself with saying, not only the Office of the day, but likewise that of the Dead, as well as the little Office of our Blessed Lady, which consumed some three or four hours daily. The Preparation and Thanksgiving for holy Mass, which he also found in the Breviary, struck him as so beautiful, that he made an English translation which he learned by heart, and repeated every day, before and after what he called " *his mass.*" He also styled himself a priest, wearing a cassock and biretta. One day two gentlemen passing the church and seeing the door open, entered, and were accosted by the pious minister, who replying to their inquiries as to whether it was a Catholic church, and if he was a priest, answered boldly, " Yes." At the same moment he was afflicted with such qualms of conscience, that he felt himself obliged to approach these gentlemen before they left the church, and to say to them, " I thought myself a priest, but I am not, and you will find the Catholic church three squares from here." This was the initial step towards his conversion, for could Almighty God ever allow such unselfish uprightness to go unrew   'ed? He was already inundating this soul of pra   special graces, which would be needed for   flict. Late one evening, it was Satur-
d   rly gentleman passing Mt. Cal-
                     home from St. Ignatius, " the
                  ay," attracted by the brilliant
                 ty to know what could be
               ng, at so late an hour.
               threshold of the door,
               id to the Mother of
               preacher. " This
               mpson to him-

self, and from that day until he heard of the entrance of Mr. Curtis into the Church, which was one year later, he never ceased praying for him, saying the rosary every day for his conversion. He ever retained the remembrance of that sermon, which had touched him so profoundly, and when Mr. Curtis was made a priest and stationed at the Cathedral, Mr. Thompson was among the first to become one of his most devoted clients and devout penitents.

About this time, a prominent clergyman of the advanced Ritualistic section of the Anglican church was visiting America, and Mr. Curtis invited him to officiate at Mt. Calvary. He followed so closely the Catholic ceremonial, and imitated so well the movements of a priest at the altar, that he was really taken for a *Roman* in disguise, by the misguided witnesses of his actions.

All kinds of rumors were now being circulated, and some of the more fervent members of the congregation, becoming alarmed, reported to their Bishop that Mr. Curtis had introduced a " *Roman priest* " in disguise, who celebrated " *Mass in English.*" Mr. Curtis was summoned by the Bishop, who, slow to believe the reports, wished to question the pastor himself. Naturally enough, this attack on his veracity aroused a just feeling of indignation in the breast of the accused, who stoutly denied the charge, and strongly resented the accusation, saying, " I do not lie, nor have I ever lied in my life," hastily left the Bishop alone, sorely puzzled in his cogitations.

An inspiriting correspondence now took place between Bishop Whittingham and the Rector of Mt. Calvary church, which gives an insight to what was transpiring, and shows how each in his turn was striving to maintain what he considered the truth, — the Bishop conscientiously protecting his flock from what he looked upon as " the ravening wolf," the Presbyter, drawn by the whisperings of

Rt. Rev. A. A. Curtis, D.D.

Who is truth itself and cannot deceive, felt he could no longer resist their attractions.

In this same year a Pastoral regarding the Holy Eucharist was issued by Bishop Whittingham; and this was to bring to a culminating point the fears, perplexities and doubts, which beset the mind of the young minister, leading him at last, after further toils and struggles, to the center of Catholic Unity and Truth, which with so much steadfastness of purpose he had been seeking from his youth. Jesus in the Blessed Sacrament was his teacher and guide, and he, responding to the call, preached and defended Him, even before he knew the full value of this priceless treasure. It has been admitted by those who knew him most intimately, that his devotion of predilection was to the Blessed Sacrament, and in his daily walks he was seen stealthily visiting a Catholic church, in the suburbs of the city. There concealing himself behind one of the great pillars of the church, he poured forth his soul, in loving adoration and prayer.

The following letter will convey in part his earnestness in pursuing the cause he had so nobly and devoutly espoused.

Wednesday, November 8, 1871.

To the Rt. Rev. Wm. Rollinson Whittingham, DD., LL.D., *Bishop of Maryland.*

My dear Bishop:

I am very reluctantly but unavoidably about to give you pain. I have at last determined to resign my Rectorship at once, and to vacate it at the end of the year. Strict consistency demands no doubt that I should immediately close my mouth, but I desire to finish the ninth year of my Rectorship, and I desire also to give the vestry some time in which to procure another Rector. In the time beween this and the year's end, I will study not to contradict the Pastoral. And I will take

13

Rt. Rev. A. A. Curtis, D.D.

it for granted that you will not oppose my teaching under this proviso, during that short time. For a little while I can be silent, but the statements of Pastoral as to the Holy Eucharist I dare not even try to accept. I could turn back and become in body and soul twenty years younger, as soon as I could cease to believe, that my Master is in the Eucharist, and presented to me under the form of Bread and Wine, that I may adore, as well as eat and drink Him. If it is not the truth that the very Human and divine Christ is Himself first offered, for the living and the dead in the Holy Eucharist, and there put according to His whole Living Person into my very hands, to be then and there adored and endowed with all I am, and all I possess perpetually — there is no truth for me, at least no truth I greatly care to know. And as I dare not and will not try to accommodate myself to the Pastoral, so I dare not undertake to go on teaching, under that to which I am down to the root of myself, so intensely and irreversibly opposed. I could not teach without contradicting intentionally or unintentionally, what the Bishops have propounded. For as my own inner life, so all my teaching grows out of, and depends upon the fact, that the Lord is actually one with and present in the Eucharist, under the form of Bread and Wine as He was of old present in the stable, one with and under the form of Babyhood. I have no choice then, if I would remain honest but to resign work, which I can no longer discharge according to the mind of my Superiors. I am then resigning my work only, not my orders as you will understand. I feel profoundly that in my present state I am totally unfit to have the care of souls. Nothing remains but to ask you if it seems right to you, to keep my resignation to yourself. I wish to create as little talk as possible. One more thing does remain, namely, to thank you with all my heart for the truly fatherly forbearance and affection which you have ever shown towards me.

Rt. Rev. A. A. Curtis, D.D.

I shall never forget them, nor ever cease in return, to pray for you and yours. I need not ask you to pray for me, for I know you will do it unasked.

Very faithfully and affectionately

Yr. son in Ct.

A. A. CURTIS.

This beautiful letter drew forth the following reply from Bishop Whittingham, which has only to be read to prove that he was, or at least seemed to be, in good faith.

MADISON AVENUE, November 13, 1871.

MY DEAR CURTIS:

You rightly judged of your letter of Wednesday last, that it would give me pain. I think I have never received one that gave me more occasion for intense anxiety and regret. Receiving it, as I did, late in the evening before a day necessarily to be entirely given to duties for which I was under previous engagement, while in an ill condition of health, I found in the opening sentences ample reason for laying it aside, to be read entirely only when better prepared for its unwelcome contents. And when, on Friday, I found myself at leisure to give it my whole attention, the communication proved to be even less endurable than had been known by the opening announcement. It was bad enough that you should be led to think of resigning work in which there seemed to be so many reasons why you should find content and satisfaction; but it sadly aggravated the distressing nature of the tidings to be informed that the resignation had been resolved on in a spirit so different from any which I had ever known you to manifest before, and for an array of reasons which seemed to me, on your own presentation, so miserably insufficient. You represent your determination as taken because you are profoundly certain that you are totally unfit to retain the care of souls.

15

Rt. Rev. A. A. Curtis, D.D.

But of such total unfitness you neither give nor in any way intimate any other ground of proof, than your inability any longer to discharge your work, according to the mind of your Superiors.

And of that inability the whole evidence consists in the asserted impossibility, that you would continue to teach without contradicting intentionally or unintentionally what the Bishops have propounded in their Pastoral Letter, on a single point of doctrine concerning the Holy Eucharist.

Surely, never did a Christian priest contemplate the abandonment of the Exercise of his high office with less apparent cogency of reason! Had the Pastoral taught a doctrine of the Eucharist contrary to that which you state to be the ground of your own inner life and of all your teaching, it would indeed have become incumbent on you to do one of two things — *Either,* cease your work, *or* enter on a serious and thorough re-examination of your own views, to see if it might not be *possible,* that one Presbyter was in error, and nearly fifty of his Superiors right.

All that I have ever known of you would have led me to expect of you the adoption of the last alternative. But there is no such procedure until contrariety of doctrine do require it. Who has faulted the doctrine of the Real Presence even stated as you stated it, in the fullest strength of language which it is possible to use, without running into unscriptural, uncatholic and rationalistic presumption in definition?

Your objection is to a condemnation of a practical inference from that doctrine. You choose to infer from it that your Master presents Himself in His Blessed Sacrament to you under the Form of Bread and Wine to be adored; and having made that inference you speak of being intensely opposed, down to the very root of your nature to the authoritative document which takes a different view — not of doctrine, but of resulting privilege and duty. You declare that you do not

16

even try to receive its statements! But you do not and will not try to accommodate yourself to it! My dear Brother: I know you do not so mean it; but let me tell you plainly, this is the very way of talking of a heretic! It is now my turn to challenge you to give a word of proof that you have the Master's warrant for your inference.

I know the subterfuges by which over-eager devotion has tried to build up for itself a right without that warrant; and the far more objectionable boldness, bordering on profanity, by which human logic works the claim out of premises gotten by its own inventions on the mode of statement; but what I demand of you is our Lord's authority for inferring from His gift of Himself to you, that He makes it to be adored in it, and holding that inference against fifty of those whom He has set over you in His name, with such temerity or rather to offend His little ones by throwing up His commission to work among them for His sake, than give up your own individual convictions and cease your own individual innovations, in the public doctrine and worship of the church in which you are a minister. Dear Curtis: your letter talks about not daring to undertake or try to do certain things; let me tell you that it is far, very far worse daring to resolve on such a course without incomparably more reason than I have as yet any ground for thinking that you can show.

Your deeply grieved, but most truly loving friend
and brother,

W. R. WHITTINGHAM.

REV. A. A. CURTIS.

This called for another letter on the part of the ardent Presbyter, which shows how deeply his grateful and affectionate heart was wounded by the thought of inflicting pain upon him whom he revered as his Superior, and whom he loved as the best of friends. But

Rt. Rev. A. A. Curtis, D.D.

with that candor so characteristic of him, and true to the light which he had received, he gives without hesitation " a reason for the [faith] that is in him." 1 St. Peter iii. 15.

Tuesday afternoon, November 14, 1871.

To THE RT. REV. WM. R. WHITTINGHAM, D.D., *Bishop of Maryland.*

MY DEAR BISHOP:

I am deeply grateful to you for the affectionateness and gentleness with which your letter overflows. That letter is of a piece with all your conduct towards me. Indeed it pains me to pain you, and the more when I see you even under the pain dealing so leniently with me. I have not yet had time to weigh as I propose to weigh what you have said. I shall do so however with a desire to find in what you concede a door of escape from my present position. I must confess your interpretation of the Pastoral was a great surprise to me. Indeed it more than surprised, it bewildered me. I read and I must confess still read the Pastoral as condemning not only eucharistical adoration, but such a Presence of the Master in the Sacrament as " allows " such adoration. This point, however, I do not presume to debate with you. You must know better than I how to interpret your own words. And it was the suppressing both adoration and the Presence, which justifies adoration to be censured and disallowed, which disturbed me so very much, and threw me into a state which rendered me, as I said, totally unfit to retain the care of souls in this communion. It never for a moment came to me that the Bishops could mean to tolerate such a Presence as I held, and as I have stated to you while condemning to me, its entirely inevitable consequent, or rather accompaniment. I cannot at all see how Christ can be received as Christ without adoration. To say that He is present but is not to be

18

Rt. Rev. A. A. Curtis, D.D.

adored is to me only a certain way of saying that He is not veritably present at all. To say that I receive Him into my hands without the most prostrate adoration, is to my mind just the same as to say that I receive something which is called Christ, but in fact is not Christ. It was the condemnation as it seemed to me, not only of adoration but of any such Presence as suggests adoration which distressed me so much, and caused me to determine to hold my peace for the future. If I can see what you wish me to see as to the import of the Pastoral I will, but I cannot now promise to see that it will be honest to teach such a Presence as calls for adoration, while at the same time agreeing to seem to disbelieve in the propriety of adoration. A word more. Of course I can produce no explicit command of the Master calling upon to adore His Eucharistical Presence, nor can I find in Holy Writ any precise dogmatical statement of any use of the Articles of our Faith. My whole faith as formalized into dogmas is simply what the Church under the guidance of the Spirit of Truth has deduced from the statements of Holy Writ. The first of all truths, that God is a simple, indivisible essence entirely present in every point of space, is a deduction. The Homoousion is a deduction. And the Arians fought against it as merely a deduction. And eucharistical adoration is so much to me because it is to me a deduction, which the Church has made from the words " *This is* My Body, *This is* My Blood." In favor of a deduction of my own, I would not presume to set myself against even one Bishop, and still less against fifty, and one of them yourself. But because the Bishops to me seem to disallow a deduction which the Church has pronounced inevitable, therefore it is that I presume to differ from them. Certainly all my reading of antiquity as well as my understanding of the Church's *loving* will is to the effect that adoration is, and ever has been rendered to the Lord's Eucharistical Presence. It is

Rt. Rev. A. A. Curtis, D.D.

then as submitting to the Church, and not as presuming upon my own individual logic. Thank you again and again for all your kindness.

Very faithfully and affectionately,
Your son in Christ,
A. A. Curtis.

The answer of the Bishop to the earnest, pathetic appeal of his doubting and enquiring disciple is severe in its tenor, and while striving to asseverate his arguments, he seems to lose in the contest by the weakness of his reasonings.

Madison Avenue, Wednesday, November 15, 1871.

My dear Curtis:

Your last note gives me a new perplexity. Your kind estimate of what you lovingly accept as the " gentleness " of my letter answering your announcement of intention to resign, seems to have occasioned a misconstruction of the purport of that letter.

You seem to have construed it into an acceptance of your views, in so far as they differ from those set forth in the Pastoral Letter, and an Endeavor to make you see something in the Letter which may enable you, retaining and inculcating those views, to continue the Exercise of the Ministry.

What I meant to do, was, first, to remonstrate against an act on grounds which, by your own showing, did not require it; and, secondly, to urge that you had no sufficient grounds for the unfounded inferential doctrine and practice which you maintain as against the teaching of the Pastoral.

I must say frankly that your present position is much less to my mind than before. You seem to me coolly to assume infallibility and absolute independence in the Exercise of your Pastoral functions, and to claim for your own individual, ministerial actions the functions of a General Council, in asserting doctrinal inferences and liturgic usages. If on deliberation you shall find the teaching of the Episcopate of the Catholic church in which you minister, capable of accommodation to your decisions on points of inferential doctrine and ritual, you will accept it — if not — not. Is that the proper relation of a Presbyter to the Church in which he ministers?

While showing you that the Pastoral Letter did not do what your first letter assumed that it had done, I had no intention to be understood to accept all the particulars of your statement of your own (inferential) doctrine of the Presence. Most certainly I do not admit that you are right in holding the belief of a Presence, capable of being put into the hands or designed to be adored in the visible Elements; still less, that you have any right, as a Presbyter of this church, to teach such belief or publicly to practise or to inculcate any ritual based on its assumption. I have long known, with intense grief of heart, that you were following a course of teaching which, in my judgment, distorted and perverted the Gospel of Salvation by assigning undue prominence to one of its fundamental portions, to the dwindling, if not exclusion, of the rest.

The spinal column is the noblest part of the human trunk; but its undue development produces a hunchback cripple. So the undue development of Eucharistic doctrine may utterly deform and cripple a pastoral system of doctrine otherwise worthy of all praise.

Testimony of every kind represents to me the existence of such an undue " dividing of the word " in your course of teaching, by sermon and catechism, in the past two years. I should be unfaithful both to you and to the people who, although your people, are also my people, if I allowed the occasion afforded me by this correspondence to pass without warning you against what seems to me so great an error.

It was to be expected that the pursuance of such a

course of partial teaching would expose the teacher to the danger of error in the exaggeration of unduly favored doctrine, and over-curious discussion, perhaps presumptuous definition, on points of faith purposely made mysterious, and so kept by the Church Catholic in all her normal teachings and ritual.

I cannot but perceive such exaggeration and rashness of definition in both your letters, in relation to the Presence of our Lord in the Sacrament of the communication of His most precious Body and Blood.

Your tone, in regard to the matter, is not what my past knowledge of your nature and experience of your conduct would have led me to expect from you under the circumstances. It is, for you, unnatural and harsh. It is clear to me that one-sided devotion and study have produced an unhealthy tone and temper in your mind, in relation to this particular department of your ministry.

Your congregation, it is my full persuasion, would be better taught and profited, and you yourself a more able and effective minister of the Gospel of Christ, if you would be silent on the subject of the Sacrament of the Eucharist, both in catechising and in preaching for half or even a whole year. Look at the proportion given to Eucharistic doctrine in the apostolic teaching. Would St. Paul or St. John have taught the Gospel as you have been teaching it the last two years at Mt. Calvary?

I know, of course, what you have to say about prevalent false doctrine, irreverence, and so on. But I know, too, that there is a bounden duty to study rightly to divide (ὀρθοτόμειν) the word of truth; and that duty cannot be fulfilled by a Pastor who spends most of his time in harping upon the one string of one side of the doctrine of one Sacrament.

My dear Curtis, I write very plainly and freely to you because I know your love for me and you know mine for you, and the time is not far off from either of us (certainly not for me) when a plain word spoken in love will be known as more precious than a lifetime of unmeaning compliment or deceptious reticence. I speak to you as a son in Christ. Weigh well a father's warning.

You are in a dangerous path. This Pastoral Letter furnishes an occasion for pause and consideration. Listen to the voice of the Pastorate in it, and lay aside the unwise reliance on private judgment which is betraying you into making a pope of A. A. Curtis, and be content to be advised and guided by those on whom the Lord has laid the responsibility of government in His Church, and believe that your Master may be served as faithfully and as effectually in other ways, as in a will worship (ἐθελοθρησκεία) of your own private inference, from the Church's inference, from His gracious Word of Promise, given to be accepted and obeyed, and *not honoured* by being made the mere hook on which to hang man's inventions of what he deems proper uses of a Great Gift offered, with no suggestion of such Employment.

Ever — in whatever perplexity and grief of heart, still none the less —

Your true loving friend and faithful brother,
W. R. WHITTINGHAM.

REV. A. A. CURTIS.

Things seemed now to have reached a climax, for after much questioning on the part of the church authorities, and great discussion among the congregation as to how matters would be settled, Mr. Curtis, after tendering his resignation, publicly announced his intention of going abroad, at the same time promising his people he would take no step towards Rome until he had consulted the authorities of the Anglican church. The following edifying letter from the vestrymen of Mt. Calvary Church, accepting most reluctantly the resignation of their pastor, proves their esteem for him, as well as the devoted attachment of the congregation he had served so faithfully.

BALTIMORE, December 30, 1871.
Vestry-room of Mt. Calvary Church.

REV. A. A. CURTIS,

REV. AND DEAR SIR:

In consideration of the motives which have prompted you to tender to us your resignation of the Rectorship of Mt. Calvary Church, we, your vestry, feel constrained to accept it.

We do so with reluctance and heartfelt pain, but not without the hope that in God's good providence the reasons which in your judgment have rendered this step necessary may be so far removed that you may be restored to the flock which so thoroughly trusts and deeply loves you.

We cannot express to you in words our sense of your self-sacrificing zeal and loving care, but on behalf of this congregation and for ourselves we would renew to you the assurance of our devoted attachment, and of our recognition of your perfect faithfulness in the discharge of every pastoral duty, during all the years of your ministry among us.

We will pray that God may always abundantly bless you, and have you evermore in His most holy keeping.

Your faithful friends and servants in the church.

BERNARD CARTER,
GEO. G. CAREY,
S. C. CHEW,
WM. D. MARTIN,
M. J. DE ROSSET,
SAML. B. FLEMING,
JAMES McANDERSON,
                    Vestry.

CHAPTER III

1872

IT was early in the month of March of 1872 that Mr. Curtis took passage on a steamer bound for Liverpool; but before leaving America he again addressed himself to Bishop Whittingham, giving him a very explicit and detailed account of his reasons for resigning his pastoral charge. He had retired to a small country town, to calm his mind amid the tempest of fears, anxieties and doubts which assailed him. His soul was oppressed with sorrow, and his heart was a prey to the most poignant grief at the thought of separating from his beloved people; nevertheless, he recognized " the Will of God in this unfortunate affair," as he afterwards said. Although weighed down by severe indisposition of body, with a superhuman energy he wrote in his strong, vigorous style the following letter, which for its clearness, integrity and perspicuity may be compared to a veritable masterpiece of wisdom and logic.

NEWTOWN, February 14, 1872.

TO THE RT. REV. WM. R. WHITTINGHAM, D.D.,
   Bishop of Maryland.

RT. REV. FATHER:

Indisposition and changes of place have combined to retard my answer to your last letter. In that letter there is one thing only of which I propose to take notice, namely, your complaint that I have of late avoided you and have given you no opportunity of saying what you have to say against the step I am meditating.[1]

This complaint is from your standpoint entirely just. I go further and acknowledge that even to myself it seems as if it might have been in some respects better had I at least made the attempt to confer with you freely, as to the things which I have been for years revolving without reaching (until a little while ago) any conclusion. Why is it then that I have studiously kept away from you and debarred you from all opportunity of giving me a single word of counsel? I will tell you. Let me remind you then that my avoidance of you is no new thing. It has been growing for years. For years you have known from myself nothing at all of that with which my mind has been most filled.

I began with thinking you the very embodiment of everything Catholic. Then I consulted you as to everything. I deferred to you as to everything. I not only did not venture to do, but I did not even venture to believe anything by you disallowed. But as time went on I was constrained to assent to things known to be extremely repugnant to you. One of those things was the goodness of the Roman Communion and the unreasonableness and wickedness of the hostility with which that Communion is by almost all Anglicans regarded. We claiming to be merely one of the coördinate branches of the Church I saw that we had no right to denounce, condemn, hate and vilify a body in antiquity at least equalling, and in size far transcending our own Communion. I acted upon what I saw, and being sure that the sin of sins in the Anglican Communion is hatred of and injustice towards the Roman obedience, I ever spoke both in public and private in behalf of that obedience. It seemed to me right to

---

[1] In a letter dated February 5, Bishop Whittingham had reproached him for not having opened his mind to him "on the subject of his doubts and perplexities, and thereby given him an opportunity of offering counsel or instruction on the step he meditated."

make a great deal of one of our faults, and as little as possible of the faults of our brethren. And when I had learned to recognize practically the coördinacy with us in the Church of the Roman Communion, I began to draw apart from you and to close my mind to you, because (you must excuse me for saying it) I know few who dislike Rome as intensely as you dislike her, and I know none less capable of doing her justice. I could not agree with you, because I stood too much in awe of you, and because too I knew you to be totally impervious to anything whatever meant to make you think more favorably of *Romanism*. Neither could I play the hypocrite and leave you to infer from my silence that I had accepted, when in fact I had totally repudiated, the dire things which upon the very slightest provocation I knew you to be ever ready to utter against Rome.

Nothing remained, therefore, but to keep my thoughts to myself, since any propounding of them to you would either have produced strife or else would have rendered me liable to the charge of hypocrisy. A single fact will sufficiently illustrate what I am saying. I went then into your study some time ago for a specific purpose, meaning to come out the moment my business had been transacted. My errand had been discharged and I was coming away when with great glee you stopped me and took me aside to show me — what? A wretched picture, wherein his Holiness Pius the IX was seated, blowing soap bubbles; Cardinal Antonelli standing at his side and holding the vessels whence the bubbles were blown. The bubbles were each labelled "*Major Excommunication!*" I looked with sickness of soul at this fearful caricature, and yet such was my awe of you that I even smiled, asked questions, and without doubt, on the whole, so behaved as to leave on your mind the impression that the Pope's "Excommunication" was almost as much of a joke to me as to you.

Rt. Rev. A. A. Curtis, D.D.

I went out fiercely angry with myself and profoundly disgusted with you, and with the whole system of which you are a fair exponent. Had I been brave enough I should that very evening have renounced you and Anglicanism. A Bishop shaking his sides with laughter, when by the profane of the profane, the Primate of all Christendom is caricatured. A Bishop making very merry when seeing an Excommunication, at least as valid as his own, compared to a soap bubble. Such a man, I said, cannot be a Bishop save in name. I ought to renounce him, denounce him and look elsewhere for Bishops who are Bishops indeed.

For days I despised myself for my cowardice in not telling you what I thought of the picture, and of you for regarding the picture as a good joke. And yet I knew that had I spoken plainly the result would have been a quarrel, and a separation once for all.

Is it wonderful then that I avoided you when at each interview I incurred the danger of falling into hypocrisy, or of provoking a collision which, on my part certainly and on yours probably, would have been a wrathful and disastrous one? For I knew perfectly if I once began to speak I should warm in speaking, and should not stop short of such an outpouring as would drive you to extremes. For the reasons given then I for years avoided you more and more. At last came the late most miserable convention. It gave me my death blow. It made me once for all see that I could no longer go on balancing myself between the Roman and Anglican Communions, but that I must choose the one and disallow the other. For years I honestly tried to believe in both, and to render allegiance to both. But when the Pastoral came under my eyes, I felt in my soul, though I did not at once clearly acknowledge to myself, that I must set my house in order and die to the Anglican Communion.

I did not consult you for the reasons already given, and for the further reason that I saw clearly you could not in the least help me — no matter how freely and fully I might bring myself to confer with you. For we not only differ radically as to what the truth is, but as to how the truth is to be ascertained. You appeal to the Bible. But I care no whit more for what *you* find in the Bible than for what you find in the Koran or in a newspaper; for though I am certain of the infallibility in itself of Holy Writ, yet I deny utterly that it was ever meant to be used by one individual to prove anything to another individual. Had we met then I should have insisted as a preliminary to discussion that the Bible should not be even once named. Again you would have appealed to the Primitive church. And to this appeal I should have declined to submit. I should have asked you to name the precise point where the line is to be drawn between the Church primitive and pure, and the Church older and corrupt. When you had named this point I should have asked by what authority the same point had been given the preference over other points. Again I should have said, granting your line is properly drawn, yet how we are to study fully and exactly the period which we have agreed to consider pure. We have but the merest fragments of the devotions, the discipline and the teaching of early times. Much has perished. Much was never written at all. How know we then that the fragments in our hands are a sufficient clue to the mind of the Primitive church? Further, how know we that we are at all likely to put a right interpretation upon these same fragments? Lastly, granting that we can with certainty ascertain the mind of the Primitive church, yet what particular concern have we of the nineteenth century with the Primitive church?

The Primitive church was for primitive people. In her own day when she needed to be understood she was understood. She was never intended to teach us, and therefore does not speak fully to us. The Church of the 19th century must teach the people of that century. And if there has been a Church at all there is a Church now, just as plain and as infallible in its teaching as was the Church even under the *twelve* themselves. And if the Church of the 19th century is so corrupt as to be unworthy of credence, neither is there any good reason for believing the Primitive church. For if the Primitive church taught the truth, it did so by virtue of the indwelling therein of God the Holy Ghost, and if that indwelling ever was a fact, it is a fact still and so will remain till the end of time. Thus then I would have disposed of your appeal to the Primitive church. I do not think you would have appealed to the reformers, and therefore it is not necessary to say that no reformer has any weight whatever with me. But you would perhaps have attempted to prove it impossible that the Roman Communion can be what it claims to be. I should have told you you were wasting your labor. So in proving Rome antichristian, you were to me proving that there is not and never has been any such thing as a Catholic Church, and that Christianity in consequence is simply a mockery, a delusion and a snare. For if so much of Christendom as is contained in the Roman Communion has become apostate in spite of Apostolical descent, in spite of the Sacred Scriptures, in spite of the Sacraments, in spite of the indwelling of God the Holy Ghost, none of which things are denied by any one to the Roman obedience; then how can it be shown that the much smaller part of Christendom which Anglicanism constitutes has not also become apostate. No promises were made peculiarly to us, we have no choicer Scriptures, no better Sacraments, no more ancient descent, and no fuller indwelling of the Spirit. If in the case of Rome then all safeguards have been unavailing, what proof is there save our own bare assertion that the same safeguards are as respects us thoroughly effective? So then all attacks upon Rome would have been worse than useless. They might have driven me a step nearer infidelity, but they would have made me think no whit better of the Anglican Communion. For I see once for all that no authority can be claimed for Anglicanism which cannot with more reason be claimed for Rome. And hence to discredit Rome is with me nothing less than to discredit every form of Christianity. I hope that I have shown you how futile would have been conference on my part with you.

I have written hastily and while still very unwell, therefore no doubt obscurely and disjointedly. Nevertheless I hope you see that my case is now past any cure you could apply. I am tired to death of uncertainty. I am sick of self will. I am weary of standing alone. I am disgusted past bearing with that thing in the Anglican Communion which calls itself Catholicism. I must find a living, speaking infallible authority to which to submit, or else I must disregard Christianity as a miserable sham. In Anglicanism I find no one note of the Church. It is not *one,* for it has almost as many teachings as teachers. It is not *holy,* for supernatural holiness it stigmatizes as superstition and idolatry. Monks, virgins, hermits it scoffs at, — scourges, hair-cloth, celibacy, vows, confessions, penances, vigils before the Sacrament, and almost all other means to preëminent holiness it disallows in no measured terms. I cannot see that the holiness it recommends goes very much beyond such a holiness as Cicero might have practised.

Nor is Anglicanism *Catholic.* It is confined to men of one Church, and it will have nothing to do with the rest of Christendom. It hates the Roman obedience and sends its emissaries wherever it can to stir up strife in that obedience, as we have missionaries forsooth in Mexico, in the West Indies, in South America, in France and even in Italy; and as you yourself have been deputed to encourage and further these miserable Germans who rebel against the Church while attributing infallibility to certain professors. Even the Greeks we have undertaken to evangelize, and for years have had in Athens an ignorant old man and a staff of women who — bless the work — have been expected to make known among the Greeks that pure Gospel for which we have the monopoly.

Lastly, Anglicanism is not *Apostolic*. In England, Parliament is supreme and churchmen literally worship God according to Parliament. Laymen say what is and what is not the Church's doctrine, and now acquit and now condemn Priests. And in this country, too, not the Bishops but the laity rule. What the laity want they always get and what they don't want is never forced upon them. They sit in all ecclesiastical bodies as coördinate with the Bishops themselves. And in almost all diocesan committees the Bishops are ruled out altogether, and are not even allowed to be coördinate with the laity.

But it is useless, I am sure, to prosecute further this indictment against Anglicanism. To you it is all profane bubble I know. To me it is simple truth, and until I can be made to see a oneness where there is infinite diversity and endless strife, a holiness where almost all that personates eminent holiness is disallowed, a Catholicity where the rights of all other communions are with intolerable arrogance continually ignored or denied, and an Apostolicity where the Bishops dare not undertake to suppress any one of the heresies which have for centuries rited at their own will — in a word, until I can be made to see what now I cannot see, namely, that Anglicanism has the notes of the Church, I must retain my purpose of looking elsewhere for that Church. It was my purpose to have sent you with this my renunciation, but as pleasing others, I have determined to go abroad for awhile and make there my submission to the Chair of St. Peter, if, after consulting with some whom I have promised to consult, my mind is still to the effect that Anglicanism is spurious and that the Roman obedience is alone entitled to my allegiance. I have thought that the making my submission abroad might spare you as well as my other friends. If consultation abroad in no way alters my mind, I will, ere I seek a Roman instructor, send you my renunciation, so that you will be able to act upon it ere I have been actually received into the Roman Communion. But if my purpose of reserving my renunciation does not meet with your approbation, please say as much, and I will make renunciation before I leave the country.

Finally, in spite of all I have said, I do love and venerate you. If I had not held you to be the very best of the whole Anglican Episcopate I should not perhaps so soon have arrived at the position I to-day fill. I do thank you for years of kindness and for very much which you have taught me. I shall never think or say other than good of you, and shall never cease to pray that the gulf between us may be abolished. In future years even more than now, I shall, I am sure, look back to you as the one who first started me in the road to Catholicism. I will even hope that hereafter at least we shall understand one another better than we have been able to do on earth.

Very faithfully and affectionately Yrs,

A. A. Curtis.

Bishop Whittingham's Answer.

Madison Avenue, February 20, 1872.

My poor Brother:

I have read, patiently, every word of your long letter. Most distressing is the conviction it forces upon me that for years I have been simply trusting a man who was abusing my confidence, for the maintenance of relations which he knew himself to be wronging.

With such an one I can enter into no discussion. We have no common ground. Every sentence of your long tirade against your spiritual Mother reveals a heart sick unto death with self-opinionated pride. It is God's just judgment upon one who has given himself over to the indulgence of that primal sin, that he should fall into the tempter's hands, in strong delusion to believe a lie.

How else could you rely on the infallibility of your own decision in favor of the unscriptural, uncatholic, unprimitive, uncanonical claims of the arch-schismatic who blasphemously usurps divine vicegerency in the Roman See, and imagine that you were thereby getting relief from distractions of your own creating, in the comfortable committal of your intellect and conscience to the disposition of a human infallible authority.

The teaching God sent you, you have had and abused. On your own responsibility you are claiming to make for yourself an infallibility not meant for man — not promised to him — not given him. Nothing can come of it but ruin. Beginning in indocile presumption such a course must end in debasing substitution of the human for divine, the outward for the spiritual, the servitude of a creature of flesh for the liberty of a child of God.

Your expressions of personal regard add poignancy to my sense of the wrong you have been doing me by your long concealments, and do but embitter the affliction I undergo in the witness of your spiritual suicide.

I can neither accept nor refuse your offer of a delay of your renunciation of your Holy Ministry. I could accept it if I could trust you, and would gladly cling to the hope that in His Merciful Providence God might yet bring you, through reflection and intercourse with men able to convince you of the shallowness and insufficiency of your past, imperfect studies, to a better mind and clearer and truer views. But how can I trust you for the future, after your revelation of the past?

Yet I cannot refuse what opens to me the only discernible door of hope for your deliverance from a most

Rt. Rev. A. A. Curtis, D.D.

miserable false step. May our Lord Jesus Christ, Whose service and work you have been so sadly mistaking and misperforming, of His infinite Mercy interpose to open your eyes before it be too late.

Your sorrowing but still loving friend,

W. R. WHITTINGHAM.

REV. A. A. CURTIS.

This answer to Mr. Curtis' magnificent tribute to Truth brought to a close the series of sad impressions and painful trials produced by one of the gravest misunderstandings that could exist between two of the noblest characters in life. If the struggle was over, the " sharp agony " caused by the severance of a friendship so long and intimate remained to remind each of the wide gulf henceforth existing between them. One, not understanding the real point at issue, in all sincerity blamed the other for what he called a lack of openness and confidence towards his superior, while the other, being no longer able to silence " the still, small voice within," deplored in the depth of his soul the sorrow he was causing his devoted Father and Friend. Only those who have passed through this same conflict can fathom the depth of that anguish, which may be likened to " a two-edged sword, reaching unto the division of the soul and the spirit." Heb. iv. 12.

To augment, if possible, the grief of the already sorely tried pastor, seven of his parishioners who had for years listened to his counsels and followed his direction felt themselves drifting in the same current of doubt and indecision. In their appeal to him they had only for reply these words spoken in the extremity of his anguish: " My children, I can no longer advise you, for I know not what I will do. You must now think and act for yourselves." In speaking afterwards to an intimate friend, he said, " I felt as though I were about to leap into a great chasm, knowing not where I would land." However, his humble prayer,

Rt. Rev. A. A. Curtis, D.D.

"Lord, what wilt Thou have me to do," had already "pierced the clouds," for, "The Lord is nigh unto all them that call upon Him; to all that call upon Him in truth." Ps. cxliv. 18. "He healeth the broken of heart, and bindeth up their bruises." Ps. cxlvi. 3.

His Ananias was to "Lead him on

> O'er moor and fen, o'er crag and torrent, till
> The night is gone."

Cardinal Newman had wrestled ten long years "amid the encircling gloom" before he saw "the morn—" He was well fitted to meet the exigencies of this case, for in passing through the same ordeal thirty years previous, he, in his turn had said, "I feel as though I am losing myself, as though I am throwing myself away, and know not what will come of this determinate step." [1]

"In his own person Newman had stated and resolved the great alternatives: either Christianity is a human invention destined to have its day, or the primal indefectible Christianity is the Roman Church. It was fitting, then, that he should have advanced to his conclusion by sure steps though slow; that logic, and history, and the voice of conscience should play their several parts, and the evidence be weighed, objections tested and passion laid to rest." [2]

[1] Letters and Correspondence.
[2] Life of Cardinal Newman by Rev. Wm. Barry, D.D.

CHAPTER IV

1872 (*continued*)

UPON landing at Liverpool, Mr. Curtis, agreeably to his promise, directed his steps towards Oxford — that center of Anglicanism, whose Universities have sent forth so many brilliant men, fired with ambition and zeal for the advancement of Anglican principles. Whilst maintaining their views, unknown to themselves, many were struggling against the light which was eventually to bring them to the door of Truth. Carried along by the tide of their intellectual reasonings some would have preferred to see Rome bend down to the Church of England if possible, rather than yield one jot or tittle of their elevated ideas concerning its teachings, and in their misguided zeal they held back numberless souls who, notwithstanding, in the end, became, with themselves, loyal and devoted sons and daughters of holy Mother Church.

The pure Catholic views of Mr. Curtis had grown and deepened with his years, for having trained his mind to commune with God in the sincerity of an upright will in all that he undertook, he was now nearer the goal of his most ardent desires than he himself realized, and that at a moment when he was well-nigh ready to believe there was no truth to be found in this " vale of exile." The great tempter of all good, taking advantage of the darkness in which this chosen " vessel of election " was submerged, spread his satanic snares more deeply, in order to precipitate his soul into the depths of eternal night.

" But the strength of his cry and the offering up of prayers and supplications to Him that was able to

save him from *death* was heard for *its* reverence."
Heb. v. 7.

"He shall cry unto Me, and I will hear him," says
the Lord. "I am with him in tribulation, I will deliver
him and I will glorify him." Ps. xc. 15.

In the vain search for a solution of his doubts, and
sick at heart with the disappointments he met on every
side, Mr. Curtis at last determined to confront the
learned convert, Dr. Newman. Arming himself with
the numberless objections and abstruse questions he
had been so long revolving in his mind, he at once
sought an interview. It was quite early in the morning
of March the 27th when he arrived at the Oratory
at Edgbaston, and asked for the Doctor. He was told
that "Father Newman had just finished saying his
Mass, and was making his thanksgiving; would he be
pleased to wait a while." The first words spoken by
the Doctor after a cordial greeting was: "My young
man, have you breakfasted already? If not, come
with me to the refectory, after that I will listen to all
you have to tell me."

This first interview was a long and interesting one,
and at its close, having referred feelingly to his own
experiences of thirty years previous, the Doctor placed
two books in the hands of his visitor and said: "Read
these if you like, but pray and pray; nothing will help
you more than humble prayer; and come to me whenever you will, I am at your disposal."

The three following beautiful letters written during
his stay in England speak volumes: telling of the peace
and repose found after so many struggles and sorrows;
of his new-born happiness and overflowing joy which
make him a "child again," and of the secure and safe
shelter he finds through the ever open door of the only
true Church.

These letters are addressed in the name of one to
several members of his congregation at Mt. Calvary
Church, who, imbibing his teachings and following his

counsels for many years, deserved now to share in his triumph. Under his direction, some years previous to this date, three devout members of the congregation had left America to enter a ritualistic convent in England, but before he reached Liverpool one of them had become discouraged, and on account of troubles in her family was returning to Baltimore, passing her holy Director in mid-ocean; the second, remaining in England, was the first of his children to greet him in a foreign land, and to encourage him in his search for the truth, for she with her companion in religion shortly afterwards found an asylum in the bosom of Holy Mother Church, and both consecrated themselves to God — one in the Order of St. Dominic, and the other as a Sister of the Good Shepherd. To the third, who had lived under his direction from her childhood, he addressed the following lines: " I have resigned my charge at Mt. Calvary — a difficulty with the Bishop; I am here in England, investigating Catholicity, and if the Roman Catholic Church is not truth, then there is no God. Write me the day and hour I can see you. There is nothing in the system you have embraced. I was instrumental in your coming here, and I *insist* upon your returning to your family when I return to the States." It is needless to add, that it was deemed unsafe, by the Superioress of the convent for the protegée of Mr. Curtis to confer with him, and she was obliged in consequence to forego that satisfaction. She did, however, after a time, sever these bonds, to embrace holier and more lasting ones, for she too entered the true fold, and on her return to America became a member of the Order of the Visitation.

This little digression is deemed necessary as it gives an insight to the workings of grace in the souls confided to his care. The three letters addressed to those he had left in America follow one another successively and portray the several alternations in his mind and heart — from depression and grief to the overflowing

peace and joy which flooded his soul when the full light
broke upon it.

OXFORD, March 15, 1872.

MY DEAR CHILD:

I am sure you and certain others whom you will
know, and to whom I trust you to show this letter will
desire to hear how I am faring. I cannot write to all
to whom it would be a pleasure to write, and therefore
I make you my agent and ask you to show my letter
to those who desire to hear from me. Don't forget
Doctor and Anna C. nor Mr. and Mrs. C—— Izzy
and Sally you will remember of yourself. I should be
glad also if you would let the Belts see this. I was
very sorry that I had not seen them for some time
before I left. But to begin. My passage was
wonderfully tranquil, the season considered. Neither
the weather nor sickness prevented me at any time
from keeping the deck throughout the whole day. I
ascribe the prosperousness of the passage solely to the
prayers of the many kind souls who were, I know, be-
seeching God in my behalf. Nevertheless, the voyage
was to me what all sea voyages are, namely, very
dreary; we had very few passengers, and none of
these few interested me much, although they were all
pleasant enough. At sea I never can think or read,
and so there was little to come between me and the
feeling that I was sailing away from all dear to me,
on an errand the most unpleasant of all that could have
befallen me. I remained in Liverpool only just long
enough to transact some indispensable things. It is to
me a hateful place on account of its being totally im-
mersed in money-making, and on account of the great
rascality of most of those with whom a traveller comes
in contact. In making the passage from Liverpool to
Oxford I found the country already very green. The
weather there was delightful and has since so remained;
there has been no rain at all. The sun has shone

40

throughout almost every day. The rooks are nesting and accompanying the process with a continual noise which is to me, however, very pleasant. To see these birds nesting in the very midst of the town of Oxford is one of the strangest things an American here finds. The skylarks are soaring and singing, robins in full song, trees coming into leaf, the hedges already green and flowers everywhere blooming in abundance. I arrived in Oxford a week ago to-day, late in the day. The next day I went to leave my letter with Dr. Pusey and to ask for an interview. But through the Doctor's son I learned that there was no chance at all of my seeing his Father, he having been quite ill with some bronchial affection, and being already so much engaged that he cannot undertake any new thing. The next thing to be done was to find, if possible, Canon Liddon, to whom I had a letter, and with whom I had promised to confer. But he was out of Oxford and also quite unwell, so there was no getting at either of the two whom I had crossed the ocean to see. I went next to call upon Father Benson. But he could do nothing at all for me. Were I to believe what he tells me I should at once fling the church and religion to the winds, and content myself for the future with the aim to make myself useful to my fellow-men in some secular calling. Father Benson, however, did me one service, namely, he told me Canon Liddon was in London. So the day after I went to London and left my letter with Mr. Liddon, whereupon he writes me that he is leaving London for three weeks and cannot see me until his return. Again I was thrown back upon myself. But in London I received a kind letter from the Bishop entreating me to confer with a Dr. Burgon, Rector of St. Mary's, Oxford, author of the "Plain Commentary," upon the Gospels. So yesterday I returned to Oxford to see Dr. Burgon. I have not yet called upon him, but shall do so this evening or to-morrow morning. But I know well enough to be sure that conference with him will be totally useless. Nevertheless I feel bound to comply with the Bishop's request; what I shall do when I have seen Dr. Burgon I do not know. For I shall not see Dr. Newman until I have conferred with Canon Liddon. But I do not think I shall spend the interim in Oxford, which has become to me extremely dreary. I have seen it before and am already familiar with all a stranger cares to visit. Indeed I have gone where strangers do not go; namely, all around the neighboring country, on foot. In one of my rambles I stumbled on " Littlemore," the place to which Dr. Newman retired from Oxford when he, like myself, had gotten totally out of tune with the Anglican Communion and was contemplating a transfer of his allegiance to Rome.

The country here is certainly very beautiful, but its very beauty makes me more lonely and homesick. I know no soul here save Father Benson, and go whole days without exchanging a word with anyone. For there is no good, as I have said, in conferring with Father Benson, not to speak of the fact that he is too busy to give much time to me. And as I am lonely in the country, so I am more so in town. For Oxford now seems to me to be what Dr. Newman styles it, " *a heap of dry bones.*"

When I want to say a private office, I have to go a long way to the Roman Chapel of St. Clement's, no other sacred place being open to me except at the hours of public service. All the churches are closed, and into the college chapels you cannot go save by feeing the verger, and even then he introduces you not to pray, but to see what he considers worth pointing out. The undergraduates too, who make up so large a part of those whom one meets on the streets, are to me very disagreeable creatures. They seem, with few exceptions, to be irreligious dogs, and to care for nothing save frolicking, rowing, cricketing and so forth. But you ask what is to be the end of it all. I answer, I see no end but my submission to Rome. I have not the slightest notion that anything can avert that result. I am postponing my final action merely to please others, and not because I see anything entitled to cause delay. I am under promise to see Dr. Pusey and Canon Liddon if I can, before I try to find Dr. Newman. I shall fulfil this promise if in my power. Conference will and must leave me unchanged, and then if Dr. Newman will suffer me I shall call upon him to instruct me and introduce me into the Roman obedience. It is to me as certain as anything can be, that I must find what I seek there, or else must give up all concern whatever as to the truth. Please say to Izzy that Helen came to London to see me and that I was with her part of two days. It was refreshing to meet her. Please tell any of my friends, yourself included, to write to me if they wish, directing care of Brown, Shipley & Co., Liverpool. I want very much to hear how they are faring. Love to Ellie and Chrissie and all others. May the good Lord have you all in His keeping.

Yrs,

A. A. Curtis.

BIRMINGHAM, March 27, 1872.

MY DEAR CHILD:

I wrote to you from Oxford on the arrival of your first letter and requested you to show what I wrote to others. But this is all for yourself and Ellie and Chrissie. Your second letter reached me some hours ago, having travelled about awhile ere catching me. I think I wrote to you from Oxford when on the eve of conferring with Dr. Burgon. I afterwards saw him twice to no good effect, except it be good that my dissatisfaction with Anglicanism should be rather deepened than removed. The Doctor scolded me very severely, but I cared so little for his scolding that I was not even tempted to retort in kind. I can, I am sure, do without a definite religion of any kind, but if

Rt. Rev. A. A. Curtis, D.D.

I am to have a definite religion at all it must be more consistent than Dr. Burgon's, or else I prefer to dispense with it altogether. In Oxford I also conferred with Mr. Beuren, but he too was totally unsatisfactory, though not so severe as Dr. Burgon. He, however, was once very sharp. Neither touched my difficulties. After seeing them I went to Bristol to meet Canon Liddon. He is a man of an entirely different kind, very lovable and very clear-headed and fair-minded. Could I think it right to follow any one man implicitly I should, I think, select him as my guide. We had two long conferences and ventilated things very thoroughly. The result was that I could not consent to acquiesce in his conclusions. He sees and deplores all I see and deplore. He recognizes the errors and dissensions among us. He sees that almost all authority is against us, and that as resting upon our own judgment, we must, to maintain ourselves at all, resist authority. In all this, and in much more to the same purport, we were at one. But here we diverge. He is in no wise unsettled, and is determined to die where he is, because he is satisfied that things are no better in the Roman than in the Anglican Communion, whereas I am not willing to believe this until I have proven it to be a fact. And should it seem to me a fact, still Canon Liddon and I will diverge. For he is content to go on in what he thinks the best place to be found, while I don't think such a place worth maintaining and shall certainly cease to lay claim to any definite religion should I find as many contradictions in the Roman as I see in the Anglican position. I can't choose the Church simply as a lesser evil among other evils. I am quite sure that the Church, as we understand it, never existed at all if Anglicanism is to be regarded as the present phase of the Church. So after finishing with Canon Liddon, I came here to see Dr. Newman, and he has been so kind as to consent to see me to-morrow afternoon. I hope he will succeed in removing the obstacles which now seem to debar me from an entrance into the Roman obedience. And every right-minded man ought to join me in that hope, for it is to me quite settled, that with me it is Rome or no definite religion. Nevertheless, the Doctor must meet me fairly and convince me fairly, or he shall not convince me at all. He must recognize facts and account for facts, for I shall not in the least shut my eyes to these facts. I know he is without guile, and I am sure too of the clearness of his head and of the soundness of his logic. So I expect great things of him in the way of dispersing difficulties. In the meantime I am glad to hear that you and Ellie have become certain as to what you ought to do, and have found peace in the certainty. It is a miserable thing to remain in doubt as to the things of the greatest and most lasting moment. Nevertheless one must be content with uncertainty till he reaches full assurance by fair means. Hence my slowness in doing what you have already done. You were certain and did right to act promptly upon the certainty. I hope to become certain, and when I am so, shall not long delay action. I am sorry to tell you that there are seats rented in the Oratory, and in all the Roman churches I have visited in England. This grieves me hugely, I need not say. The weather for the last week or two has been very dreadful. To-day is as dreary as any day can be — dark, cold and sleeting. Yet the country is very green, frost does not seem to blight here as it does with us. Please make my congratulations and give my love to Chrissie. I hope she has chosen well. And, indeed, Mr. C. impressed me very favorably when I saw him, and I was unprejudiced, for I did not know he was laying siege on Chrissie. Love too to Ellie and to your mother. Please convey my warm remembrance and my affection to the Beams. I can't say now when I shall start home. But I am thoroughly tired of wandering about England all alone. There are other countries where a solitary traveller could find it more comfortable. May the Lord have you all ever in His keeping.

Yours faithfully,
A. A. CURTIS.

BIRMINGHAM, April 20, 1872.

MY DEAR CHILD:

I have delayed writing to you for the reason that I was in retreat when your last letter came, and then I wrote no more than was necessary. I thought too that you would sooner have a letter when all was well over, and I at last safe at home, than one telling you of my being still unreceived. I was received last Thursday, perhaps in the same way you were received. I was first conditionally re-baptized. That I might have escaped had I made a point about the matter, but I did not want to leave open any door whatever for the entrance of a scruple. I made a mistake. I first made a confession to one of the Fathers in his room, then I went into the chapel and was there baptized, kneeling before the altar, then versicles, collects and the Miserere were said; after which I made my profession in the creed of Pope Pius. Then Father Newman absolved me from excommunication and interdict, and finally in the confessional I received absolution. On Friday I made my Communion. I was to have been communicated by Father Newman, but he was too unwell to celebrate in the chapel, and my confessor communicated me instead, for Father Newman would not hear my confession, that is, he preferred not to hear it. On Thursday, after my reception, we went to see the Bishop Ullathorne, or rather His Lordship, as to my confirmation. He was perfectly charming, but we had to behave ourselves, I tell you that. He was as cheery and as kind as a father, but behind it all was the authority ready to be asserted, but not in the least asserted, for the simple reason that there was no need of its assertion. He talked to us a deal, and as to

Rt. Rev. A. A. Curtis, D.D.

much I knew nothing in the world about, and it is my belief, but you need not mention it, that Father Pope, my confessor, who was with me, did not know either. But both of us were too smart to betray ourselves. Going in and coming out we knelt and kissed the Bishop's ring, and he did give us his blessing so lovingly, and just as if he thought it was going to do us good. I could not help thinking that somehow we were the better for it. The Bishop said I was to come to him on Saturday and be confirmed in his own private chapel at 8 A. M. So Father Pope and I were off early this morning. The Bishop was as tremendously learned and as genial as ever. As we arrived before eight o'clock we went into the chapel a little before the time, and a delightful little place it is. The Bishop celebrated Mass first, which he does usually in the chapel when at home. He has a magnificent voice, and has the clearest pronunciation of Latin I ever heard anywhere. I could follow him perfectly without a book; he vested of course at the altar. His chasuble was very large and heavily embroidered. He won't wear, I am told, the cutaway chasubles now most common, at least in America. Many of the priests here use the full chasuble. After the Mass I was confirmed, kneeling before the Bishop seated at the middle of the altar. And again he made me feel through and through he was giving me something worth having. We stayed and breakfasted with him, and it struck me that he showed much less care for our stomachs than for our souls. The breakfast was tea first; I was afraid to take two cups, for it seemed to me that there was danger of the tea-pot giving out; then there was toast. I did n't consider that there was more than enough of that for two, and so I would not have any of it at all. Thirdly, there was a good chunk of cold bread, and seeing there was plenty of that I helped myself liberally. The last thing was a dish of fried bacon, and not a large dish either. I got some of that, but not so much as I would have been glad to have, for I doubted the capacity of the dish to suffice for all if each took as much as he desired. On the whole I did not think it much of a breakfast for " my Lord " to set before his two guests. But he did not seem to know at all that it was anything less than princely. And so I took it into my head that " my Lord or not," yet he was not much used to making luxurious breakfasts, at least not at home. Now, whatever you do, don't let this breakfast story get out, for if you do, it will go all over Baltimore that the Bishop was so shabby that he would give me nothing to eat. I myself was quite charmed with the breakfast, and thought it very much to the credit of the Bishop that we got no better one. He is very poor; they put him in jail once for debt, and worst of all, for a debt he did not make. Some lady died and left him a thousand or two pounds of stock in some bank. He did not know much about banks, I suppose, and so he kept the stock just where it was when given. But the bank failed, and not being a limited bank each stockholder was bound for the whole debt of the corporation. And so they came after the Bishop when his stock was good for nothing, to pay an immense sum. He gave them all the money he had in the world, but they said he must call upon his people to make up the rest. He declined, and they answered that he should go to jail if he did n't. So he made ready and went to jail and stayed there, till they became disheartened and turned him out. While he was there the jail was full of grand visitors, and there was no end of the hampers of game and champagne, etc., that came for his use. I think it will be a good notion to have him sent to jail again, just before I next breakfast with him. Perhaps he will bring some of the hampers home with him. At breakfast he discoursed in his usual erudite way. He was a Benedictine, and they get their living mainly out of books. He told me some things about the late Council which surprised me no

Rt. Rev. A. A. Curtis, D.D.

little. One was that the Council was determined upon
first, with a view to revising the Canon Law, and that
the prerogatives of the Holy See were defined as an
after-thought, when the bad people began to get up a
hubbub. And that struck me as so like what the Church
ought to be and all along has been; namely, she lets
people alone, till they begin to contradict, deny and
rebel, and then instead of humoring them, as is the
case in places known to me, she wakes up and says:
" What is all this stir about? What for are you quar-
relling as to my meaning? This is what I mean and
what I meant all along. And now stop your noise, and
go along and do your work in your own place. If you
don't I 'll deliver you to Satan. Rest you certain of
that. If you quarrel before I define I will forgive you
if you yield with a good grace, but if you presume to
quarrel after I have spoken, I will cut you off to a certainty." Among the many things the Bishop told us,
was one to the effect that we had no full vows in
America. I was rather inclined to bristle at this until
he said neither were there any in England. In neither
case have they what are called solemn vows; though
in both they have vows just as binding on the conscience.
I did not understand Canonical distinction. One of
the chief benefits of becoming a Catholic is just the
fact that you find so much you don't understand, and
that makes you feel as if you had gone back a long
way, and turned baby again. And it 's very nice to be
a baby when you have such a grand thing as the Church
to take you in its arms and carry you along. I am intensely happy every hour in the day for my second
babyhood. It is so very nice to leave off pretending to
know and to judge, and to be quite certain that you are
where the judging will be done for you. I just believe
whatever I am told, and I have been told nothing that
I find any difficulty in receiving. When you do thoroughly give up your self-conceit and self-will, and without any reserve say to Holy Church, "Mother, I don't

know and I don't want to know, and don't dream of trying to know; it's your place to know for me," you do get so happy. Then the feeling that you have found the real thing at last, and need not sneak any more, that is just delightful. You don't have to *sneak* out your invocations of the saints any more. You don't *sneak* to confession, you don't adore the Master in the Sacrament in a half-surreptitious way; what your heart longs to do you may do to your heart's content, and nobody will dream of calling you names. Yes, this secure feeling that you have found the reality, and this way to Catholic things in an open way is a very great rest. You feel not only as if a child again in ignorance, but a child also in truth and simplicity. It is a hard battle to put to death totally self-will, but when you have conquered, and you are really and finally submitted, and are quite sure that nothing can ever make you undo your submission, there comes so great a calm and so full a joy, such certainty, such blessed incredible faith, that you don't know your own self. And you almost wonder whether you are not dreaming. There are only two or three things that *try* to bother me now, and they don't succeed in the least. One is, " What right has such a sinner as you to all this blessedness? " I answer, I have n't any right, I don't even fancy I have. God called me just because I was such a sinner that there was no chance at all out of the Church Catholic. So now, Satan, take that and be off. Another thing is, that one feels so utterly contemptible when he sees how good many Catholics are without suspecting it. I wonder why the devil don't tell them they are good. Not one of the Fathers here has any notion that he is good. They do great things in such a matter-of-course way, they don't seem to make any effort. They don't make the first particle of fuss over you, not they. They seem to think you have done a wise thing, but at the same time a thing you could not help doing; it was so much the only wise thing to be done. They come in at dinner and put you down in the place of honor, and put on an apron and serve. But there is no *air* in the way they do it at all. They are all converts from Anglicanism, save one, and he is the only one who has any drollery about him. He has found out I like fun, and at dinner, where we are not allowed to speak, he sometimes casts his eye so comically at me, that I could titter if I were not afraid of disgracing myself. Father Newman rarely smiles, but he is as far as possible from anything approaching moroseness. He all the while sees the tremendous things of the invisible world so plainly that there is no place left in him for mirth. I don't suppose he knows at all what a joke means. But some of the others do. But my man is the only one who brims over with fun. And he never had to fight like all the rest of us, such a long way through the toils ere he found his rest. But the Fathers don't astonish me quite as much as some others. I went the other day to see the Little Sisters of the Poor, and I sneaked away feeling like a whipped dog. I did not think myself worth even a whipping. They had eighty of the most horrible creatures to care for that one could find anywhere. I would not live among the dreadful things on any account. It made me miserable just to take one look at them. But the sisters were just radiant with joy. They bubbled over with happiness; they evidently like the creatures the more, the more horrible they are. They fondled them, petted them, just as if they had been nice clean babies, or spic-and-span new angels just made, and not having had time to ruffle their feathers. And why on earth don't these miserable old creatures quarrel and fight, I asked. I am sure if I had the managing of them they would do nothing else but growl and snarl the whole day. I could not understand it at all. But the poor seemed almost as happy as the sisters themselves. Twenty or thirty old women in one room and not the faintest approach to a squabble. As many more old men all together too, and just as cheery and good-tempered as if each was just waiting to be crowned a king. I could not admire the sisters very much, because their goodness went too clean beyond me. It just puzzled me out and out. If they had been putting on anything I should have detected them in a second. But they were not putting on, that was certain. I sneaked back to the Oratory, and went into my private chapel, and made a meditation about the sisters, but I could not see even afterwards how they contrived to be so good and so happy.

You must know I, being the prodigal son come home, have extra privileges. And on the same floor with myself, and only a few feet off, is a little chapel whence I overlook the Blessed Sacrament. And there like a king I meditate, or pray or hear Mass without being exposed to the gaze of the community. I always go there and make my manners to my Master before I lie down at night. I tell Him that home is so nice and I am so glad to be there, and that I do feel so safe and happy. And I never go without reminding Him about those in Baltimore who were so good to me, and whom I love ten times more than ever. I tell Him they must *all* come Home, and that I shall never leave off remonstrating with Him until He brings them. And it is so much like Heaven to be there, when all is so still and so sacred, and to talk to Him as long as one wills, face to face. And I can't help, for I don't try to help, thinking that He answers back so gently, and congratulates me for having returned from doubt and wandering to certainty and peace. What could be more like Heaven than to sleep under the same roof with Him!

I went also to see a little first seed just planted of a Passionist monastery. There are only two Fathers and one lay brother. They are in a mean little house with only two little boxes of rooms below. Behind is a small schoolroom and alongside a little chapel.

Rt. Rev. A. A. Curtis, D.D.

There was only one Father at home. And he too was disgustingly good and happy. There he was in his black robe and leathern girdle, with the white heart and the other symbols of the Passion, looking as if he never ate, or slept or did anything else that other mortals do. And then, besides, he has to go through scourgings and what else I don't know, and, between ourselves, hope to be excused from knowing; but he was just like a lark, as old daddy Krebs used to say. He was heir to wealth, but the poor fool gave it all up to starve and whip himself every day, and, strangest of all, he did not know, evidently, that he was an uncommon creature. He just sat down and talked as cheerily as if he had enough to eat and had good clothes, and was not living in a hovel, and never expected to be whipped any more. And yet it was: " Now you must be hungry. Do let me make you a cup of tea; I can do it directly. Well, then, may I get you a glass of wine? " I did n't intend to demean myself by eating and drinking in his presence. Neither would Father Pope.

When he could not do anything else for us he raced off upstairs and came down with a snuff-box, and made Father Pope fill his nose as full as it would hold, and he did really take one little snuff himself, and that was the only thing human about him I saw. I was made very happy by that pinch of snuff, for that proved that he was flesh and blood, which I had before been inclined to dispute. And yet there can't be much flesh and blood about him either, or he would not keep the snuff-box upstairs, but in his pocket. The Bishop takes snuff. But once in a while he gets fearfully virtuous and won't snuff, and then the chapter meet and notify him, that if he don't fill up his box they prepare to strike at once, because they find him cross unless he mollifies himself with a pinch now and then.

But I must use up the rest of my paper in telling you about a man who is just opposite me on the other side

53

of the corridor.[1] He is somebody, — an Oxford fellow, head of a large congregation not far from here. But he has been a great sinner; I am nothing in comparison. He had incense, copes and closed chasubles, and half a bushel of candles all burning at once. I don't know what he did n't do, and all under the Bishop of Lichfield's nose. He came over to America and wanted to know why something was not done with me, and here in his diocese was this man, and plenty more, doing what I never dreamed of doing. This poor soul and I came here by the same road. Neither of us could find out what we were obeying, and both looked out for something to obey, and neither could find anything he felt entirely safe in obeying save the Holy See. Like me, he groped about, hoping to find something else, because again, like me, he did not fancy at first the being obliged to receive any and everything the Holy See had said or might say. But it was no use, so he gave in at last and came here to be made over into a little baby. And again, like me, he finds the process not dreadful at all. He comes and talks to me and asks me what he will have to do. He is so simple-hearted and ready to believe what he is told, that I am half inclined to tell him that the very first thing done to him will be to give him a most tremendous flogging; the next to put him down in the cellar for a week, and so on and so on. I think if I did he would believe me and begin to prepare himself for it all. You know I put on a very superior sort of air, as being in the Church some time before him. He thinks the Ritualists here have run out their line and will smash up soon, which has been my opinion also for some time. But you must have had more than enough of nonsense. I am coming home ere very long, and am going to do just whatever I am told. If the authorities feel disposed to make me a street sweeper

---

[1] Rt. Rev. Mgr. W. Croke [Robinson, M. A. "Roads to Rome," Raupert, page 218.

Rt. Rev. A. A. Curtis, D.D.

I don't think I shall much care. But I am resolved that I won't be either a Little Sister of the Poor or a Passionist monk. I have written a deal of fun, but indeed I am as happy as a beggar.

Like him, I don't know and I don't care what is to become of me.

Love to Ellie and Chrissie and all others. God bless you all.

Yrs,
A. A. CURTIS.

Only one letter in answer to these intimate communications seems to have been preserved, and it should be given in full, as it depicts in such lively colors the workings of a sincere and disinterested soul, zealous for the greater good.

This letter seems to have crossed the one written by the venerated pastor after his visit to the Oratory, for it refers only to a " promised interview," thus keeping his correspondents in longer suspense. Be it said to the credit of the seven members of his congregation, who with him were forced by their religious convictions to abandon themselves to an uncertainty in seeking the truth, they did not permit themselves to be influenced by his movements, but, on the contrary, delayed not in making investigations, and by earnest prayer and fidelity in following the light, they were safely housed in the true Ark even before their beloved pastor returned; and when Mr. Curtis was made a priest, not one of them chose to show a preference for him who had known and understood so well their individual needs and difficulties.

BALTIMORE, MD., April 12.

MY DEAR FATHER:

I read last night your letter to the Haywards, written on the eve of your interview with Dr. Newman. It seemed strange at first that you should have written before rather than after you had seen him, but seeing

55

one must face the fact that there were two possible issues to your conference, it was good of you to do it. At least in the interval one may hope and pray for all things. I heartily hope I may have read your letter wrong — it has greatly saddened no one but me. The others see only the former assertion that if you cannot render allegiance to the Roman Church there is nothing else left to you — I mean as regards religious faith. To me you seem to say more now when you say that unless facts are accounted for and difficulties cleared away you will not believe. Of course I don't even know what your difficulties are. When I had to decide the question for myself I saw after a little thought that the only rational thing for me to do, as to all difficult questions resting on ecclesiastical history or anything else which I could not myself examine, was simply to put these aside. Before we went to Mr. Lee it had with me come to this — if our Lord Jesus Christ is a verity He established a church; if there be on earth the church of His founding it is the Church of Rome. Then I had only to go to a living authorized teacher of that Church, and when I found that her doctrines as stated and explained by him neither contradicted anything I knew to be true nor contained anything I could not conscientiously accept — to render her full and unquestioning submission. Of course your case altogether differs from mine, your responsibilities and difficulties are immeasurably greater, but this never alarmed me — only the making conditions — the demanding that *all* should be cleared up seemed fearful. Dr. Newman's silence on a question that tortures so many hearts seemed to show that he could not utterly explain and clear away difficulties — that he was constrained to say to the church sent by the Son as He had been sent by the Father, what Simon Peter had said to our Lord when the many fell away before the great mystery proposed to them: "To whom shall we go? Thou only hast the words of eternal life."

Rt. Rev. A. A. Curtis, D.D.

I do not see where the little child is, if one is to take nothing on trust. I dare say I have read you wrongly and shall have to beg your pardon; besides, your case is settled before this, and if it were not I could not say anything. What were you doing all the early part of to-day I wonder. Something very prosaic, I have n't a doubt. One rarely finds extraordinary coincidences outside of books. Did you know you wrote your letter to me the day of our confirmation? We speculated as to the time of its writing — eight o'clock with us would be about one with you. Becky has doubtless told all about the pews — that the seats are free throughout the week, and at the four first masses on Sunday — locked only at High Mass, Benediction and Vespers. If this does n't alter the principle (and I don't see that it does) at least it makes one to go to church without at all concurring in the system. Indeed, practically it does n't touch me at all. I am physically so strong that I am a good subject for the aisle, and then one is not obliged to be present at High Mass (though one certainly wants to be); and in most of the churches there 's a children's Mass with an instruction at nine o'clock, and since the instructions are very good and the sermons rarely so, in one point of view one might gain by the exchange; lastly, by going early one is sure of the last seats at the Cathedral, which are out of hearing and therefore not rented; here, too, there are a *plenitude* of very devout poor people for immediate neighbors, though I can't say the advantages arising therefrom are unmixed. I have not spoken to Mr. Lee about the pews since I got your letter, for two reasons: First, now our instructions are over I don't see him except in the confessional, and he is so overworked, now that he and Mr. Dougherty are in sole charge of the Cathedral,[1] that I would n't ask

---

[1] Archbishop Spalding died on the 7th of February, 1872, and until the installation of his successor, the Very Rev. James Dougherty administered the diocese.

57

to see him except it were absolutely necessary, and secondly, I have already said, though perhaps not with your vigor, what it, pew renting, was in our eyes, and he said, what perhaps was all he could say, considering that he is least in rank at the Cathedral (the Arch-Bishop, Vicar-General and Mr. Dougherty all ranking him), that beyond all question it was wrong — churches should be free; then, with a sigh, shelved the difficulty in what seems the usual way: " It is unknown in Catholic countries." I don't think less and I feel infinitely more than I ever did before the enormity, the horribleness of the system. There is but one place in town where the pews are not rented, and there I am afraid we are out of place. I mean the Seminary. I have never been there except once to Vespers and Benediction. There is everything to make it immeasurably dearer than anywhere else, — the congregation of Seminarians below in their cassocks, cottas and birettas; the full, strong chanting; the perfect unanimity and profound reverence; the greater fullness of the service; then one's own surroundings — the dark, bare little gallery with only very poor people for its occupants, and the Seminarian boxed up to himself — who plays the organ. After all, outsiders are expected to come or the accommodations provided would be inexplicable. I, too, was surprised at first at the absence of any peculiarly Roman teaching in the sermons; but it is not in the least neglected. Manuals, for instance, are essentials and there is no authorized manual that does not fix it all. Even matters not defined as of faith but universally received, as the assumption, are indirectly enforced. One is not required to profess faith in it but one is required to keep the day as a holiday of obligation, and is advised to say the Rosary, of which that is one of the glorious mysteries. One cannot confess without using the invocation of Saints, and the multitude of prayers to which indulgences " applicable to the dead " are attached demand at once a practical faith in purgatory and in the power of the Pope — then the abundant provision for instruction to children makes it unnecessary to reiterate it perpetually when they are grown.

I wonder greatly that the spectacle of the lives of the priests does not carry greater weight with it. Such a life in a single man works wonders, and how much greater is the miracle witnessed in a whole class. Take Father Lee's Easter. He was in the confessional from nine o'clock in the morning to midnight Holy Saturday (I suppose of course he may have come out for something to eat at twelve); but one of the Cathedral ladies told me she went to his confessional at two in the afternoon and could not get in until eight, the service which commenced at nine and lasted till two being handed over to the Seminarians. To me 't was out of question the most beautiful of all the services — more so than Maundy Thursday even; the blessing of the new fire and relighting of the Sanctuary light and altar candles; the prophecies, the blessing of the font, and then the Litany of the Saints so simply, grandly and heartily chanted, when, verily, Heaven and earth seemed thrown into one; and finally the Mass with all its joyful accompaniments. It is strange that according to the nowadays arrangement all the Easter gladness should come so early on Saturday. To return to the confessional — Mr. Dougherty too came to his place at nine. He had broken down Friday, so that some one in the choir had to take his part of the Tenebræ, and he looked worn out to begin with. Easter, Father Lee had the two first masses at six and seven. Owing to the immense number of communicants, there was scarcely five minutes' interval. We stayed for both, and then after breakfast I went to the Archbishop's house to see about Haynie; I hated to add to the day's labors, but was afraid to wait. For once he was not engaged — said he was not at all busy, his Easter work was over (he had told us a week before that Mr.

Rt. Rev. A. A. Curtis, D.D.

Dougherty was to preach the Easter sermon); but while we were talking a man came for him, and I heard what passed in the hall. He wanted Father Lee to see a girl in some alley who was dying. Father Lee asked how old she was, whether she had made her First Communion; the man did n't know; could she swallow the Blessed Sacrament? Her teeth were clenched — he did n't know. He came back and finished with me, making an appointment for Haynie, then went in the Cathedral for the Blessed Sacrament. After High Mass I remarked to the Haywards that the sermon was the best we had heard and that the preacher was n't Mr. Dougherty after all, for *he* had a black head, whereas this preacher's was light. I got laughed at in return and was told it was Father Lee. Mr. Dougherty had proved too ill to leave the house, and Father Lee preached at twenty minutes' warning. That evening he sung Vespers and Benediction. We found the pith of part of the sermon or meditation rather in Challoner's meditation for Easter Monday. Of course I am not founding my opinion as to the priests' lives on unusual occurrences like this. It is the insight into every-day cases that impress me.

Dear Father, I have been trying to put your present, perhaps now your past struggle from my mind, and write as I would if there were no fear, but I cannot do it. I can neither write what I want nor as I want; in spite of everything I *do* believe I read your letter aright. If your case rested with Dr. Newman I would not have the shadow of a hope. But it does not. It is, as you said yourself, of the judgment, and surely this is your fiery trial — nothing but "invincible faith in, and invincible love to the Person of Christ" can enable any man to stand it.

Yesterday — I am writing this on Sunday — was fixed for our second Communion; by an accident I could not communicate then and went to-day instead. Truly, as Ellie says, the trial is over by this, and what can prayers avail now — and yet I could but carry with me but one thirst and one petition. As St. Paul could wish to become accursed for Israel's sake, I would to God I might be wrecked if so you might be saved from this. All day there has been in my mind your own reading of the legend. The child who at the setting forth was scarcely felt, a weight that well-nigh crushed the giant's strength before the end was reached. Surely what we see is only the staggering that shows the human strength is nearly spent — the end is nearly reached. Since He who is the burden is the strength and He who sends the darkness is the Light, there is nothing we may not hope — His love and power and truth never can be questioned. To doubt is simply to doubt you, and that I neither will nor can until the end. You must be called to great and hard service to be so tried. I both believe and hope as to the end — not through Dr. Newman but through Christ our God.

Faithfully yours,
I. B. M.

It is to be regretted that the several interviews which Mr. Curtis had with Dr. Newman during his stay in England cannot be told in full, for they must have been of a most interesting character. It may, however, suffice to sum up all in the words spoken by him years afterwards to an intimate friend in the priesthood: To his various enquiries concerning the subjects which most occupied him at the moment, such as the Popes Honorious and Liberius, Bishop Dupanloup and Père Gratry, the learned doctor replied that, " There were answers to these difficulties which he did not thoroughly study himself because there was so much else true in the Church that these did not bother him." " Do you," he continued to say, " believe in the Scriptures, and do you understand all contained therein? " " This closed my mouth," said Mr. Curtis, " except to ask for baptism at once."

Rt. Rev. A. A. Curtis, D.D.

After being baptized conditionally, made a true soldier of Christ by the "imposition of hands," and strengthened with might through the indwelling of the Holy Spirit, the fervent Neophyte felt himself fully equipped to begin anew. Desiring to make of his life a perfect holocaust for the salvation of souls, he conferred with his newly found Director regarding his aspirations towards the religious state, in following the rule of St. Bruno, whose austerities and love of solitude he so greatly esteemed.

From this laudable desire he was, however, gently but firmly dissuaded by Dr. Newman, who, recognizing the benefit his virtues and talents would be to the world at large, with the superadded influence of his example, advised him to return to America and put himself at the disposal of the Archbishop of Baltimore.

CHAPTER V

1872 – 1875

THE dawning of the year 1872 brought mourning to the Archdiocese of Baltimore by the passing away of its beloved Archbishop, the Most Reverend John Martin Spalding, who, by his amiable character and gentle manner, endeared himself to all. He was succeeded by the Right Reverend James Roosevelt Bayley of Newark, who was consecrated Archbishop of Baltimore on the 30th of July, and installed on the 13th of the following October. During the interval the Very Reverend James Dougherty, rector of the Cathedral, was administrator, and to him Mr. Curtis tendered his obedience on his return to America. After a short vacation passed with his mother and sisters, he spent the rest of the summer at St. Charles College, Ellicott City, Maryland, where he prepared himself to enter St. Mary's Seminary in Baltimore, conducted by the Sulpicians, that venerable society whose members have for long years so well prepared and admirably fitted innumerable young men for the priesthood.

These two landmarks of Maryland Catholicity would seem to deserve at least a passing notice, having been connected so intimately with the subject of this biography; indeed one of his last acts of kindness was in favor of an inmate of St. Charles. The land for the building of a college where young aspirants to the priesthood might be educated was given to the Sulpicians by Charles Carroll of Carrollton, one of the signers of the Declaration of Independence, and cousin of John Carroll, the first Archbishop of Baltimore,

63

who as early as 1791 welcomed and encouraged a colony of Sulpicians to open a seminary in the newly formed diocese. This seminary in time became known as " St. Mary's Seminary of St. Sulpice." St. Charles College, a preparatory seminary, or, as called in foreign countries, " Petit Seminaire," owes its origin to the zeal of Archbishop Marechal, third Archbishop of Baltimore, furthered by the venerable " Signer," who added to the generous gift of two hundred and fifty acres a handsome donation in bank stocks with the following fervent prayer: " May this gift be useful to religion and aid our Church in rearing those who will guide us in the way of truth." How fully the prayer of the fine old patriot has been answered is now a matter of history. The names of hundreds of famous alumni, including His Eminence, Cardinal Gibbons, testify to the devoted, self-sacrificing efforts of the saintly Sulpician Fathers who dedicate their lives to this beautiful work.

St. Mary's Seminary enjoys the singular privilege of occupying the same premises purchased in 1791, though new buildings have, in course of time, been erected, but the historic college at Ellicott City was swept out of existence in 1911 by inexorable flames, its destruction being an immense loss to the hard-working Fathers. Not only did it mean the disbanding of their school, but likewise the sacrifice of valuable manuscripts and priceless paintings, together with a library of more than sixteen thousand volumes. The indomitable spirit of the sons of Monsieur Olier was not crushed, however, and soon from the ashes of old St. Charles arose the foundations of the new, under the protection of " Maria Spes Nostra," not indeed at Ellicott City, but at Cloud Cap, Catonsville, where it will continue that sacred mission, " stamped with the seal of the divinity." Mr. Curtis was in his forty-second year when he presented himself at St. Mary's Seminary, filled with hope for the future and quite ready to begin

again his studies for the ministry; to become one
with the seminarians, whose senior he was, not only
in years, but, in many cases, in virtue, talent and
experience. The kind reception of the Fathers who
were to be his teachers, and the hearty welcome of the
students made Mr. Curtis very happy, while the sweet
quiet of his new surroundings charmed him. His long
settled meditative habits of mind and former earnest
reading of the Scriptures and Fathers of the Church
helped to make him feel at home in this delightful retreat of solitude and prayer; and his many years of
self-discipline, coupled with his energetic character and
faithful correspondence to grace, smoothed away the
difficulties of this new life.

In those days the students rose as early as five
o'clock, and made an hour's meditation before hearing
holy Mass; they were obliged to keep their room in
order, to sweep it and make their own bed, as well as
their fire in winter, carrying the wood themselves.

Lacordaire once said to a friend who could not
adapt himself to the life at St. Sulpice: "A priest
who has not passed through the Seminary will never
acquire the ecclesiastical spirit." "I loved the Seminary life," Bishop Curtis often remarked in after
years, "and I found nothing very difficult, not even to
take my place beside the young fellows on the bench."

But what better authority for these edifying reminiscences of Mr. Curtis' life at the Seminary, than quotations from the notes of one of his fellow seminarists,
who says that among the fortunate events of his life
he counts not as the least his acquaintance with the
humble, learned and saintly Bishop Curtis, with whom
he was raised to the sacred priesthood, at one and the
same ordination. "The room assigned to Mr. Curtis
at the Seminary," he adds, "was on the third floor at
the extremity of the south wing of the building, a part
of old St. Mary's College. Like the other seminarists he had to keep his room in order, sweeping it

himself, making his bed and attending his fire in winter. It was in this room, as I well remember, that on the day of his ordination he heard his first confession; the humble, hasteful penitent being Mr. Tabb, afterwards the noted poet priest. Mr. Tabb had already as a Protestant been his penitent, he was now eager to claim his old Confessor's first care." " I received so many absolutions before that did not count, I wanted one at least that did," was his remark to the students.

Mr. Tabb had been from his earliest years one of the closest friends of Mr. Curtis, and was associated with him in the Protestant Episcopal church. Though so unlike in every respect, except in their love of retirement, simplicity and unworldliness, the peculiar temperament of the one called forth the benevolence of the other, and years after when Father Curtis was made a Bishop he could be seen regularly wending his way to St. Charles College to visit his friend, sometimes even walking the five miles which covered the distance between the railroad station and the college. Although Mr. Tabb had entered the Church six months earlier than Mr. Curtis, his elevation to the priesthood was much later, and he had in the meantime retired to St. Charles College, where he pursued a more varied course of study and finally became a professor in that institution. It was here his long trusted friend visited him, and by his solid counsels and patient ministrations became his consoling angel in the hour of his greatest trial and darkness, when threatened with the total loss of sight. Together they took long walks through the country, recreating each other in exchanging reminiscences, one submitting to the criticism of his friend his latest verses, while the other cheered him by his encouragement.

Indeed the Bishop was occupied with his sorely tried friend up to the last moment of his life, sending him kind and encouraging words from his death-bed, and even bequeathing to him his chalice. Strange to say, Father Tabb survived the Bishop only one year, dying at St. Charles College, among the devoted Sulpicians. The chalice of the venerated Bishop then became the property of the faculty, who came near losing their relic at the time of the disastrous fire. Having with great difficulty succeeded in saving the Blessed Sacrament, the President, Reverend F. X. McKenny, spoke of the chalice which was kept in a room on the third floor. One of the students rushed forward and offered to ascend to the room above, hoping to rescue the sacred vessel from the flames; immediately three long ladders were spliced and placed against the wall of the doomed building; the young man quickly mounted, and making his way through the dense volume of smoke to the place indicated, returned with the coveted treasure, and then sank exhausted to the ground.

But to return to the notes of Mr. Curtis' fellow companion at the Seminary: " In the lecture-room he was seated close up to the professor's rostrum and to his left hand. Lectures, as well as recitations, were in Latin. Though quite familiar with the language, our student in the beginning experienced not a little difficulty in expressing himself with fluency. In fact, he was more conversant with Greek, and was also a good Hebraist. He was rather reserved in class, not venturing to express an opinion unless called upon by the professors. In the prayer hall, as I remember, he was posted near the lower door of entrance — was in fact door-keeper — and very prompt was he, as all well knew, to shove the little bolt into place when the time limited for entering there had expired; and they who were late for the exercise had now to put in their appearance at the upper door, directly under the eyes of the Superior.

" I cannot recall distinctly the place usually occupied by him in the chapel, though in his last year, when already a sub-deacon, he must have been in one of the

Rt. Rev. A. A. Curtis, D.D.

rear stalls, where also he was, probably, the year previous. He was profoundly religious and the very soul of piety, but I think his general deportment at prayer and divine services was in no way remarkable, and has left no special impression upon my memory. Nor can I with certainty point to his place in the refectory. His acts of self-mortification at table, however, I do remember, for they could not be hid, and were frequently commented on by the students. We thought his fasts rigorous, while he considered them slight, and not to be compared with those to which he had been accustomed. In many a former penitential season his practice was to partake neither of food nor drink all day, until toward sunset. It was from the high desk in the refectory that at dinner we used to deliver our practice sermons, and these we were obliged to memorize and preach just as they had been written. Mr. Curtis found this requirement irksome; yet, such was his childlike obedience that he conned his manuscript, word for word, as the merest tyro. Indeed he was ever a close observer of the rule, a shining light and beautiful example to us all.

" From the start Mr. Curtis became a favorite with us students, and his manners and conversation a source of edification. He associated freely with the various members of the community, and by most of us it was esteemed a privilege to pass one's time of recreation in his company. His talk was instructive, entertaining and often quite amusing. He was not opposed to banter, and he seemed to enjoy a joke. When he first appeared in clerical garb, we noticed that he wore a birettum with four lobes — a doctor's cap — instead of the regulation cap with but three lobes. He avowed he was not aware of the distinction, and had made the purchase in good faith, and he laughed heartily at his apparent presumption. He said he had used birettum, cassock and sash as minister; the sash, however, had served him for stole instead of belt or waist band. He always spoke of his former co-religionists in the kindliest manner, and insisted much on their good faith respecting the Church. As far as he, himself, was concerned, he assured us he was not one hour in bad faith; still, he could not deny that in his earlier days he was greatly prejudiced against Catholics. He used to tell with considerable amusement how he managed to get his first glimpse of a real, live Papist. A circus was coming to a distant town, and it was reported that a certain gentleman and family down the country, who were Catholics, were expected to be amongst the audience at the performance. Mr. Curtis, then a good-sized lad, walked many a mile to town, not so much, said he, to see the circus, as to gratify his curiosity with respect to these individuals. He wanted to see for himself what Catholics looked like; he had heard and read such shocking things about them, that he felt quite sure they must differ from other folks, and prove more exciting and novel than the show. Again with regard especially to priests, he said, although he had learned to reverence them in his heart, the sight of one on the streets, even up to recent date, greatly agitated him. If he turned a corner and espied one advancing on the same side, he crossed over to the other side if possible; for he felt his flesh ' a-creeping if he passed close to the man.' Such was the enduring power and force of inborn prejudice."

Notwithstanding these prejudices of his early education, his inherent love of truth and overflowing charity prevented anything like bigotry influencing his actions. The following instances in his life at Mt. Calvary Church will prove the truth of this statement. One of his spiritual children brought him a rosary to be blessed, saying that it had been given to her by a Catholic relative, who had it blessed by the Holy Father Pope Pius the IX in a recent visit to Rome. " You say the Pope has blessed it," he replied; " his blessing is above mine, I cannot put mine over his," and he returned her the rosary. At another time, remonstrating with two of his young parishioners who had trifled on the subject of religion by engaging a priest to enlighten them on the teachings of the Catholic Church, and who had procured from him some books for the purpose, he said very gravely: "If you are in earnest, and believe your present position false, you are right to investigate the truth and obey the voice of conscience, but you are entirely wrong to trifle thus with a priest of God and holy things. If God is leading you into the Roman Catholic Church, follow Him; if not, then take back the books and trifle no more with so sacred a subject." One of the two receiving the fullness of light entered the true fold many years later. Yet one more striking instance of the broadness of his views he, himself, relates: In his frequent visits to the penitentiary he was struck by the effect that the Catholic faith had on the prisoners who professed it, and pondering within himself, he said: "If a Catholic priest can have such an influence over the minds of these men, that in obedience to him they refuse to listen to any other teacher, he must speak with authority. What power there must be in that church, and whence comes this power?" These reflections made so deep and lasting an impression that in one of his visits, coming upon a Catholic prisoner who was in danger of death, he went in great haste to procure a priest, and this with considerable trouble and inconvenience to himself. As the penitentiary was not under the jurisdiction of the parish to which he applied, Mr. Curtis was directed further, and while somewhat astonished at such a refusal, he did not desist from pursuing his charitable errand to the end. But to resume the touching notes on his seminary life: "Mr. Curtis was quite affable, and he seemed never to take amiss our freedom in plying him with questions. We were, of course, greatly interested in the history of his conversion and we questioned him accordingly. Had he

ever suspected that he would one day find himself
amongst us? He had frequently, indeed, he said,
passed the Seminary, and the thought had come to
him, how happy must be the inmates behind those
walls; but he had never dreamed that he, himself,
should at any time be numbered amongst them. He
had been drifting for years, it is true, nearer and
nearer towards the true fold, but it was all unaware,
though others claimed to see it, and failed not to utter
their warning. He believed himself truly an ordained
priest, and hence did not marry. He spent much time
studying the early Fathers of the Church, and he saw
more clearly, as time went on, how their teaching was
exemplified by our Church in her doctrine and practice. He began to use our books: the Missal, the
Breviary, the Catechism of the Council of Trent. This
last was the text-book for the preparation of his sermons. Strange as it may seem, in all this he himself
perceived no inconsistency at the time, nor had he any
misgivings until his eyes were finally opened, and that,
suddenly.

"Bishop Whittingham was holding Communion service at Mt. Calvary Church, and the rector, Mr.
Curtis, while assisting him, made profound reverence
to the elements of bread and wine. This was observed
by the Bishop, who, after the service was ended, took
Mr. Curtis to task privately, assuring him, however,
that if he acted similarly on a future occasion he would
feel himself constrained to reprove him openly before
the assembly in church. The rector revered his ecclesiastical superior as a father; he felt himself, moreover, under personal obligations to him; he grieved
much to differ with him on such a momentous matter;
yet come what would, he could not promise to do other
than he had, for he believed Christ to be Very God
and to be truly present under the Eucharistic elements;
and, hence, standing in His real and awful Presence
— the creature before his Maker — he could not but

71

worship and adore. The Bishop insisted upon his imperfect view and the teaching of his Church: Christ is there to be communicated, not to be adored. The rector held, if He is there at all, He must needs also be taken note of and adored. Mr. Curtis now, at length, felt the ground cut from under him; he must be untrue either to his conscience or to his Bishop, and the Church he represented. The following Sunday he announced to his congregation that he had resigned his charge, and that he would look for light and guidance outside the Church to which thus far he had been submissive."

The result of this resolution is already made known by his visit to England, and through his several letters written at the time of his abjuration; therefore, it is needless to quote the writer of these notes in this matter. But what he says regarding the temptation which so suddenly and strongly beset Mr. Curtis while in England is too explicit to be omitted. It seems that Satan made one last attempt to turn his feet from the way of Truth and Life. During his visit to Oxford, while standing on a bridge and gazing down upon the water, a temptation to despair settled darkly upon his soul, and the evil one seemed to whisper, " Why not cast yourself down, and so put an end to this anxiety and doubt?" Speaking of this moment of terrible trial to a friend in after life, he said that it was the sound of the beautiful chimes from the neighboring towers of Oxford that roused him from this hideous revery. It was Sunday, and the bells were ringing the morning service, forming a never-to-be-forgotten harmony as he stood on the bridge studying the flowing current beneath that wound silently in and out, and over every obstacle in its way. Suddenly straightening himself, he flung off the tempter's snare, and passed over the bridge with such rapid strides that before he realized his speed, he had crossed a ploughed field planted with potatoes. Finding himself unexpectedly in the neigh-

Rt. Rev. A. A. Curtis, D.D.

borhood of a modest little Catholic chapel, where the Holy Sacrifice of the Mass was about to be offered, Mr. Curtis entered and found peace and calm after the tempest.

To return to the notes of his colleague: "In his changed condition and novel surroundings at the Seminary, some things undoubtedly must have been very trying to our student. After years of active life to come in middle age back to school again; to have been a long time at the head, and now to hold only a subordinate place: to get accustomed to community life and all it implies; to be under a strict rule and to apply ever and anon to Superiors for trifling permissions; to render humble services — dusting the chapel, waiting upon table, etc., to go on the community walks through the streets of the city where you have become noted, and where every one is free to point you out or stare at you. In one of these walks, passing near Mt. Calvary Church, a beautiful little boy of three or four summers was playing on the sidewalk. Mr. Curtis stooped and picked up the little fellow, imprinted a kiss on his forehead, gently set him down again, and with a smile remarked to his companions, 'I baptized him.' What stronger proof could he give of the tenderness of his feeling and the unalterableness of his affection, which neither time nor place had changed? Mr. Curtis used sometimes to remark that he enjoyed the uncommon distinction of having been christened no less than three times in his life — as Catholic in his mature years, as Episcopalian in his youth, and as Methodist in his infancy. Of one or other of the latter administrations he himself, it would seem, had little, if any, misgivings; but the Cardinal,[1] in view of Mr. Curtis' intention to prepare for the priesthood, deemed it advisable to repeat the Sacrament, at least, *sub conditione*, so as to make assurance doubly sure, and safe-

---

[1] Dr. Newman was created Cardinal by Pope Leo XIII in 1879.

guard the validity of any ordination that might thereafter be conferred on so promising a subject." But to conclude these notes: "Such was the heroic soul of the man, in passing through a life which daily furnished him subjects of greater or lesser trials; in the many months of my class association with him, I do not recall a single word of complaint from his lips, nor the expression of a single adverse criticism. His deep piety, profound humility and spirit of faith and self-obliteration carried him safely through all difficulties, so that peace, serenity of soul and abounding joy seemed to be his happy portion from the beginning to the close of his term at the Seminary."

During those two years he seemed to have deeply imbibed the Sulpician spirit of mildness and simplicity, and he always spoke with great appreciation of the ecclesiastical formation given by the Fathers to the Seminarians. As the time of his ordination drew near, Mr. Curtis wrote to his venerable friend, Dr. Newman, acquainting him with his approaching happiness, and asking for his baptismal certificate, which the Doctor kindly sent in his own handwriting, of which a facsimile is shown on the opposite page.

It was by predilection he made choice of Paul for his name in baptism, and he was henceforth to model his life on this great apostle, walking even more closely than ever in his footsteps, so that after his example he could say indeed and in truth, " Be ye imitators of me, as I also am of Christ." 1 Cor. iv. 16.

On the 19th of December, 1874, with three of his companions, the Revs. A. J. Frederick, J. Cunningham and F. Fowler, he received ordination at the hands of the Most Reverend James Roosevelt Bayley. The first-named of these Fathers is the only one of the class who has outlived the Bishop, and it is he who has contributed to this biography the pleasing reminiscences of Seminary life. The Most Reverend Archbishop immediately made Father Curtis one of his household and

I, John Henry Newman, Superior of The Oratory of St Philip Neri, in Birmingham, certify that Alfred Paul Curtis, of Baltimore, in the United States of America, sometime a minister of the "Protestant Episcopal Church," was reconciled by me to The Church on the 18th April 1872, having previously made abjuration of his errors, and received conditional baptism, in my presence.

John H Newman

The Oratory,
Birmingham,
10 May 1872

appointed him his secretary. A convert himself from Episcopalianism, and for some time a minister of this denomination, he understood and appreciated the struggles through which Father Curtis had passed, nor did he hide from his newly appointed secretary what it had cost him to leave the diocese of Newark. Indeed the Archbishop made no effort to conceal the reluctance he felt in coming to Baltimore, and for this reason he was misunderstood by many of his new flock; few penetrated beneath the surface, and consequently did not know nor appreciate the wealth of goodness and affection hidden under a reserved and cold exterior, while his failing health left much of the work of the great Archdiocese in the hands of his assistants.

CHAPTER VI

1875 – 1886

THE newly anointed of the Lord entered upon his appointed field of labor with a spiritual zest springing from his magnanimous courage, and strengthened by the distinctive graces which the Sacrament of Holy Orders confers. The parochial work of the Cathedral was very laborious, owing principally to the extent of territory it covered, while the failing health of the Archbishop added to the burden of the three priests who constituted his household — the Reverend Thomas S. Lee, Reverend William E. Starr, now Monsignori, and Father Curtis.

Besides the duties of their respective offices, they vied with one another in their devotion to the work of the confessional, the care of the sick, the direction of uneasy and perplexed consciences, the instruction of the young and the ignorant, and of those whom God sent them for introduction to Catholic truth. The harvest indeed was great and the laborers few; nevertheless, they seemed to multiply themselves in proportion as the work increased. Father Curtis was made assistant rector, and "his conscientious discharge of even the least of his duties was a continual reproach to the rest of us," says one of his co-laborers. Their intimate companionship made them recognize the imperfections of one another, and in bringing them to light, put to the test the virtue of each. Although Father Curtis was so much esteemed, they would occasionally laugh at what they deemed his peculiarities, taxing him with them, and rather enjoying seeing him roused; but when his indignation was cooled, he, him-

77

self, was the first to laugh at the provocation. He was always ready to retract and apologize after an outburst of his impetuous nature, or when his inability to excuse the foolishness of men caused him to deduce unfavorable conclusions. " Still with it all," relates one, " the beautiful tenderness and compassion which were striking features of his character were daily exemplified. I recall his tireless endeavors in the service of the poor, and his unflagging considerateness with the perverse and the tiresome. I remember what his Lents were, not limited to the bare requirements of the Church's law, but putting into rigorous practice what her spirit insinuates. He took the words of the Breviary as his rule, and gave up all conversation except what courtesy and necessity demanded. And we may well imagine that when he put so close an embargo over his tongue he was not less careful to mortify his eyes and his ears, his curiosity and his imagination. He was towards the end of his life not much of a reader of newspapers; in Lent, not at all."

The room he occupied was devoid of all heat in winter, owing to a defective flue which prevented connection with the furnace; here he passed all the time not devoted to parochial work and the confessional. That " he practised what he preached " was evidenced by the effect produced on a religious priest who visited him in his room. " It was in itself a sermon," he remarked, " so bare of every comfort."

He arose every morning at four o'clock, made two hours' preparation for holy Mass, and was " always the first to be seen kneeling before the Blessed Sacrament when the church was opened, while his visit in the afternoon was a revelation of absorbed devotion," says the same observer.

Unconsciously to himself he became the very center of innumerable souls whom he drew to God as their director, guide and comforter, for his natural gifts, as well as his supernatural powers, were hidden in his

The Bishop when Priest at the Cathedral of Baltimore.
– 1875 –

humility. Nothing was too little, and nothing too great in the service of his penitents who flocked in crowds to his confessional, where he could be found every afternoon of the week, and in the morning after his Mass. He devoted all his energies to their interests; the old, the feeble, the blind and the troublesome, white and colored, all alike were the objects of his care and solicitude. Every Saturday afternoon he would leave his confessional to lead in a poor old blind man, and after hearing his confession and comforting him he would conduct him back to his pew. A "lady of color," who regularly took up her station on the platform of his confessional for holy Mass and other services, was invited by him to use his velvet cushions, to the astonished indignation of one of his "Philotheas," who had them upholstered for his use alone. On hot summer days he would fan his penitents, taking care that they got the full benefit of the current of air, while unmindful of himself. To the weak he became weak, making himself so entirely one with them as to give the inward persuasion that he himself had experienced the same infirmities. He never went in advance of grace, knowing so well how to "wait on the Lord," and to allow the Holy Spirit to do His work in the soul. He was, notwithstanding, very prompt, when the exigency of the case called for it, in urging those engaged "in the race" to "so run" as "to win the prize." To such, after the example of his beloved St. Paul, he gave the following counsels:

"Put ye on the Lord Jesus Christ." Romans xiii. 14. We must put on Christ that we may no longer live in ourselves, or of ourselves, but that Christ may live in us, operate in us, accomplish His Will in us, so that we may say, not in the way the great St. Paul said it, but in our little way, "I live, now not I; but Christ liveth in me." Gal. ii. 20.

And again:

In the Epistle to Timothy (I. vi. 12) we are told " to

Rt. Rev. A. A. Curtis, D.D.

lay hold on eternal life." We must not wait till death to enter Eternity, the door is open now; and let us remember what it cost our dear Blessed Lord to open it, that it may help us to enter it before it is closed forever. We must enter Eternity now, and " lay hold of eternal life," that is, lay hold of God in our own soul, and live there with Him that life that we shall live forever.

His preaching drew crowds to the Cathedral, and his appearance in the pulpit was inspiring. His clear, penetrating eye and strong sonorous voice called for the deepest attention, and the result was a hushed silence as the flow of his beautiful language revealed the fullness of his heart. Although not possessed of any great oratorical power, his strong, vigorous style made a deep and lasting impression on his hearers, while his impetuous zeal, tempered by his benignant love for souls, caused him often to give a good blow suited to the occasion. " I have been many times reproached for showing anger in the pulpit," he said, " but I am wholly unconscious of it," so that he knew how to " be angry and sin not."

If to deaden the sense of self-complacency Lacordaire scourged himself before ascending the pulpit, Father Curtis did more; he humbled himself, he humbled himself to the very depth of his being. As the moment approached for him to preach, his head was seen to lower and his whole attitude betrayed the humility of one sinking into the depths of his nothingness and unworthiness before the Majesty of God. " I could scarcely repress my tears when at the first note of the ' Veni, Creator,' sung by the choir, I caught a glimpse of him," says one who witnessed it. His seven minutes' sermons given at the Gospel of the early Mass, Sunday after Sunday, were gems of practical spirituality, and are still brilliant in the recollection of one who heard him in those days. His visitation of the sick was marked with the greatest kindness and gentleness, and these visits were continual. Night and day, in season and out of season, he was ever at their service, spending himself in comforting and fortifying them, and when the illness was of long duration, or the invalid was convalescing, he would bring sunshine into the home by a certain playful cheerfulness. " He was unfailing in his attentions, coming every day during an illness," says one who for years had enjoyed this privilege, " and timing his visits so as to say the night prayers or some other devotions." A family weighed down with sorrow and affliction he surrounded with a father's solicitude, visiting them regularly, making it a pleasure to join them at the family board, while ingeniously diverting them by his cheerful conversation. The following little mementos of those days have been carefully preserved by one of the grateful survivors :

This note accompanied a box of bonbons at Christmas, and the children — so called — were children of a larger growth.

MY DEAR CHILDREN :

When Santa Claus consulted me as to your merits during the past year, I told him that on the whole you had been reasonably good children, and entitled rather to sweets than deserving of switches. And he, being a good Catholic and not venturing to differ from a priest, has accordingly sent you the sweets, and I hope you will enjoy them and will not forget to repay the good word I spoke to him for you, by praying for me.

Yrs. faithfully,
A. A. CURTIS.

Another with confectionery :

Be good children and eat your goodies properly. Don't mess yourselves up, but use the tongs like little women, and when done eating, pray for

A. A. CURTIS.

Rt. Rev. A. A. Curtis, D.D.

And yet another:

MY DEAR CHILDREN:

I fall back upon first principles. I am, you know, in a small way, an apostle of *first principles*. I send you, therefore, a box of goodies in remembrance and as a token of all sorts of things, too many to be written. The large card, mind, is for Stannie and " Mont," the house dog. And please assure " Mont " that the card in no wise reflects upon honest " Tonsil " dogs, such as he himself is; but solely upon dogs setting up to be cultured and " fin de siècle." Pray for me, too, a little out of common to-morrow.

Yours faithfully,

A. A. CURTIS.

On another occasion:

To speak in a feminine way, the mending " is just perfectly splendid," and the note equals the mending. I am more than half disposed to tear the umbrella again for the sake of having it still further ornamented. I might, but that I don't like to impose on affection as willing as yours. But when I shall have any rents, *honestly come by,* I shall certainly give you a good part of my custom, etc., etc.

Yrs. faithfully,

A. A. CURTIS.

This humorous strain in his intercourse with others was frequently enlivened by the pleasure he took in relating his little experiences, even at the cost of being bantered about them.

In his regular visits to an infirm maiden lady, according to his usual custom he kept such a good guard over his eyes that she was heard to say to her companion, " Father Curtis has a well-shaped foot, and I think he is a little vain of it, for he is always looking at it." No one enjoyed better than himself her misapplied appreciation of his modesty.

His ministrations to the dying were most consoling; strengthening their faith and confidence in God, he would impart comfort and hope to the bereaved ones surrounding the death-bed, by the beautiful and touching prayers he poured forth with so much fervor. One soul, entering the "valley of the shadow of death," he encouraged to victory in the combat by sending the graceful, waving palm he had that day (Palm Sunday) carried in procession. To another, to whom he believed himself indebted, he wrote the following message, "My first Mass of Christmas will be offered for you."

In the latter part of his life, when feeling the infirmities of age and the fatiguing labors of the missionary work which he still pursued, he was immensely consoled in bringing the grace of the Sacraments to a wanderer, for whose return he had patiently waited and perseveringly prayed for fifteen or twenty years. The summons came quickly at last, but in God's Providence the Bishop was at hand, and in his ministrations to the sufferer — for he paid him several visits before the end came — revealed the light of God's countenance signed upon him. "The light of Thy countenance, O Lord, is signed upon us." Ps. iv. 8. Turning to his wife, the stricken man whispered: "I see Jesus in the Bishop's face," while the Bishop on his side was lost in admiration on beholding the reverent faith and deep humility of him whose whole attitude bespoke the presence of his Lord and God. For weeks afterwards the holy Bishop spoke of the impression produced upon him on this occasion, and said it was a forcible reminder of the strong faith of St. Peter, who, on seeing the miraculous draught of fishes, exclaimed in his deep humility, "Depart from me, for I am a sinful man, O Lord." Luke v. 8. If the "light" in his countenance brought God to the soul, his burning words of zeal and charity were not less powerful, and the miracles of grace he worked in the souls of those who heard him would fill a volume. The following extract, taken from a sermon, made a deep and lasting impression on one of his hearers, who repeatedly referred to it and who fervently prayed that these consoling words of the holy Bishop might be known to all poor sinners throughout the world.

"This Man receiveth sinners." Luke xv. 2. "The Jews said this to our Blessed Lord as a reproach. Yes, this Man receiveth sinners. He not only receiveth sinners, but He will come to the sinner; the vilest, the most wicked, the most abject, the most abandoned has only to call upon Him, to desire Him, to long for Him, to believe in Him, to hope in Him, and this Man who receiveth sinners will come to him; even one sigh, one desire for forgiveness will make Him come instantaneously to the aid of the most abandoned sinner on his death-bed."

Three days after this sermon was given, the one who had been so deeply impressed was suddenly confronted with death, and being wholly unconscious, there was time only for the final absolution. Although not an abandoned sinner, it was most comforting to those who surrounded that death-bed to recall the fervent desires which the Bishop's consoling words had inspired.

But to return to his labors at the Cathedral: Father Curtis took especial interest in the children of the parish, catechising and instructing them for an hour every Saturday morning, when he could be seen listening in the liveliest manner to their simple questions and answers. He was passionately fond of little children, and when the pattering of their tiny feet was heard on the stone floor of the great Cathedral he would leave his place to go after them, take them up in his arms, caress and even kiss them.

One afternoon a little "tot" of four or five years

running up a side aisle of the church, with her head thrown back, caught sight of the window in the great central dome, where the Eternal Father is represented as a venerable old man, bending over the world; the little one clapped her hands and cried aloud, " O Santa Claus! Santa Claus! " This proved irresistible to the loving heart of the good priest, who, snatching her up in his arms, and placing her on the back of a pew, began smiling and talking to her of the great " Santa " or Father of us all. " I know not," he once said, " what the world would do if it were not for the old people and the little children," and it was in his dealings with them that he revealed the charming simplicity of his noble character.

He knew how to bend down to the little and the lowly, and to accommodate himself to their ways, while his great deference and respect for Superiors appeared in the admirable humility with which he seemed even to efface himself that *they* might appear, and this he did in so gracious and affable a manner as to attract the admiration of all who witnessed it.

The Archbishop and his three assistants were greatly attached to one another, and they made a very congenial household, so that when the untimely death of Archbishop Bayley came, only two years later, they were all but inconsolable in their loss, and as one of them remarked: " We never quite got over it." This was the first great cross of separation for Father Curtis after becoming a Catholic, and he deeply lamented one who understood him so well, and to whom he felt himself bound by strong ties of sympathy and affection. Their characters were strikingly alike, and "it was necessary to have an intimate knowledge of both men, in order to overlook their seeming peculiarities, and to esteem their just worth," says one who knew them well. This was the happy portion of those who had learned to look up to, and lean upon their guidance, for *they* could not regard as peculiarities actions performed from a sense of honor and uprightness of intention, even at the cost of disfavor and criticism.

Father Curtis revered the memory of his first Superior in the Catholic Church with undiminished affection and respect to the last days of his life. For years after the Archbishop's death, in his daily walks he carried the cane which his Grace had used and given him, as a souvenir of the friendship which existed between them.

In 1877 the Right Reverend James Gibbons of Richmond, our illustrious Cardinal, succeeded to the Archiepiscopal See, and to him Father Curtis now gave his allegiance, remaining his obedient servant until death. In the spring of 1881 he had the inexpressible sorrow of parting with his mother, who passed peacefully away on the 23d of May, after an illness of several weeks. He had hoped against hope to see his beloved mother die a member of the true Church, and in his great disappointment he could be reconciled only when assured of her good faith by a friend in the priesthood, who frequently visited her during this illness. The intensity of his grief was manifested not only in private, but in public also. Seated in the confessional, and giving comfort to others, the tears flowed down his cheeks, revealing the depth of his sorrow; and in the evening devotions of the month of May, which he attended most faithfully, he was seen silently weeping.

Cardinal Newman says in his article on " Religious Parties ": " You cannot make others think as you will, even those who are nearest and dearest to you," and like this great man, Father Curtis had to suffer the want of sympathy on the part of those nearest and dearest to him, even until death. He remarked at one time that he felt confident that had his father ever met a Catholic priest he would have entered the true fold; doubtless he meant that his father's great mind and broad views would have made him amenable to the teachings of Holy Church, and, consequently, had he

Rt. Rev. A. A. Curtis, D.D.

ever come in contact with a priest, he would have investigated the truth and embraced it.

In the declining years of his life, however, Bishop Curtis had the consolation of hearing of the admission to the true fold of his long lost brother, who, dying far away from home, had the happiness of securing his salvation. In a letter written about that time the Bishop said: "Forty years or more ago my only brother quitted us all to take up his abode in Montana; he never did anything for us, and would not even write to us. Early this year I got a letter from one, a total stranger to me, informing me that he, my brother, was in a certain town of Montana, quite ill and entirely without money, and that he must go to the poorhouse unless I could otherwise provide for him. I wrote to Bishop Blondel, since dead, and got entrance for him into St. John's Hospital, Helena, where he has been ever since, and is likely to stay as long as he lives, which cannot now be very long. . . . I am glad to say that he has been baptized since he went to the hospital." Later, for his brother lingered some months, the Bishop heard that he had received all the privileges and rites of a true member of Holy Church.

To the great Mother of God, for whom he entertained a peculiarly touching devotion, Father Curtis must have turned most confidingly in the overwhelming sorrow, caused by the loss of his beloved mother. In Her, the "Comforter of the Afflicted," he surely found that solace which all true devoted sons of Mary experience when under the pressure of the Cross.

It was through his marked devotion to the Blessed Virgin that he organized a Sodality at the Cathedral. There each week, on Friday evening, he led the devotions, manual in hand, uniting his voice in singing the English hymns with the assembled multitude. The evening chosen was not without a purpose in the mind of the pious director, for, he said, in naming the

87

day, " we may at least lessen the number at the theatre on Friday night by paying devotion to the Mother of God instead."

About this time a rather novel and interesting meeting took place between the two future bishops of Wilmington. It was a lovely afternoon in the month of June when Father Curtis, according to his weekly custom, wended his way to St. Mary's Seminary. He was told at his entrance that the Fathers had gone with the students for a walk, but that there was a young priest in room No. — who would doubtless hear his confession. After this sacred duty was accomplished, the following conversation took place between confessor and penitent: " And who are you?" asked Father Curtis, with his genial simplicity. " I am Father Monaghan of South Carolina," answered the smiling confessor, who was twenty-five years his junior, " and I am here collecting for a church, I am trying to build in Spartanburg." " Well," was the answer, " I have n't anything much with me; let me see," — and putting his hand in his pocket, Father Curtis drew forth a five-dollar bill, saying, " Take this, Father, it may be of some help to your project." Both were in the early years of their priesthood, and were destined to succeed each other in building many churches for the glory of God, and in laboring for the salvation of souls in the same Episcopal See.

The three weeks' vacation allowed the clergy of the Archdiocese was taken advantage of by Father Curtis to get away from the crowded city, to lose sight of the newspapers and his mail for a time, by taking to the woods, or, preferably, to the water, where, laying aside all formality, he could indulge in his favorite pastimes of boating and fishing.

From boyhood he was a good fisherman and an expert yachtsman, and often ventured out in the bay by himself in a little yawl where few would dare to go, and now in these summer outings he chose a companion who, like himself, was a good sailor and willing to rough it.

Providing themselves with a small sailboat, in which they stored the necessaries for saying holy Mass, some hard-tack, and other dried provisions for a three weeks' cruise, they sailed to the mouth of the Chesapeake Bay, a distance of some two hundred miles. He and his companion, an aspirant to the priesthood, were good swimmers and did not mind risking a heavy blow, while the element of danger lent zest to the adventurous sport and caused the old boatmen to shake their heads and express surprise that those daring sailors were not drowned.

Towards evening, when twilight settled on the sea and the day's toil was at an end, they found some little cove or quiet nook where, pitching their tent, they made their bed on the ground, with an armful of pine branches. Several times their frail little craft capsized, or stranded on an unknown bar; but after a good ducking they recovered themselves, and securing their skiff, feared not to hazard further dangers.

On one occasion they made an attempt to shoot the rapids of the French Broad River from Asheville to Hot Springs, North Carolina, but failing to accomplish this exploit, nothing daunted, they determined to conquer, as indeed they did, the following year. The river runs in a strong current among the rocks, and it is only necessary to float in a dugout and avoid the rocks by using an iron-pointed pole. There are several narrow passages through which the whole river plunges, and the boat was swamped in one of these, after having successfully jumped a rather formidable waterfall. Shoes, stockings and many other articles were lost, and the last ten miles of the journey had to be made over a hot and dusty road. Clothed in knee breeches and rough flannel shirts, their limbs burned and blistered by the blazing sun, these intrepid seamen, with sails lowered, and looking like tramps, made their way through the town to the main hotel, where their baggage, which they had shipped ahead, awaited them.

There was nothing striking in the cut of their garments, and while the guests of the hotel wondered at their novel appearance, none suspected that such a forlorn pair of travellers could be bent upon pleasure.

In 1883 Father Curtis accompanied Archbishop Gibbons to Rome, and while nothing remains to tell of the impressions made by this visit to the Eternal City, it may be readily imagined that it played an important part in the life of this holy ecclesiastic. He once remarked that his only desire in going abroad was to see St. Peter's, and to have an audience with the Holy Father. Undoubtedly this visit served to increase his love for that supreme authority, vested in the Vicar of Christ, and strengthened the bonds uniting him to holy Mother Church. In the fall of the following year the Third Plenary Council of Baltimore was convened, in which Father Curtis acted as theologian and secretary to the Most Rev. Archbishop Seghers, a zealous and holy prelate, who afterwards sacrificed his life when serving the Indian missions of Alaska.

He was much beloved and greatly revered by his companions in the same field of labor, who styled him "the St. Francis de Sales of the United States," on account of his great meekness and condescension, combined with his priestly zeal and episcopal dignity. Father Curtis was much attracted by his amiable qualities of mind and heart, and spoke most feelingly of him, upon hearing the sad and untimely death of this self-sacrificing apostle, who fell a victim to an assassin's bullet, having been shot by his guide on their journey to Alaska.

This occurred on the 28th day of November, in the year 1886, at the very time the burden of the episcopacy was laid upon the shoulders of Father Curtis, and naturally produced a sad impression on one already weighed down by the thought of the new and unlooked for responsibility imposed upon him. He was ever averse to any office bearing in its train dignities and honors, for the deep humility of his soul filled him with distrust of self, and he was heard to say, " I care not how many I have over me, provided I have no one under me."

When he received the news of his elevation to the Episcopal dignity, with characteristic humility he made a threefold appeal to escape the responsibility, representing to his superiors the consciousness he felt of his inability to hold the office, but when his objections were gently but firmly overruled, with that ingenuous frankness which was one of the guiding principles of his life, he said, " I promised my Mother, Holy Church, when entering her fold, ever to be her obedient son, and now at the call of duty in her service, I must submit; although I feel that Almighty God will not compel me to carry this heavy burden more than ten years." Was this a prophecy, or could he have known by some secret intuition that in a decade of years his words would be verified? Whether a prophecy or not, the sequel proved the correctness of his statement, for after ten years of arduous labor his health was so impaired that he found himself unequal to the work, and making application to the Holy See, was relieved of his charge. These ten years were to be, perhaps, the most strenuous of his whole life, for during this time he was to give full scope to his apostolic zeal and unbounded spirit of self-sacrifice in the labors of a struggling diocese.

He was accustomed to take the heaviest part of the burden upon himself, choosing always that which was most humble, obscure and laborious, and when urged to ask the assistance of others, he replied, " I never exact of my priests that which I find too hard for myself."

He was justly styled " The Ideal Champion of the

Rt. Rev. A. A. Curtis, D.D.

Missionary Life," while his predecessor, the Rt. Rev. Thomas A. Becker, bore the title of " Pioneer Bishop and Staunch Defender of Higher Education," to which the beautiful bronze tablets erected to their memory in St. Peter's Cathedral of Wilmington bear testimony.

These handsome memorials of the first bishops of Wilmington were placed in the Cathedral and bear the following inscription:

" Erected in Saint Peter's Cathedral on July 4, 1909, by the gracious generosity of the Bishop, Clergy and Laity of the Diocese of Wilmington, to the sacred memory of the Most Illustrious and Most Revered Bishops
Becker and Curtis.

" Though dead yet do they speak."

CHAPTER VII

1886

IF Delaware on account of its size is named the " Diamond State," [1] having been formed out of the three lower counties of Pennsylvania, what honor and glory are due to the rugged pioneers of Catholicity in those parts, whose spirit of faith and self-sacrifice helped to smooth and polish that diamond, which with the growth of civilizaton, education and religion would dazzle future generations by the beauty of its lustre and the solidity of its setting? But their labors were not confined to this narrow territory, for they extended throughout Maryland, and over a good portion of the State of Pennsylvania.

Notably among these missionaries were the Jesuits of Bohemia in Cecil County, Maryland, who in the year 1772 purchased the ground in Delaware, on which they built a little log chapel near Coffee Run, just six miles from Wilmington, the remains of which were standing until recently, serving as a relic of early Catholicity in Delaware.

The first pastor of this little church was the Reverend Patrick Kenny, who had, besides, five other stations, or missions, included in three counties and two states, and one of these stations was Wilmington, which was usually attended monthly. His successors were the Reverend George A. Carrell, the Very Reverend P. Reilly, and others who have left a glorious example of disinterested zeal and magnanimous courage in embracing the hardships, fatigues and troubles in-

---

[1] Delaware is affectionately called by its people the "Diamond State," to signify that it has great value in a small compass.

Rt. Rev. A. A. Curtis, D.D.

separable from the labor of breaking the soil of a new and rough country.

This spirit has been bequeathed by these generous missionaries, as a rich inheritance, so that when in the year 1868 a diocese was created, separating Delaware from the Archdiocese of Philadelphia, to which it had hitherto been subject, and adding to it the counties of the eastern shores of Maryland and Virginia, it still retained its missionary character. The Wilmington diocese is known as the "Delmarvia Peninsula," so called after the three states which contribute to its formation — the whole of Delaware, nine counties of Maryland, and two counties of Virginia, east of the Chesapeake Bay.

" Its first Bishop was the Right Reverend Thomas A. Becker, D.D., whose indomitable will and unbounded zeal fitted him to cope with the difficulties of a new and only half cultivated field. He was a man of brilliant talents and great scholarly attainments, with an unusual facility for acquiring languages. He spoke several of the modern languages fluently, was a master of Greek and Latin and had some knowledge of Irish, Sanskrit, Syrian, Chaldaic and Hebrew. Before his conversion to the Faith he had studied with much success in the University of Virginia, and after his reception into the Church, and some preliminary training given by his life-long friend, Father Plunkett of Martinsburg, West Virginia, he was sent to Rome by Bishop McGill, where he distinguished himself among a galaxy of other intellectual giants, who like himself became eminent as theologians, and were elevated to the highest dignities in the Church.

It is no matter for surprise that a Bishop of such gifts, to which were united much piety and fervent uncompromising faith, should be fully equipped, to face all obstacles and trials, and ready to spend himself for the glory of God and the good of souls." [1]

[1] Dedication Souvenir of St. Peter's Cathedral, Wilmington, Del.

Rt. Rev. A. A. Curtis, D.D.

The administration of Bishop Becker, continued for eighteen years, during which time the diocese became solidly established, only, however, at the cost of untold sacrifices and indescribable labors; yet Divine Providence had other and even more arduous and self-sacrificing work in store for the zealous Bishop. In the spring of 1886 he was asked by His Eminence, Cardinal Gibbons, if he would be willing to accept the administration of the Savannah diocese, which had become vacant through the promotion of the Rt. Rev. William H. Gross, to the Archiepiscopal See of Oregon City. Upon his generous consent, he was transferred to the government of this See of such vast area, but with as scant resources as little Wilmington, which he had so successfully pioneered to a condition of self-dependence and progress.

His successor, the Right Reverend Alfred A. Curtis, called the diocese of Wilmington his " Wilderness," and so it was, being still in many places, " a diamond in the rough." On one occasion in a conversation with some friends, the poverty of the diocese, the scarcity of priests, and the extra labor imposed upon the Bishop being remarked, he replied with great feeling: " My labors and trials are nothing when compared with those of my good predecessor. He laid the foundation and paved the way for me, he did the hard work, and when I think of the extreme poverty of the diocese as he found it, without churches, without priests, without money, I marvel how he accomplished what he did. All that has been done is his work, not mine."

If for eighteen years Bishop Becker tilled the rugged soil of this poor diocese, it was his holy successor, Bishop Curtis, who watered it with the sweat of his brow, while under the government of its present Bishop, the Right Reverend John J. Monaghan, God has given the increase, this pious Prelate having chosen for his motto: " Deus incrementum dat."

Six months after the transfer of the Right Reverend

Rt. Rev. A. A. Curtis, D.D.

Thomas A. Becker to the diocese of Savannah, the consecration of the Right Reverend Alfred A. Curtis took place in the Cathedral of Baltimore. The 14th of November was the day chosen for the solemnity, which happily coincided that year with the feast of the Patronage of the Blessed Virgin Mary, under whose auspices this great missionary Bishop was to begin his labors. The morning dawned bright and beautiful, and the great doors of the Cathedral were thrown open at an early hour to admit the immense concourse of people who thronged to the brilliant consecration ceremonies. Besides the innumerable friends of the Bishop Elect and a few relatives, there were five hundred persons from the See of Wilmington, who had made the journey for the purpose of witnessing the consecration of their new Bishop. A daily journal [1] of that city gives the following details of the great event:

"The ceremonies were grand and most impressive, the consecrator being Cardinal Gibbons, assisted by Bishop Kain of Wheeling and Bishop Moore of St. Augustine, Florida. There were present also Bishop Chàtard of Vincennes, Bishop Becker of Savannah, Monsignor McColgan, eighty clergymen, two hundred students from St. Mary's Seminary, and a vast congregation.

"The participants and attendants formed in processional order at the Cardinal's residence, and walked slowly around the southern side of the property into the Cathedral through the main entrance. Censer-bearers led the way, followed by sanctuary boys in white surplices and black cassocks. The clergy, Monsignor McColgan, Bishops Chàtard, Kain, Moore and Bishop Elect Curtis came next, preceding the Cardinal, who wore the imposing insignia of his rank, including the Cappa Magna. His long train was carried by four little boys in white surplices and red cassocks.

"When the Cardinal entered the Church the choir of fifty or more voices sang with grand effect, ' Ecce Sacer-

[1] Morning Journal.

Rt. Rev. A. A. Curtis, D.D.

dos Magnus.' Passing through the sanctuary gate, the seminarians went to the right and left of the main Altar and occupied seats in the recesses. The clergy were seated along the sanctuary rail, and on chairs in the cross aisle facing the Altar. Bishop Elect Curtis with Bishops Kain and Moore, took positions in front of the small Altar on the south side, and the Cardinal sat upon his throne to the north of the main Altar, with the Reverend Dr. Magnien and Reverend M. Walters, deacons of honor, seated either side.

" A good number of the Clergy from Wilmington were in attendance, showing by their presence the desire they had to honor and welcome to the diocese their new Superior, to whom on this day they pledged their allegiance.

"When all were seated the spectacle thus formed was brilliant and imposing, the center of the scene being the resplendent main Altar, with its polished marbles, burnished ornaments of brass and silver, hundreds of lighted candles, and artistic decorations of smilax, chrysanthemums and growing plants. To the north and south were the lesser Altars, the prelates, clergymen, seminarians, and sanctuary boys, while in the foreground of the vast Cathedral were the people, so numerous that every pew was crowded and all the aisles filled. Only pew-holders and invited guests were admitted before the procession took place, but after the Cardinal reached his throne the barriers were removed, and in a few minutes thereafter this throng extended from the aisles out into the street.

" The Ceremony of Consecration was long and solemn, embracing the anointing of the head and hands, the blessing of the crosier, which is the staff of the pastoral office, the ring, mitre and other sacred insignia; after which the new Bishop was led to the episcopal chair, to signify that henceforth he holds the office of judge and ruler.

"At the Gospel of the Mass the pulpit was moved

Rt. Rev. A. A. Curtis, D.D.

to the front of the Altar, and the Right Reverend Thomas A. Becker of Savannah ascended and preached the sermon. He began by reading the text from Matthew xxviii, 16th to 20th verses, inclusive, as follows:

"And the eleven disciples went into Galilee, unto the Mountain where Jesus had appointed them.

"And seeing Him they adored: but some doubted.

"And Jesus, coming, spoke to them, saying: All power is given to Me in Heaven and in earth.

"Going, therefore teach ye all nations: baptizing them in the name of the Father, and of the Son, and of the Holy Ghost. Teaching them to observe all things whatsoever I have commanded you: and behold I am with you all days, even to the consummation of the world."

"The Bishop began by saying that Jesus Christ claimed, and had proven His claim to all power. Having the power, He transferred it through St. Peter and his successors to the Church. His mission is not only all-powerful, but perpetual, and ample provision had been made for the continuance of this work, in which He promises His perpetual presence. An eternal commission like this requires eternal existence. The Catholic Church alone can show a direct succession from Leo XIII, tracing backward to St. Peter, embracing some two hundred and thirty pontiffs. Her genealogical pedigree is direct, clear, concise. She has a more perfect succession than even this favored republic of ours, in those who have at least been acknowledged in its succession. When we see the serried columns of twenty general Councils march before us, and note how rapidly the Church has spread over the world, it is evident that however small it may have been in the beginning, it was breathed upon by the divine power and has ever since grown in majesty. . . .

"In matchless purity it still continues, for it has an immortal life. The Catholic Church has also been the guardian and preserver of all that has been handed down to us of what was precious, in the literature of

98

the world — the literature of pagan Greece and pagan Rome — and most precious of all, the manuscript of the Scriptures. The Apostolic succession is a perpetual continuance by the order of Jesus Christ. The Roman Pontiff is the direct successor of St. Peter, and has by divine right the Apostolic Jurisdiction. The Bishop then went on to state the work that had been done by the prelates of the province in selecting worthy names to be sent to the Sovereign Pontiff. He said: From among them, one has been selected; one who is near and dear to you. Never can a calling and avocation be more firmly assured, than when to the divine vocation which drew him to the dedication of himself to the service of his Master, is added the mandate of the Vicar of Christ, the visible head of the Church.

" In conclusion Bishop Becker spoke highly of the good report given the new Bishop, by those among whom he had labored. ' He has worked both in season and out of season, and with gifts innumerable; his talents are devoted to the service of his Master. You may be sure his consecration is from on high'; and, then addressing himself directly to the newly consecrated, the Bishop said: Go, feed the flock which has been entrusted to your care. I know well that your modesty would ask me to keep a gracious silence, but I cannot forget to say why you are raised to this high dignity. Placed in the peculiar position of addressing my successor, I ask in the first place most earnestly the benefit of your prayers. May the shortcomings of your predecessor find ample correction in your zeal, earnestness and judgment. Go, teach and preach and perform the works of the apostle. Your sheep only ask to know your will in order to perform it. The people to whom you are sent are generous and well-disposed, and even those who are not of the household of the faith are generous and open-hearted, and without bigotry or ill-will.

Rt. Rev. A. A. Curtis, D.D.

" May the peace of God remain with you, the communication of the Holy Ghost accompany all your labors and bless them, that you with your flock may be found at the right hand of the Father when Christ shall say, ' Come ye blessed of My Father, possess the kingdom prepared for you from the foundation of the world.' "

After Mass the newly consecrated was attended along the main aisle of the church, by the assisting Bishops, giving his blessing to the congregation as he passed. Then the procession reformed, and wended its way back to the Cardinal's residence, while the congregation repaired to the sacristy where the beautiful episcopal gifts were displayed. They included four costly rings, three of which had unusually fine stones, surrounded by diamonds of the first water; the fourth was a remarkable Egyptian seal. In addition to these was a magnificent gold cross set with diamonds, representing a halo, the gold chain from which the cross was suspended being heavy and elegant. There were besides a jewelled mitre, two crosiers set with brilliants, laces, embroidered slippers, Bibles, Breviary, Missal, gold and silver candlesticks and many other beautiful gifts.

In the evening the Bishop sang Pontifical Vespers, after which a number of his friends called to offer congratulations.

On the following Sunday, November 21, Bishop Curtis was installed in St. Peter's Cathedral at Wilmington by Cardinal Gibbons, assisted by Archbishop Ryan of Philadelphia, Bishop Moore of Florida and Bishop Becker of Savannah. The Cardinal preached the sermon, at the conclusion of which he delivered a glowing eulogium on the great learning, piety and zeal, combined with extraordinary humility and meekness of his former secretary, " whom none knew but to love, and to love all the more, the better he was known."

Rt. Rev. A. A. Curtis, D.D.

In the course of a conversation after the ceremony His Eminence spoke of the esteem in which Bishop Curtis was held by the people of Baltimore, how all parted from him with deepest regret, adding that he, himself, could only become reconciled to this loss by the knowledge that he would have a larger field in which to display his extraordinary learning and virtue.

Bishop Curtis had now reached the full prime of his vigorous manhood, and was of a magnificent physique and commanding appearance, with a certain dignity and gravity of bearing which inspired reverence, even something akin to fear; that fear, however, which engenders respect, and makes impossible any undue familiarity. His benevolent countenance mirrored the peace and serenity of his well-ordered soul; for the unceasing warfare he maintained in his interior, unknown to others, was the secret of that gentle and benignant charity which showed itself on every occasion.

If as a holy contemplative says, " for every act of self-suppression God gives an action of His own," what abundant graces must have fallen upon this soul, who possessed the land of his heart, by a meekness for which he had ever to strive; thus acquiring that strength of virtue which was to influence so many coming in contact with him, or living under his direction.

CHAPTER VIII

1886 – 1888

THE first care of the newly consecrated Bishop was to regulate his household, choosing from among the clergy those whom he thought best fitted to compose it, and to work with him in advancing the interests of the flock committed to his guidance. After mature consideration he concluded to adopt the plan of promoting the pastors of the country districts to the city parishes, choosing them according to seniority; this plan he admitted had its drawback, but on the whole presented the fewest difficulties. It was his purpose, likewise, to have only willing workers in his diocese, and as soon as circumstances would permit, to allow any priest, who would so desire, to transfer his allegiance to any other Bishop who would be willing to accept his services, for he would force no one to change his work.

"When summoned to give up a pastorate in a country district, to which I was much attached," says one of the older priests of the diocese, "my first thought, which later became a fixed determination, was to decline the honor; five minutes' conversation with the Bishop compelled me to surrender completely, and from that day I have thanked God, and will forever praise Him for the incomparable blessing bestowed upon me, in being permitted to live under the same roof, and enjoy an intimate intercourse with this holy servant of God, and that for the space of eleven years. The impression made upon me in this first interview," he continues, "never left my mind and

Rt. Rev. A. A. Curtis, D.D.

heart, but rather quickened admiration and affection as the years passed away. His frankness and simplicity, his earnestness and zeal, together with his paternal tenderness, took possession of all who constituted his household. I had no sooner taken up my residence with him, when he entrusted to me the whole management of Church and house, saying in his great humility, that he had never attended to such duties, and that he possessed no aptitude for them; moreover, if he had an especial vocation it was to serve the wanderers of the poor country districts who were in greater need, and as this would necessitate his being absent a long time, he wished me to concern myself particularly in looking after the interests of the city clergy and people. This, however, did not prevent him from being present and officiating Pontifically in his Cathedral at all the important Festivals, when he generally preached his original, direct and practical sermons, very carefully thought out as a rule, but never memorized, because his soul was an overflowing fountain of salutary waters of divine grace and human erudition.

" In these discourses, as in every other relation of life, he was averse to all display, and whatever degree of intellectuality and scholarship he possessed, and these were of no mean order, he was always very modest and unassuming. Although he had never passed through the training and discipline of a College or University Course, and had been given but two short years of the Seminary Curriculum, which was at times painfully manifest, he nevertheless always appeared equal to every emergency, whether in the pulpit or rostrum, whether addressing Bishops, Priests, Seminarians or Religious bodies, learned Judges and Lawyers or professional Scientists."

He seemed to have read everything and to have retained what he read, his memory being rarely at fault, so that he was at home in all questions that came up in every branch of literature, and likewise had made

103

himself familiar with all the Greek and Latin Fathers, as well as the Scriptures which he seemed to know by heart, reading every day a chapter in Hebrew. Whilst a priest he had read most carefully the works of St. Thomas even seven times over, and every day a sermon of Bossuet, besides having absorbed the works of standard ascetics, just as he had very early in life devoured the English poets and Blackstone's Commentaries.

His "Vade Mecum" was St. Bernard and his ideals St. Paul and his Divine Master, Whom he ever strove to imitate, so that while drawing others to walk in the same path, he seemed to say by word and example, "Be ye followers of me, as I also am of Christ." 1 Cor. iv. 16.

The Bishop could be, when he chose, a clever disputant, but he rarely argued, especially with the opponents of our faith, for he was convinced that the best way to reach the understanding is through the heart, hence he discouraged controversial preaching in his clergy, enjoining upon them in order to make converts, to preach plain, practical sermons, as if all present were Catholic, and to make their own people faithful and devout members of the Church, adding, ". Verba movent — exempla trahunt."

During the Lenten Season he invariably preached the full course of sermons, likewise the "Three Hours' Prayer" on Good Friday, in addition to sermons at the morning and evening services, and besides these a "ferverino" on the other nights of Holy Week, and in the morning and evening of Easter Sunday.

Although his labors at home and throughout the diocese were more exacting and incessant during the penitential season, he nevertheless maintained the strict olden time black fast, taking no meat from the beginning of Lent until Easter and denying himself the use of milk, butter and eggs, allowed by holy Church, and yet he naïvely declared, "He had not fasted since he

Bishop Curtis as Bishop of Wilmington.

became a Catholic." As a Protestant he allowed neither food nor drink to pass his lips throughout the whole season of Lent, until the meal taken at sundown, having been taught according to his own words, " it is only Christian to fast," but as a Catholic it seemed to him he did not fast at all, so light and easy is that done through obedience, when compared with what is done by one's own will, " When the Bridegroom is present there is no fast."

At the midday meal the Bishop used nothing but vegetables, fruits and jams, which he invariably mixed together to make the most uninviting and unpalatable repast, and in the evening he took a small portion of fruit and a cup of tea with a biscuit or two, occasionally. He must have used the discipline unsparingly, one having been found in his room, which he evidently forgot to hide, armed with steel prongs, and much stained with blood. He also wore a hair shirt and heavy chains which caused him at times to walk with difficulty.

It was his custom to retire to his room a little after nine o'clock in the evening, and he was the first of the household to rise in the morning, being up as early as half-past four, and after making two full hours of preparation, celebrated holy Mass at eight o'clock, assisting at three and sometimes four Masses besides.

Several times when the clergy of his household were called in the night or the early hours of the morning to visit the sick or to assist the dying, they found the Bishop prostrated in the middle aisle of the Church, face downwards. There in the silence of the night and the solitude of the Sanctuary, he kept his vigil with the Prisoner of Love, and poured forth his soul for the needs of his diocese, knowing full well " that no weapon pierces the heart of God like earnest, humble prayer."

He had his trials from the very outset of his Administration, but he knew how to bear them alone, never permitting others to be afflicted by them, for he could not endure to give the least pain to any one. His strong irascible nature was often roused by the force of contending circumstances, but almost instantly quelled by the energy of his vigorous ascetic life, so that it could be said of him as of the gentle but firm St. Francis de Sales, " he had passions — violent passions — but he had them only to put them to death."

Although the most charitable of men, he was heard to say openly in a sermon that there was no sin for which he chastised himself more severely than for uncharitableness. " There are times," he would say, " when we cannot help having uncharitable thoughts, but it is always in our power to refrain from expressing them." With what fidelity he reproduced this virtue traced by his divine Model is seen in the unselfish sacrifice of himself in the service of his neighbor.

One out of many instances may be related here. With inexhaustible tenderness and patience he sought, uplifted and encouraged a young soul already lost to family and friends, surrounded by a thousand pitfalls, and beset by violent temptation. How he waited, prayed and did penance for that soul, guiding and safely leading it forth from sin, ruin and despondency; until at last he had the joy of placing the repenting one in a haven of safety, where several years of heroic penance and holy living were followed by a happy death.

The greater the sin, the more hopeless and tempted the soul, the stronger burned the zeal of the saintly Confessor to gain such a one for Christ. Truly may it be said that the words of the great Saint Dionysius found a living echo in his heart, " Of all divine things, there is nothing more divine than to coöperate with God in the salvation of souls."

The great control he exercised over himself and the virtues he practised amid the exigencies of occurrences were often manifest. Having generously consented to perform the functions of a religious ceremony on one occasion, at which he was to preach, his surprise mounted to a feeling of just indignation, when upon reaching his destination, after a walk of two miles, he was informed that several were waiting to make their confessions before the ceremony. He positively refused to go to the confessional, saying it was not the moment, and besides he had heard the confessions only a few days before, but after some further importunity, he finally relented and bracing himself up for the ordeal, walked quickly to the confessional, where he was confronted by two tall candlesticks and a large armchair, which had been hidden there and forgotten in the preparations for the festivities. The Bishop's feelings may be more easily imagined than expressed, as he struggled to remove the barriers to his entrance.

As soon as he reached the Gospel of the Mass, turning to his audience, he gave a beautiful discourse on the acceptance of the Will of God at every moment, which he said should be recognized and embraced even in the unexpected events of life. "When I came out here this morning it was with the intention of saying Mass and giving a little instruction, but I did not expect to hear confessions. I was not prepared for that, and I acknowledge my fault that I was not pleased when I found I had to do it. So let us make up our mind to be prepared to accept that which God asks of us at the moment, and beg of Him to give us the grace to receive what He sends, whether it be pleasing to us or not."

When the Bishop took possession of his See, he found that all church property stood in the name of the Bishop of the diocese — a most unsatisfactory state of affairs at best, one which in case of the Bishop's death could cause great complication, and to which he determined to apply a prompt remedy.

For this purpose, and with great inconvenience to

himself, he took steps to obtain from the legislatures of the three states in which the diocese lies, namely, Maryland, Virginia and Delaware, the passing of a law, that would permit an incorporate title for each separate church and dependent property.

This appeal the Bishop pushed perseveringly for several years, until at last his untiring energy was crowned with success. Then came a second and still more laborious task; that of visiting every church of his diocese, and taking the necessary legal steps, to have the title, standing in the name of the Bishop of Wilmington, changed to the recognized incorporate title.

Not such an agreeable work for the one who undertook and carried it through, but a work which has been of the greatest benefit to all concerned; thus straightening out matters, from which unpleasant consequences could easily have arisen. Finding that many of the parishes were carrying heavy bonds, mortgages and other forms of indebtedness, the Bishop determined to make personal application for financial help to the neighboring dioceses that were in a more flourishing condition. He made constant and eloquent appeals as liberty was granted him, to different congregations in New York, Baltimore, Boston, Philadelphia and received considerable help, although in diminutive instalments. His next movement was to hold a diocesan bazaar which netted him $28,000, which with some handsome donations from personal friends, enabled him to clear away the greater part of the debt throughout the diocese.

Thereupon he made a law at his first Synod, that no more debt should be contracted beyond $150 for any purpose whatever, for he contended that it is no more justifiable for a church or religious organization to make unnecessary debt than for individuals. All are bound to practise economy and live within their means, and especially ought this to hold good with regard to bishops, priests and religious, who in this, as in all other matters, should be the leaders and exemplars.

One of his clergy offered him the bulk of his modest little patrimony, which the Bishop declined to accept, and noticing the painful effect produced by his refusal, he made the singular observation that he had already been accused of promoting this priest because bribed to do so by a fabulous sum. "This bequest," he said, "ought at least to be held sacred, as it does not belong to the diocese, and will be needful later," which proved a very fortunate prophecy.

Writing to a priest of the diocese on the subject of debt, he said, "The longer I live the more I am opposed to debt anywhere, and most of all in the case of country churches."

On one occasion, when preaching, his words seemed to apply so directly to the officiating clergyman that the latter could not conceal his displeasure; upon observing it the Bishop accosted him, and demanded the cause of his offence. In his turn, the Bishop felt deeply moved to think that he could be accused of any such dishonorable procedure, and assured the Father that every word of the sermon had been addressed to himself. He had often been heard to say, that when he preached it was more for himself than for others, and that if one wished to reform others, he should begin with himself. "Let each one reform himself," he said, "and that will be the best way to reform and convert the country."

The Bishop imposed upon himself the duty of visiting the County Almshouse to hear the confessions of the inmates, and this he did twice a year, choosing Christmas Eve and Holy Saturday for his visits. His indulgent kindness and tender sympathy drew all to him, and gained many hardened sinners. None feared to approach him, for he could not speak an unkind word, but on the contrary seemed to say like his prototype: "My heart is enlarged for you all." 2 Cor.

vi. 11. Men and women who had remained away from the sacred tribunal of Penance for years, returned weeping, or sobbing like children, so much touched were they by his love and paternal tenderness. He offered the first holy Mass at this Institution, giving the chalice, vestments and altar cloths, and that the inmates might have the consolation of assisting at the holy sacrifice more frequently, he appointed one of his priests to say Mass there every month. He had the stations erected for their benefit, and when he preached to them his sermons were full of charity, and the love of one another. Nor was he less solicitous for their bodily comfort, sending them fruit, confectionery, nuts and raisins, and even tobacco for the old men, and this he did every year at Christmas and Easter, providing at the same time for the whole Institution. On Holy Thursday he gathered twelve of the old men in his Cathedral, to wash their feet immediately after the long morning services. Before drying them he kissed them, notwithstanding the fact that some were gangrenous and of a very repulsive appearance; then he dismissed them with a *liberal* alms.

Every year he held a Diocesan Synod, which lasted three full days, in which the laws and regulations of the diocese were promulgated, religious questions discussed, and social intercourse kept up between the clergy. Mass was celebrated each day and a sermon preached to which the laity were invited, and this was productive of much good in manifold ways.

At the close of these synods the Bishop, seated on the predella of the Altar, and vested in cope and mitre, holding his crosier firmly in hand, made the final address. Never at any time did he appear to be more fully invested with all the power and majesty of Apostolic succession. In clear, powerful and even impassioned words, he addressed his clergy as one bearing authority, deeply impressing all present with the solid-

Interior of old St. Peter's.
–1886–

ity of his vigorous sentiments, while his strong, stentorian tones seemed to make the very walls of the Cathedral vibrate.

The Bishop delighted to show hospitality to his clergy and to have them around him, and these meetings truly resembled the reunion of Father and Sons. On one of these occasions Father Gaffney, a pious Jesuit, who was then stationed at the old Bohemia Manor, remarked that he could not understand how people generally were so dissatisfied with their past life. " He had," he said, " not done anything out of the common, but had he to begin life over again he did not know how he could manage any better." The Bishop clapped his hands, declaring enthusiastically that he was most delighted to hear one hold this opinion, which he shared with him from the fullness of his heart. " I, too," remarked the Bishop, " can conscientiously say that I have tried to live the best I know how, with the lights and graces given me, and I would not know how to do any better, if I had to begin my life over again." He was ever the good and faithful steward and kept himself in readiness for the summons, which for him might come at any time, or in any way most pleasing to the divine Will. The following simple but forcible comparison which he once made use of when speaking of keeping oneself always ready for the call, will prove the truth of this assertion:

" Just as a school-master might say to his pupils when leaving the class-room, I will return, but without letting them know whether it will be in an hour or less, fearing that they would give themselves up to amusements if they knew that they had a certain length of time, and would do their duty only when they expected him to return; so our Lord mercifully conceals from us the time of His coming, for if people knew that they had several years to live, they might spend most of the time in earthly enjoyments and prepare for death only when it is near; thus they would lose the reward that might have been theirs had they always kept themselves in readiness for His coming at any hour." Our Lord says, "Watch ye therefore, because you know not *what hour* your Lord will come." Matt. xxiv. 42.

Although a lover of his country and scrupulously obedient to every law, the Bishop was not blind to her demerits. He called himself "An American of Americans," possibly alluding to the day of his birth in connection with the "Day of Independence," but he did not fear nor hesitate to cry down that spirit of independence peculiar to the American nation. "There is in every one of us," he said, "that spirit of rebellion, what we are pleased to call American independence. I feel it every hour of my life; I have to crush it and trample it down. We began in rebellion, we were born in rebellion, and we glory in it, saying like Lucifer: 'Who shall rule over us? Who shall be Lord over us?' That spirit which we see everywhere, that is the spirit we've got to crush out." This spirit of independence which the Bishop so forcibly condemned had reference in his mind, principally to the effect it has on individuals, in their duty to God and religion, emancipating them from all submission to authority, without which there is no true order — "God's first law."

He was essentially a candidate for the Eternal and Heavenly Country, and strove to lift all, who were subject to him, above the narrow limits of earthly boundaries to seek first and always, the Kingdom of God and His justice.

It will not be out of place to quote here from one of his letters in which he is ready to apologize for any offence his strong expressions, regarding American independence, may have given; at the same time corroborating his decided opinion on this subject: "It relieves me a good deal to know that my opinion of the American spirit did not make you angry. I have been scolding myself ever since for having been so unwise as to say such a thing. But in my own case I do feel so profoundly the misfortune of having grown up, not only as an American, but as a Protestant, that sometimes my feelings contrive to get the use of my tongue."

These humble remarks of the Bishop bring forth another beautiful trait in his character — his consideration for the feelings of others, which always distinguished him, for he lived by the rule of austerity to self and mildness to the neighbor. Writing to a friend who with him had been implicated in a misunderstanding which brought much anxiety and trouble to both, he says: "The late complication caused me trouble too, but I can't say I suffered. I think I am incapable of anything which you would call suffering; nevertheless I had what you did not have, *viz.*, self-reproach. First, on account of hastiness in writing. I am getting old, and have known much as to the mischief coming of precipitancy, so I was without excuse in not waiting. Secondly, I accused myself of cowardice as to the matter. When writing at all, I should have written straight to you or to C———. When I am cool, I am morbidly afraid of paining others, and am always considering how I can escape inflicting upon them anything likely to hurt. And I weakly yielded to the dread of hurting either of you, and made a request which I ought not to have made of M———, and after all caused both a good deal more suffering than would have come had I written frankly to either or both, and this is usually the result of cowardice."

It is easy to recognize in the Bishop what Cardinal Newman is pleased to style his idea of a true gentleman — "one who never needlessly inflicts pain." But the most striking characteristic of the Bishop's holy life was undoubtedly his humility, for humility was the foundation of his spiritual edifice as well as the crowning glory of his old age; it led him not only to a complete forgetfulness and abnegation of self, but even to that sublime degree of virtue which made him love to be despised and counted as nothing for Christ's sake.

Like all great souls he loved truth, therefore he loved humility and walked in its truth, showing forth in word and deed the practice of that admonition of St. Paul. "In humility, let each esteem others better than themselves." Phil. ii. 3. St. Francis de Sales tells us that, "Charity is an ascending humility, and humility is a descending charity," a teaching also exemplified in the life of God's humble servant, who found nothing too mean or too low when there was question of serving the neighbor. "Menial occupation lowers no man," he would say; "the only thing that lowers a man is sin." One of his priests relates the following incident: "On a certain occasion, when rooming with him in an out-of-the-way country place, I was astonished upon awakening in the morning to find that the Bishop was already up, and quietly blackening my shoes. 'You shall not do that,' I cried in dismay. 'And why not,' he replied, with his usual simplicity; 'I may as well do it, since I have finished my own.'"

Among the many instances of his inimitable condescension one recalls having seen him peel and quarter an orange for a little girl, then take the greatest pleasure in watching her eat it. This little one verified the words of the Psalmist: "Out of the mouths of babes and sucklings Thou hast perfected praise," for turning to her mother she whispered, "The Bishop is a Saint." Doubtless this was the thought, also, of another of God's little ones, whom the Bishop was seen relieving of her heavy basket and helping across a muddy crowded thoroughfare.

At another time a bevy of children ranging from six to ten years gathered around the benevolent Bishop during one of his visits to a home where he was always welcome. He looked exceedingly pleased, and smiling on the innocent upturned faces entertained them with a number of interesting anecdotes, after which he engaged each one to relate some little incident, according to the capacity of their young minds, helping and encouraging them to find their words, and form their thoughts. This innocent and simple entertainment was a source of keen enjoyment to the children, and no small cause of astonishment to a fond Mama, who seeing her bashful, timid boy transformed into a young Cicero under the kindly encouragement of the Bishop, could not restrain her enthusiasm. The Bishop not only loved to bend down to little children, but even the dumb animal had its place in his sympathetic heart. He used to say: " the humble docility of the domestic animals always touches me; we can learn from them many a lesson," and again: " I could almost love the toad, because it is so humble and despised," and stooping to the ground, he spoke gently to that lowly creature.

On another occasion, in the depths of winter, when the sidewalks were covered with sleet, the good Bishop was seen rescuing a drowning kitten. Stepping cautiously along the slippery pavement to a barrel near the curbstone, he plunged his arm into the icy water and drew forth a half-starved, pitiful looking kitten. He rubbed its back, smoothed its fur, and setting it on its feet, clapped his hands, saying, " Run now, run for your life, lest some naughty boy again play the same trick on you." This little scene was witnessed by the occupants of a snow-bound car, who were greatly impressed with such an exhibition of humane kindness on the part of the Bishop, who was wholly indifferent to the gaze of the spectators.

That ardent lover of all God's creatures, the great St. Francis of Assisi, who embraced the folly of the Cross for Christ's sake, did not consider it beneath him to preach to the birds of the air, and the fishes of the sea, whom he called his little brothers and sisters. The Bishop shared in this love both for bird and fish.

Rt. Rev. A. A. Curtis, D.D.

"Some people do not like the sparrow," he once remarked, "but I do; he is such a sturdy little fellow, and then his chirping always takes me back to the days of my retreat at the Oratory in England, where praying and meditating in the church I heard the continual chirp of the sparrows from the yard below. They always remind me too of our heavenly Father's care, and of His ineffable Providence over His children — "
"Better are you than many sparrows" . . . "and not one of them shall fall to the ground without your Father." Matt. x. 29, 31.

Love, not only for whatever was poor and lowly, but for poverty itself, held an exalted place in the Bishop's heart. Few persons knew to what an extent he practised personal poverty, so carefully did he hide his self-denial, especially during the last ten or fifteen years of his life. He gave away clothing until he had for himself what was barely necessary; he was "better pleased not to be bothered with superfluity," and he "liked what was coarse and common"; yet those who knew the Bishop well are quite aware that this was not a natural attraction, but entirely supernatural.

Like every true preacher of the Gospel, he despised the world, and trampled under foot all earthly grandeur, for he well understood that a Bishop should give an example of evangelical poverty. His grave attire, modest mien and plain living, as well as his poor Episcopal residence gave evidence of that interior detachment and abnegation of self, which he loved and practised so well. In later years on more than one occasion, to his great delight, he was taken for a beggar, for the outfit he adopted in riding the bicycle so completely disguised him, that his most intimate friends failed to recognize him. Speaking of these little episodes in a letter, he says: "I rode out to Notre Dame to see the children, and the doorkeeper more than half-suspected me to be a tramp, though it seems to me I was respectably clad." At another time, going out

Rt. Rev. A. A. Curtis, D.D.

from Baltimore on his wheel to the country home of some devoted friends, he was mistaken for a beggar by the servant who opened the door, and whose manner intimated that he should enter the house by another way. A little later what amusement on one side, and what embarrassment on the other!

The Bishop himself tells the following story: He went to call on a suburban priest to make arrangements for Confirmation, and when he asked for Father X the good housekeeper looking at him doubtfully replied, " he is very busy, sir, and I don't think he can come down " — the bicycle had been left out of sight. She announced, however, " a poor man at the door," and returning, offered him a nickel, saying, " Father X is preparing his sermon and cannot be interrupted." " Please tell him that Bishop Curtis wishes to speak to him," said the smiling prelate, at the same time showing his pectoral cross. The consternation and embarrassment of the good woman may be more easily imagined than expressed.

How edifying to behold this humble Bishop hiding under so poor and lowly an exterior such rare and exceptional gifts of mind and heart! One of his brothers in the Episcopacy said of him: " he is the kind of saint anybody can live with," for his forgetfulness of self and consideration for others had become in him a second nature.

CHAPTER IX

1888 – 1893

IT would be impossible to speak worthily of the events in the active life of Bishop Curtis in the country districts of the diocese, and his invaluable services to religion, which endeared him to the hearts of all, whether in or out of the household of the Faith. His tender solicitude extended to the whole flock committed to his care, for every member was dear to him, but like the Good Shepherd he rightly considered, there were other sheep outside the Fold, and these also he must bring in.

They were all his children, and no father's heart ever warmed with more generous affection; hence in season and out of season, he lived, labored and sacrificed himself to serve them. He brought all his ingenuity and energy to bear in devising ways and means to benefit them, gathering them together from the highways and byways, into public halls or private dwellings, in saw-mills and even in the open air, when no shelter could be found, and there ministering to them.

He induced his friends to build churches and chapels as memorials to their dead, in towns and villages where no Catholic resided, maintaining quite rightly, that these edifices would serve as silent Missionaries in the absence of a resident priest. He ever contended that the country required priests of tried and sterling missionary virtues, and whenever possible he assigned the pick of his clergy to such places, saying: " If we would have good citizens and politicians, we must make the country people good," and as he never failed to set the example, he became the leader in the field, bravely bearing every burden and enduring all kinds of hardships.

On one occasion, being accompanied by a young priest who was little accustomed to the Bishop's austere way of living, and who, feeling the pangs of hunger as the hour for the evening meal approached, was greatly astonished to see the good Bishop draw forth from his pocket some apples, cheese and crackers, which he offered to share with him. The young man looked aghast, but became still more embarrassed when the Bishop insisted upon his going to the hotel, where he would perhaps find a better meal, but, as for himself, he needed nothing more, being accustomed to such fare. Father X having found a meal " according to his taste" at the country inn, after engaging rooms for the night, returned to the church in search of the Bishop. As it was growing late and both were fatigued from the labors of the day, Father X proposed retiring to their quarters at the hotel, upon which the Bishop replied: "You may go, but I have a place right here," pointing to the foot of the altar. " I will just roll up this old cassock, which will do for a pillow, and wrap myself in this rug, and I am fixed for the night."

How many times in making the rounds of his " Wilderness " did he not pass nights in a similar way at the foot of the Tabernacle, not thinking of his own comfort or convenience when there was question of the Master's service?

His intense love for the eastern shore of Maryland as being the place of his birth, together with his experimental knowledge of its spiritual destitution, made his heart yearn for the salvation of its scattered inhabitants. He, therefore, set to work to make a foundation in that section of the country which extended one hundred and fifteen miles from the Delaware line on the north, to Cape Charles, Virginia, on the south; and on the east and west, from ocean to bay. The first church built by the Bishop was a neat little brick edifice erected at Cape Charles, the farthest point south of his diocese, about two hundred miles from Wilmington.

Although no Catholics resided in the village, he conceived the idea of making it a center for several neighboring missions on the eastern shores of Maryland and Virginia. Providing a resident pastor for St. Charles, the Bishop continued to serve this mission in conjunction with him, visiting it as often as practicable.

Reverend Edward Mickle of Baltimore, who had just finished his studies, and been ordained in Rome, was chosen for this post, which he has continued to serve most faithfully to the present time. Father Mickle had enjoyed the friendship of the holy Bishop several years previous to his appointment to the See of Wilmington, and now his example was to be an inspiration to the newly ordained, whose love and admiration for his Superior caused him to follow close in his footsteps. "Who could help learning in such a school, and with such a teacher?" he remarked in his eulogy of the Bishop, one year after the holy Prelate had passed away. "He did not command us," he continued to say, "but invited. ' Follow me,' he seemed to say; ' fear not failure, but let us do our duty,' and as our leader, he went on ahead, and led the pace. If through weakness we sometimes falter, yet, the infection of his example has been contagious, and such an impetus has been given us, his priests and people, as shall not soon wither away and perish." [1]

On the occasion of the dedication of this little church, followed shortly afterwards by its consecration, the Bishop's remarkable spirit of piety and penance shone forth conspicuously. Though so far removed from the seat of his See, he had everything suitable for a Pontifical Mass transported to the town, from his finest outfit of vestments, mitre and crosier, to the slippers, gloves and gremiale used by him on

[1] Anniversary Mass at St. Peter's.

great solemnities in his cathedral. He invited as many of his clergy as could be spared from their parishes, engaged his Vicar-General to preach on the occasion, and did everything in his power to make the ceremony one of real splendor.

On the eve of the great day he crossed the bay to Norfolk to engage a choir for the Mass, and returning was seen making the final preparations; sweeping the church and lighting the lamps, for there was no gas, much less an electric button to operate then; this he did by means of a board which he placed across the back of the pews, and springing upon it, he accomplished the work in an incredibly short time. This feat was repeated six times, as he moved up the aisle, board in hand. One more task remained to be done ere the energetic Bishop could take some rest; this was to pave a way over the mud to serve as an entrance to the church, a work he accomplished alone, laying down straw and making it solid by stamping upon it, after which, missing his handsome episcopal ring, he searched, and found it deeply imbedded in the straw.

Some years later the Bishop had the consolation of seeing his zealous, self-sacrificing labors at Cape Charles blessed a hundred-fold, in spite of the prejudice and criticism to which he was subjected, regarding the inopportuneness of building a church in such a waste. The town became the terminal of a new railroad to the South, and this brought trade to the place, which, with the increase of population gave it considerable importance.[1]

The Bishop made preliminary arrangements for the building of a school, which later was enlarged by the

[1] The flourishing town of Cape Charles in Nottingham County, East Virginia, is the extreme southern point of the Delmarvia Peninsula, and occupies the site of what was known as "Old Plantation," in the days of Captain Smith and the Jamestown settlers, who made it their resort for vegetables and other produce. This section of the country is very rich and fertile, and is to-day a garden not for Jamestown alone, but for all the great cities of the north and west. Farm land has increased in value sixfold in the past fifteen years, and is not for sale at any price.

pastor to accommodate the increased number of pupils. Writing at this time to one who felt an interest in his work at Cape Charles, he gives expression to the immense satisfaction he enjoys at its success: " I told you that twenty-five years would prove us right and give us the name of sagacity in so early founding this outpost in the desert, and it appears now that my prognostication is going to be verified. Please give my love to all and warn them again how much I depend upon their prayers always and especially here in the ' Wilderness.' " This name of " Wilderness " which the Bishop gives to his Missions signifies its spiritual destitution, not its want of material prosperity; for the eastern shore of Maryland is so abundant and prolific in its resources, as to be called by its people the " flower garden " of the state.

Some friends of the holy missionary visiting him in his " Wilderness," he took pleasure in introducing them to the beauties of his favorite spot on the peninsula — a secluded forest of beautiful towering pines, interspersed with rich clustering holly. The sturdy old trees had been shedding their needles for years, and had formed a soft brown carpet, which rendered noiseless the passage of the carriage, while the gentle sighing of the breeze through the forest inspired a reverent silence. But what added more to the impressiveness of the scene was the view which met their astonished eyes on coming forth from this silent retreat. Immediately facing them was the broad expanse of the great Atlantic with its wide-spreading beach, inviting the impetuous wave to rest under the spell of this awe-inspiring scene.

Breaking the silence, which was almost prayerful, the Bishop exclaimed, " This is the place of my delights, here I would willingly spend my days." And what more beautiful spot for elevating mind and heart to God, where forest and sea praise Him, and no creature intervenes to mar that silence, so aptly called the

Rt. Rev. A. A. Curtis, D.D.

" voice of God." The two great attractions of the
Bishop's life may here be recognized — the active, in
his laborious devotedness to these rough country missions — and the contemplative, in his adoring love of
God in His creation. Truly could it be said of him,
that he was enamoured of solitude, and yet when the
moment came for action, he gave himself up to it with
such earnestness, that one might say he cared for naught
else.

A second mission dear to the heart of this devoted
shepherd was Salisbury, where in toil and weariness he
spent himself for the sake of a few scattered sheep of
his fold. " It was here," relates one of his clergy,
" that the Bishop built a little church, though there was
but one Catholic family, very poor and indifferent, in
the place, the only other Catholics being an old man
and a good old woman, an invalid. The Bishop attended this mission once every month, setting out Saturday morning and going by rail to Delmar, within six
miles of the place. There he invariably left the train
and made the rest of the journey on foot, in all sorts
of weather. He returned on Monday in the same way,
as he considered walking the most Apostolic manner of
travelling.

" While at the mission he slept in the sacristy, making up his own cot, sweeping out the church, and in the
winter cleaning the stove and kindling the fire. Needless to say there was no sexton. Before leaving Wilmington, he would put some apples, cheese and crackers
in his pockets, and this served as his only food until
his return.

" The congregation at Mass was sometimes two
and rarely more than five or six souls. After an hour
or more spent in catechising a class of three, he would
pass the rest of the afternoon in prayer before the
Blessed Sacrament. In the evening a number of Protestants would come to hear him preach.

" This he did for years, with no apparent fruit from

123

his labor other than that he thus became an example to his priests, whom he always led rather than commanded."

It should be told how this little mission so inauspiciously begun, where the Bishop uncomplainingly endured so many privations, has in its turn, become quite a flourishing parish. From the two or three Catholics who composed the congregation it has increased to more than a hundred souls, and the pretty little church named in honor of St. Francis de Sales, has a resident pastor, who with his assistant, both Oblate Fathers of the holy Missionary Saint of the Chablais, devote themselves to the parish of Salisbury, and several neighboring missions.

Ten years after his resignation of the See of Wilmington, in speaking of this little mission so dear to his heart, the Bishop says: " I am very glad my Successor proposes to cultivate Salisbury. If he accomplishes much, and I trust he will, it will be the case of some sowing and others reaping. For all in all there has been for many years a good deal of sowing in that place, but until lately nothing came of the sowing, save, perhaps, some increase of merit on the part of the sowers themselves," and he adds, " You will soon have Salisbury erected into a ' Suffragan See ' with a resident pastor." [1]   Indeed this last took place in 1910, two years after the holy Bishop had passed away, when his worthy successor, the Right Reverend John J. Monaghan, placed two Oblate Fathers at Salisbury.

The increase of Catholicity in the place, though not great, was a source of joy and consolation to Bishop Curtis, to which he reverted many times, even speaking of it on his death-bed. One of the last acts of his laborious life was to visit his former diocese at the invitation of Bishop Monaghan, to dedicate a little church at Westover, Maryland, which is but a few miles

---

[1] This was merely a little witticism of the Bishop at the expense of his clerical friend who then had charge of the mission at Salisbury.

from the place of his birth. He liked what the world calls little works more than great ones, and would show his displeasure whenever a place of commercial prosperity was praised and spoken of as God's country. "God does not look at things in that way," he would say, "for we know He chose Nazareth for His country."

Writing to one who shared with him the toils and labors of these missions he says: "I know nothing more discouraging than a purely rural mission such as yours. How to reach and move the people of such a mission I do not know, nor so far as I am aware does any one else know. To suppose that the country is to be abandoned and nothing cultivated but the towns and cities, seems dreadful, and yet labor appears wasted everywhere else; yet even in the towns and cities we are not doing so much as some imagine. The only thing is to live in God, and do moment by moment whatever comes to hand. Work for God and leave the results to Him; do not look for success in what you do, but work for God alone."

At another time speaking of the Missionaries invited to preach in the country districts the Bishop says: "The Missionaries may apply the spark occasioning the explosion, but it is to the pastor that the manufacture and accumulation of the powder are to be ascribed. I have little admiration for an ambulatory goodness, now here and now there, and without responsibility, monotony or burden anywhere. Such a thing is necessary, no doubt, but it is not in my eyes a thing of high grade. That grade I ascribe to the man, who, in spite of all discouragements, stays in the same place and spends himself, so often as it appears in vain, for the same people. The travelling man has no permanent weight to carry, he sees the best of everything and if he finds anything unpleasant, he knows that in a few days he will leave it behind. But the stay-at-home sees the worst, as well as the best, and he must

Rt. Rev. A. A. Curtis, D.D.

all the time face everything and run away from nothing. Men cannot be found who are able, or who, if able, are willing to give themselves wholly and forever to work in the country places, and in the absence of such men little can be done by any mere perambulator. The difficulties and discouragements in districts where the people are not only so apathetic, but so far apart from one another, are so very great that one may be well excused, if he come to believe himself simply wasted in such a region. All honor to any who prove superior to the temptation to seek better places."

But as example is stronger than precept, what more forcible illustration of the Bishop's hidden, unselfish labors and practice of his own teaching can be given than the account contained in the following letters, written by him upon his return from those " expeditions down below," as he humorously terms them.

These letters were addressed to one who fully understood and appreciated the difficulties of the surroundings, being well acquainted with the habits and customs of the people, as well as with the inconveniences attending the journey. While the Bishop's taste for adventure and the simple life is apparent amid these labors in the rural districts, the irksomeness and fatigue were none the less felt as was also the monotony, and seeming uselessness of his unsparing devotedness.

WILMINGTON, DEL., March 19, 1888.

The blizzard caught me at Snow Hill. Notwithstanding the pouring rain the Court-house was half full, and that night I thought I was going to be turned out-of-doors. I was going to Berlin at 7.20 A. M. So I got up about 4 A. M., and between 5 and 6 began to say Mass in my room at the Inn. I had to drag the bureau across the floor and place it in front of the fireplace in order to keep the candles lighted. During Mass the storm did rage and I thought the windows would certainly come in, even if the whole side of the room did not give way. But I held on and finished without mishap. I got to Berlin safely, but there was no walking for me next day. The Mass was to be at 6 on Tuesday, that I might get the train at 7.50. Word had been sent to Patrick, but I never dreamed he would come. About 5 A. M. I heard some vehicle crunching into town from his direction, and by 5.30 he was on hand. I stuck him close to the stove, thawed him, and heard his confession; and really I thought he had come as near as a man well can, to earning his Communion. After waiting an hour and a half I got off and reached Harrington about midday; there I stayed until 7 P. M., when a train came poking along and I got on board. Some miles below Dover we stuck fast, and they sent to Clayton for somebody to dig us out; we waited in a car not quite as cold as out-of-doors. They liberated us in time and I got to Wilmington between 1 and 2 A. M., Wednesday.

The next day I went off again to Queenstown for a sort of Mission there. They told me the road to Centreville was open, but they were false. When I reached Townsend they had just begun to clear the road, and no one knew when a train would get through, so I set off and walked over nine miles to Massey's with the intention of going farther if there should be no speedy prospect of a train. Fortunately I found the Kent Road cleared to Massey's, so I went to Chestertown by the train. There I stayed all night and took steamboat to Centreville, from which place in a wagon carrying the mail over the fields, through the woods and across ditches, I got within a mile and a half of Father Scott's and then walked the rest of the way.

The next morning we were due at St. Joseph's, nine or ten miles away; we tried it first in a carriage, no thoroughfare, so we went back and saddled the horses and tried again. By all sorts of turnings and windings, scrambling over ditches, jumping fences, and scrambling through the woods we got to St. Joseph's a little after 11 A. M. I said Mass and gave them a homily and then we remounted and returned after the same fashion. Yesterday I was at Queenstown, and this morning I took the boat thence to Baltimore, and from Baltimore came home. So you see I made out pretty well. Anyhow the weather did not beat me much.

Yrs. Faithfully,
A. A. CURTIS, *Bishop of Wilmington.*

WILMINGTON, May 1, 1888.

I am glad the Jesuits turned up at last and hope they got the cottage, for it would be good for them and for the place too. I am sure you don't miss Salisbury so much as it misses you. I went first to Westover, and said Mass there on Saturday; there were at least ten Communions, and two or three were absent who ought to have been present. I went to Salisbury by the mixed train, and certainly it did not mix any speed with its pokiness. Do you remember Forrest Hall? Mr. F—— got that for me, and a dreary place it is. I went at once to fix up things for Sunday, and found something with four legs, a piece, I think, of an old counter. I lugged it on the stage and then hunted up two blocks for a super altar. Mrs. S—— brought a tablecloth large enough to cover all, and my bag supplied the rest.

When I had done the best I could I went out to refresh myself with a stroll on the river bank. I saw a small schooner or bug-eye coming down, and I made up my mind she was going to get into a scrape, so I picked out the place where she was coming to grief and waited to see how she would fare; sure enough the wind headed her off and she tried beating; she missed stays, went aground, drifted back and did everything except to make way in the right direction.

Finally I heard the skipper say to the one man constituting the crew, we must run to the bank and you must get ashore with a rope and drag her through the reach, so he attempted this. But while the man was out on the jibboom to get ashore, the wind drove her from the bank, and he could not get off save into the water, so the skipper seeing me asked if I would not catch a line. I consented and dragged the boat in till the crew got ashore when he and I pulled the boat to a place where she could sail; so she went off and left the Bp. with the dignity just so conspicuously shown.

Sunday morning I found the hall cold so I foraged all over it first, and gathered everything useless and burnable. But not finding this enough I went out to the vacant lots and there gathered enough to keep fire going; the people enjoyed it but did not suspect they owed it to me. By the way, Mr. F——'s dog objected to my taking away anything from the church lot, and barked around me furiously.

There were but one or two besides the Catholics in the morning. X and his eldest son came, but not fasting. I lambasted him well and told him to bring all fasting Monday morning. After all he left one boy at home and came with his wife, and the other one. There were ten Communions and neither Mrs. F—— nor Mrs. C—— were present, both being too unwell.

In the afternoon I went home by the boat via Baltimore, which was as cheap, and not counting the night quicker. I was at Denton last Sunday, and had the court-house full at night, and the church more than full in the morning. There seems a rather good spirit in the place, and we must try and get a new church there next summer. The old one is too small and very dilapidated. I am sorry Mr. T—— is under the weather, the sea-side will cure him I hope.

Love to all, and mind that you pray for us.

While the famous bicycle was yet a novelty, a friend of the Bishop thought to give him some exercise of a recreative character by presenting him with one of these little machines; besides, he was beginning to feel the inroads of rheumatism, and the benefit he might derive from the exercise was urged as a sufficient reason for adopting the wheel. It was not then so common a means of conveyance as it became later, when so many indulged in its use, so that when it was rumored abroad that the Bishop of Wilmington was deliberating as to whether he should accept a bicycle or not, it created quite a panic among his feminine friends who besought him to decline the gift. Notwithstanding their remonstrances and fears, and even their prayers, the good Bishop accepted the much decried vehicle, resolving to make it serve a double purpose — a means of travel to his far-away missions, as well as to provide the necessary exercise. It has been said that he rode several times from Wilmington to St. Charles College, near Ellicott City, by way of Havre de Grace, a distance of some eighty miles; that he travelled to and from the "Protectory" — an Orphan Asylum in his diocese — every week, where work awaited him, and that he thought nothing of a stretch of sixty or seventy miles a day. When questioned as to how he felt about riding the bicycle, he replied, " It gives me the best kind of exercise, and I would be glad if our young priests would adopt the same method of travel, and thereby be relieved of the expense of keeping a horse, which is an item of some consideration."

He penetrated into the roughest parts of his diocese on the wheel, and was once seen carrying a portable altar on his shoulders, that he might offer the Holy Sacrifice of the Mass in some out-of-the-way place, where the people were too poor to get to church. It was a hot Summer day, and the good Bishop " looked the worst for the wear " as he approached a cottage on the roadside, where some friends were seated. Their sympathy being excited, they began expostulating with him, begging him to accept a purse, which would enable him to adopt a more suitable and easier mode of travel in such weather. He graciously declined, saying, "If you give me this for car fare I must refuse, but if for my people I will use it."

The natural dislike the Bishop had to preaching did not prevent his faithfully fulfilling this sacred duty of his holy calling. In his visitations of these isolated parts of his diocese, he employed freely the great gifts of his soul, for the enlightenment and encouragement of his hearers, adapting the subjects to the particular needs and condition, of each of the districts that he studied and knew so well.

The following list of texts selected for his sermons shows with what care and precision he prepared his work, and gives some idea of the manner in which he spent himself in the faithful service of his people:

March, 1888, St. Joseph's, Talbot Co., " Penance."
Sts. Peter and Paul, Queenstown, " Passion as all Wisdom."
March 28, St. Peter's, Wilmington, " Judas."
March 29, St. Peter's, Wilmington, Evening, " Gethsemane."
March 30, Good Friday, St. Peter's, Wilmington, " Pontius Pilate."
April 1, Easter, St. Peter's, Wilmington, " Peace be to You."
April 1, Evening, St. Peter's, Wilmington, " Blessed are They Who have not Seen and have Believed."
April 8, Dover, " The Real Presence."
April 8, Dover, " The Catholic Church the Incarnation Asserted."
April 22, Denton, Same under another name, " What is Christianity? "
May 13, Dover, P. M., " Mistaken Industry."
May 20, St. Peter's, Wilmington, A. M., " He that hath My Commandments, etc."
May 20, St. Peter's, Wilmington, P. M., " We will Make our Abode with Him."
May 27, St. Patrick's, Wilmington, " Oneness of Confirmation."

Rt. Rev. A. A. Curtis, D.D.

June 3,	Delaware City, A. M., " Oneness of Confirmation."
June 3,	Newcastle, P. M., " The Great Supper."
October,	Chestertown, " What is Christianity? "
December 9,	Denton, " Blessed Virgin Mary."
Christmas,	St. Peter's, Wilmington, A. M., " The True Light which Enlighteneth, etc."
Christmas,	St. Peter's, Wilmington, P. M., " Power to become the Sons of God."

1889.

Jan. 6,	Smyrna, " Catholic and Non-Catholic Christianity."
April 21,	Easter, St. Peter's, Wilmington, A. M., " If Ye be Risen with Christ, etc."
April 21,	Easter, St. Peter's, Wilmington, P. M., " In the Garden was a Sepulchre."
Pentecost,	Confirmation, St. Peter's, Wilmington, " Light."
Pentecost,	High Mass, St. Peter's, Wilmington, " Let not Your Heart be Troubled."
Pentecost,	Vespers, St. Peter's, Wilmington, " Not as the World Giveth, do I Give."

Thirteenth Sunday after Pentecost, Denton, " Purgatory."
Christmas, 1889, St. Peter's Wilmington, " How shall We Escape if We Neglect so great Salvation? " Heb. ii. 3.

" The personal labors and saintly influence of the late Bishop Curtis," says one of the missionaries working in these same districts to-day, " have left an indelible imprint on the Catholicity of the people in these parts, and an inspiring example to young pastors." Who could doubt this statement, when reading of the innumerable trials, hardships and sacrifices borne by the Bishop, whilst he planted and cultivated the mystical vines and olives on the eastern shores of Maryland and Virginia?

In the declining years of life, feeling that the infirmities of age no longer permitted him to spend himself to such an extent, he was heard to say, " Now that I am old and no longer able to work as I once could, I take delight in ordaining young priests and sending them out into the vineyard." Work was not, however, to cease for this great lover of missionary life, until his last sigh. He was to labor unto the end, even to the total extinction of his being, for he literally gave his " whole substance " for the love of his God, to the complete exhaustion of strength, long undermined by great sufferings, silently endured. He knew the value of suffering, above all when united to labor, so he suffered and worked on, for the glory of his Master, and the salvation of souls, dying on his feet, as the sequel will show.

In 1889 the Bishop invited the Josephite Fathers to work for the colored people of his diocese, and through the energetic labors of Father John de Ruyter, St. Joseph's Church was built, and in connection with it an orphan asylum for colored boys was established. A few years later St. Joseph's Industrial School at Clayton, Delaware, was founded, where the boys were taught a trade, or worked on the large farm connected with the school. During the years 1889 and 1893 no less than ten churches were built in the country districts.

In the city old St. James' was abandoned and a new church dedicated to St. Ann was erected on another site, in the same parish.

In 1892 a beautiful edifice for the benefit of the large influx of Polish people was raised and dedicated to St. Hedwig.

CHAPTER X

1888 – 1893 (*continued*)

THE unceasing activities of the Bishop were not confined to his Cathedral and the country districts; for like his divine Model, the true Shepherd of souls, he knew how to bend down and accommodate himself to the little ones, the least and last of his flock.

The orphans were the special object of his paternal tenderness, and the two asylums of the diocese always held the first place in his thoughts, sharing equally in the temporal and spiritual assistance he was able to give, not only during his administration, but long after his resignation of the See.

If our Lord has promised an eternal reward even for a cup of cold water given in His name, what treasures must have been amassed in heaven for this true pastor of souls by his innumerable acts of charity towards the least of God's little ones.

A short time before the appointment of the Rt. Rev. Bishop Curtis to the See of Wilmington, relate the Sisters of St. Francis, a Protectory for Catholic boys had been founded by his predecessor, the Rt. Rev. Thomas A. Becker. This institution was in charge of the Sisters of the Third Order of St. Francis, Philadelphia Foundation, and was located at Lovering Avenue and Du Pont Street, Wilmington.

On Bishop Curtis' arrival in the diocese, the Sisters of St. James' Protectory desired to offer him a little gift. One of the orphans was sent with it to the Cathedral. The good Bishop, after expressing his gratitude, immediately asked the little boy to accompany him to the Protectory. The child in his innocence, answered, "Bishop, I cannot go with you, because Sister told me to meet her at the shoe store; but I shall be glad to show you which way to go." The Bishop was much amused at the child's answer, and afterwards told the sisters how obedient the boy had been. Following the child's directions, Bishop Curtis arrived at the Protectory; it was his first visit to any place in Wilmington. This incident occurred the day before his installation as Bishop; and St. James' Protectory has always considered it a great honor that, small as it was, it was the first institution to receive a visit from the saintly Bishop Curtis.

This good Prelate did not forget his little flock at St. James'. Having noticed the poverty of the place, and the crowded conditions there, he at once planned to aid the sisters in their care of the orphans. The need of a more commodious building had already engaged the attention of his predecessor, who had ordered stone to be hauled to the present site of St. Ann's School, Wilmington, for the purpose of erecting a Home there. This was as far as Bishop Becker's hope was realized, for the erection of the building was never begun.

Bishop Curtis, fearing for the souls of the boys, should they remain within the city, decided to seek a place outside its limits. After carefully considering the matter and realizing its necessity, he selected as a site for the new home a pleasant spot about two and a half miles from the Delaware river. On account of its high situation, pure air and secluded position, this place seemed admirably adapted for an Orphans' Home. On a farm of ninety-six acres, standing well back from the road, is the double brick mansion now known as the " Roman Catholic Male Protectory." The front is graced by a beautiful lawn, while the sparkling waters of the Delaware arrest the attention; the vessels on the river can be plainly seen from any part of the lawn. The building having been a private dwelling, it was necessary that some remodelling be done. For the purpose of ascertaining just what improvements would be needed, the Bishop accompanied Mother M. Agnes, Superior General of the Sisters, and Sister M. Rosalia, Superior of the Protectory, to Reybold. After the completion of the improvements, the boys were removed to Reybold on the eighth of August, 1888. During the Bishop's ten years' stay in the diocese, he took a lively interest in all that concerned the Protectory. He seldom failed to go down weekly to hear the sisters' confessions, but he would not allow the carriage to be sent for him, preferring to walk from the station. He often walked all the way from Wilmington, a distance of about twelve miles. In later years he rode down on a bicycle. He never left the Protectory without visiting each class-room, not forgetting the baby tots. He always gave a short, but practical instruction in each room. Were there any boys who had given particular trouble, he would call them and speak to them privately. During the summer, when the boys were not in school, the Bishop would go out to them on the playgrounds. All the little ones would run to him and he had a pleasant word for each. The children felt how true a friend they had in this good Bishop.

During the first year that the Bishop was in the diocese, one of the Protectory boys, while playing with a cartridge, met with an accident which caused him to become totally blind. The Bishop always took a special interest in this poor, blind boy, and at each visit showed himself a father to the little sufferer. When the boy was old enough, the Bishop himself took him to the Blind Asylum where he could learn a trade, and even then the Bishop's care of this blind orphan did not cease, for the boy was often visited by his beloved Father and friend.

Sometimes the Bishop would come to the Protectory and remain for several days in order to allow the chaplain a vacation. During this time he often went out fishing, enjoying this, his favorite sport, a whole day at a time. "Indeed an invitation to preach in a country church, or to take the place of a country pastor for a Sunday or two, was far more likely to be accepted by him, than an invitation to a great gathering of prelates," says one of the clergy of the Wilmington diocese. Once on his journey homeward from ministering to the Catholics along the eastern shores of Maryland and Virginia, the trains were blocked by a snow storm, and the Bishop had to walk to Wilmington, a distance of sixteen miles. He had nothing to eat all day, and it was after midnight when he reached home. As he wished to say Mass the next morning, he would partake of nothing, and three times during the Holy Sacrifice he was overcome by weakness.

In the evening he preached his regular Lenten sermon, and it was to fulfil this engagement that he had pushed his way home.

It was the earnest wish of the Bishop to have an additional building erected at the Protectory, for he saw the extreme necessity of such, and was always most solicitous for this choice portion of his flock. Although this hope was not realized during his time, yet in his first interview with Bishop Monaghan, Bishop Curtis spoke of this need, and asked the Bishop to supply it. Bishop Monaghan did erect an additional wing affording the sisters and their charges many conveniences.

The departure of Bishop Curtis for his new field of labor in 1897 cast a gloom of sadness over the inmates of the Institution, for they realized that they were losing a kind and loving Father.

After leaving the diocese, the Bishop continued until the time of his death, to show his interest in the boys of St. James' Protectory.

He also encouraged and helped the Benedictine Sisters in purchasing a new place at Ridgely, Caroline County, Maryland. They were affiliated to the Wilmington diocese in 1887, the second year of his ad-

ministration, and he always took a lively interest in
their large farm, aiding and assisting them by his
advice.

Among their recollections of the holy Bishop, the
Benedictines relate the following incidents: "A young
sister in our community had always expressed a great
desire to die at the age of thirty-three. She was particularly strong and robust; but, indeed, as she entered
her thirty-third year, this dear Sister was suddenly
stricken with pneumonia; the case proved serious and
was soon pronounced hopeless; then temptation came,
and the ardent longing for Heaven gave way to fear
and anguish, until it seemed that not even resignation
remained. The good Bishop hearing of her illness,
visited the sick sister, and on being told of her great
dread of death, he exclaimed in a tone of holy impa-
tience: 'A spouse of Christ should not fear death!'
Immediately, her interior dispositions changed; she
became perfectly resigned and shortly after died in the
greatest peace and joy.

"On another occasion the Bishop had made an engagement with us for the morning of February 14,
1895, the day appointed for a ceremony of Religious
Profession. Perhaps, many still remember the terrible
blizzard of that year. Our convent is situated four
miles from the station, from whence a beautiful winding drive leads to the convent, but on that day all signs
of a road were entirely blotted out, the level snow
covered the fences, the white plain broken here and
there by immense drifts. No communication with the
outer world had been possible for a fortnight, so when
the great day — ardently looked forward to by the
virgin hearts, longing to consecrate themselves to God
— at last arrived, it seemed that their cherished hopes
must be deferred. But no! our sainted Bishop was
on his way to us. Although warned before leaving
Wilmington of the impassable roads and blockades
along the line, he nevertheless set out, nothing daunted,

and reached his destination through many difficulties. When told at Ridgely that the roads were unbroken, and that no vehicle could pass, he ordered a horse and rode through the snow banks to our convent, and so fulfilled his promise."

Such an incident but exemplifies the Bishop's own words to a religious: " I am not very demonstrative as you well know, but I may truly say that whenever a service is to be rendered I never fail a friend."

The Sisters of the Visitation also found in him a kind friend, Father and Confessor, having enjoyed the same privilege under his predecessor, the Right Reverend Thomas A. Becker, who gave them a gracious welcome to the diocese in the year 1868, shortly after his installation. The Very Reverend Patrick Reilly of Wilmington had previously invited them, as he wished to secure a teaching community in place of the Sisters of Saint Joseph who had been recalled to Philadelphia.

Although Bishop Becker could promise little or no material assistance to the new community, he nevertheless took a deep interest in the success of the school, aiding the teachers in their preparation of class-work and even imparting some of his linguistic knowledge by giving lessons in German, Latin, etc.

Nor did his interest cease during the eighteen years he governed the diocese, so that when the Right Reverend Alfred A. Curtis succeeded him, the sisters were fairly established and had a fine Academy, though they had always to work hard, and even to struggle to keep above debt. To quote from the Annals of the Visitation at this time: "Our dear Lord had us in His keeping when he gave us the Right Reverend Alfred A. Curtis for the shepherd of this flock. Shortly after his installation he made his first visit to us as our Bishop, and won all hearts by the gracious suavity of his manner. With charming simplicity he took off his ring and pectoral cross and handed them to each of us to examine while telling their history. Some of us remarked that our sisters of Baltimore were very much grieved to part with him, that he had been so kind to them. He answered sweetly with a paternal smile, ' They think I was kind to them, but you know I will do much more for you, because you are my own, you belong to me.' He inquired about the temporal and spiritual affairs of the community with great interest, and said he wished everything to continue according to the arrangements which Bishop Becker had made, and that he would do just what Bishop Becker had done. With one voice we all exclaimed, ' Then, Bishop, you will have to hear our confessions.' With a look of surprise he said, ' Hear your confessions! Did Bishop Becker find time to do that? Then I will be your Confessor until you can get some one to suit you better.' "

Knowing the limited resources of the community the Bishop did everything in his power for its advancement, not merely in the shape of material help, but intellectually and spiritually likewise; for with his usual abnegation of self, he found time to participate in all the important festivities of the community, preaching, singing High Mass and performing the religious functions of Clothing, Profession, Renewal of Vows, as well as the Retreats and Canonical Visitations. Indeed, it would be impossible to give any idea of the kindness of this good Bishop to the community, collectively and individually.

The lively interest he felt in the affairs of the community is depicted in the following charming little notes, written at various times during the first years of his administration. The first of these is an acknowledgment of a set of vestments received for one of his priests just ordained.

June 11, 1887.

DEAR REV. MOTHER:

I am sure our young man will be proud of the vestments, especially if he finds out whence they came. As

Rt. Rev. A. A. Curtis, D.D.

for me, you are right in supposing that I want very
little of some things. But one thing I want very much,
and that is prayers, such pay as I may be entitled to
is to be made in that currency. You must never do anything for me which costs you any money, I am not in
need of that and you have none to spare. Anything
which costs you merely work, I shall value, but anything implying the expenditure of money on your part,
I don't want, not that I don't value your kindness, but
I want it shown in such wise as will benefit me most,
as well as embarrass you all the least, so if you feel you
owe me anything, prayer will more than pay.

Yrs. faithfully in Xto.

✠A. A. Curtis, *Bp. of Wilmington.*

Among other good works undertaken by the Sisters
of the Visitation was the organization of a Tabernacle
Society,[1] for the benefit of the more needy churches of
the diocese, which attracting the attention of the various congregations of the town caused the convent to
become a real center for this laudable work, which was
blessed with marvellous success.

The kind patronage of the Bishop is manifested in
the following lines in answer to the query as to what
might be most useful.

Dear Rev. Mother:

I think the greatest need will be vestments, including copes, but if this should be too high a flight for the
infant society, altar-cloths will probably be the next
most useful things. For these, you may as well measure your own Altar, it will probably come as near
suiting all as any other to be found. Third, some puri-
ficators, corporals and finger towels. After them, anything else suggesting itself to the workers. Pray for
me.

[1] This Society is still maintained by the ladies of the various parishes
and is under the patronage of the Ursulines, who succeeded the Sisters of
the Visitation in their Academy on Delaware Avenue.

Rt. Rev. A. A. Curtis, D.D.

In the month of July he sends his recommendation of the school, permitting the sisters to use his name in the cause, " as much as they please."

DEAR REV. MOTHER:

Perhaps this recommendation will be better than my mere name; if so, use it, and if not then you are free to use my name as much as you please.

I most earnestly commend the school of the Sisters of the Visitation of Wilmington to all the faithful, here or elsewhere. I am sure that their daughters cannot be in better hands, either as regards the acquisition of secular knowledge, or as to what is so much more important, a training in faith and piety.

Again he writes relative to a promised retreat for the sisters:

OCEAN CITY, August 6, 1887.

DEAR REV. MOTHER:

I write to say that the friend whom I hoped to get for your retreat, can't act. I am sorry I need not say, but I think you will do as well to make the retreat of yourselves. Next year I may be good enough, and have leisure to justify me in becoming your preacher, especially if you all pray hard enough that I may overcome my long and deep hatred of preaching.

I am now getting pretty well, indeed more nearly well to-day than I have been for two months. Please give my love to all, and don't forget or let them forget how much I depend upon the prayers of the community.

In December of the same year he writes to thank the sisters and children for their prayers, and to make arrangements for their Christmas Masses.

DEAR REV. MOTHER: December 22, 1887.

Will you please thank the children and the sisters for me. It scares me to find myself no better after so

142

much prayer for me. I must be an uncommonly "hard case," or most certainly so many prayers would have me almost, or quite a saint, instead of leaving me still profoundly a sinner. I think you will get your three Masses on Xmas. day, but they may possibly be a little late in beginning, as both our young men will be needed here for the Solemn Mass at 5½ A. M. But one will go to the convent as soon as that shall have been finished. Please present my best wishes and prayers to all.

_____

It is edifying to see the confidence and humble dependence the Bishop places in prayer, and most interesting to note the variety of original ways in which he asks the alms. The following little epistle, however, is very characteristic of his idea regarding multiplicity of devotions, and serves to accentuate the great simplicity of his life, in which every hour was one of prayer.

WILMINGTON, January 25, 1889.

DEAR REV. MOTHER:

Fr. N—— and Fr. N—— will no doubt together do all required for the Guard of Honor. Very likely they will become members also, and choose, or take of your choosing, each an hour. As for myself I would rather not be enrolled, I am much too stupid for such refined devotions, and must just blunder along as I can. Besides, I don't like nominal things, and my membership would be, or would soon become nominal; as there is no hour which I would be certain to remember and keep. You, yourself make your own requests to Frs. N—— N—— then, and content yourself, as to me, with praying that God's grace may, in my case, make up for the want of sense.

Yours faithfully in Xt.

✠A. A. CURTIS.

In explanation of this "refined devotion," as the Bishop calls it, the Visitation Convent had been made a Local Center for the Guard of Honor, by which means the devotion to the Sacred Heart of Jesus was spread in a marvellous manner. Over two thousand members have responded to the call, and faithful to their Hour of Guard, are to-day zealous in propagating devotion to that Heart which uttered this sad complaint: " I looked for one that would grieve with Me and I found none, and for one that would comfort Me, and there was none."

On February 27, 1889, the Bishop writes again:

DEAR REV. MOTHER:

Better late than never, so I send you $35.00 which ought to have come to us before the drawing, but they are still in time to be of use. The Bp. of Savannah would not promise me to come to us earlier than Friday evening or Saturday morning. I am afraid our charms are losing their effect upon him. Pray for me, or you will have reason to think still less of me, than the little I now deserve.

This little note with enclosure has reference to a raffle organized by the Bishop and his Vicar-General in behalf of the community, to liquidate their heavy debt, and is another example of his thoughtful interest in their material necessities.

When he paid his weekly visits to the Convent for the confessions of the sisters, the smaller children always managed to escape from the class-room to get a peep at the Bishop, for they soon perceived what favorites they were, as he could not pass them by without addressing some playful words. This was the beginning of a series of visits which they called confession, for with child-like confidence they carried to him their little grievances and displeasures, and it sufficed for the teachers to keep order in class, to threaten the withdrawal of this privilege; so that such strange utterances as these were heard in the class-room: "You have been too bad to go to confession this week," or "You are not good enough to go to confession."

On his way to the convent one morning meeting one of the children carrying a covered basket, the Bishop addressed her, and when she told him she was taking two little kittens to the sisters he offered to help her carry the load. It had been raining and the crossings were muddy and slippery, so with one hand the Bishop conducted the little girl across the street, and with the other carried the basket all the way to the convent.

The following series of short notes written by the Bishop at this time reveal a wealth of kindness, consideration and thankfulness known only to those to whom he felt himself indebted, and as according to the words of Cardinal Newman, "the true life of a man is in his letters," this little correspondence with his spiritual daughters unveils the characteristic traits of one who ever studied and imitated so closely the Heart of his divine Master.

The sisters feeling their inability to repay their kind Father and Benefactor for the sacrifices he made of his time and person in their behalf, often begged the favor of doing some little work for him, and his admirable condescension to their modest request is cordially expressed in the following lines, which have reference to some collars he needed:

WILMINGTON, May 1, 1889.

DEAR REV. MOTHER:

I was sure I had forgotten something this afternoon, and this is it. I want some collars. I send you one rather the worse for wear, but which will serve as a pattern. But they need not be of linen so fine as that of the former ones, such linen does not wear well. And I don't like things that are worn out, as soon as or sooner than one has become used to them. I send all my blessing, and in return beg every one's prayers.

On December the 24th of the same year he returns thanks for their remembrance at Christmas.

DEAR REV. MOTHER: December 24, 1889.

The rochet seems to me most uncommonly fine — certainly more than fine enough for such a tramp as the present Bp. of Wilmington. I tried after I left you to-day to get a picture for your Xmas gift, but it was not to be had.[1] One is promised however in time for New Year's day. My thanks and love to all for their prayers and the rest of their kindness. I hope they may not feel discouraged at seeing so little improvement in me as the result of their prayers. They must remember how much it often requires to keep one from getting worse.

Whenever prevented by his round of duties from serving the community on the day prescribed for confession, he would acquaint the sisters in time, or appoint one of his clergy to take his place. It happened once when the Bishop was away longer than usual that the sisters' confessions were overlooked, or forgotten, and complaining to their kind Father of this neglect, he promptly wrote at once, expressing his surprise and regret by a quizzical allusion to their long fast.

DEAR REV. MOTHER: September 1, 1890.

I am very sorry you have been all so long wasting away in your sins. But I shall come to your relief on Wednesday, at which time I hope to find you all still living, though perhaps much attenuated. I am at a loss

---

[1] The picture spoken of in this little note was a photograph of himself, which he had promised the sisters, at their earnest solicitations. True to his word he sent it at the New Year, and it has been most carefully preserved, as a souvenir of his condescending kindness.

Rt. Rev. A. A. Curtis, D.D.

to understand why you have been so neglected, and will see that such a long fast from confession is never again visited on you.   My love to all — and all pray for me.

Yrs. faithfully in Xt,

✠A. A. Curtis, *Bp. of Wilmington.*

Another note of thanks at Christmas of 1890:

WILMINGTON, DELAWARE, December 24, 1890.

DEAR REV. MOTHER:

I am afraid you must have mortgaged the Convent over again in order to send me what I find when I returned from the Protectory this morning.   I am sure I have never aspired to anything half as fine.   I shall have to filibuster for a new diocese in order to get rid of the incompatibility between cassock and the rest. If fine feathers make fine birds I shall be indeed a gorgeous bird.   I need not say how much I thank you all, nor tell you how much I have the welfare of all at heart.   As the most I ask of you is just your prayers, so I suppose I can promise you nothing better in return than mine.   The prayers of the man are not much, but those of the office will surely be worth something.

If the spiritual welfare of his daughters was so near to his heart, nothing being too little or too trifling for his close and undivided attention, he was not less concerned when they were ill, for then he assumed the manner and tone of the tenderest of mothers.

When the grippe prostrated nearly every one in the house, the Bishop came himself, or sent every day to inquire for the sick sisters, told Mother to give them every alleviation and relaxation in her power, and sent word to the chaplain to say the daily Mass an hour later, so that the sisters could have more rest.

On December 24, 1891, he writes: The veil is exceedingly beautiful, and the other things quite as useful.

Rt. Rev. A. A. Curtis, D.D.

How, I do not know, but somehow I manage to spoil and wear them out very fast. I send you St. John Baptist de Rossi. Perhaps you have it already; if so, it will do to give away. I beg the prayers of all, and promise all a special memory to-morrow.

Grippe in addition to Xmas. does not leave me much time, so I end.

Yrs. faithfully in Xto.

✠A. A. CURTIS, *Bp. of Wilmington.*

At Easter of 1892 the Sisters having sent him some useful articles of their own making, he returns an abundance of thanks:

WILMINGTON, April 16, 1892.

DEAR REV. MOTHER:

Many thanks for the collection of fine things sent me, and more for the affection and the prayers which the things, I am sure, signify. But I am afraid you somewhat forget that fine feathers are for fine birds, and it is not possible to make of me a fine bird. If anything should promise to become the better for alteration I shall tax you to make it. Please get everybody to do some of their very best praying for the soul of my old, and much esteemed friend Miss Harper, who died at the foot of the Cross yesterday.

And if some of the same sort of praying be done for me, I should be the less likely to become a reprobate. My love to all, and best wishes for an Easter, first good, and then as happy as shall be consistent with its goodness.

———

Again at Christmas of this year, he remembers his beloved daughters, speaks of his deep interest in the community, and expresses his grateful acknowledgment of their kindness, in the following beautiful note:

Christmas Eve, 1892.

MY DEAR CHILDREN:

I have not time to-day for much writing. I had a tussle with the blizzard this morning on the road from

Rt. Rev. A. A. Curtis, D.D.

the Alms-House to the town, and a tussle too with old men and women inside before I undertook to overcome the northwester outside. I tried to be as angelic as possible, but no doubt the old people did not think the wings or harp at all conspicuous.

At home I have still much to do, and so must content myself with the shortest of Xmas. greetings, and with the most meagre expression of thanks for the rochet, etc. I think I must be specially hard on that garment. Anyhow, I always regard a new one as very soon to be needed, if not at the moment necessary. But as my best testimony of gratitude, I promise the community one of the two Masses at my disposal to-morrow. I think I need not protest my deep interest in you all, nor avouch my willingness to do for you anything in the world, except to preach to you. I draw the line there. At the same time I must say that I deem my good will towards you much more than repaid by the prayers you make, and are going to make for me, and mine. I give you the largest blessing I can bestow.

Yrs. faithfully,

His pen steeped in the sweetness of charity traced words of deepest sympathy and strong encouragement in occasions of trial and sorrow, and some of his religious daughters received his treasured teachings with great reverence, reading them kneeling, for they felt that the Holy Spirit inspired each of his words. Receiving news of the death of a sister he writes:

" At noon yesterday, I found your letter telling me of the death of Sister ——. I should not, I suppose, have been surprised, but I was. It goes without saying, that she shall have the benefit of everything I can accomplish in prayers, Masses or otherwise. She was always an edification to me, and was, I am sure, a still greater edification to the community. We must all thank God for the graces given her, and try as well as we can to follow her in her more than simple patience

149

under disability and suffering. She seemed to me to do much more than simply to submit to the inevitable, rather instead to choose and embrace it. May she rest in peace! And I am sure she will rest in peace."

Upon hearing of the death of an out-sister of the community he writes as follows: " I was very glad to say Mass for Sister —— and shall continue to pray for her. I liked her. She was a good soul, much better than she ever thought herself to be, and a great deal better than other people imagined her to be. I am sure she did a great deal of good in the town, and much that will never be known."

The Bishop's characteristic humility is apparent in the following lines, where he speaks of the edification he receives from the virtue of the deceased:

" I am so sorry that I did not again see Sister ——. I would have given up my holiday perhaps had I supposed that she would pass away in my absence. I fully counted upon finding her still with you when I returned, not that I should have been of any use; but for my own edification simply, I hoped to find her still among you. But it is better so since the Lord has thus willed."

The Bishop strongly combated any leaning towards discouragement, gently detaching the soul from self, and firmly raising it from dejection or sadness to thanksgiving and confidence in God. To teach the soul to recognize and love her own nothingness, then to leave and forget self in order to dwell with God and in God, to be occupied only with His interests to the exclusion of all self interest; such was his practice and precept. Christ dwelling in his soul was his light and love, giving a heavenly unction to his simplest words.

" You don't seem to be thanking the Master enough for the light He has given you," he said to one of his spiritual children, adroitly turning her from discouragement and self-introspection to the sight of truth and goodness in God. " This is the very first return to be made. I don't mean that you should feel thankful; to render thanks and to feel thankful are two things by no means always coinciding; one signifies little — the other everything. And certainly we should by faith and main strength make ourselves see that there is no good but truth and what comes of truth, and that of all truth none is more necessary than the truth as to ourselves. Try to be thankful first then, and next aim to become even glad of the recognition of your own nothingness. And if you genuinely try to be thankful for a better sight of your own self, you will not fret or chafe under the recognition of your own nothingness, but you will become patient with yourself, humble and full of confidence in Him, who knowing you so much better than even you can ever come to know yourself, notwithstanding has not merely borne with you, but heaped all blessings upon you. He having given so much when His goodness was less appreciated can but give more still when you begin to see better the greatness of His love towards you."

CHAPTER XI

1893 – 1896

IN the fifth year of the Bishop's administration of the diocese he was consulted regarding the preliminary steps to be taken for establishing a Convent of the Visitation of exact observance, according to the original idea of its Holy Founders, Saints Francis de Sales and Jane de Chantal, where no provision is made for teaching.

With this object in view he made several journeys into other dioceses, consulted eminent Ecclesiastics, and laid the proposition before those in authority; for that disinterested zeal peculiar to great souls made him refrain from mentioning his own community of the Visitation in connection with so important an undertaking. Knowing the desires of the sisters and appreciating their untiring efforts to provide a means of support during the twenty-five years they had been in the diocese, naturally his mind reverted to them. Finally when his efforts proved unsuccessful elsewhere, and he was modestly asked, if he could not find a little corner in his diocese. "Gladly will I become your agent," he replied, "and do everything in my power to make the work a success." When questioned afterwards as to why he had apparently maintained so much indifference regarding its establishment under his jurisdiction, while encouraging the work elsewhere, he replied, "Well I did not feel free to act, and thus possibly stand in the way of the Will of God, until a more explicit avowal was made to me."

The Bishop was an infallible advocate of religious discipline, and a firm upholder of its strict observance, and now that he was to take the work in hand, his indomitable courage and persevering zeal made him fearless in the face of opposition and difficulties, even to open criticism. After eighteen months of anxious solicitude, indefatigable labors and constant prayer, he had the happiness of seeing the obstacles removed, and the work of the establishment begun. To quote from the Annals of the Convent: "How many times in the past had the dear Bishop told us that God would hear our prayers, and that although humanly speaking there was no prospect of a Monastery, God never refused the petitions of those who prayed earnestly, and made good use of the graces offered them, and that in His own good time He would give us all that was necessary for the exact observance of our holy Rule." The Bishop always added: "God does not ask impossibilities of you, my dear children, and although you have not the material surroundings for exact observance, you desire it; you have the spirit, and in time God will grant you all you ask of Him."

Realizing the necessity of spiritual assistance in an undertaking of such importance, and wishing to conform in everything to the desires of our holy Founders, seconded by our Bishop, we applied to our holy Source, at Annecy, for the requisite assistance.

Indeed the Bishop was the first to accede to this proposal, as a letter written by him at the very moment he consented to accept the work, will prove.

WASHINGTON, D. C.

MY DEAR REVEREND MOTHER:

First, write at once to Annecy and ask for the Mother to retire in May, asking for her as long as she can be spared, urge the matter with all your might. I enclose a note from myself which you can send with your letter. I think we may now consider your transfer and your reduction to the strict observance as

Rt. Rev. A. A. Curtis, D.D.

settled. But don't say anything save to those who already know of the matter till I see you. Finally, pray for me, and for all the clergy of the diocese. We begin our retreat, Monday week. Pray too for our enterprise, but don't talk of it, save to our Lord who never tells secrets.

Yrs. faithfully in Xt.

✠A. A. CURTIS, *Bp. of Wilmington.*

The Bishop lost no time in procuring a suitable place in his diocese for the erection of the new Monastery, and the present site on Gilpin and Bayard avenues in Wilmington was purchased, plans and specifications for the Convent were drawn up, and the work of the building begun. On the 30th of June in the following year, he presided at the installation of the new Superioress from Annecy, Mother Marie Alexandrine de Butler,[1] and ever true to his word, he supported, upheld and encouraged this holy undertaking during the rest of his life. He well understood that such a transition as the community had made could not be accomplished without great suffering. By his wisdom, prudence and fatherly devotion he smoothed the way, rendering the souls desirous and capable of the greater good which God was preparing for them. He made it a duty not to leave his Episcopal city during many weeks, that he might be, not only the Father, but also the Guardian Angel of each of his daughters, and with a delicacy similar to that of those heavenly spirits, he encouraged, consoled and made plain, that so great a blessing as the primitive spirit of a Religious Order, must be purchased at the rate of the greatest sacrifices.

---

[1] As this book goes to press God has called to Himself, July 22, 1913, the great and noble soul of Mother Marie Alexandrine de Butler. Ever full of zeal for the glory of God and the good of souls, Mother Marie Alexandrine seeing the benefit already derived from the Instructions of the saintly Bishop Curtis, gave an obedience to one of her daughters to prepare them for publication. These form the second part of this biography, having been deemed by this zealous Superioress' too precious to withhold from the many souls, who would doubtless reap from them fruits of salvation and sanctification.

Rt. Rev. A. A. Curtis, D.D.

Replying to one who at that time spoke of her weakness in the face of sacrifice, he said: "Yes, you make a great renunciation, but remember that our Lord rewards good with higher good, and hence rewards one act of renunciation with a call to a higher act of the same kind. The renunciation made is not equal therefore to the renunciation to come." As a Director of souls the Bishop was in his element, so well did he understand from his own personal experience the interior life of union with God, and the state of purification through which the soul must pass before she can attain her end.

A religious deeply versed in the Science of the Saints, addressing the community spoke thus: "What shall I say of your holy Director? Although your spiritual graces are incalculable, you might include them all in this single fact: God has given you a Bishop according to His own Heart, a Bishop formed by Himself in the zenith of His divine Charity, for the work which His love had resolved to accomplish in Wilmington."

The Bishop ever continued to be the protector, guide and even Cyrenian of the community, deeming it the greatest privilege that his mortal remains should one day be laid to rest within the sacred precincts of its cloister, as he himself signified when acceding to the request, that after death he would, "as the Founder," accept a resting place in the convent cemetery. "You will gain nothing," he said, "but I shall gain much, for I shall have the prayers of the sisters, which is all I ask."

It was not until the summer of 1893 that the new Monastery of the Visitation was completed, and on July the 31st of that year the translation of the community took place. In the meantime, the Bishop had invited the Ursuline Nuns of Bedford Park, New York, to succeed the Sisters of the Visitation in their school, and to this end had induced his devoted daughters to

155

resign their Academy on Delaware Avenue, Wilmington, in favor of these teachers, who have since conducted a boarding and day school for young ladies with success. On August the 3rd the altar was consecrated and the chapel dedicated to St. Joseph. Pontifical Mass was sung by the Bishop, and the sermon for the occasion preached by Rev. Fr. Haugh, S. J., who took for his text: "Holiness becometh Thy House, O Lord."

On the same day strict enclosure was established and the sisters began the exact observance of their holy Rule, in which they were seconded by their saintly Spiritual Father, the Bishop, who made the first Canonical visit of the Monastery in the month of September, of that year. Taking for his discourse the words of the Apocalypse, " Behold, I make all things new," he made them admirably applicable to the sisters in their new retreat, deeply touching their hearts with the unction of his words.

It may be of interest to reproduce here a portion of his beautiful exhortation:

" Behold, I make all things new." Apoc. xxi. 5.

" My dear children, we do not gain our crown by patience exactly, but by perseverance, for our Lord Himself tells us that, ' he who perseveres to the end shall be crowned.' As one who would serve his country, make great sacrifices, or perform heroic deeds, and in the end betray his country, all that went before his treason would be obliterated, and would only make his treachery more odious.

" There are many good people who have a mistaken idea of perseverance. After making good resolutions, if they fail sometimes, they think they have no perseverance. Perseverance does not mean success, and no failures. God does not expect this of us, nor does He want it, because it would not be good for us, for it might lead us into pride, and none of us know how much pride there is in us, and it 's not likely we shall

Rt. Rev. A. A. Curtis, D.D.

know, until we have been burned for it a long time in Purgatory.

"Exterior perseverance is not sufficient, for there are some people, who go through their duties and exercises from doggedness, too proud to be beat. If I want to go to the country there might be mountains, there may be rivers in the way, morasses to cross; if I should oscillate for a while, even fall or lose the straight way for a time, but still keep my purpose in view and gain it in the end, then I persevere. To persevere, does not mean that we are never to make any mistakes, never commit any faults and never fall; you all know the wise answer of the old negro, when he was asked what was the difference between a good man and a bad one, since the Scripture says, 'The just man falls seven times a day': 'Oh, the good man gets up after his fall, but the bad one is willing to remain in his sin.'

"Now, how can we persevere? May God help me a poor sinner, you know more about this than I do, for the more I have thought about perseverance, the less I feel able to speak about it, but this I will say, I do not think any one who thinks profoundly can speak easily. Some can make use of the thoughts of others, and speak of them with great facility, but I cannot. But I will tell you what I mean, and you can think it out for yourselves, perhaps you have already done so better than I have myself, for though I have tried to think it out for you, I have not had sufficient time to do so, at least to put it into words.

"It may be a crank of my own, but I don't think it is, that any truth taken and studied throughout, thoroughly from top to bottom, from bottom to top, becomes always new. This is what our Lord meant when He said: 'Unless you become like little children, you cannot enter the Kingdom of Heaven.'

"What is it that gives that freshness and charm to little children, which makes them so attractive? It is

157

because everything is new to them, they are always learning something, and they are always interested in what they see, because it is new to them. So it is with us, when we take any point of truth, study it, live in it, live up to it; it reveals always new lights, it becomes always new, each day we see something we did not see before.

"This is what spiritual writers mean when they say there is no standing still, and the Holy Scripture says: 'I make all things new.' Observe that our Lord does not put it in the past or future tense, but in the present: 'I make all things new.' Take for instance our Lord's presence, not around you, or about you, but in you, in your bodies, in your souls; or His presence in the Blessed Sacrament, or in the study of yourselves; not in your sins of the past — from them you learn nothing — but study yourselves in the present moment, and see what revelations God will give you.

"Take this thought of the presence of God within you, not only to the choir, to meditation, but take it everywhere, in every act of your daily life, and thus you will make your life new. It is the custom of those who give Retreats to clergymen to appeal to their feelings, by saying: 'Think of your first Mass, of the fervor you had then,' and I must say that in many cases it seems to be very efficacious, though for my own part, I never could understand why they should go back to their first Mass, for they ought to be able to say after each Mass, This Mass is the best Mass I have ever said. I have offered to God more for souls this day than I have ever done before; more love and more zeal for the conversion of souls; I have sacrificed to Him more of my own will. Although all this will be done without feeling, without the same warmth of heart, or the same effusion of tears, it will however be the continual renewing of our good will, and an advance in the way which leads to perseverance.

"God can take from you all things but one. He can

take your money, your possessions, even your life, but your will He cannot take; from this one thing He has debarred Himself — but this one thing we can give to Him. Now I leave you to think out this one point; maybe some other time I shall be able to think it out with you, or for you, but to-day I have not time."

On a similar occasion, a year or two later, the Bishop exhorted his children "to pray for the grace to love to be nothing." Growing eloquent with his favorite theme, he spoke thus:

"There is a thought that has been in my mind, it has always been there, but more so of late. It may be an error, or a notion of my own, like many others, but I don't think it is. I don't see enough of that real, earnest striving to reach sanctity by the only means by which it can be reached; and to me it is the supreme test of sanctity; it is not to wish to progress in sanctity by this means or that, it is not to have this virtue or that, it is not to pray well, nor even to have great zeal in the service of our Lord; for it seems to me that half the time these good works and great desires are nine parts for self, and one part for God — but it is to be simply nothing for God, and to be sweetly content to be nothing, and to be recognized as nothing, to be treated as nothing by others, to be set aside as useless, and under this, to be sweetly, patiently, resignedly content.

"But there is a step further, it is not only to know you are nothing, but to be willing that others shall take you at your word and treat you as nothing, and to rejoice that others are something, and that you are nothing, and to be sweetly content to be so. But this is to die and we don't want to die, and the longer we live the less inclined we are to die, and the older and more useless we are, the more necessary we think we are. Here we see an old man all worn out, who can do nothing, clinging to life, waiting to do something yet.

"People are not content unless they are doing something, and yet what was the greatest work that was ever done — the Incarnation when God became nothing — and what is He doing here in the Blessed Sacrament so still and silent, while others around Him are busy — striving, working to promote His glory?

"And what did Mary do that made her so lovely? She was nothing, she was content to be nothing, willing to remain in the house, cooking, scrubbing and washing, while the Apostles went out in the world preaching, converting and making a noise. And what did Joseph do? He was nothing and content to be nothing. Children, pray for this grace, to love to be nothing."

On the 23d of July, in the year 1896, the Sisters of the Visitation learned from a newspaper report that their holy director had resigned his See. He had heard their confessions the day before, and had not even hinted at the possibility of such a change. Could it be that he would leave without even preparing them for the awful blow? Several days were spent between hope and fear, and finally one of his devoted daughters wrote to ascertain the truth, and received this reply:

WILMINGTON, DELAWARE, July 27, 1896.

Your letter came into my hands a little while ago. I don't think I have contradicted myself. I always said I would never renounce jurisdiction here to accept it elsewhere, and I say just the same now. I have always said, too, that I would never retain a place I found myself clearly incompetent to fill. I am incompetent, and all the while am becoming more and more incompetent to furnish what Wilmington has the right to demand, and is in duty bound to demand of its Bishop. I have failed, and I am failing more and more all the time, particularly in that most indispensable — the throat. I never gave myself more than ten years of service. I knew from the first that the Lord, or the Pope would free me at the end of that time.

In the beginning of this year, therefore, with the

Rt. Rev. A. A. Curtis, D.D.

knowledge and consent of Father Dissez alone [his Director], I sent my request for a discharge. On the 10th of June last, the Cardinal Prefect wrote me that my petition had been granted, with the condition that I go on as heretofore, till my successor shall have been appointed, and shall be ready to assume jurisdiction. This will certainly keep me till Xmas, and perhaps some months longer. Now, as to you in particular, I shall be able to do almost as much as ever for you. I shall remain your Director in general, and your Confessor, at least extraordinary, unless my successor forbid, and that is not likely.

You know I have to earn a living, for self and my sisters, and the Cardinal, for the sake of the use he can make of me, has promised me a living. I am to stay with him and take any functions he may wish to assign me. But I am to have no jurisdiction, and upon purely private agreement between ourselves I am to help him as he wishes and as I can, in return for the support he grants me.

My love to all, they must now pray that a better man may follow me.

Yours faithfully in Xto.,

✠A. A. Curtis, *Ad-Ap. of Wilmington.*

Could there be anything more touchingly beautiful than the true humility which pervades every line of this letter? Is not the whole action of the Bishop the simple putting in practice, his exhortation at the late Canonical visit? Recall his own words: "To me the supreme test of sanctity is to be simply nothing for God; to be recognized as nothing, to be treated by others as nothing, to be set aside as useless, and to rejoice that others are something, while you are nothing."

As Administrator Apostolic of the diocese he was "to go on as heretofore," he said, "till my Successor shall have been appointed and shall be ready to assume jurisdiction." For another year then he continued to work, keeping himself more and more hidden while weighed down by the oppressive labors, which seemed to multiply as the time drew near for his departure.

Although he was to lay down the arms of jurisdiction he would still glory in working for his Master. If he was to change his field of action, there was plenty of work awaiting him in the adjoining field.

CHAPTER XII

1896

"IT was in the heyday harvest of the Bishop's work," says the Chronicler [1] of the diocesan records, "when everybody was looking forward confidently to many more years of its prosperous continuance, and even if possible, its greater increase, the news was flashed over the diocese and the country, that Bishop Curtis had resigned; and was now only 'Titular Bishop of Echinus.' Clergy and people were simply paralyzed. The secret was so well kept that it was known only to two individuals before the newspapers had announced it, namely, Bishop Curtis and his Spiritual Director.

"Every one regretted it, most of us looked upon it as a calamity, and there was not a single individual with a ray of hope of its recall, for it was so like Bishop Curtis. The work he had accomplished in every field of duty in a very few years, silently, unostentatiously, but none the less perseveringly and successfully, was much more than is allotted many Bishops to do in a lifetime, with all the advantages of large resources and extensive territory.

"In less than one decade of years the clergy of the diocese were doubled in numbers, the list of clerical students was increased from nothing to twelve; three new churches were added to the city of Wilmington, and three others, including St. Peter's, St. Mary's and Sacred Heart, were renovated and remodelled, the magnificent Convent of the Visitation was built and

[1] Dedication Souvenir of St. Peter's Cathedral.

163

endowed; Ursuline Nuns were introduced at the Academy of the Visitation on Delaware Avenue; the attendance at parochial schools doubled; several new and elegant school buildings were erected, including the institution for colored children at Eleventh and French streets; other houses were added to the diocese, such as the Mother House of Benedictine Nuns at Ridgely, Maryland, the Catholic Male Protectory at Reybold and the Industrial School or Colony at Clayton; twelve new churches were built in the diocese outside the city of Wilmington, and several priests' houses, a number of church edifices were enlarged and improved; the amount paid for new buildings and in extinguishment of debts on others is somewhat more than one million dollars.

"These are practical results which make up a very creditable roll of honor, yet are but the shadow of the deep and abiding interest in the spiritual welfare of the diocese, the results of which cannot be estimated by any earthly standards of number, weight or measure. The Annual Retreats, Synods and Conferences, the frequent missions to our own people in every parish, and uninterrupted Missionary Work in behalf of Non-Catholics; all this Apostolic work, a reminiscence of that of olden times and of our immortal pioneers, joined to a noble leadership of holy life and unbounded erudition, of untold self-denial and saintly love for souls, all this, and much more than a volume can detail, must have reaped a harvest of good to souls and of glory to God which only the intelligence of Angels can comprehend, and the goodness of the God of Angels sufficiently record."

All sorts of rumors were now current as to the possible cause of the Bishop's resignation, but these were one and all set at rest, in the farewell address he made before his departure from Wilmington. It was given at the Cathedral on Sunday, May 2, 1897, one week before the installation of his worthy successor, the Rt.

Interior View of St. Peter's.
— 1905 —

Rt. Rev. A. A. Curtis, D.D.

Rev. J. J. Monaghan, of which the following is a re-production in part:

" In making the present explanation of, and apology for myself, I am giving the people of Wilmington such a proof of esteem and affection as I have never in all my life bestowed upon any other people. As a Catholic I held one only, as a Protestant four places before taking charge of Wilmington. All these places I left when the time came without even mentioning in the pulpit that I was going. But it is not uncommon that the last child of many is more loved than any of the children preceding, and hence it is not strange, if like Jacob, I especially favor you, the children of my old age.

" At the same time if you find me lame and halty in this, the single farewell address of all my life, you must not be surprised. What one does but once in a life-time, he cannot be expected to do well. Let us then without further preface attack the question which I propose to answer: 'Why do I quit Wilmington?' It may be well then, if I first discuss something which may be supposed to have impelled, but in fact did not impel me to ask and find relief from the charge of this diocese.

" First, then, I do not go because I prefer to reside elsewhere. I know and am sure that I can never be better off or more content anywhere than I am in Wilmington. Besides, all places are to me now nearly the same. Again, I did not ask for a release because I was disappointed in and disgusted with the clergy of this diocese. I have always said and still say that the clergy of Wilmington will not suffer in the comparison with the clergy of any other diocese in the country. I have the respect of them all, and in most, if not in all, I find affection as well as respect.

" As I am not, and never have been at war with the clergy of Wilmington, still less am I disappointed in the laity. Not only at home, but everywhere else, I have never mentioned them save to express my admiration of their docility, and my surprise at their large and persevering generosity. I have uniformly said, and I now repeat, that I would not exchange them for any other people on the face of the earth. Once more, I do not go hence because I have found myself frustrated as to my designs and expectations, and because I regard my work here as an utter failure. On the contrary more has been done during my episcopate than I ever ventured to promise myself would be accomplished. As my predecessor, by his signal ability, and his long and hard labor, made it possible that I should effect something, so under God, I have, I trust, rendered practicable that my successor may effect a great deal more than I have done or could do. So much then as to some of the things most likely to be falsely imagined causes of my retirement.

"Now the real cause, first, age. I am nearer seventy than sixty. I am far down the other side of the divide and every day accelerates the descent. In particular, my throat is simply and irretrievably worn out. After a long rest I may be able to preach now and then, but I am not equal to the incessant public speaking required of all Bishops, and very especially necessary to the Bishop of Wilmington.

"Next, I am older in soul than I am in body. I forget and become bewildered. I am no more fit for anything save to ensconce myself in some still nook, there to think a little, pray a little and prepare thus for the death which cannot now be long coming.

"'But why cannot you stay and take things more easily?' If I attempted this I am sure you would all be very patient with me, and very far from accusing me of neglecting my duties. But in the first place I simply cannot stay here and spare myself. Next, I ought not to do this, even were I equal to doing it. If it were a question of myself or no one at all in my place, of course, I should stay with you, as perhaps I might be somewhat better than nobody at all. But this is not the question. It is shall I stay, thereby barring out one in every way more efficient, or shall I regard the diocese more than myself, and so go whither I shall not be absolutely useless, at the same time making room for a successor, fully and happily, I am sure, meeting the needs of the diocese?

" It would be very good in you to let me stay, and want me to stay, having become what I am, but it would be bad in me to use your patience and your affection to the injury of the whole diocese. Therefore my part is plainly to go. But be sure that whithersoever I go I shall carry my interest in you, my gratitude to you and my duty to pray for you, and besides my obligation to further the welfare of Wilmington in every way I may in the future find within my power, and in return I beg that you will all continue to pray for me, living and dead."

In these few words we have a vivid portraiture of Bishop Curtis' character and preëminent virtue, given unconsciously by himself.

No one who knew the holy Bishop could doubt that humility was the motive which prompted his resignation. Even Protestants were struck with this, and a prominent non-Catholic journal in an editorial commenting on the " Resignation of Bishop Curtis to become again a simple parish priest," used these words: " This desire of the humble-minded Delaware ecclesiastic could only have its parallel in a general, who would ask to be reduced to the ranks, on the ground that there he could better serve his country; but neither in secular nor religious life do we recall actually a case corresponding to that of Bishop Curtis. He must indeed be a man of God, who seeks to lay up treasures in Heaven rather than on earth." [1]

On the eve of the Consecration of his Successor the Bishop paid his farewell visit to the Sisters of the Visi-

[1] New York Sun.

Rt. Rev. A. A. Curtis, D.D.

tation, in company with His Eminence, Cardinal Gibbons, the Bishop Elect and several Ecclesiastics, who were to take part in the ceremony on the following day. Showing traces of the struggle so recently endured, the Bishop looked careworn, weary and ill, but always forgetful of self, he had words of comfort and encouragement for those who found it hard to give him up, and replied to all inquiries: " I am quite well, only an old man."

One of the sisters said to him: " Bishop, why don't you stay here? Bishop Monaghan would be so glad to have you, and you could help him so much." The good Bishop laughingly replied: " My child, a handsome young Bishop like Bishop Monaghan won't want an old fellow like me knocking around." An aged sister grieving over the resignation and departure of her holy director, exclaimed: " Bishop, we never thought you would give us up." He answered: " My child, I am an old man, and worn out," upon which the sister interrupted him and said: " Oh Bishop, that was not the cause of your resignation, I know all about it." " You know all about it! What do you know? " he inquired. " I know this, Bishop, that for eleven years you have been trying to teach us to be nothing, to wish to be nothing, to love to be nothing, and you remember last year, *that one thought* was the sum and substance of all your instructions and exhortations, and now you want to practise what you have preached, that is the whole secret of your resignation."

The Bishop bowed down his head and after a moment's silence said: " Yes, my child, you are right, that had something to do with it, but that in itself would not have been a sufficient reason to ask for my discharge. I am old and worn out, and so is my throat."

How often he had been heard to give utterance to these pathetic words, and now when repeating them on this occasion he appeared like a venerable old patriarch, with head bent down as if in deep thought, and living far above this world, his heart, mind and conversation in Heaven.

To the great edification of his worthy successor, the good Bishop asked to be allowed to continue serving the community, and in speaking of it later to an eminent Ecclesiastic, Bishop Monaghan remarked: " The Sisters of the Visitation are blessed in having so holy a director, and the only request he made when leaving the diocese was to continue as their Confessor."

Writing to the Sisters shortly after his installation he said: " It gives me great pleasure to learn from the saintly Bishop Curtis, that in leaving Wilmington, he will not give up the kind interest he has always manifested in the welfare of your community."

Even as he had eleven years previous despoiled himself of all his little personal belongings in favor of his friends when leaving Baltimore, so now the holy Bishop would retire from the Episcopal See of Wilmington divested of everything, save his books. He would not allow the generosity of his devoted people to be taxed for his personal benefit, although earnest endeavors were made to give some public demonstration of respect and gratitude to their self-sacrificing shepherd.

The Congregation of St. Peter's succeeded, however, in taking up a collection quietly, by which it was enabled to present the Bishop with a magnificent Episcopal outfit, which he carried with him to Baltimore and treasured as a souvenir of his devoted people, having it carefully preserved in a special apartment at the Cathedral, and under his personal supervision.

He remained in Wilmington for the Consecration of his successor, taking part in the ceremony, after which he would have slipped away unknown to all, had not the vigilant eye of the devoted Vicar-General kept a close watch on his proceedings. Knowing well from eleven years' intimacy the favorite proclivities of his saintly Superior, he followed him to the station, and insisted upon accompanying him to Baltimore.

The 10th of May in the year 1897 was a day of mourning for the diocese of Wilmington when the venerated Bishop left the city for his future home. " Ever true to his promise he kept up an active and generous interest in the welfare, spiritual and temporal, of the Wilmington diocese, continuing to visit St. Peter's and preaching occasionally to the people, at the request of the Rector. He distributed gifts and spiritual favors and rendered substantial assistance to the country missions. A large school, a sisters' home and two pastoral residences were the gifts of his munificence.

Several of his friends blessed with the gift of fortune were happy to have their benefactions pass through his trusted hand. It was with peculiar satisfaction that the Bishop distributed these revenues, and in the discharge of this pleasant duty, he always showed especial discretion and prudence, seeking out the most needy, the bashful poor who had seen better days, and managing affairs with so much delicacy, that the recipients of his bounty seemed rather to be doing him a favor.

None were dearer than the " children of his old age," as he loved to call those who belonged to the Wilmington Diocese. This affection was seen strongly dominating him on his death-bed, when too weak and prostrated to receive the numberless visitors who came for a last word or blessing, he gave strict orders that not one of the Wilmington priests should be refused, saying: " I must see them, they are my boys."

[1] " Bishop Monaghan did not come as a stranger to Wilmington, for he had no sincerer or warmer friend to greet and welcome, to assist and comfort him, than his Right Reverend predecessor. In this welcome, he was joined by the clergy of the household, the reli-

[1] Dedication Souvenir.

gious, the laity of St. Peter's, and by the whole diocese, clerical and lay. Some of the clergy were his classmates, and others made their studies in the same Seminary. It may be said in truth that the diocese has continued to prosper, from the first day of his prudent and benevolent administration."

The new Bishop retained the faithful Vicar-General in his Office, also leaving him Rector of St. Peter's. In 1905 the old Pro-Cathedral, after being remodelled and greatly beautified, was dedicated on October 5th, at which the Bishop Titular of Echinus presided, coming from Baltimore to take part in the ceremony of old St. Peter's. Subsequently Bishop Monaghan obtained from Rome, for its Rector, the Very Rev. John A. Lyons, V. G., the honor of Domestic Prelate to His Holiness Pope Pius X, with the title of Monsignor. The venerable priest, his snow-white hair contrasting with the Roman purple, is a striking figure in his own sanctuary, and in others, where he sometimes appears on days of feast and ceremony.

Bishop Monaghan took upon himself, for a time, the pastoral direction of St. Paul's Church and congregation. In two years the heavy debt had almost disappeared, a fine home for the Franciscan Sisters was erected and the school rebuilt. This work was one that required signal energy, ability and tact; circumstances having greatly complicated affairs. Bishop Curtis was in admiration at the success of his Rt. Rev. successor, and said, with his characteristic humility and directness: " Indeed he has accomplished what I never could have done. I assure you, Bishop Monaghan is no jelly-fish! "

Many other good works show how abundantly God has blessed his zeal; new parishes, churches and schools, not to speak of the growth of Catholicity in the diocese. The Bishop has secured the services of the Little Sisters of the Poor, for which application had been made by Bishop Curtis, and he purchased for the aged poor a comfortable home with ample grounds. He also seconded the wishes of his holy predecessor in allowing the good Oblate Fathers of St. Francis de Sales, to live in community and open a college in the diocese. A suitable Episcopal residence with private chapel has been organized within late years, thus greatly facilitating the labors of the Episcopate.

CHAPTER XIII

1897 – 1907

"I AM receiving an Angel into my household, who will dispense graces on every side." Such were the words of Cardinal Gibbons when referring to Bishop Curtis' return to Baltimore. For his part, the Bishop gave himself up to be used according to the good pleasure of the Cardinal, for the benefit of the Archdiocese. The humble Prelate laid down for himself even stricter rules of life, from which he was never to depart. At the Cardinal's residence, he chose a room in the third story, notwithstanding the remonstrances of His Eminence and the priests of his household, who had prepared a more suitable apartment for the Bishop. Situated in the southeast corner of the building, just under the roof, this room was to be his place of holy seclusion, where he would spend the time left free from active duties in reading, writing, studying and praying. One of the clergy of the Cardinal's household, who admired and appreciated the Bishop's spirit of self-abnegation, tells, how he collected some scanty furniture from the lumber room nearby, and improvised a book-case from three old peach crates.

Many hours out of the twenty-four were passed in the presence of the Blessed Sacrament, and he frequently, if not habitually, rose during the night, crossed the yard that separates the house from the Cathedral, and entered the Sanctuary where several hours were spent near the Tabernacle. There he drew in long draughts of the life-giving spirit, which he again gave forth to all with whom he came in contact. One bitter cold night, when freezing sleet had made walking almost impossible, he was seen crawling on hands and knees over the icy way that led to the church. In reply to an inquiry as to how he passed those many hours in the Sanctuary, he answered simply: "Oh, I just stay there like a dog at the feet of my Master!" A truly characteristic answer, worthy of one so well versed in the heavenly art of prayer. His work continued to be, much of the time, of a missionary character, often requiring long and fatiguing journeys throughout the area of the large Archdiocese; for, although having no jurisdiction, as he joyously remarked, he was nevertheless to exercise the functions of a Bishop of the Church, preaching, confirming, ordaining and consecrating. The Cardinal treated the Bishop with the utmost consideration, placing him on his right hand at table, and showing him at all times the greatest kindness, while the Bishop appreciated to the full the benevolent and lovable character of his Superior. It cannot be said that Bishop Curtis was by nature dependent; on the contrary, a certain freedom and independence of mind and action were a part of his very being; yet, through long years of struggle and effort, such real humility had been acquired, that in later life, dependence and submission were marked characteristics. "To depend and submit to the will of another is my safeguard and delight," he said, "for then I am sure of doing the will of my Master."

The Cardinal made him Vicar-General of the Archdiocese, and the duties of this onerous charge were faithfully fulfilled by the Titular Bishop of Echinus, until a few days before his death. When not on his missions, the Bishop celebrated Mass in the Cathedral at six o'clock, the holy Sacrifice being always preceded by his usual long preparation.

One who received ordination at his hands, writes thus: "To see the Bishop say Mass and administer Holy Communion was a sight never to be forgotten; his faith, his reverence, his devotion were so saintlike, as to inspire a sentiment akin to awe." He was alone with his God, bending low in love and adoration. " I always begin my Mass at the same moment," he once said, " trying in this way, though ever so little, to imitate the unchangeableness of God." Ever a strict observer of Church laws, the Bishop took no breakfast during Lent, not even the small cup of black coffee urged upon him, and often spent part of the day visiting hospitals, the poor and invalid friends, who depended upon his counsel and comforting words; looking eagerly for the gentle presence, and genial hand-clasp of their never-failing friend, who, in his unostentatious way, went about doing good, leaving behind him blessings of hope and peace.

The Bishop's great learning, combined with his almost childlike simplicity, made him a delightful companion at the Cardinal's table, where the young priests took pleasure in drawing him into discussion with His Eminence, on difficult and varied questions. He kept in touch with current topics, as well as with new publications, that he might be able to advise those who consulted him, although personally he entertained a certain indifference for modern literature.

When giving a rule of life to a soul whom he was directing in the world, he appointed a regular time each day, for the careful reviewing of all books that would fall into the hands of the children of the family, saying, that though the task might be tiresome, it was a sacred duty too often neglected by parents and guardians of the young, and one which would safeguard the budding minds, and prevent many sins in later life.

The Bishop was very orderly and methodical in the arrangement of his affairs, and the distribution of his time; never appearing hurried or anxious, however pressing his engagements might be. From the pile of mail lying on his table, he would take up the letters one by one, just as they came to hand, without a useless glance; putting aside such as called for deeper thought or reflection, and proceeding at once to answer the less important, unless the former called for immediate attention. He must have carefully read his letters over after writing; as erasures and slight changes of expression sometimes appear, with an occasional word or two above the line. Part of his day was spent in work appertaining to his office of Vicar-General, and in receiving visitors on matters of moment. After dinner, taken at half-past one, instead of retiring to his room for an often much needed rest, he would go over to the Cathedral, and remain in prayer until it was time to enter the confessional. He was frequently seen pacing between the pillars of the great Sanctuary, reading his Breviary, which he always tried to do standing, and with uncovered head. Even when travelling he managed to find some corner in the train, where he could stand to say the Divine Office, manifesting in this, as in every duty prescribed by holy Church, his deep reverence for God's divine laws.

The Bishop was far from being pessimistic in his views, as some have thought. Although serious and perhaps inclined to introspection and living on a plane elevated above the ebb and flow of worldly interests, he had nevertheless a deep fund of humor, and told an anecdote remarkably well; his serio-comic air when relating a story often provoked more laughter than the subject itself. He was once invited to lecture on St. Patrick's day in behalf of a charitable cause. The Bishop was very reluctant to appear on the platform, but after much persuasion accepted the invitation, determining at the same time to make the affair a success, as far as lay in his power, and declaring it would be his last appearance as a Lecturer. Some days before the appointed date placards announcing the entertainment were posted throughout the city of brotherly love — " What the Irish know nothing about," by the Rt. Rev. A. A. Curtis. Needless to say, the hall was filled to overflowing, the curiosity of the Irish-American being aroused by the novel announcement. They were soon enlightened, however, for the Bishop's great store of natural history was unfolded during an hour's talk on "snakes," of every description, size and color, their habits, instincts, etc., from the deadly boa-constrictor to the harmless little snake of our garden. The speaker retired amid the loud applause of his enthusiastic audience, an applause which helped somewhat to cover the chagrin of many. "I would not have cared had they hissed me off the stage," the Bishop afterwards said, with a merry twinkle in his eye; "considering that the two-fold object was gained; viz., a crowded house and a well-filled money box." It is not generally known that the Bishop was also a poet, of no small merit — both in Latin and English verse. But all such work he destroyed with his own hand, commencing with some poems written during the civil war, which expressed warm sympathy with the South. He was so upright and so conscientiously loyal that he thought later such sentiments should not see the light of day.

The Bishop always shunned notice, and studiously avoided whatever might draw upon him any personal attention. At the time of the Silver Jubilee of his Ordination, he left town and passed a few days in a quiet country place, where he said Mass and had time for undisturbed prayer and recollection. It must not be imagined, however, that the Bishop had no spiritual trials; like all great souls he passed through hours of darkness and agony, through that refining fire which purified the gold of his heart, preparing him for an exceptionally close union with God, and leading him to great detachment, and a holy indifference for visible and material things. He was now to experience that which often falls to the lot of those who grow old in the service of the Lord, causing keen suffering to hearts not already dead and insensible to human sympathy. Death had claimed many from amongst his circle of friends and penitents during the years he held the Episcopal See of Wilmington, and with the changes brought about by time and circumstances, a new set of people had largely taken the place of those who had known and venerated him. As it is in the nature of all human things to change, the young flocked to the young, thus leaving comparatively little work in the confessional, so besieged in former years. Did the Bishop feel this change? No word ever expressed his sentiments, but his loving and sympathetic heart undoubtedly offered to God the sacrifice of a much loved work, and for which he had a special predilection, and as is well known, a marked gift. Now, he would often slip away alone in the afternoon, to some fishing stream, there to cast his hook and line, while contemplating God and nature. Or, again, he would mount his wheel, and spin off to some quiet country road. One who knew the Bishop well, and admired his total absence of human respect, gives a pen picture of him in these later years, which is sketched as follows: " An old gentleman, in a short coat and close fitting cap, trousers tied at the ankle with a piece of twine, might be seen issuing from the Cardinal's house, mounting a bicycle, and hastening away. After a ride of forty or fifty miles, he would lug his machine up to the garret room, don his cassock, and proceed to the Cathedral for an hour's visit to the Blessed Sacrament."

The friend who so kindly furnishes many letters and sayings of the Bishop for this biography, together with valuable reminiscences, adds: " Possibly many foreign Bishops and perhaps some American prelates, to whom Bishop Curtis was not known personally, might consider certain of his ways too unconventional to be in keeping with the dignity of his office." Such, however, was not the judgment of a distinguished Monsignor, Vicar-General of an important French diocese. The scene of their meeting was the parlor of the Visitation Convent, where the French ecclesiastic was paying a visit. At three o'clock in the afternoon of a hot July day, the Bishop arrived from Baltimore to hear the confessions of the religious. He was fasting, having sung a Requiem Mass at the obsequies of a dear friend in the priesthood. He had accompanied the remains to the cemetery, and then fearing to be late for his engagement, had, without dining, boarded the train for Wilmington. Perhaps he never looked worse than when he entered the parlor, tired, overheated and wearing a long linen duster. Certainly he bore a striking contrast to the elegant Mons. X——, and after a short conversation, made awkward by the Bishop's small knowledge of French, and the Monsignor's still smaller knowledge of English, the Bishop withdrew to the chapel. " Ah! " exclaimed Mons. X——, " Cet Evêque est un Saint."

He possessed the distinctive traits of a true gentleman, combined with the highest virtues of a Priest and Bishop, which coincides with his definition, that, " Only a thorough disciple of Christ can be a true gentleman." Yet he did not deem it beneath his dignity to ride in a baggage car, for the sake of fulfilling an engagement, when there was not standing room elsewhere; to take a spin on the wheel and even a pinch of snuff. He suffered always from a catarrhal affection of the head and throat, to counteract which — as well as " to keep me awake," he laughingly said, " during the long hours in the confessional " — he used snuff, but with moderation; for he was most ingenious in finding means of mortifying his tastes. Regularly at the beginning of Lent, he would hide his snuff-box, not allowing himself even a pinch until the fast was over; anticipating the time, however, by a few hours — for the little box could be seen in his hand on Holy Saturday — when engaged, till the late hours of the night, in the confessional.

He had very little knowledge of music, not being able, as the common saying is, " to turn a tune." " I was almost the despair of those who had to teach me the chant in the Seminary," he said, to a party of friends gathered around him, at the same time making this singular little boast, " but I tell you, I can tune a fiddle as well as any of you." He abhorred the performance of music of an operatic or worldly style in church, and remarked once, half-quizzically, yet with displeasure: " When I am pontificating, and the soprano begins to squeal up there," making an expressive gesture towards the choir, " I feel like turning around and telling her to close her mouth. There is no more soul in such singing than in the squeaking of a cart-wheel." [1]

Whatever was poorest and most ordinary, the Bishop thought best suited to his needs. Who amongst those that knew and loved him, does not still remember the thoughtful, kindly face, under the common broad-brimmed beaver; the red bandana, which he always used, through a spirit of mortification, his hands chapped, and often gloveless in the severest cold; while in place of the fine polished linen of former days, the china buttoned wristband of coarse outing flannel, disappeared above the sleeves of soutane or coat. A silver chain attached to a two-dollar watch, was the gift of a friend, otherwise it, too, would probably have been discarded. That same friend tells how the good Bishop tried to use a one-dollar watch, but disappointed in its service, added a second dollar to a new purchase. It must be remarked, however, that when occasion required, the Bishop did not fail to dress well, and doubtless those who knew and loved him equally recall his great dignity and striking appearance when vested in full pontificals.

On the other hand, how lavishly he distributed alms! What abundant help given, just, when sorely needed, help known only to God and the recipient; food, coal, warm clothing, money; and last but not least, kind words and personal service uplifted many a despairing

---

[1] This was before the Holy Father Pius X had forbidden music of such stamp to be sung in the Church.

Rt. Rev. A. A. Curtis, D.D.

heart, and won many a soul back to its Maker. The Bishop practised literally the counsel of our Lord, for he let not his left hand know what his right hand gave. It was only after death that his many benefactions were, in part, revealed. The greater number inscribed in the book of life by the recording Angel will only be manifested on that great Day — when the deeds of all, good and evil, shall be made known. Among the many pathetic scenes witnessed after the Bishop's death, while his body lay in state at St. Agnes' Hospital, was that of a poor old man, who hobbled painfully out from the city, with the crowd of visitors. Weeping bitterly, he stood gazing on the prostrate form of his holy benefactor, crying aloud, " Oh! you have kept me alive by your charity."

During the ten years the Bishop administered the diocese of Wilmington he allowed himself no regular vacation, only varying his daily routine of hard work, by supplying, now and then, for some of his priests in the country districts. But after the resignation of his Episcopal See, a devoted friend, owning property on the Gulf coast of Florida, persuaded the Bishop to take a few weeks' rest every year in the early spring. There on the southern coast in the land of sunshine and flowers, he could indulge in his favorite pastimes of boating and fishing. The invitation was gratefully accepted, for the Bishop was beginning to suffer much from rheumatism, and to feel the weight of advancing years.

The following letters speak of the pleasure he experienced in these visits to the sunny South, but do not tell of the sacrifices made in behalf of others, both in a material and spiritual line, for he never lost an opportunity of doing good, but scattered blessings wherever he passed.

"Sarasota, May 4, 1902.

" It is better to do more than less than one has promised; I promised to write you as soon as I had taken

181

a tarpon. As yet not one has been taken and yet I write. We have tried faithfully for four whole weeks without any success. Again and again tarpon were all round about us in great numbers, but they were impervious to any bait which we were able to present them.

"Sharks and sharks we have killed, relieving the waters of one or more every day nearly. Other fish we have taken also, of many kinds, but no tarpon. I should have despaired and abandoned the quest, but for Mr. McKee to whom I owe the trip, and whom I promised I would stay and try till strictly obliged to return.

"This I am not forced to do save in time for Pentecost, when I am under promise to pontificate in the Cathedral, so at present the probability is, that I shall not reach Baltimore till May 16th. But when I appear, I shall be such a mulatto in face and hands, that you may all refuse to have anything to do with me, till I have had time to undergo some bleaching. . . . But to go back, one side of the account is no tarpon; moreover, as soon as I had arrived I was taken ill; even yet, I am not entirely well, though nearly so. Besides my right shoulder has been much more than ever before, rheumatic and aching. It is better now, but not yet well, and indeed I fancy never will be. This is the debtor side of the account, the other side is, — weather all the time exquisite. We have missed but one weekday, and Sundays, of course. Every other day we have been on the water from 8.30 A. M. till nearly, or quite 6.00 P. M. We have had splendid sailing, usually enough and rarely too much wind. We have had perfect quiet. Mass every day, of which you all have never missed your share. Birds and flowers in abundance, and on my part, at least, some bathing. This I think states the items in general, but I am looking forward with no little pleasure to return home, where I am sure I am going to stay till some clear duty summons me elsewhere. Some recreation is, I suppose, necessary, but of recreation simple, I tire very soon." The Bishop, as is easily seen, was a great lover of simple, country life, and said that when he pushed out on the water, hook and line at hand, he felt like a school-boy on a holiday.

Writing a little later of his success in fishing, he says: " I have landed a Jew-fish weighing thirty pounds, and have fought a number of sharks, but they usually cut the line and cleared themselves. I have struck but one tarpon. He leaped magnificently five times, and then went his way, leaving me a hook turned and so bent as to be wholly useless. Seeing the size and strength of this hook, you would begin to understand what a tarpon is, and what he can do. We begin in earnest this week to pursue the animals, and as they are now more numerous, we hope to master some of them before we quit."

This brief relaxation only made the Bishop return with renewed zeal, to the labors awaiting him in the hidden parts of the vineyard of the Lord. One of these spots was Solomon's Island, located in the Chesapeake Bay, and quite difficult of access. For the benefit of the few scattered Catholics, the Bishop repaired at stated times to this out-of-the-way place; where he offered the Holy Sacrifice and administered Confirmation. Arriving late one Saturday afternoon, he found that it had been raining for more than a week, and the downpour still continued. There was no one to meet him, nor was there a conveyance of any kind in sight. The good Bishop looked at the muddy roads which were almost impassable, and, as he afterwards said, " My first impulse was to return to the boat, but thinking of the poor country people who would come so far to hear Mass, only to be disappointed, I changed my mind, took off my shoes and stockings and waded for more than a mile through the deep, heavy mud." He did not mention that he carried a large travelling case, and when asked if there had not been danger of cutting and bruising his feet, he only laughed and replied: " Oh! yes, some danger " — then quickly changing the subject spoke of the edification he received, on seeing so many poor people coming so far to Mass, in the pouring rain — some fasting until after mid-day, while, on the other hand, those in better circumstances, and living nearer the church, did not arrive until after Mass, when all the ceremonies were concluded. The following week the Bishop was so ill in consequence of cold, and exposure to the inclement weather, that he was unable to officiate in the Cardinal's place at the solemn Requiem Mass for the deceased Pontiff, Pope Leo XIII. Neither was he able for several days to perform any of the official duties which devolved upon him, during the Cardinal's absence in Rome. Under a burning sun in the hottest days of summer the self-forgetting Bishop could be seen pursuing his way, and returning from most fatiguing journeys, to occupy for a short respite his room " under the eaves," until another engagement should call him forth.

Writing at this period to one who enjoyed his confidence, he speaks freely of his labors and sufferings, in connection with the summer heat: " The thermometer stood 91 at 4.30 this morning. It has been near that in my room for a day or two. My sleep is much and often broken, otherwise, I am so far as I know not any worse. I think relief is not far off, but it must be preceded by a tremendous storm. I shall stay here now, till after the retreat, then I shall go for a week to do various things at Oakland, Piedmont, Cumberland. Hurrying back from Cumberland on the 9th of September, I go on the 10th to Mt. St. Mary's for Ordinations on the 11th, 12th and 13th."

On September the 21st he writes: " If it was cool in Norfolk it is a pity you did not stay there longer. At 8 P. M. the thermometer stands at 88 in my room. Add humidity to the heat, and the most cunning and venomous of mosquitoes to both, and you may understand our case. I don't think I have ever known a Summer and Fall so oppressive."

In the early part of the year 1905, the Bishop's hitherto strong and vigorous constitution began to fail. During the preceding years, he had met with several accidents while riding his bicycle, and a series of falls which followed, must have been the prelude to that dread disease, which was now beginning its insidious inroads, and which three years later would set free that great and noble soul.

Writing to a priest, an intimate friend, and speaking of these falls, he says: " Misfortunes come not singly. My fall from the wheel was little as compared with the fall I had yesterday. How it happened I am totally unable to say. I started down stairs to dinner. That I remember — after that, nothing till I found myself in Russell's room, with him and Louis beside me. There was a pretty bad cut on the right side of my head. The Doctor soon came and stitched and dressed this. Save for some smarting of the wound, I have since been as usual. I not only said Mass this morning, but afterwards carried Communion to my friend, Mrs. X., whom I am serving in what seems to me to be her last illness. But how long it will be in reaching the end, one cannot say. It seems to be an *internal cancer.* . . .

" Once before, years ago I fell from the wheel, and did not remember falling at all, and the Doctor says this is not at all uncommon. I have been keeping my room to-day under the Doctor's advice. Every day I am made more and more aware of the fact, that life is full of accidents, which no wisdom can foresee, and no strength or skill can avert. Just as on the other hand one often escapes damage in the most marvellous way, when prior to the fact, escape would have seemed nearly impossible. The one I suppose implies the evil, and the other the good Angel."

It was at this period that the Bishop drew up his will, a document so characteristic of its author in simplicity, and so touching in its spirit of poverty and humility that it cannot fail to edify.

April 14, 1905.

I owe no man anything which can be paid in money.

My sisters will pay the expense of my funeral. I will and demand that this expense shall be the very least practicable. Let the coffin — not casket — be of cheap wood — uncovered with cloth, and having upon it nothing of silver — nor anything simulating silver. Let the Mass be a low Mass if permissible — I demand and insist that no one whatever shall at the time of the funeral, say a single word save in the offices themselves. If I die in Baltimore, the Visitandines of Wilmington will, I suppose, claim that the interment shall be made within their enclosure. I promised them this. If they fail to make their claim, there is a place reserved for me in the lot of the Misses Hayward, in the Cathedral Cemetery, Balto.

I give my Chalice to the Rev. John B. Tabb. All my vestments of every kind, not Episcopal, I give to the Rev. Edward Mickle. I desire that the Rev. John A. Lyons may be permitted to select anything and everything he wishes of the rest of my things.

Let the Episcopal things go to any Bishop who may desire them, or any one of them. Let my books be free to all the household, to choose as each shall will. If the remainder be worth anything let them be given to anybody who may want them."

✠A. A. CURTIS, Bp. of Echinus.

Referring to the Bishop's instructions regarding his coffin, it is almost needless to add that his Administrator, the Reverend William Fletcher, D.D., Rector of the Baltimore Cathedral, could not bring himself to carry them out to the letter; but provided a casket, in keeping with the dignity of a Bishop of the holy Catholic Church. Bishop Curtis left no money, and never valued it, save in as far as it enabled him to assist God's poor, and make necessary provision for his sisters. With this end in view, he managed to save enough to give a moderate sum to a Catholic Seminary, stipulating, however, that a life interest should be paid to his sole surviving sister, — an interest which, since his death, she has regularly received. During his last illness, indeed the very day before he died, the Bishop laid his three Episcopal rings in the hand of a trusted friend, saying faintly: " Sell these, and give the value received to ——," naming certain needy persons, whom he had been accustomed to aid. Then stretching out his hand, and selecting from among the number a large and very handsome amethyst, set with diamonds, he said: " But, no: this one was given me by Mrs. X—— on the day of my consecration. She who was so liberal in gifts and alms while she had means may now be in need of this; see that it reaches her, with my blessing." It may truthfully be stated that the heights which the Bishop had attained in the spiritual life did not lessen the tenderness of his heart, and at this epoch the long and painful illness of his youngest sister touched him deeply. She was said to be the favorite, if the Bishop could be suspected of making any distinction, having loved and cared for mother and sisters since the father's death, which occurred in his eighteenth year.

The following lines from letters penned to a friend during the different stages of this sister's malady, depict the alternate hopes and fears which moved him, without, however, altering in the least that serenity and repose of spirit in God which he ever enjoyed.

" My sister M—— keeps out of bed and goes out of doors a little, when the weather does not forbid, but the old spells have returned, and altogether I have fear, that at any time she may become as she was before." Then encouraged by signs of improvement, in another letter he writes: " My sister has become wonder-

fully, and to me and the doctors, unexpectedly better."
Again: "My sister Maggie has not improved. She
now says nothing at all, and sleeps nearly all the time,
but happily, as tranquilly as a baby, which is a great
comfort to us." And later: "There is no notable
change in the condition of my sister. I have no hope
whatever, though none can tell how long or short the
decline is going to be." When two years later, death
came to her relief, the end was, as is so apt to be
the case in a prolonged illness, sudden and even unexpected; so sudden that the devoted brother was
not present, for there was not even time to summon
him. He made arrangements for the funeral of his
dearly loved sister, in conjunction with one of his
nephews, and accompanied the remains to their last
resting place in the family lot at Pocomoke City.
After her decease, expressing his gratitude for the sympathy and prayers offered him, he remarked solemnly
and gravely: "My sister Maggie never sinned against
the light." And this seemed to be a source of great
consolation to his otherwise deeply afflicted heart.

Extracts from letters to one of his most intimate
friends, a holy priest, give some idea of the amount
of work the Bishop still accomplished, while infirmity
and suffering increased rapidly. In October of 1906
he writes: "I am just back from Mt. St. Mary's,
where I laid the corner-stone of the new Seminary. I
am in Charles County next Sunday. Two confirmations, with some ten miles between — the Sunday after,
three confirmations in Cumberland, and after that a
confirmation every day for a week, and a little more.
How things good and bad do bunch themselves."

On December the 9th of the same year he writes:
"I was on the go last week. Wednesday to Wilmington and back. Thursday to Frederick for the annual
visit, Friday home, and away at once to pontificate yesterday, at the University. I stayed over till this morning to make a priest of a Holy Cross deacon, ordered

Rt. Rev. A. A. Curtis, D.D.

to Bengal and to sail next Wednesday. I made one for the same Mission a year or two ago, and already he is in the hospital, a hopeless invalid, but he will get his reward, for the Lord no more needs our health than our sickness. Pray for me."

If one reflects on the amount of work spoken of in the above lines, and realizes that each of these ceremonies of which the Bishop speaks, means a double class of persons to be confirmed; the administration of the Sacrament, always preceded by Holy Mass; a short address to the confirmandi before and after the ceremony, a practice the Bishop never omitted. Add to all this the fatigue of long rides over the rough country roads, so much dreaded by him in his weakened state of health, the holy Bishop's zeal and remarkable fortitude cannot fail to be recognized, and it may easily be believed that he could say with the great St. Paul, " I die daily"; and again, " I can do all things in Him who strengtheneth me." 1 Cor. xv. 31; Phil. iv. 13.

CHAPTER XIV

1908

WHEN Bishop Curtis wrote: "Age teaches us humility, making us feel our incapacity and nothingness," he was doubtless expressing his own personal feelings; not realizing, as did others, that he was already a finished master in that Christ-like virtue, of which he was to give, yet, one more striking example.

The Bishop had a strong presentiment of his approaching death, though no one else dreamed of it, also of the nature of the cruel disease that was slowly consuming him, but concerning which he had not yet seriously consulted any physician. On May the 26th he wrote the following answer to an anxious inquiry about his health: "I really do not know what to say. I have no appetite and am often so weak and giddy that I am afraid of toppling over. On two mornings at the altar I seemed on the verge of going down from giddiness. What is the root of the matter I can't determine; the stomach, I know, is seriously implicated, but whether as principal or accessory I can't determine. . . . The worst is that this spell is much longer and more obstinate than any previous one. I hope, however, by the help of God to keep on my feet, and to do the great deal I must do between this and the end of June."

The willing spirit and iron will upheld the rapidly weakening body, enabling him to perform the long and exhausting functions of his office, preaching, confirming, ordaining, while literally dying on his feet. God allowed him to fulfil an oft-expressed wish: "I hope I shall die in harness, doing the Master's work." In view of increasing infirmity the Bishop had silently begun to make preparations to resign his office of Vicar-General, and leave the Cardinal's house, " to make room," he said, " for a better and younger man." But when he announced his intention to Cardinal Gibbons, His Eminence would not hear of it, nor would he release him from his charge. The Bishop was glad to work on, and between the 26th and 29th of May, confirmed twice. On the 29th he wrote: " I find I can always do what I feel I must do, and moreover, that I am none the worse for doing it. I had two confirmations yesterday, but both small. The second was at Mt. de Sales, where everything was very beautiful. I have but two more, one at the colored church of St. Barnabas, and the other at St. Joseph's, Emmitsburg. But I have three ordinations, two of them, each of three days, besides, I have two commencements, one at Mt. St. Mary's, and the other at St. Joseph's."

The following extract from the letter of a holy daughter of St. Vincent de Paul gives a little account of the above mentioned confirmation at St. Joseph's Academy, Emmitsburg. " The brief instruction given on that occasion was singularly impressive, so much so that the Priest who waited on him said that his words seemed those of inspiration, voiced by a saint, even the children themselves remarked it, in their own simple way. After explaining to them the nature, graces, gifts and benefits derived from the Sacrament of Confirmation, the Bishop said: " We all desire a friend, we look about for one that we can trust, for one that will be a right arm, a support, a comfort, a help, a defence, a guide, a protector. Now, this you will have in the Holy Ghost; He comes to be the truest and best of Friends, an unfailing one. He comes to be to you more than any earthly friend could possibly be. All other friends, however true, would simply be such only in name, in comparison with the Divine Friend who comes to you to-day. Keep Him then always in holiness and truth, never sadden Him, nor force Him to deny His All-powerful Friendship, by the commission of any grievous sin, but try to deserve His most intimate communications by great purity of life and manners. This Friend will never abandon you, but will ever be at your side, within your heart, to give you any spiritual help you may need. Think of this, and cherish with jealous care a love and friendship absolutely essential for the salvation of your soul. This divine Friend will never depart from you, unless by sin you chase Him away. May God grant that such a misfortune may never happen to any of you, but that having had the happiness to become the temples of the Holy Spirit of God, you may ever cherish and preserve the help of the divine Friend, by fidelity and perseverance in God's grace."

Sister C—— adds: "What our Fathers remarked as characteristic of Bishop Curtis was his total indifference to the ways of the world, there seemed to be nothing of this earth about him; his manners, his words, his appearance, his opinions were totally averse to those of the world, and most adverse. Our good director who is a man after God's own Heart had the most unbounded veneration and esteem for the saintly Bishop Curtis, and loved to speak of his virtues. In his instruction to the community he has spoken of him as a living model of poverty, humility and utter contempt of the world. He told us how edified our reverend father confessor was, on the occasion of his business visits to the Bishop, when admitted to his bedroom, to see not even the ordinary comforts of life. . . . We possess his plain, black straw hat and his old, faded umbrella. These we have placed in a glass frame and venerate as relics. Father S. keeps his common pocket knife about his person, as a sacred object and souvenir of the saintly Bishop."

From all sides comes the testimony that the Bishop's increasing sanctity was something almost tangible; the hasty temper was subdued and the strong irascible nature had become so meek and humble, that those who came in contact with him, felt he might have said in truth: "I live, now not I; but Christ liveth in me." Gal. ii. 20. The bodily powers grew weaker as his soul drew nearer to God, and the purification was to be in proportion to the high place destined for it. God spared not him whom He had predestinated to conformity with the image of His beloved Son, and laid upon His faithful servant not only the cross of physical pain, but the cross of keenest suffering of both heart and mind. The Bishop accepted the Chalice and the Cross, in perfect conformity with God's holy will, even joyfully; and his desire is well expressed in these other words of the great St. Paul: "That I may know Him . . . the fellowship of His sufferings, being made conformable to His death." Phil. iii. 10.

For the sake of the Religious family, so devoted to him, the Bishop bore the cross in a series of misunderstandings, which sprang from the best intentions on the part of all concerned, but of which God formed the instruments of this final purification.

On June the 3d, Bishop Curtis, already too weak to trust himself to travel alone, though the secret was so well kept, none surmised it, made his last journey to Wilmington, accompanied by the Very Reverend F. X. McKenny, President of St. Charles College. He paid what proved to be his last visit to the Visitation Convent, of which he was for so many years Spiritual Father and Director, and where he was eagerly expected by his devoted daughters. To quote from the Convent Annals: "Our hearts told us he was suffering; the tall hitherto erect form was stooped and emaciated, but the gentle smile remained unchanged, and he had his usual kind, fatherly word for each sister, as she advanced to kiss his ring. When it came the turn of an aged domestic sister, the Bishop rose and went forward to meet her. After a pleasant talk in the assembly room, the Bishop and his companion, surrounded by his children, passed into the beautiful garden. Upon reaching the little cemetery, he counted the graves of the religious, praying at each one, and raising his hand in blessing; then, with arm resting upon the iron gate, his eyes dwelt long and with an inscrutable expression on the green sod at the base of the stone crucifix, the spot destined and reserved for his tomb. In six short weeks that spot was to open its earthy walls to receive his mortal remains.

The meditation lasted long, and the Bishop was so lost in thought, that he roused himself with difficulty. Continuing to walk through the winding paths, he said very gently: "I did not think it so far around the enclosure. I never realized the walk so long." How little those who accompanied him, thinking that the pure air of the lovely June morning and the freshness of the flowering garden would refresh him, dreamed of the effort being made. Entering the Ante-Choir the Bishop leaned heavily for a moment upon a large bracket, which bore a statue of the Infant Jesus, then recovering himself, he said with much animation: "Now I want to visit the sick," and with perceptible difficulty ascended a staircase leading to the Infirmary, where he conversed cheerfully with an invalid sister long confined to a rolling chair. Leaving behind him the benediction of his holy presence and uplifting words, he passed out through the enclosure door with hand raised in blessing; through that enclosure which was so soon to open to his coffin. Between this date and the 27th he continued to work, going through the long ordinations mentioned in his letter of May 29th, thus fulfilling his last engagement. Having finished the work God had given him to do, the Bishop at last consulted a physician.

To quote again from the Convent Annals, " June 29th, 1908: To-day we stand in the shadow of a

Rt. Rev. A. A. Curtis, D.D.

mighty cross, which came to us in a letter from our saintly Bishop Curtis, telling us of his mortal illness. In his last visit of June 3d we were shocked by his appearance, but, in spite of our pleading, he refused to see a physician, saying, he knew what they would say, and that he had engagements every day until the 26th. On June 27th the Bishop consulted a noted specialist, and the worst fears were confirmed; his disease was an internal cancer, and the announcement pierced our hearts like a two-edged sword. In the following letter he gave the dread tidings:

BALTIMORE, June 29, 1908.

For some time past I have thought myself to have an internal cancer, either of liver or stomach. Saturday last, I consulted the expert, Doctor Friedenwald. After two examinations, the second one including the pumping out of the stomach, he ratified my conjecture. He seemed, however, far more hopeful as to an amelioration and prolongation of life than I myself am. I am going this afternoon to Ocean City, rather with the wish for, than in the hope of benefit. It is with loathing and difficulty that I can take the smallest quantity of food, and when taken it seems to do rather harm than good. So, as it to me appears, it is simply a question how long I shall be in starving to death. I am in no wise disposed to resist or impeach the will and sentence of our ever Blessed Lord. But I want more than this, and I beg that you and all the rest will pray, that I may not have merely resignation, but that according to my littleness and unworthiness, I may share in that strong desire which St. Paul had to depart and be with Xt., more than I can be with Him on earth.

If I shall find it practicable I shall try to see you all before I become totally disabled. My love and blessing to all.

Yrs. faithfully in Xt.,

✠A. A. CURTIS, *Bp. Tit. of Echinus.*

195

Rt. Rev. A. A. Curtis, D.D.

The heart of the reader can comment on such a letter better than a weak pen. On June the 29th the Bishop accompanied by a faithful friend went to Ocean City as the guest of his successor, the Right Reverend J. J. Monaghan of Wilmington. Although everything possible was done for his comfort during the five days of this visit, he suffered greatly from extreme weakness and exhaustion, being unable to retain any food. But the love of God, burning in his soul, so supported him, that he succeeded in saying Mass every morning, until July the 4th. On the 3d, the " First Friday " of the month, that day specially dedicated to the Sacred Heart of Jesus, the holy Bishop said his last Mass. What that Mass must have been, one may safely conclude from his own words uttered years before: " We ought to be able to say after each Mass, This is the best Mass I have ever said. I have offered more to God, more for souls *this* day than I have ever done before; more love and more zeal for the conversion of souls. I have sacrificed to Him more of my own will."

On July the 4th, the Bishop's 77th birthday, his devoted companion, the Very Rev. John A. Lyons, his former Vicar-General, celebrated the holy Sacrifice, at which the Bishop not only assisted, but even served, after which the Very Rev. John A. Lyons conducted the dying saint to St. Agnes' Sanitarium in Baltimore.

The day was excessively warm, and the fatiguing journey was accomplished with difficulty, owing to the weakened condition of the brave sufferer, for whom few comforts could be procured. The Bishop had long exercised himself in abandonment and holy indifference, having taken for a special practice during the last years of his life the admirable maxim of St. Francis de Sales: " Ask for nothing, and refuse nothing." He found in this exercise all the virtues combined, and without choice received all the events of life with loving indifference as coming from the Divine Hand.

Rt. Rev. A. A. Curtis, D.D.

The following letter of Monsignor Lyons speaks of that last journey:

St. Peter's Cathedral, Wilmington, Delaware,
July 4, 1908.

Dear Sister:

Your very kind letter I found on my desk a few moments ago, on my return from St. Agnes' Hospital, where I had the honor of escorting our beloved saint, father and director, to what, without a miracle, will prove his last resting place this side of Heaven, where he belongs.

So sure was he of this, that he had already arranged to go there before starting off with us Monday last for Ocean City. He is now in the hands of God, of the expert physicians and the devoted sisters. All is possible to grace, but among the cherished feats of my life is the one just concluded of bringing the martyr of suffering into a sure asylum of ministering angels. I will call to-morrow and say what I have not heart now to put on paper. Our cross is mutual.

Sincerely in Domino,

J. A. Lyons.

When the Bishop reached St. Agnes' at about 2.30 P. M., he was greeted with the words: "O Bishop! I am so glad that you have come to us, we are going to be very good to you, and do everything possible to benefit you." "Oh, yes! dear child," the Bishop replied, "I know very well you can do the first, but I doubt the second." He was urged to go to bed, but with the submission of a child, he said, that if it did not matter, he preferred to remain on the lounge. About an hour later one of those "ministering angels" going to the chapel to make her meditation, found the venerable Bishop kneeling as straight as though in perfect health and reading his Office. After supper he spent some time in the chapel, and requested to be awakened in the morning for the Community Mass, since he was not able to offer the Holy Sacrifice. He was urged to receive Holy Communion before Mass in order that he might retire immediately when the Holy Sacrifice was finished, but he said, fearing to give any trouble: " I would rather communicate when the community receives." Then with faltering steps he approached the altar where he received Our Lord with angelic fervor. " Every hour of the holy Bishop's stay at the Sanitarium was marked with subjects of edification, and evidences of his sanctity," said one of the nurses. " When in an agony of intense pain, and the burning fever consuming his very vitals, he asked for a little ice to allay the terrible thirst, but seeing that the sister in attendance would be obliged to descend the stairs for it, he forbade her to go, saying, " Sister, I give you an obedience not to go for the ice now, I can wait."

On Monday he sat on the lawn for a short time, but as he was returning to his room, he said to the one who accompanied him, " This is the last time I shall go out." His words were prophetic, for on Tuesday the holy Bishop took to his bed, never again to leave it. " Every morning," says one who had the privilege of waiting upon him, " I took the Bishop his mail, and knelt as I handed it to him; he would say: " God bless you, thank you, dear child." On July the 7th he wrote with his own hand to his dear daughters of the Visitation of Wilmington, who, unable to leave their cloister, sent emissaries almost daily to see their beloved Father.

St. Agnes' Hospital, Baltimore,
July 7, 1908.

My dear Daughters:

I am trying to write you my last letter. But it must be a very short one since I am so very weak.

1. I must thank you for the affection, trust and docility you have for so long always shown to me. The Lord takes all this to Himself and will not be slow or niggardly in reward.

Rt. Rev. A. A. Curtis, D.D.

2. Cleave without flinching to your purpose to live by the ancient rule of your Order. . . . Be always loyal, trustful and affectionate towards your Bishop. Neither lend nor borrow, but give whenever you can and all you can. In particular I commend to you —— and —— See that neither ever lacks anything necessary to his comfort.

3. All the rest you must take for granted; viz., how I love you all and depend upon you all to procure mercy for me at the judgment seat of the Lord Jesus, and how I count upon soon meeting you all, if not in Heaven, yet in the Vestibule thereto.

Many, many times love and blessing to you all. As I have told you how you should stand towards your Bishop, so now I tell you to cleave to your Mother, be she who she may. Confer with her, confide in her — obey her, and so far as practicable, let there be no film of alienation between any child and the mother of the family.

Yours faithfully in Xt.,

✠A. A. Curtis, *Bp. Tit. of Echinus.*

At the Bishop's request, the attending physician at St. Agnes', a Protestant, was asked not to resort to any extraordinary means for the alleviation of his sufferings or prolongation of life, for, said he, " My days of usefulness are over, and my age is such as to assure me that God wants me now."

" The saintly Bishop suffered much," his chief nurse wrote, "but not the least complaint escaped his lips; ever most patient and resigned, his only trouble seemed to be the anxiety he caused others." His Eminence Cardinal Gibbons called at the Hospital on Saturday, the day of the Bishop's arrival, and again on the following Wednesday. Coming out of the Bishop's room, the Cardinal said: " Sisters, God has favored you, in permitting you to care for a saint, and a great saint."

After the first few days at St. Agnes' the Bishop

was unable to go to the chapel for holy Mass, and his devoted friend, the Reverend Edward Mickle, having taken up his abode at the Hospital, that he might be near the holy invalid to serve him in every possible way, offered to say Mass in his room. The Bishop refused, saying: "There must be nothing extraordinary, nothing out of the common for me. I know my Lord and my God is on the altar in the adjoining room — there is only a wall separating us, and I can assist from my bed at the Mass going on there."

He made only one personal request during his illness. Upon being told that the Apostolic Delegate then in Washington, now Cardinal Falconio, had telephoned to ask news of the Bishop's condition, he expressed his gratitude; and the one who brought the message asked if he had any special reply. "Yes," answered the Bishop, "please ask him to send me the Holy Father's blessing." Visitors flocked to the Hospital in great numbers, hoping to receive a last word and blessing from their saintly Father, friend and benefactor. The clergy of the Wilmington diocese, and faithful friends amongst the laity, were greeted with special affection, for although so weak and prostrate, he would not allow them to be turned away, saying: "Yes, let them come in, they are my children." As they knelt for his blessing he bade them sit close to his bedside, and to stay until he should dismiss them.

Answering a question addressed to him by one of the Wilmington clergy, he said: "I am starving to death, yes, starving to death; but, there is something which gives me a little fear." The good priest interrupting him, said: "O Bishop, if *you* have anything to fear, what will become of the rest of us?" "Well," said the holy dying one, "I fear that I do not sufficiently desire to go to God and I will have to answer to my Master for this." Was not that momentary

Rt. Rev. A. A. Curtis, D.D.

fear of a soul that had always longed, " to be dissolved and to be with Christ," the last touch of the Divine Refiner?

When asked if the pain was very severe: " Awful, awful, awful," was his only reply, and then, as if regretting having spoken so plainly, he asked quickly: " How long do they say I shall hold out?" Father Mickle answered: " The head nurse thinks you will live a month." The Bishop said slowly: " Yes, that would be little to pay God what I owe Him; yes, little, but I have only three days more, then all will be over." He said the same to the Cardinal, who visited him again on Wednesday, the 8th of July. When His Eminence spoke with doubt and indecision of his approaching voyage to Rome, the holy Bishop answered: " In three days all will be over, and you will sail on the 15th as you have planned." His Eminence having expressed deep regret and compassion for his terrible sufferings, the Bishop said he " reckoned them to bear no comparison with what he hoped and expected."

That same Wednesday Father Mickle, noticing a great change in the saintly sufferer, asked him if he would not like to be anointed. When the Bishop assented, Father Mickle wished to know why he had not asked himself for Extreme Unction, to which the Bishop replied: " Oh, it is not for me to say! I am in your hands and leave to you to decide and to administer when it shall be the proper time."

Kind, consoling words to those surrounding him were ever on his lips, and when strong men broke down and wept like children, it was the dying Bishop who encouraged and strengthened the grief-stricken, while his feeble, emaciated hand was continually raised in blessing.

When the end came at last, on Saturday, July the 11th, at 8.45 A. M. it was, as is so often the case, even in mortal illness, unexpected at the moment. The Chaplain of the hospital, the nurses and a few others, near and dear, were around him, but so sudden was the summons, there was no time to call the household.

" The change," says one who was privileged to be present at that bedside, " was instantaneous; the holy Bishop put his blessed hand under his head, which he turned to an opposite side, raised his eyes towards heaven, and passed to God, like a child who finds the longed-for rest on the bosom of its mother."

" After his holy death, upon looking over his little belongings," writes the same pen, " nothing could be found that might be given as souvenirs to the many friends who cherished and revered him. His Breviary had absolutely nothing in it, a pair of common black Rosary beads with a much worn cross attached, seemed to be his greatest treasure. It had been blessed and given to him by Pope Pius IX, and he had always carried it, in sickness and in health. While at St. Agnes' it was never out of his poor, tremulous fingers, even to the last moment, which ended his beautiful life on earth."

The Bishop died gloriously poor; as one testifies, whose happiness it was to minister to him to the last: " A Rosary, Breviary and Ordo, one suit of clothes, a few changes of underwear of the poorest kind, and a gun metal watch were all that he left behind him."

A small steamer trunk contained all his worldly possessions, with this was a fishing-tackle, which he left to Rev. Louis O'Donovan of the Cathedral, for, said he, " Louis is young and loved to accompany me in this innocent diversion." " Two old pocket-books were also found, one containing a few one-dollar bills, folded separately and carefully; the other held a few five and ten cent pieces and quarters, arranged seemingly for distribution among the poor."

The good Bishop told one who was with him throughout his illness to give each of his male attendants five dollars, and to say to them, that he would beg God to bless their kindness to him. " As for the Sisters," he said, " they are working for the same recompense as myself."

"Nothing could be more beautiful than the sequel of this blessed holy life," continues his "ministering angel." "I thought I had met saints in my life, but I have certainly met the greatest, in the wonderfully humble, learned, modest and holy man of God, Bishop Curtis. I think St. Vincent de Paul's last hours must have been like those of the holy Bishop. Such was my impression as I ministered to him."

Immediately after the great soul went forth, St. Agnes' bell tolled the sad tidings, and the flag was lowered to half-mast. The news was sent at once to the Cardinal's residence, from whence the priests of the parishes throughout the city of Baltimore were informed, and the bells of more than forty churches were soon tolling in memory of the dead Prelate.

The Cardinal was deeply affected at the sad tidings, as were also the Priests of the Archdiocese, numbers of whom were greatly attached to the Bishop, who lay in the stillness of death at St. Agnes' Hospital.

Messages of sympathy poured in at night, and several prelates arrived in Baltimore the next day. Thousands viewed the holy remains while they lay in state, at St. Agnes' on Sunday, July the 12th. Eminent prelates, the clergy and laity, young and old, rich and poor came to show their respect, veneration and esteem for the beloved dead.

Yes, the heroic soul of the saintly Bishop had passed forever from the land of exile, and had tasted the fruition of a promise he loved to quote: " His servants shall serve Him, and they shall see His face, and His name shall be on their foreheads." Apoc. St. John xxii. 3, 4.

CHAPTER XV

1908 (*continued*)

BY order of Cardinal Gibbons, the holy remains of the deceased Bishop were removed on Monday from St. Agnes' Hospital to the Cathedral, where they lay in state until the funeral, which took place the following morning. If thousands viewed his body at St. Agnes', what can be said of the throngs that passed around the bier in the old Baltimore Cathedral! Books, rosaries and objects of devotion were eagerly and reverently laid for a moment on the casket, or brought in contact with his Episcopal robes. At the funeral services the church was filled to overflowing, with members of the Cathedral congregation and other Catholic churches of the city; and there were also present many of those who were under his care when he was Rector of Mt. Calvary Church. With that extreme simplicity, which he himself so much liked, the services were carried out. The altar and holy images were draped in black, and at 9 o'clock the Office of the Dead was said by the clergy, Bishop Monaghan of Wilmington presiding. The Cardinal celebrated the Mass of Requiem, during which he was deeply moved; his assistant Priest was the Very Rev. John A. Lyons of Wilmington, and his Chaplains the Very Rev. Dr. E. R. Dyer of St. Mary's Seminary, and Rev. O. B. Corrigan, Vicar-General of the Archdiocese, now Auxiliary Bishop of Baltimore, the Revs. Thomas S. Lee of Washington and William E. Starr of Baltimore, now Monsignorii, were respectively Deacon and Sub-deacon of the Mass. The Cardinal occupied his throne, and one was erected on the Epistle side of the Sanctuary for the Apostolic Delegate, now Cardinal Falconio. Other Prelates, among them Archbishop P. J. Ryan, and Bishops Kenny, Van de Vyver, Monaghan and Keiley, occupied seats in the Sanctuary, with the regular and secular Clergy behind them. There were likewise representatives of the Benedictines, Franciscans, Dominicans and Jesuits.

The Rt. Rev. P. J. Donahue of Wheeling, West Virginia, a former rector of the Cathedral, preached the funeral oration. He chose his text from the Acts of the Apostles ix. 15. "This man is to me a vessel of election," and spoke in part as follows:

"We are all familiar with the sublime recital from which the foregoing words are taken. Paul going up from Jerusalem to Damascus, 'breathing out threatenings and slaughter against the disciples of the Lord'; the light from Heaven which struck him in terror to the earth, and the voice from Heaven calling, 'Saul, Saul, why persecutest thou Me!' of his sublime baptism and his glorious career in the after time, as Apostle to the Gentiles.

"In the nineteen centuries intervening God has not ceased to call at one time by exterior vision, at another by interior illumination, chosen souls, vessels of election, whom He intends for some great vocation — not indeed as sublime as that of Paul, but still for His honor and the salvation of souls; and as I gaze upon the mortal remains of our dear Father in Christ, Rt. Rev. Alfred Allen Curtis, the words of my text arise in my mind irresistibly and spring to my lips. For we who look back upon this noble life of threescore years and seventeen now ended, without presuming to search too deeply or curiously into the ways of Divine Providence, must perforce believe that the soul once inhabiting this prostrate tenement of clay was a vessel of election, designed by God for a very special work, and that He so preordained the character, environment and history of that soul, as to fit it for the high destiny it was to achieve.

"Alfred Curtis was born in this Commonwealth, of sturdy stock on July 4, seventy-seven years ago, and throughout his long life preserved something of the spirit of freedom and independence for which that day stands. He was a studious and retiring child and youth, fond of books, solitude and self-communings, and of a deeply religious turn of mind. Born and reared in the Episcopal faith, as he advanced to manhood there was a great religious movement developing in England. John Henry Newman, thirty years his senior, was beginning to shake the religious world of Oxford to its foundations. He had taken orders in 1824. Nine years later, in 1833, while returning to his home from Sicily, by way of the Mediterranean in an orange boat, as he lay in a dead calm of a week's duration in the Straits of Bonifacio, broken in health, but still more harrowed and broken in spirit, he wrote those immortal lines:

> Lead, kindly light,
> Amid the encircling gloom
> Lead Thou me on.
> The night is dark
> And I am far from home —

which have ever remained a comfort and strength to souls doubting and unsatisfied, groping and stretching out helpless hands of supplication, like the babe stretching out its hands for its Mother in the night. After twelve more years of spiritual struggle, he was received into the Catholic Church, October 9, 1845, to be followed later by Manning, Faber, Oakeley, Ward and others in great numbers. Nor was the influence of this movement unfelt on this side of the Atlantic.

"Young Curtis was fourteen when Newman joined the Catholic Church. When the Catholic hierarchy, after a suspension of three centuries, was again set up in England, and Newman preached the memorable

Rt. Rev. A. A. Curtis, D.D.

sermon, ' The Second Spring,' he had arrived at man's estate. God forbid, dearly beloved brethren, that I should seize upon this occasion to indulge in the bitterness of religious controversy. If the cold right hand of that sacred form prostrate here could be lifted, it would be in stern disapproval of such a course. I am merely endeavoring to trace the history of this man's soul and God's dealings with it.

" I believe then that it was caught and swayed by the tide which first began to set from Oxford, and that the heart of our departed one was subjected to long periods of questionings, self-examinations and doubts. I believe that he trod a like rough and thorny path with Newman and his followers, and for many years; till after consultation with his leader in England, he himself made the great sacrifice, and from a zealous, most devout and ardent Episcopalian clergyman became a Catholic, and later, after due preparation, a Catholic priest.

" Thus he broke suddenly and irrevocably with all his former life. He gave up friends, and doubtless made some critics, if not enemies. His might have been domestic love, sweet home and children climbing his knee, fame, position and all that this world holds dear, but true to his convictions, he gave up all. We may not know the whole history of that great renunciation; it is written in the Book of Life. He became a priest, and what a priest! This is within the knowledge of many of you — his love of the poor, his patience with sinners, the fiery eloquence and depth of his pulpit utterances, he himself being a perpetual sermon as he went about in his sacred ministry.

" I dare to say that even if he had been born and had lived without the pale of Divine revelation, he would have been a great and lovable man. He had a brave and tender heart, a finely disciplined intellect, a great capacity for friendship.

" A Bruno or a Benedict in his love of solitude, he

Rt. Rev. A. A. Curtis, D.D.

was a Saint Francis of Assisi in his love of all the furry creatures of the woods, the birds of the air, the fishes that go to and fro in the paths of the sea. And when this solid foundation of the natural man was exalted, spiritualized, ennobled, by the superstructure of divine grace, then you had the man of God, the man of prayer, the unselfish man, who recked not of the honors, riches and pleasures of this world. And I think his special vocation, the reason of his being marked out as a vessel of election, was to show the world the faithful and the unfaithful, and especially the clergy of this great Archdiocese, the model and the exemplar of a Christlike priest in chastity, poverty and sobriety in utter self-sacrifice, in unabated zeal for the house of God! Candor looked out of those mild eyes, and truth sat enthroned upon the lips. Modesty and quiet dignity were atmospheres round about him. To him indeed could superior associates and inferiors point and say with holy pride: ' There is the true Priest.' "

Bishop Donahue passed over the period of the episcopate of the deceased, partly because, he said, he was not well acquainted with it, and partly because it would be appropriately dealt with, when the body was borne to Wilmington, his former Episcopal See. " He was as true a Bishop as he was a Priest, loved and revered by us all," continued the preacher. " When he laid the burden down after eleven years, he came back here to the scene of his former labors, and here in his love of solitude and prayer, in his unfailing kindness and fatherly tenderness, he has been an Angel among men."

At the close of his sermon the eloquent preacher made an earnest appeal for the prayers of the Cardinal, whom the deceased had served for so many years as secretary, priest and Vicar-General, for those of the Suffragan Bishops, of the Clergy of the Archdiocese, and of the faithful to whom he had devoted so many

Rt. Rev. A. A. Curtis, D.D.

years of labor, attending their sick, instructing their little ones, burying their dead and breaking to all the Bread of Eternal life.

After Mass the Cardinal in a black cope and attended by his Chaplains performed the absolutions of the Church around the bier, after which the Clergy, followed by the congregation, filed down the middle aisle to view once more the body of the holy Bishop. The honorary pallbearers were the Hon. C. J. Bonaparte, Messrs. Michael Jenkins, Austin Jenkins, Dr. Felix Jenkins, Dr. Charles O'Donovan and Charles B. Tiernan. At four o'clock the remains were removed to the Union Station, and escorted by Rev. Dr. Fletcher, rector of the Baltimore Cathedral, and the active pallbearers, as a Guard of Honor, to Wilmington. Bishop Monaghan had chartered a special car, beautifully fitted up, wherein the casket was placed, the attendants occupying the remaining space. The active pallbearers were selected from the St. Vincent de Paul Society and were Messrs. J. R. Wheeler, D. N. Sullivan, C. I. Dunn, E. Kreamer, Mark O. Shriver, P. J. McEvoy, W. G. Groeninger, and Dr. C. J. Grindall.

Back to his loving and beloved people came the dead Bishop, to the seat of his former See. His body for the third time was laid in state at St. Peter's Cathedral; and the numbers of those, Catholic and Protestant alike, who filed past the plain black casket for a last look at the beloved face could scarcely be estimated. The Guards of Honor alternated during the night, in watching, until the Clergy began the Office of the Dead the following morning.

The Pontifical High Mass of Requiem was celebrated by Bishop Monaghan, whose assistant Priest was the Rev. Dr. Fletcher.

The church was heavily draped in black, but, knowing the desires of the late Bishop, everything was conducted with marked simplicity. Could he have spoken, how tenderly would he have greeted the great number of children from the Orphan Asylums, he so loved, gathered there to honor their devoted Benefactor!

An eloquent eulogy was preached by the Rev. William Temple, D.D. (beloved by the deceased as one of " his boys "). The preacher took for his text:

" Give, and it shall be given to you: good measure, well pressed down and shaken together and running over shall they give into your bosom. For with the same measure that you shall mete withal, it shall be measured to you again." St. Luke vi. 38.

" Could the lips that are now closed in the coffin be unsealed for one brief moment, and give utterance to the wishes of the soul that dwelt therein, well we know that they would forbid the paying of any tribute to his memory. And yet, great soul, so retiring and averse to the applause of men, forbear and forgive beyond the grave as you were wont to do in life. Not for your sake, but for ours, allow some words of grateful appreciation, on the part of the faithful clergy and people of this diocese.

" You are ours. Your boyhood days, your early ministry, your ten years of episcopate, your last Mass, all took place within the confines of the Diocese of Wilmington, and now you come to give us the remains of that body whose heart loved so tenderly the land of its birth and the field of its labors.

" From the Rt. Rev. Bishop of the diocese, through all the ranks of the clergy to the humblest member of the laity, we are all of one mind and one heart this morning. We are of one mind in our sincere admiration of the nobility of your life, each eager to chant the triumphal song of the Saints even while the strains of the Dies Iræ ring in our ears. We are all of one heart, grateful to God for the royal gifts showered upon you, and grateful to you for the royal way in which you wore the King's purple and bore the King's passion. We are of one hope, too, that God will give into your bosom good measure well pressed down and shaken together and running over, the exceeding joy of his exultant Saints, for the generous way in which were meted out to Him the wealth of your soul and the health of your body.

"There are two ideals of life around us, of *giving* and of *getting*. Success, so measured by the world, is to get. To get joys and toys, goods and gold and glory, houses and lands, renown and raiment, on these are set the hearts of the children of men. For these they labor and spin, these are the treasures they love and lay up on earth. Success, as taught by Christ our Lord, is to *give*. To give, body and soul, to give hopes and home and heart, to give service and sacrifice, these are the delights of the children of God. To take the lowest seat at table, to forego and forget self in waiting upon the neighbor, these are the treasures they lay up in heaven where neither the rust nor the moth doth consume, and where thieves do not break through, nor steal. 'Give and it shall be given to you.' So spake the Master. So lived his disciple. He gave up one thing after another to God and his neighbor. He gave up the call of the world for the call of Christ, and few men had greater natural gifts for a distinguished career in the state. He gave up the joys of family life, and no man had a tenderer heart than he for the charms of a child. He gave up his early religious belief, and no one had been a more faithful follower of its creed than he. He gave up the peace of his parochial work in the city of Baltimore, and no man's soul was more sternly set against the privileges of high places. He gave up the powers and prerogatives of the head of this diocese, and no man was more keenly sensitive to the criticism of good men that would ensue. He gave up comfort and convenience, his own way and will, whenever an opportunity occurred that would not injure the cause of Christ; and what he gave up was but a fraction of what he wished to give up for the love of God and in imitation of Christ Jesus.

Rt. Rev. A. A. Curtis, D.D.

" Nor was this generous outpouring of himself due to any weakness. He was a very Ajax among men, full of fire and fiber, but he humbled himself by prayer and penance, and the strength of the natural man became the sweetness of the heart of Christ.

" The Saint of Assisi said he so loved Lady Poverty because she alone stood by the naked Christ on the cross. Our dear Bishop so loved the Lord Truth, that for his sake he became naked, divesting himself of all things that he might cleave to Him. It was the dominating principle of his life. Were an artist to sketch the workings of his soul he would need but to trace a straight line, the shortest distance between his conscience and his Creator. Whatever records may leap to light in the great Judgment Day, nothing little or low will be brought against him.

" It was this love of truth that made him so impatient of pretence and sham, of newspaper notoriety and passing applause. What is man in the sight of God but a frail and failing creature? Pride, parade, pomp are but a form of lie, and against any kind of lie he unsheathed his sword, as against a personal insult.

" It would be a chapter from the life of a missionary, were we to recount the devotedness and the privations of his loving and lonely visits to the country parishes of this diocese. It would be a page from the history of a Confessor were we to speak of the depth of his faith, the earnestness of his zeal and the shame that bowed his head at every scandal in the church.

" It would be a narrative from the annals of the martyrs, were the story told of his penances and privations, of the unceasing warfare by which he overcame the vehemence of his passions, and made them subject to the law of God.

" It would be a passage from the lives of the Saints, were an account given of the lonely vigils and the lengthy prayers, by which he hallowed the Sanctuary of this Cathedral Church, prone on his face before the altar during the long watches of the night, making this place indeed a house of prayer and the gate of heaven.

" It would be the echo of the voice of a Master in Israel were we to recall the splendid words of persuasive and penetrating power, that bursting from a heart overflowing with God's love so often touched the soul of the sinner and spurred on the flagging footsteps of the Saint.

" Men do not come from God except through the agency of their fellowmen, nor do they return to God ordinarily except by the same way. Supernatural as well as natural life comes from the ministrations of men. If it is a great grace to have a good earthly father, it is a still greater one to have a good spiritual father.

" What a blessing to the priests and people of this diocese have been the sanity and sanctity of their late Father in God! It is not so much the written Word of God, as it is the walking and working Word of God in a man's life, that keeps virtue alive in the world, makes the Church attractive to those outside the fold, and increases the piety and devotion of the faithful. The life of Bishop Curtis was an open Bible, illustrated with the deeds of the Saints, and illumined with the inspiring and inspired Word of God. His practice of the Gospel precepts drew many souls after him in the narrow and rugged way that leads to Eternal life, and his memory will continue to be a benediction on this land of his birth and burial.

" But like all the servants of Christ, he had his cross to bear. The one great desire of his soul was to carry the gift of Catholic faith to the eastern shore of Maryland. For this he labored and was not ashamed to beg. For this he preached and prayed, that God might spread the precious gift of Catholic faith along the marshes and among the pines of his native land. For this he founded the Religious Community of the Visitation in this city, that it might by its prayers and sacrifices obtain one day from God the wish of his heart. For this he left his body to dwell among them, that his tomb might be a torch to keep aflame towards God the deepest desire of his priestly soul. It did not please the Providence of God to grant his request, but he persevered in his prayer till the end. A soil that grew such a soul is well worth converting to the Church, and who knows when God will deign to hear his prayer and turn the light of His Countenance upon the level lands he loved, and make them flourish with the glorious heritage of Catholic faith.

" God cannot be outdone in generosity. ' Give and it shall be given to you.' If God did not give him his native land, He gave him the riches of His peace and joy; He gave him the friendship of many saintly souls; He gave him the respect and confidence of all who came into contact with him; He gave him the loving admiration of the people of this diocese and of many of the great Archdiocese of Baltimore. But what God has given him is as nought in comparison with what God will give him. And we are gathered here to-day to beseech our good God to be generous to him, to give full measure, well pressed down and shaken together and running over into his bosom, that he may know now the height and the depth, the length and the breadth of the love of God, that he may taste how sweet God is and enjoy forever the good things that God has prepared for those that love Him, that he may rest from his labors, and that his works may follow him to be his crown, his glory, his exceeding great reward."

Bishop Monaghan read the absolutions after Mass, and then, preceded by a Guard of Honor, including the Catholic Societies of the city, members of the Hibernian Knights, Knights of St. Lawrence and St. Hedwig's Cadets, the body of the dead Prelate was borne in solemn procession, amid the continual tolling of

Bishop Curtis' Tomb,
Cemetery of the Visitation Convent,
Wilmington, Del.
–1908–

Rt. Rev. A. A. Curtis, D.D.

many bells, to its last earthly resting place, in the cemetery within the enclosure of the Visitation Convent. Bishops Monaghan, Keiley and the clergy followed the pallbearers in closed carriages, and an immense multitude lined the streets as the funeral cortége, with its precious burden, moved from the Cathedral to the Monastery, a distance of about two miles.

Through the kind and thoughtful arrangement of Bishop Monaghan, who wished to give his bereaved daughters every possible consolation, the blessed remains were first carried into the black-draped Convent Chapel, amid the plaintive chant of the Miserere by the clergy, and placed on an inclined bier, close to and directly in front of the open Communion window of the grille.

There his devoted children assembled in the choir, advanced to look once more upon that kind and gentle face, to touch with their beads and medals the dear feet, which had so many times brought to them the glad tidings of peace and reconciliation.

The last absolution pronounced, and final ceremonies being concluded, the holy remains were carried to the enclosure door, accompanied by the two Bishops and all the clergy, who entered the Monastery, passing out to the humble cemetery where the religious with lighted candles and lowered veils waited near the open grave. The burial service was read by Bishop Monaghan, amid the tears of clergy and religious, and the body of the great and humble Servant of God was lowered into the tomb, while the impressive chant of the Benedictus echoed through the quiet Convent garden. The Bishops and clergy then withdrew, and the nuns re-entered their choir, there to chant the Office of the Dead for the holy deceased, being more inclined to pray to him than for him.

This sentiment was most feelingly expressed in a sermon preached at the month's mind of the holy deceased in St. Peter's Cathedral, Wilmington, by the Rt.

Rt. Rev. A. A. Curtis, D.D.

Rev. Mgr. W. E. Russell, Rector of St. Patrick's Church in Washington, who closed his remarks on this occasion by saying: " While we feel more like praying to him than for him, let us nevertheless pray for dear, good Bishop Curtis, who fought the good fight, ran the race and kept the faith."

Many petitions have been sent to this hallowed spot, and the religious love to kneel in prayer on the massive granite slab at the foot of the great crucifix; which in summer is surrounded by fragrant flowers and waving willows, and where the " sturdy " English sparrow he so loved is continually chirping; while sweet songsters, the thrush and robin, seem to choose that spot for their most beautiful evening song.

That many graces and favors, not miracles, have been obtained at the holy Bishop's grave, is incontestably true, and it sometimes seems as though his gently voiced promise, " I shall be here, I will not leave you," were indeed realized. It may not be amiss to speak of the widespread " story of the birds." It is one which has been greatly exaggerated in its details; but the fact remains, that two very young aspirants to the religious life were recreating, a few days after the Bishop's burial, like little children, not far from the cemetery hedge. They entered the gate, and confidently asked the good Bishop to help them catch some of the many beautiful birds flitting through the grounds and resting in the trees. After the petition they tested their faith, and their loved Father's remembrance, and indeed their childlike, spontaneous prayer was heard. They took in their hands, and without difficulty, several birds which at once flew down and allowed themselves to be fondled and gently caressed by the little girls before they were launched again in the air. This happened not once, but many times, birds even remaining on their heads and shoulders when so placed. And this is the true version of the story. Similar favors, if cited, might not be credited, while countless " Miracles

Rt. Rev. A. A. Curtis, D.D.

of Grace " in answer to prayer are the secret of hearts which may one day be revealed.

The faithful souvenir of the saintly Bishop's heroic virtue and holy direction lives ever in the hearts of his spiritual daughters, and in the memory of many others as well. His sacred remains, as a relic reposing in the Convent cemetery, are a precious pledge of his oft-repeated promise to intercede with God for those he loved and cared for here below, and who hope for a participation in those endless joys of which he must already be in full possession.

Among those who knew the saintly Bishop best, some have thought his death was one of pure love, and this, the touching inscription on his tomb would seem to confirm.

Expectans · Beatam · Spem
Et · Adventum · Gloriæ · Magni · Dei
Hic · Jacet
Corpus · Illmi · Et · Revmi · DD ·
Alfredi · Allen · Curtis
Qui
Episcopus · Wilmingtoniensis
Die · XVII · Martii · A · D · MDCCCLXXXVI
Renunciatus
Decimo · Post · Anno
Onus · Pastorale
Ultro · Deposuit
Titularioque · Ecclesiæ · Echinen · Præfectus
In · Civitatæ · Baltimoren · Decens
Ab · Emin · DD · Card · Gibbons
Vicarius · Generalis · Creatus
Multis · Laboribus
Potius · Quam · Annorum · Pondere
Oppressus
In · Osculo · Domini
Die · XI · Julii · A · D · MCMVIII
Ætatis · Suæ · LXXVII
Requiescat · in · pace

Rt. Rev. A. A. Curtis, D.D.

Expecting the Blessed Hope
And Coming of the Glory of Almighty God
Here lies
The Body of the Right Reverend
Alfred Allen Curtis, D.D.
Who was appointed
Bishop of Wilmington
the 17th Day of March in the Year of Our Lord 1886
After ten Years
He of his own accord laid down
The Pastoral Burden and
Was made Titular Bishop of Echinus
And Vicar General to His Emin. James, Card. Gibbons.
Weighed down more by Labours than by
the weight of Years
He expired
In the kiss of the Lord
The 11th Day of July in the Year of Our Lord 1908
In the 77th Year of his age.
May he rest in peace.

✠

With the heartfelt wish that this humble attempt to portray the saintly Bishop's " Life and Characteristics," may increase an hundredfold the number of his admirers and imitators, these pages shall be closed in his own devout words:

" Let us honor all the Saints, but especially that numberless army of unknown Saints. The canonized Saints, who are few compared with the former, have been capable of practising heroic virtue, virtue which is beyond our attainment. But we will consider the vast army of unknown Saints who have no history, who lived the same common life that we do, who did common things uncommonly well, who toiled, waited, suffered; who believed, hoped, loved and repented, these we can imitate."

PRAY FOR THE SOUL
OF THE
RT·REV·ALFRED·A·CURTIS·D·D
SECOND·BISHOP·OF·WILMINGTON
CONSECRATED·NOVEMBER·14·1886
DIED·JULY·11·1908
IDEAL·CHAMPION
OF·THE
MISSIONARY·LIFE
FOR·THIS·COUNTRY
MAY·HE·REST·IN·PEACE

Bronze Memorial Tablet
in St. Peter's Cathedral, Wilmington, Del.

LETTERS

IN this very incomplete collection of personal letters to various friends will be found many of the Bishop's characteristic traits; his unswerving uprightness, tender, affectionate heart, pleasure in innocent recreation and loyalty to his friends.

"His last days were spent in making sure that there should not be left a jot or tittle of his writings," says one of his admirers.[1] This is confirmed by the holy Bishop in a letter written a short time before his death when learning that some of these valuable epistles had been preserved: "Those letters contradict, I fear, my intention to leave no writing behind me when I go. I have already had several auto-da-fé and nothing will be found in my own possession save some annotations here and there, of books which no one will be likely to find, or be able to read, even if they should be found. But the letters I have been so unwise as to write I can't control. I have not erred of late even as to letters. But time was when I was not so careful as to putting myself on paper as I at present am."

The five letters which follow were addressed to a Religious:

WILMINGTON, DEL., October 25, 1890.

MY DEAR M.:

I am very glad indeed to hear that you are well, and no doubt as happy as it is safe to be. I did not mean to complain at all of your silence, though what I said may have suggested as much; for writing often implies, or seems to imply, what one does not really intend; to say nothing of the greater defect of not suggesting what one does really mean. I am very far from wanting you to write for my pleasure. Do so only when you wish it for any reason whatever, and even for no reason at all, should you have the slightest desire to communicate with me. I am never burdened with letters, first, because I do not receive very many, and next, because I answer them as soon as received.

What I said when I last saw you was very far from the intention of suggesting greater reticence to you. It applied to my-

---

[1] Taken from notice of "Lights and Counsels" in "Extension Magazine," by Rev. Thomas V. Shannon.

self, and not to you, and signified that I had taken up as much of your time as I feel free to claim. . . .

I am sure you pray for me as I for you. How strangely things come about! You are glad that you are in religion, and I am every day more thankful that God would not let me become a religious.

Yrs. faithfully in Xt.,

✠A. A. CURTIS, *Bishop of Wilmington.*

EASTON, MD., January 4, 1891.

MY DEAR M.:

I heard the sad news yesterday at the Station in Washington. I would gladly have returned to —— or remained in —— had I been able. Not that I could have done anything for you or the others, but simply because thereby I should have more evidently shown my sympathy with you all. But duty in the most imperative way forbade this. And hence nothing is left me but to write you a line to say, what you know without my saying it, namely, that my heart and my prayers are with you in your trouble. I said the Mass for him this morning as much as I could, it being a people's day. I have also said my office for him since I heard of his departure. I was so glad to be assured that for a good while he has been regular in his use of the Sacraments. You must try not to be too much cast down by the suddenness and unexpectedness of the blow. Some with little sense might see in it a bit of divine disapproval of what you were doing. But you know better, and understand that it is merely God's taking you at your word, and giving you at the start the opportunity of signally showing that you know and mean what you do. May He bless you.

Yrs. faithfully in Xt.,

✠A. A. CURTIS, *Bishop of Wilmington.*

WILMINGTON, DEL., March 30, 1891.

MY DEAR CHILD:

Your letter reached me when I was so very busy that I could not well find the time in which to answer it. Besides I thought it as well to wait awhile ere answering. The older I get the more I become afraid of myself, and the less disposed to counsel others, if I can fairly avoid doing so. In taste, as well as in principle and conviction, I am so much at variance with so many far better than myself, and am so much disposed to see nothing but my own view of a question, that I fear more and more to advise others and fear most of all the having to advise at once and without prior consideration. And this combined with much more work than I ought to have undertaken, caused me to defer writing to you till to-day. And even now that I am writing I can think of nothing better than such mere generalities, as will, I am sure, be of small service to you. First, then, anything not evidently sinful is better than singularity unnecessarily incurred, so while you yourself seek no indults or dispensations, yet I am sure you should cheerfully accept, and in good faith use all of both recommended you, it being understood, of course, that you are first free to represent frankly why you suppose yourself not to need or desire exemption. But this being done, you should accept willingly the verdict of authority, however less exacting than your own judgment. Secondly, you remember what I tried to inculcate when you were vested, *i. e.,* that religion is the sacrifice of the will itself, and very specially its sacrifice as to things in the abstract good or even the very best of all. So then you have but one thing to consider, viz., whether or not you are inwardly and loyally submissive to authority, or trying to be thus submissive in the life you are leading. If so, that is the end of the matter. In the pursuit of sanctity you may be deceived, and you will be deceived if you pursue it according to your own lights and after your own bent. But you cannot incur mistake or suffer real detriment, no matter what the apparent loss, as long as you are thoroughly and strictly under obedience. Finally, I am obliged to be in Savannah for the annual meeting of the Bishops on the 15th of April. As I return I shall, if possible at all, see you, and we can talk over things more fully. I shall pray for you, as you will, I am sure, for me.

WILMINGTON, DEL., July 1, 1891.

MY DEAR CHILD:

I do not see why anyone should be very grateful on account of a visit from me. And certainly you seemed to value my late visit to you much more than I myself fancied to be worth.

I fully believe that every one should be loyal to his own steadfast inspirations, be the opinions of others what they may, and the more loyal, when as in the case in question, the fulfilment of those inspirations implies no conflict with or possibility of injury to one's neighbors. Therefore, I decide without hesitation that you do right in adhering to the purpose so long ago formed, and since remaining with you. And in the fulfilment of the same purpose I shall account it an honor and a benefit to be your agent and instrument, depend upon that. I have not yet been able to make my visit North. But I think I can accomplish it ere the expiration of the month, and will then find a day to run over to you.

Rt. Rev. A. A. Curtis, D.D.

As to the other matter, I am upon principle much in favor of doing charity when one can, ere death. F—— will, I take it, have told you about the consecration. All things considered, we went through the function marvellously well. F—— was exceedingly kind, and gave for expenses of consecration a sum out of which I hope to have enough over with which to buy a bell. I am well enough. Don't forget that next Saturday will be my sixtieth birthday. Besides your own prayers, get me all the other help you can. I do not forget you. May God bless you.

WILMINGTON, DEL., October 15, 1892.

As to the Salesian Oblates: If I can get the means of establishing them, and they are willing and fit to be established in the country, or even in some country town, I shall be glad to establish them just as soon as practicable. I shall be most happy — indeed much more than is commonly understood by being happy — in furthering to the utmost of my power any project, looking to the introduction of the Oblates into Wilmington.

As to the general confession, think no more of making it. No such confession would in the least tend to make me know you any better than I do. Of that rest certain. To know one really now, it is not at all necessary to know that he used to have certain warts, or even ulcers of which he is at present free. Use your retreat then, not in disinterring and dissecting the dead past, but in trying to bring your present living heart into more complete and permanent union with the most Sacred Hearts of Jesus and Mary.

The Oblates of St. Francis de Sales, here mentioned, are now established in Wilmington, where they conduct a flourishing College for boys, besides exercising many offices of the sacred ministry in the Diocese.

CP. CHARLES, October 11, 1893.

MY DEAR CHILD:

Yours of the 9th I found here yesterday when I arrived; we were frustrated in our purpose to give two nights to Chincoteague Island. The hall there is in use every night on the part of some society, and hence we could not hire it. So after finishing yesterday at Pocomoke, we came to this place to stay till to-morrow, when we go up to Onancock, and the day after to Eastville, returning on Saturday to Cp. Charles for Sunday. Monday I cross over to Fortress Monroe to get the boat up the bay at night to Baltimore, where, on Tuesday, we are to nominate for Wheeling. Wednesday morning the Cardinal has his

Letters

jubilee Mass; I must assist at that, but by cutting the dinner following, I hope to get home Wednesday afternoon.

It will be well to notify the Oblates that we cannot see Bohemia before Friday, the 20th. I shall notify the Frs. to expect us on that day. We can, after a fashion, lodge two Frs. at house, and if necessary put two more just across the street; I don't want them to stop at a hotel. I do hope they may take to Bohemia. I am sure I should not object to finishing my own days there. Having been so long in use on the part of the Jesuits, there must be some virtue and blessing attached to the place itself. I am not obliged to go to Rome till '95, though it does not look well to postpone a duty till the last possible moment. Hence I have thought of going, or getting permission to send a commissary next year. But as yet I have settled nothing. I am writing this in the new house. It is really very nice and quite sufficient. Altogether the place is immensely improved, grass, pavements, drains, etc., etc. I told you that twenty-five years would prove us right, and give us the name of sagacity, in so early founding this outpost in the desert. And it appears now that my prognostication is going to be verified. Please give my love to all, and warn them again how much I depend upon their prayers always, and specially here in the wilderness. God bless you.

The Bishop here refers to a journey to the Benedictine Convent at Ridgely, Md., of which mention is made in the Biography.

February 15, 1895.

I managed to get to Balto. to-day after all, though more than once yesterday it was doubtful when I should again arrive even at Wilmington. The travelling from the station to the Benedictine house was through or around any number of snowdrifts. I returned to the station yesterday on horseback, as the easier and safer form of locomotion. To crown all, after waiting for hours for the train we stuck fast and had to be dug out. I reached home, however, at 1.30 this morning. Don't forget nor let the others forget our mission in Onancock, Va., beginning next Monday and lasting till Thursday evening. Besides, all of you combine to get me first a little more faith, hope and charity, etc.

The Bishop loved truth for the sake of truth, and could not bear that it be tampered with or made light of, as will be seen in the concluding lines of the following letter. They have reference to a party purchasing secretly some property for an individual, who had been refused the right of purchase by the owner.

St. Charles' College, September 21, 1895.

I have already written to —— promising, God willing, to be with you on Wednesday, October 2, and begging the prayers of you all for myself and the retreat I am to give here and for which I am, with as yet small success, trying to prepare. I hope my cry for aid will rouse you all to do the very best you can in my behalf.

I remember Miss B—— very well. Being as fit as I take her to be to die, I am not sorry to hear that she has been in effect called hence. Even could we stay here forever it would be well to besiege Heaven for permission to die. And since on the other hand die we must, and life means nothing save as preparing for death and being consummated in death, the sooner we die the better, always provided that we die when and as the Lord willeth. I don't like anything savoring of trick even when the device promises to be successful, and of course I no more like the device when it is sure to fail of its purpose. And in this case it certainly would fail. I have time for nothing more than to say that I send my blessing to all.

This letter speaks of work done while the Bishop was Vicar-General to His Eminence Cardinal Gibbons:

St. Inigo's Manor, St. Mary's Co., Maryland, July 11, 1898.

I am now nearing the end of my tour; I have three other confirmations and then can return. Fortunately we have had but one day of real heat, and no rain at all. Hence there has been nothing to diminish the classes for confirmation. Up to the present I have confirmed more than a thousand. The dust and the driving in carriages and the much diversified eating expected of one, have been the only disagreeable things. Since work this morning, I was driven nearly, or quite fifteen miles. Of those confirmed, the colored largely exceed the whites, for which I am not sorry. One confirmation to-morrow will be on St. George's Island, where the first Mass in Maryland was said. And the confirmation will be the first ever had on the Island. I am fond of the Jesuits; they always edify me, and treat me as I desire to be treated, viz., with real kindness and respect, but without fuss or undue formality. About half or rather more of the men in service in St. Mary's are very efficient, and to the people very attractive.

Letters

The following letter portrays the Bishop's reverence for the exact observance of religious rule, and the determination to maintain it *" en rigueur,"* even to the denial of the seemingly legitimate desire of one of his spiritual daughters, who, prevented by a passing indisposition from descending to the confessional grate, expressed the wish to have him enter the cloister to hear her confession.

November 28, 1898.

I feel myself specially called upon to maintain the cloister with all practicable strictness, and this for several reasons. It is totally against nature, and nature will always, as we say, bear watching, and sleepless watching too.

But all the tendencies good and bad of the present time are against the cloister, and multitudes in most ways abler and better than I am scout it, as an anachronism. On all hands among the best you will find plenty who will tempt you to forego strictness, but very few who will encourage you to stand by that strictness.

As therefore the strictness began under me and in some sort through me, I feel myself the more bound not to relax it save for a very sufficient reason, and I did not regard your confession, knowing well what it would have been, as such a reason.

The two following letters written to the Visitation Nuns at Wilmington contain some original reflections:

January 20, 1900.

Your letter, like most things in this world, is mixed. Good news that some one has been found promising to fill the place, which as yet I myself have seen no chance of filling. It is the old story. Have you a vacancy? You look in vain for one willing and able to fill it. Have you a person in want of a place? Search how you may, no place can be found. It is good news then that for once, place and person come together. But it is not, humanly speaking, good that Sr. —— has been so suddenly smitten; she is indeed a very good soul, honest and earnest, two qualities not always found in the same person. For my experience is that very earnest people are not always to the core honest, and less still to the core unselfish. We must simply ask our Lord to make her well again for the Community's sake.

His Lordship dined with us yesterday and deputed me to fix the conditions upon which you are all to gain the indulgence of the jubilee. It will be as well to write down these conditions now, so that you may begin at once to fulfil them. Each then will make seven visits to the Pieta — one in honor of each of our Lord's wounds, the sixth in veneration of the thorns and their punctures, and the seventh of the scourge and the gashes it left. Length of visit and prayers during the visit are left to the choice of each. Love and blessing to all.

BALTIMORE, December 14, 1900.

To be faithful when one is not greatly, if at all, tempted to become otherwise, does not signify very much. And I am not often or much tempted to spend money upon myself. Instead of spending upon myself, ever since my seventeenth year I have found my duty and pleasure in trying to make and save for the benefit of others. I can the day after Xmas postpone starting home till the 2.09 P. M. train, and this will give me time enough in which to go and stay awhile within. As I have to act for the Bp. otherwise, it will be quite the thing to make his Xmas visit for him. I pray that at Xmas you may all arrive at a deeper and more prevailing conviction that there is nothing much worth while but the love and lowliness which made Xmas.

" Blessed are the poor in spirit:
for theirs is the kingdom of Heaven."

One of his spiritual daughters having drawn this beatitude for the Bishop on the eve of All Saints, and mailed it to him on a card, received in return the following beautiful reflections on poverty:

BALTIMORE, November 3, 1901.

Thank you for the Beatitude. If it were really my Beatitude! If I could but become as poor in spirit as I am in fact. If we all could but recognize more and more how poor, and more than merely poor we are. Had we this the first and germ of all Beatitudes, the rest would surely follow it, and grow out of it.

The following characteristic note has reference to the loss of his pocket-book, which the Bishop thought he had left in the Convent Sacristy, and after writing to inquire about it, found it safe in his overcoat pocket:

January 15, 1903.

DEAR REVEREND MOTHER:

" The number of fools is infinite," says Holy Writ, and I am daily more certain that I must be included in this number. I have found my pocket-book; in my overcoat pocket it was, as I discovered a moment ago. I looked for it there yesterday, as I supposed, carefully too, and did not find it. But I looked again this morning, by accident, and certain that I should not find it; and yet there it was, and discovered at the first touch. And yet how it got there is more than I can divine, for I am sure I did not have it in hand from the time I quitted home yesterday till I returned, as I never carry it in my overcoat. Perhaps, Sister found it in the Sacristy on the floor, and put it in my overcoat while I was in the cloister. I don't think Saint Anthony did it, because he knew it did not belong in the overcoat. And if he had undertaken the job he would not have botched it, and virtually hidden from me what I wanted to find.

Love and blessing to all.

Xmas, 1903.

The expressmen are over-burdened, and besides, are getting, I trust, to-day a well earned rest. Hence they are reserving our package till to-morrow, when it will no doubt appear unharmed. I promise to use the contents when I shall need them. I am doing well enough at present. You may infer as much when I inform you that I this morning waked the others at 4.30, and then myself went to the confessional to gather in any stragglers; I waited a good while, and bagged after all but three or four. Then I said my own Masses and was in time for a solitary breakfast at 8 A. M., the usual time with us for that meal. I need not say that you and all the others had your place in the Masses, as indeed you have place in all Masses as well as in everything else. I wish I could be more sure of being able thereby to procure you the good I wish and intend. Love and blessing to all.

True as the needle to the pole, the Bishop set out for Wilmington in the face of a terrible blizzard, and after having been delayed hours on the way, he reached his destination only to be driven back by the storm, for the snow-drifts were so deep that it was impossible to reach the Convent, although in sight of it. The next day he sent the following letter, explaining the reason of his non-appearance on the day appointed for the Sisters' confessions:

BALTIMORE, January 25, 1904.

I made an attempt to reach you to-day, but afterwards thought it the part of wisdom to retreat beaten. I even got to the station at Wilmington. There I found no cab and the cars were not running. I forced my way towards you for a short distance. But the wind was so high, the snow so dense and the drifts so deep that I deemed it prudent to turn back and shelter myself in the station. Thence I took the first train to Baltimore. It should have reached Baltimore at a little before 1 P. M. As it was, we arrived a little before 4 P. M. And there were times when I thought we should be even later, if we should arrive at all. When nearly half way they put on a second engine, and thereby we managed to get through in time, if not on time. I don't think I am any worse for the buffeting, and hope to do better next Wednesday. Love and blessing to all.

BALTIMORE, February 28, 1904.

You will, I am sure, have heard ere this reaches you, that Mr. —— passed onwards and upwards early this morning. For Purgatory is far above this present state of things. He went as I thought he would, very easily and quietly. I did everything I could for him, seeing him always once and sometimes twice a day. I was with him yesterday evening between 7 and 8, and gave him absolution and the last blessing, and then we all together said in full the prayers for the departing. I was at the house this morning and saw W——. He thought that the funeral will take place on Wednesday. But could not then determine details. I suppose I shall be expected to take the Mass, and anyhow I shall want to assist even if another take the Mass. Love and blessing to all.

To a dear friend in the priesthood the Bishop addressed the following lines:

BALTIMORE, April 2, 1904.

MY DEAR NED:

I start early on Tuesday: I shall go not unwillingly in the hope of shaking off grippe once for all. I am not over the fourth return thereof. I have at once catarrh of chest and head. But it may be my luck to strike cool, disagreeable weather in Florida. And there is the more danger of this, as the winter there was, I learn, rather warm.

I am very glad that you are going to leave Snow Hill, not only because you could not have rightly sold it for Protestant purposes, but because it may yet be needed. You remember when we were sorry for the interference which saved Salisbury. But you will soon have Salisbury erected into a " suffragan see " with resident pastor. And no one can tell how soon Snow Hill may outstrip Salisbury and become the second suburbican " see," appertaining to Cape Charles. Necessary expenses at Snow Hill for repairs and insurance I will try to meet if you notify me of them. Are your emigrants going to buy land at once, or are they to be mere laborers for a good while to come? The former I hope, but the latter I fear. As laborers merely they are likely to be more restless and fractious. I trust that you may get good people. Our weather to-day is splendid, and there is good hope that H. E. will be able to go all around out of doors. This will do him heaps of good. Medicine would not benefit him half so much. If I catch an uncommonly large tarpon I shall send you one of his scales. I have left myself free to stay longer if the fish should be late in coming to the hook. But I hope this will not be the case. Pray for me.

To the Same.

June 18, 1904.

I find your letter of the 4th on my return from St. Mary's, which happened at 3 A. M. to-day. The trip was rather fatiguing on account of so much driving in carriages — a thing which I hate bitterly. But I had some consolation in the confirmations which came in all to 1060. I had, moreover, a restful day on the steamboat yesterday. I went across from St. Inigo's to George's Island and embarked at 8 A. M. We spent the day in running up and down Virginia rivers, the Yoacomico and Coal rivers, and returned to St. Inigo's at 5 P. M. yesterday, or rather we went by St. Inigo's at that hour, for the boat does not stop at the place itself.

I am glad your statement shows a balance on the right side, and I quite agree with you that we should be well off if we could manage the spiritual as we do the material. But most Priests, as it seems to me, do not recognize that the two are very distinct, and that while the one may advance by leaps and bounds, the other may be lagging, languishing and dying. We have, I suppose, become conformed to that by which we are encompassed. For the whole American nation boasts only of material advances. It certainly has not advanced in lowliness, and in the recognition of the futility of all efforts and achievements, merely and solely human. Pray for me.

To the Same.

Baltimore, September 7, 1904.

I am very sorry the cigars were so very bad. I want to help the poor fellow. But I cannot do so by accumulating weeds that no one will smoke. If he would permit me to give him his commission and let him sell, if he can, the cigars to some one else, he would be as well off, and I should be saved money. But this I am sure he will not permit. I heard that Semple S. J. is to preach your retreat next week, and this I hope was no mistake. For you will like him, I know, exceedingly. He is a southerner, which means a good deal to me, and no doubt quite as much to you. He is simple and frank and kind. . . . I am very glad the Bp. proposes to cultivate Salisbury. If he accomplish much, and I trust he will, it will be the case of some sowing and others reaping. For all in all there has been for many years a good deal of sowing in that place. But until lately nothing came of the sowing, save perhaps some increase of merit on the part of the sowers themselves. Pray for me.

To the Same Friend.

BALTIMORE, June 19, 1906.

I don't believe a word as to fish biting at or near Cape Charles. I will undertake to catch more in Bush River at one fishing than you will get in both your outings. I got two dozen there yesterday, and if I could have begun two hours earlier, I am persuaded I should have much more than doubled my catch. Among the two dozen were a two-pound bass and a white perch of one pound or nearly. The rest were mostly of fair size. Besides, I had not much if any less, than eight miles of rowing. There was but a whiff of wind now and then, and the whiff was now from one, and now from another quarter. Much of the time I fished without an anchor, so sailing was impossible. But it was hot as blazes. I go on Saturday to McNamara at Benedict, and thence with him early — very early on Monday to Solomons. We propose to sail back to Benedict on Tuesday, there being no steamboat up till Thursday. Since the Pennsylvania came to include the Chesapeake among its many other possessions, the schedule is much altered. Pray for me.

To the Same.

July 4, 1906.

I reserved my answer to your last letter till my return from Benedict and Solomons. I got back late yesterday afternoon. I found McNamara as good and efficient as ever. He is making quite a name for himself as a speaker. Sunday was given to Benedict. I had to make three speeches: the first at 8 A. M. Mass, the second at the 10 A. M. Mass, the third at the Confirmation at 4 P. M. At 5.30 A. M. on Monday we started on the steamboat to Solomons. At night another speech and small confirmation. All the time it was hot, hotter, hottest. We had proposed to sail back to Benedict after the Confirmation, starting about 8.30 P. M. But one of the congregation consented to run us up in his gasoline launch. This we deemed better, so at 8 A. M. on Tuesday we set out. I stood and steered the launch the eighteen miles; we made the trip in 2½ hours. From Benedict we drove seven miles to Hughesville, and there got train at 1.30 P. M. With two changes of cars and a wait of half an hour at each junction, I got to Baltimore about 5.45 P. M. Sullivan has given up his boat and taken the hotel instead. I am afraid the change will not be to his advantage pecuniarily. During the summer the place will be filled, and after that nothing. And as he has no accidentals in the shape of bar, billiard-table, etc., he is certain to be rather out than in, at the end of the year. Pray for me.

The following choice lines on the death of an infant show that a poetical vein existed in the Bishop's great mind, otherwise so matter of fact:

August 6, 1906.

L——'s baby was a wise little thing when, having sipped a little of life, she resolved to take no more of it, and to exchange it at once for a better life, where the sweet is not so often overpowered, and more than simply nullified by the bitter and nauseous.

To a Clerical Friend.

BALTIMORE, August 17, 1906.

I am not long back from fishing. I was obliged to be an hour or two late and so got only a dozen, whereas had I been two hours earlier I should have filled my basket with good fish. Nothing can be done at Bush River save on the last of the flood tide. And that tide was a little past when I began fishing this morning. I thought of going early enough to get the high tide. But I found myself wanted to say the 6 o'clock parochial Mass, F—— having a funeral at a later hour. But anyhow I had the break and the air and exercise, and they are the main things. Our retreat begins Monday the 27th, and a Paulist, Fr. Smith, is to take charge of us. He is a good fellow and I like him, but when we had him before he seemed to me to lack ginger. I am very sorry for J——. But after all is it not the good people who cause us most solicitude and anxiety. So it seems to me. And certainly he is in the main a good fellow. I hope he

Rt. Rev. A. A. Curtis, D.D.

will do the square thing, *i. e.,* admit his fault and cast himself on the mercy of the court. We have had a most oppressive August. It has been consistently and continuously hot, day and night. And to make things worse, the mosquitoes have been unusually numerous and venomous, withal, they are so dreadfully cunning. How they get into the screened room no one can say. But they do. And not only so, but they hide by day, and at night so long as a light burns. Pray for me.

To the Same.

BALTIMORE, August 29, 1906.

We are in the midst of our retreat under the guidance of Fr. Smith, Paulist. He is doing very well, and showing more ability than I had been disposed to ascribe to him. Moreover, he has some of the ginger and spice in which I imagined him lacking. I confounded some one else with him. For this is, it seems, the first retreat he has ever undertaken in behalf of the clergy of this diocese. I am glad J—— was let off so easily, and I hope your prognostications as to similar escapades in the future may be falsified by his conduct hereafter. But a bad marriage is certainly a dreadful thing, and is never rendered the more tolerable by the reflection that it was due entirely to one's own fault or stupidity. K—— has a large practice, and so of course an excellent reputation. Besides, our boys tell me that he is an excellent Catholic. I do not myself know him at all. Saturday next I hurry from the retreat to get 9 A. M. train to Oakland, where I bless a bell on Sunday. On Wednesday after, I consecrate Altars at Westernport. On Saturday and Sunday following I ordain for the Capuchins in Cumberland. After the ordination I come home at once, and the day after at 8 A. M. I go to Mt. St. Mary's for ordinations, on the 11th, 12th and 13th. During the rest of this month, therefore, and all of the next I shall be on the hoof. Pray for me and assure Mrs. —— of my sympathy and prayers.

October 31, 1906.

Last Sunday's weather could not have been called with truth a snow storm, but there were gusts and flurries of snow more than once, and the thickest and worst of the flurries came just as the Confirmandi were out of doors, passing from the place of assembly into the Church.

The round was rather a long one, but netted very nearly 1200. On the whole I went through it fairly well, but I was none the less glad to reach my own place yesterday, at or a little after midnight. I am not nocturnal at all in my flittings, but I ciphered it out, that as some hours had to be taken from the night, it would be as well to take them from its beginning as from its end; *i. e.,* it seemed as cheap to stay up longer as to get up an hour or two sooner.

At Christmas of 1906 he writes to one of the clergy engaged in country missions: " I am going to send you for your Xmas gift two tubs of candy, so that you may be able to make ever so many of your little ones, at least for awhile, happy. And after all one cannot, I think, on earth expect to be more than temporarily happy." A little later the announcement of the arrival of the tubs called for the following:

BALTIMORE, December 28, 1906.

I am glad the tubs reached you safely and in time. I was beginning to get uneasy lest they had failed to reach you. Just now expressmen are under a cloud, and are, I fear, justly accused, not only of collecting when things have been prepaid, as your tubs were, but of wiping the things out and out, now and then. My Xmas gift came in the form of a very bad back. It does not bother me much when I am still, but any turn or twist tempts me to scream, and in fact does make me grunt and groan a little sometimes. I am afraid Russell and you may collide with another freeze, in which case the duck will be not only few, but worthless.

Our Xmas was as usual. The Cardinal pontificated morning and afternoon. The Vespers were good, but I missed the usual volume of sound. The students are much fewer, and among them not many good voices. Pray for me.

The following lines show what a close embargo the Bishop kept on nature and its cravings to the very end of his life, even denying himself that which was necessary to him who was literally dying on his feet — for it was in this year he began to fail rapidly:

BALTIMORE, May 11, 1907.

You do well to fear the nipping habit. I fear it too, so much so that I never buy whiskey for my own use. More than once some has been sent to me and I have used it. For more than a month I have felt in my wrestling with grippe that a little whiskey two or three times a day would be a great help to me. But I had none and would buy none, so I have fought on without any. I am about the same, on my feet and doing

Rt. Rev. A. A. Curtis, D.D.

what must be done, but never myself and sometimes much less so than at others. To-morrow afternoon I shall confirm from five hundred to seven hundred Poles, and how I dread the task. There should be a confirmation in such populous places every year, otherwise the numbers are too great. It is hard on the people who pack the church till it is hardly possible to supply them with breathable air, and it is nearly killing to the Bishop.

Yes, the trouble is to find one who is so unvitiated by city life, that he can content himself happily with rural work. If the mission houses do nothing, as you say, save to convince men that some one must look after the scattered sheep, they will have earned the deepest and best gratitude of the Church. It puzzles me to discover what people find so attractive in large cities, with their racking noises and evil smells, to say nothing of their great masses of dire poverty, and loathsome vice. Pray for me.

June 27, 1907.

Is Jim going to better himself as policeman? I am sure the town will be the better for him, for he is strong, honest and fearless. But will he be the better for undertaking to supervise the town? I hope so, but I have a great fear as to the permanent good of office holding in these times. In fact, I cannot recall any one during my long life who was ultimately the better for office.

I am fairly well and so glad for the country's sake that the summer seems to have arrived at last. I don't like the heat, but it does not hurt me, and for the country people who always have my greatest sympathy it is nothing less than necessary. They have already suffered much. I saw not a single cherry, for example, in all St. Mary's County, and the pears fared no better.

I went to Bush River yesterday and hooked two eels at one time. One being such a bother, imagine what were two.

Writing to a Visitandine nun from Florida, where he had been persuaded to go for a little rest, he says:

SARASOTA, FLA.

The day is most exquisite. At 9 A. M. the thermometer at 70 degrees, the sky brilliantly clear, and the air still. Birds all around us all day long: mockers, red birds, robins, jays, doves and one dear little fellow which with the most musical of voices, all day long sings nothing but: " St. Peter, St. Peter."

It has been too early for tarpon, so instead of toiling strenuously in pursuit of them, I have taken it easily. In the air and sun nearly all the time save when in bed, and even then I have been almost out of doors, for the three large windows of my room have been all fully open day and night. Mass every morning, beads and prayers in the evening. A little rowing and fishing after breakfast, and then a good floating on the gulf water. In the afternoons, from five to eight miles of walking and exploring. I have been hoping to find a rattle snake, but the nearest I have come to it is to have met a man in a path I was following, who had in his hand the skin of one killed at the side of the path a few minutes before. He proposed to sell the skin for at least two and perhaps three dollars. One of the fads of the women is to have belts of snake skins. It is, you see, an ill wind which blows good to none. Even fads and rattlers profit some of the very poor people here. My love and blessing to all, and thank all for having by their prayers made things so nice for me here.

> Yrs. faithfully in Xt.,
> A. A. Curtis, *Bp. Tt. of Echinus.*

PART SECOND

I
SPIRITUAL COUNSELS

INTRODUCTION

THE reader of these salutary Counsels of the late Bishop Curtis cannot fail to recognize that the holy Prelate is revealing the inner sanctuary of his own soul. To those who enjoyed the blessed privilege of living under his spiritual direction, and who tasted some of the secrets of his daily, nay hourly, communings with God, the sweet task of compiling these reminiscences has been reserved.

In the Spiritual Entertainments held with his daughters at the grille, during little retreats preceding the various feasts of the year, at the Annual Visitation, and on other occasions, he revealed the strength of a very sweet and tender piety, which gave unction to his every word, while in his more familiar conversation with them, he spoke of himself and his happenings with a spontaneity of which he seemed little possessed when dealing with the world.

In his visits to the Community, where he filled the double office of Spiritual Father and Confessor for a number of years, many were the pious subterfuges resorted to by his children, for exploring the rich mine of his wise and solid counsels. At such times he would respond to their various questions with an abandonment charming in its simplicity.

These encouraging lessons have been carefully gathered, and faithfully preserved as so many precious maxims, which may serve those who, having the same needs and desires, require help and encouragement.

For example, what a depth of interior life is contained in the following: " Make of your whole soul an eye, and fix it on Christ." Or: " Find God in the

239

depths of your soul, and then leave yourself to Him, just in the state that you are in at the time."

Again: " Yield yourself up to our Blessed Lord a thousand times a day, cleave to Him, keep the desire of union with Him, but leave to Him the choice of the means to effect it. If we choose them, we will make mistakes; let us leave the care of success to our Lord." What more original and forcible for gaining the attention of his hearer than the following: " Write this in the bottom of your heart and keep it there." Or at another time: " This is for always."

But the pet theme of the holy Director and of which he never tired speaking, was the lowly, hidden virtue of humility, in the practice of which he, himself, excelled, to the complete forgetfulness of self. " True sanctity," he says, " consists in being sweetly, sweetly content to be nothing. Any other kind of sanctity is one-tenth for God, and nine-tenths for self."

The following collection of charming extracts taken from his instructions and advice given at various times, contains the quintessence of true virtue, and the solid manner of practising it.

It is impossible in reading these salutary counsels not to feel that the speaker is revealing his own beautiful soul, all steeped in charity, humility, detachment and other solid virtues. To those who knew him the very tone of his voice will be recognized, and his quaint, original expressions may be likened to some old adage or striking proverb.

SPIRITUAL COUNSELS

THE value of time. "Let us try to get a clear idea of the value of time, especially valuable, since it is limited, and going at each moment; precious, because it is limited, and by no possibility can we recall the moments when once passed; infinitely precious, because unlike any other good, it cannot be stored up and put away. Let us ask the Blessed Virgin to help us to be more steadfast in our determination to employ each moment, as it is given us to merit, to use each moment as best we can, till we come to the last moment upon which the whole of eternity depends."

"If we seek God everywhere, we will everywhere find Him." "Let us ask for the grace to find our Lord in everything and everywhere; not only in what is called a Sacrament, but in all our duties. Our Lord wished to teach us this in the Gospel, when He fed the multitude.

"It was not done in a temple, there was no priest connected with the ceremony, there was no rite, nor sign, nor symbol, no religious ceremony, but it was in the desert. He wished to teach us to find God, not only on the Altar, in the Sacraments, but everywhere; for He is in all things, and in them with His tenderness, His goodness and His beatitude, to make a real and intimate communication of Himself to us."

Fidelity to little things. "Let us honor the babyhood of our Lord, that from His littleness and weakness we may learn the value of little things; for this world, vast as it is, is made up of little things. So our lives are made up of little things, one breath at a time, never two; one minute, never more at a time;

one heart throb, one thought, one action — directed and bound together by purity of intention, become great in the sight of God. The world is made up of atoms, and life is a series of little things; we must not wait for a great action, but practise fidelity, fidelity, fidelity, my children, to little things."

"*Blessed are they who hear the word of God and keep it.*" *Luke xi. 28.* " God is continually speaking to you in your own soul; you must listen to Him and then obey Him. But to hear Him you must keep yourself very recollected and in peace, and then do what He tells you, for ' Blessed are they who hear the word of God and keep it.' "

Detachment. " Let us try to learn better and better what Christ is to us. Let us take to heart the lesson taught us in last Sunday's Gospel; that it was not the successful, wealthy and joyous that partook of the Feast, but the wayfarer, the lame, the blind, the halt and the constant; so if we are attached to anything but God, we will not partake of this Feast. Detachment! Oh, how we are attached, and to so many things, we cling to so many things; but, we will try to learn this lesson of detachment from all things, that we may partake of this Feast, which is made by God, and is God Himself."

"*It is expedient for you that I go.*" " If we keep this lesson before our minds, it will give us the dispositions to allow our Lord to take from us *all,* even Himself; then there will be no eagerness, no hurry, no blaming others, but we will remain in repose and in equality of mind. In all that the Lord takes from us, He never does, nor never will, nor never can take from us, but to give something better in its stead; taking from us in life to give us more in death, and having always our greatest good in view."

" In the prayer of Holy Church we find these words: ' You are dead and your life is hidden with Christ in

God.' ' If ye be risen with Christ seek the things that are above.' Col. iii. 1. Ah! if we wish to rise with Christ, we must die with Christ. These and similar prayers Holy Church gathers at this season of the year, to teach us to die to all things, and thus to acquire the peace and the rest of the dead. They are not disturbed by the troubles, agitations and turmoils of this earth, so in the measure we detach ourselves from good and bad, perfect and imperfect, within and without, God will do His part, which is, to reward us, by giving us peace and rest of soul."

Fraternal Charity. " Let us take to heart that awful command given by our Lord in the Gospel. If you come to the Altar to offer your gift, and there remember that your brother has anything against you (not that you have anything against him) leave there thy gift. That is, leave that solemn, awful duty of the Holy Sacrifice of the Mass, to go and be reconciled to thy brother, then, come and offer thy gift."

" *Ask for nothing, and refuse nothing.*" *St. Francis de Sales.* " That wisdom which we see practised by the leper in the Gospel, is the same as that contained in the saying of St. Francis de Sales: ' Ask for nothing, and refuse nothing,' although the leper lived so many years before St. Francis.

" When the leper presented himself before our Lord, he did not ask for anything, nor did he refuse anything. He simply said: ' Lord, if Thou wilt, Thou canst make me clean.' Now this will be our attitude before our Lord, who knows better than any one else, what we need to please Him."

Fidelity. " If we were always faithful to our vocation, if we lived up to our vocation, if we were always faithful to our duties, we would be among the Seraphim in Heaven. Let us keep our mind open towards Heaven to receive light and grace, paying no attention to created things, determined to do the Will of God

Rt. Rev. A. A. Curtis, D.D.

in all things. If we cared only for our Saviour and His inspirations, and for nothing else, we would be with the Seraphim and the Lord would be our God and Creator, and our All, forever."

Patient Waiting. " We see our Lord in the Blessed Sacrament waiting, sweetly waiting for years, not only for the multitude, but for each individual soul, and when we go to Him, He receives us as if we had not kept Him waiting. What a contrast to our natural activity, which wishes to have everything at the moment. We hurry and even take things out of the hands of God; instead of waiting, we spoil everything. Still more must we wait for ourselves, until God's work is done. He will care for it, if we will only leave it in His hands."

" The grace recommended us to pray for in the Gospel is patience. Patience, not in pain and suffering, but patience in waiting for the development of our spiritual growth, moment by moment, without anxiety. We ask for God's love, and we expect it right away; we ask for humility, and we want it right away. No, we have to labor through life, to reap the fruit in Eternity."

Charitableness does not depend on our feelings but on our will. " Well, it is not when we feel most charitable, that we are charitable, nor when we feel the least so, that we are so. Often people look like devils when they are Angels within, and on the contrary, often feel like Angels, when they are devils within. So, I say, we cannot judge by our feelings. Our feeling charitable does not make us so, but we are charitable when we will it. Let us be encouraged by the fact, that when we *think* ourselves the greatest sinners, we are most pleasing in the sight of God."

We are blind when we wish to govern ourselves. " We are nothing and can do nothing; we are blind, dull and insane when we want to govern ourselves;

244

and only in proportion as we become conscious of this truth, shall we have that true wisdom, which comes only from God. I say only in proportion as we shall be thoroughly convinced of our utter weakness, shall we have possession of God. Let us then abandon ourselves absolutely to God, that God may be ours; for God and self cannot dwell together."

Our Lord's life in us. "We share in the office of Saint Joseph in protecting the life of our Lord, by preserving His life within our souls. We can nourish it by doing His will. His life in our souls, in one sense, is more precious than the life that Saint Joseph protected from Herod, for He gave up that life, to procure His life in our souls."

The Will of God. "This life is called the land of many: Heaven is the place of oneness. Here we are at one time happy, — again unhappy; one moment patient; the next moment impatient; sometimes charitable, another time uncharitable; now we remember, again we forget, ever shifting back and forth. Let us beg the Spirit of God to give us that spirit of oneness, that we may have the grace to persevere in this warfare. . . . It is difficult to know the will of God, when things please us, satisfy us and give us consolation; but when in pain and suffering, burns and heart-stings, we obey, Ah! then we are sure and certain that we are doing the Will of God."

On Silence. "Let us ask Mary to help us to get the gift of silence. How she kept silence! never telling Saint Joseph what had been accomplished in her favor. She was silent! And we see in the Gospel that our Lord was jostled on all sides; all were anxious to be heard and helped by Him; and there came up behind Him a lowly soul, in silence, and touched Him as lightly as a leaf touches the ground on which it falls, in silence. Our Lord said: 'Who has touched Me?' So we will strive for that exterior silence as far as it is compatible, but still more for that interior silence. In raising the dead, our Lord would do nothing until He had dismissed the crowd, that in silence He might work."

The Gift of Fear. "We should ask for fear, the right kind of fear; not fear of God, for He is always the kind, beneficent Father; He has never been anything else to us but infinite Goodness. We should ask for the salutary fear of ourselves, — ever changing, never to be trusted, weak, cowardly, selfish, useless; — never more to be suspected than when we feel ourselves secure. There is still another fear which should be combined with this fear of ourselves; it is the fear of the devil; ever on the watch, never wearied out, cunning, knowing well our weak points, and how to render them useful to his designs to destroy us. It is this fear combined with the fear of ourselves that we should ask for. It was when the house was swept and garnished that the devil returned with greater force."

Have we anything in the place of God? "Let us pray that we may learn more thoroughly the lesson in the Gospel of St. Matthew, namely, watchfulness, to test and discover whether we are really in earnest. We find this servant cast out for not having on the wedding garment, which shows us that though we may be doing just what God calls us to do, we may still be in fault. The farmer was called by God to be a farmer; the merchant to be a merchant. They may have begun well, but in time, put something in the place of God. It may be one thing now, and something else further on, but if it takes the place of God, it has destroyed the wedding garment. We all have need to watch and to test ourselves by this rule: Have we anything in the place of God? for we are always taking His place from Him. It may be our method of prayer, our meditations or our Communions. They were for God and we put ourselves in His place; then our wedding garment is not on. In everything however good, it may even have been ordered by God; if we do this very thing for another purpose, then we have taken God's place by that thing. So let us test ourselves, that we may not be cast out even for doing good things, which if we did not do, we would be in fault."

Our failings are more useful to us than success. " Let us ask the Blessed Virgin to help us to make good use of our faults and failings, without which, perhaps, we would not be saved. Our failings are more useful to us than success, for success only engenders pride, which hides from us what we are; our faults and failings cause us to see and know ourselves just as we are, and this leads to humility, without which, all we could do, would avail nothing for Eternity. In the Gospel our Lord said: ' Let the wheat and the cockle grow together, lest in rooting up the tares you destroy the good grain.' So our little faults and failings grow side by side with our little efforts for good; let us ask Mary to show us how to make the best use of them."

Little Infidelities. " We never fall notably all at once, we come to fall by degrees. As we reach perfection by degrees, so we go backward and downward by degrees, by little infidelities. Let us keep ourselves humble. Oh, if we knew the depths of our ignorance! As soon as we have suppressed or cut off one thing, we find ourselves face to face with another, for we are an inexhaustible mine of misery. Let us try to realize this. Let us take to heart all that may be said of us, or to us, even in jest at recreation; sometimes these words are real revelations, and our Lord means them for us, and we must take them to heart, even though they may be uttered inconsiderately. *O—h, to get rid of self* is the work of a lifetime! "

On Prayer. " October is the month of prayer, not so much the prayer of petition, as the prayer of life.

Rt. Rev. A. A. Curtis, D.D.

The older we grow, the wiser we become, and we are so permeated with the truth, that God does all things for the best, that we do not feel the need of asking for one thing more than for another; and when we cannot do this, we can do that which is greater, that is, we can behold God, we can withdraw from all that is not God, in order to be able to behold Him in silent contemplation. Only try to love our Lord more, and to become more one with Him, then you can trust yourself to His mercy, and you will never have more to trust to Him, than His mercy is equal to."

"Put ye on the Lord Jesus Christ." Romans xiii. 14. "Oh, the wonderful Epistle of Saint Paul! which does not tell us only to contemplate Christ, to be in union with Him, or even to live for Christ; but to put on Christ, to clothe ourselves with Christ, to be identified with Him, as a garment becomes identified with the person who wears it. Where the person goes the garment goes; in whatever the person does the garment takes its part, in the movement or act. So we must put on Christ that we may no longer live in ourselves, or of ourselves, but that Christ may live in us, operate in us, accomplish His will in us, so that we may say, not in the way the great Saint Paul said it, but in our little way: 'I live, now not I; but Christ liveth in me.'"

"We should ask for grace to learn the lesson given us in the Epistle of Saint Paul, which shows him to us in sufferings of every kind that could come to him from man and nature; in scourgings, in cold, in hunger, in stonings, in perils by land and sea; and in all this, rejoicing, rejoicing that he is thought worthy to bear the cross of Christ. So we will ask him to help us to learn this secret sweetness found in all that could crucify and immolate nature. He knew that his end would be premature, but he was willing that his natural life should be lost, that he might gain Christ."

248

Spiritual Counsels

"*Blessed are the poor in spirit.*" *Matt. v. 3.*
" Let us take to heart the words of our Blessed Lord,
they are the first words He spoke in His sermon on the
Mount: 'Blessed are the poor in spirit.' In no way
can we better practise poverty of spirit, than in making
a good use of our time; for time once gone can never
be recalled. Oh, how precious is time! we have but
one dot at a time, the heart gives out but one drop at
a time, and when the last drop fails, then we have no
more time. So let us make good use of our time as a
thing most precious."

"*The Kingdom of God is within you.*" *Luke
xvii. 21.* " We do well to pray at all times, but especially now, during the Octave of the Blessed Sacrament, that we may be more and more grateful for the
presence of Jesus, ever abiding with us; but above all
to be grateful for His presence in the soul of each one
of us, so that we are not obliged to go here or there
to seek Him; we have only to turn to Him within,
where we may always find Him at all times and under
all circumstances."

"*They returned into Jerusalem, seeking Him.*" *Luke
ii. 45.* " We find in the Gospel Mary and Joseph
seeking Jesus. Let us ask them to help us to seek
Jesus, for the misfortune is, we are always losing
Him in our eagerness, losing Him in the hurry and
bustle, losing Him in our labor, losing Him even in our
solitude; but like Mary and Joseph, we must be ever
on our guard to seek Him as soon as we perceive that
we have lost Him."

" Let us ask the Blessed Virgin to obtain for us the
grace to do as she did when she found our Lord was
not with her. She did not waste her time in wondering
why, or how she lost Him. No, she did nothing of the
kind, but she dropped everything and went to seek
Him. So let us do, making a sincere act of sorrow
for our negligence, and then keeping a closer guard

over our heart, where we wish to keep Him, so that we shall never be separated from Him."

"I must be about My Father's business." *Luke ii. 49.* "And great must have been this business, since it was the Father's. How did Christ set about doing this business? He did not go about showing Himself and talking about this business. No. He sat silent, and when spoken to, He answered sweetly and gently like a good, dutiful child. He asked questions as a child. So we will take these words as the Church presents them, not doing our business, but our Father's. And this will make it sweeter and easier to rise promptly in the morning, going to Mass, office, recreation, refectory and to our work, as each in its turn presents itself, not before it presents itself, because it is our Father's business."

"Whatsoever He shall say to you, do ye." *John ii. 5.* "We will ask the Blessed Virgin to do for us always and everywhere, what we find her doing in the Gospel; controlling, arranging and directing in the midst of the feast, and giving in secret, unperceived, the notice to supply the failure of the wine, that the want might not be observed by the guests. We will beseech her to see that the new wine of grace, which has been given to us, may not grow less under her eye, but instead, that it may grow and increase in time and Eternity."

"Why are ye fearful, O ye of little faith?" *Matt. viii. 26.* "Let us take to heart the lesson set before us in the Gospel. We there see our Lord, contrary to His custom, manifesting His displeasure and rebuking His Apostles for their fear, since He was with them. How can you fear or be troubled when I am here? Where is your confidence? Now, our Lord is with us, not in a little boat, but in the Blessed Sacrament, and in our souls, ever, ever there. No matter what goes

on around us, our Lord is ever there, in our souls, and He is displeased when we do not trust Him and turn to Him. Let us look to Him, let us trust in Him and the storms will cease, and we shall find eternal peace in the haven of everlasting happiness."

Root out the Tares. "We are told in the Gospel to root out the tares, while our Lord says, No, leave them alone, lest you root up the wheat also. This our Lord says to the world in general, but more especially to each individual. If we were to root out the tares, we would take for tares what are not tares, so our Lord tells us to let them grow together till the harvest. If we were left to ourselves, we would root out all our past sins, all our infirmities, all our inabilities, all our peculiarities, all our incompatibilities, all that draws upon us humiliation; these we would take for tares, these we would root out. But if these were all gone, then we would have no ground for self-abasement, self-mistrust, penance or humility; therefore our Lord says, Let them, the tares and the wheat, grow together, that we may have the wheat of perfect obedience, and a true and generous contrition for all our faults."

"*Having agreed with them for a penny a day, he sent them into his vineyard.*" *Matt. xx. 2.* "The Master of the vineyard went out at different times to hire laborers. He agreed with them for a penny a day. It was only for a day; our Lord wishing to teach us from this, that this life is but a day, and just as surely as night follows the day, so will death follow the day of this life; just as the day moves on, life moves on, and inevitably death approaches. Then even at the eleventh hour, the last hour, if we turn to Him we shall find Him propitious, and He will say to us: 'I will be your reward exceeding great.'"

"We should ask for grace to understand the lesson taught us in the Gospel of St. Matthew. The laborers were faithful, they came early, they gave perfect satisfaction up to a certain point, but they were wanting in charity, without which we cannot see God. They murmured because others who came late received the same reward as they, who had toiled from the beginning. Let us pray for that charity which will enable us to be pleased when we see others more favored than ourselves; yes, preferred to ourselves, that we may rejoice that the good is being done to others, while we are overlooked, neglected and forgotten."

"*Jesus was led by the Spirit into the desert to be tempted.*" *Matt. iv. 1.* "We should ask the Blessed Virgin to obtain for us the power and knowledge to make good use of temptation. As we see from the Gospel, Jesus was led into the desert to be tempted, and as we are here to be tried and tempted, we must use temptations as God intends us to use them, that we may reach the end He has in view, and that we may know that the time spent in overcoming ourselves is well spent, and that all our struggles are measured out by an all-wise Providence, who always sends sufficient grace for us to conquer ourselves. We, too, shall be tempted as Jesus was, in strange ways. He was tempted to adore satan, so it will be with us; but as the Angel came to Jesus and ministered unto Him, so too, it will be with us, when our pilgrimage is finished, the Angel will come to us, and we shall see that the time taken away from pleasure, enjoyment and rest, for a higher purpose, was well spent, and then we will thank God for the temptations and for the grace He gives us to resist them."

"*He was transfigured before them.*" *Matt. xvii. 2.* "Our Lord gives manifestations of what He wishes to do in our souls. In the mystery of the Transfiguration, He wishes to transfigure our souls by prayer and silence. By prayer we speak to Him; in silence He speaks to us. Let us, therefore, beg the gift of interior silence, that we may learn to recognize and understand His voice and follow Him."

"Let us ask for the great and inestimable grace to see more and more clearly that only when we have left behind all that can change, then only shall we reach to the unchangeable; that there is no rest; on, on, — always going, — never at rest, not even in enjoying our Lord.

"We see in the Transfiguration that all was clear, bright and peaceful, and the Apostles thought to remain. No, they have to come down to work and toil."

Feast of the Good Shepherd. "This Good Shepherd has travelled so far and so long. He left Heaven, renounced so much, undertook so much, suffered so much. You must not take it that He did this for a whole flock of sheep, all souls in general, but for one sheep — your soul. What journeys, what watchings, fatigues and sufferings did He not endure until He found this sheep, and then lifting it up with His divine arms, with His own strength, He pressed it to His Heart, and placing it on His shoulders, He carried it until He reached home, to enjoy it for all eternity. Our Lord does not do things by halves, He does not divide things as we do. He gives all to each one of us, all His merits, His graces, His Incarnation, His life, death, His Church, His Gospel, the Sacraments, His own sweet Mother, His own Body and Blood, Soul and Divinity — Himself entirely, and all that He has, past, present and to come, throughout all generations. If we are penetrated with this thought, by the Spirit of God, then it will help us to love God and also our neighbor; for all that was done for us, was done for our neighbor, and we will consider them being carried home by the Good Shepherd."

"As there is one Lord, so there is one Good Shepherd, whose power nothing can overcome, whose wisdom governs all, whose tenderness, long-suffering, love, patience and goodness nothing can change, and these are inexhaustible. He gives Himself entirely to each one of us. God cannot divide Himself. He gives Himself with all His possessions; let us reflect upon this, that we may love Him and understand how much He bears from us. Let us think how safe we are, and that we have nothing to fear. For what could harm us? We who are not only folded in the arms of the one great and wise Shepherd, but enclosed in the innermost depths of His tenderly loving Heart."

"Let us take to heart the two lessons in the Gospel of the Good Shepherd. It has two sides. The good Shepherd goes to seek the lost sheep, not the whole flock, but just one foolish sheep which has strayed away. Let us remember that we are just as senseless before our Lord, as sheep in regard to man. And our Lord goes to find each one of us, and carries us in His blessed arms. He wishes to do all for us. He wishes to carry us, that is all He asks, and that is our Lord's side. Now our side is, that we must lie still in our Lord's arms and let Him carry us. We cannot do great things, we cannot be strong or valiant, but we can be simple, helpless and meek like sheep, and let our Lord carry us. But we don't want that, we want to go our own way, we think it is the best way, because like sheep we are senseless. So, my children, we will try to lie still in our Lord's arms, and let Him carry us where He will, feeling sure that we are His sheep, and that He is our Good Shepherd."

"*For many are called, but few are chosen.*" *Matt. xxii. 14.* "Let us ask the Blessed Virgin to obtain for us the gift of Faith spoken of in the Gospel. There was only one who was so destitute as to be cast out, but there were many more who did not partake of the feast of God, because they were taken up with grumbling; some were not satisfied with their places; others were dissatisfied because some were preferred before them; some were dissatisfied with the cooking, or with the servants, which prevented them from partaking of the feast. Now, all these are ourselves; so taken up, that we do not realize the feast found in the Church. The feast is Faith, which is either dead or languishing in certain souls. So we will ask the good Mother to help us to vivify that faith spoken of in the Gospel."

Hunger for Christ. "Ask our Lady to obtain for us that hunger for Christ which is so beautifully portrayed in the Gospel, the sixth after Pentecost. Their own food lasted two days, and then the multitude looked to Christ; and depended on Him alone, when all else failed. So with us; we have reached the first and second day, but the third day we have not yet reached when we can do without all created things whatsoever, and look to Christ alone. Then we shall be fed with that food, that heavenly food, which creates a hunger, a hunger for Christ alone, and for nothing else. Let us ask our Lady to obtain this hunger for us."

"Thou hast not known the time of thy visitation." Luke xix. 44. "Let us ask our Lord to teach us to understand and value His visitation. We see Him lamenting the blindness of the Jews, who would not recognize the time of their visitation. Not recognizing that blessed moment, we lose what can never be regained; it has gone forever; for all Eternity we have lost what might have been ours. And if we are so blessed as to recognize this visitation, we shall be what we never could have been without this knowledge; and this blessed acceptance of God's visitation will bring us peace, joy and rest. It will teach us how to get God, to keep Him, and without knowing it ourselves, to communicate Him to others."

The tears of Christ. "Yes, we will be thankful for the tears of Christ. We see Him in the Gospel shedding tears over Jerusalem; notwithstanding all the ingratitude of the chosen people, His bearing with them all along, before and after their captivity, He is loth to depart from them; He still clings to them, and it is with tears we see Him looking upon the Jewish city. So with us, though at times it seems to us that there is only a weak, feeble desire to be all His, still we can be assured that He will not leave us, even though we are often tempted to leave Him."

"He hath done all things well; He hath made both the deaf to hear, and the dumb to speak." Mark vii. 37. "We ought to beg for grace not to make the great mistake which we see was made by the people in this Gospel. Our Lord when He had cured the deaf and the dumb had said: 'Now tell this to no man.' But they thought, Oh, what a pity not to let people know what a great One is in our midst, thinking that the knowledge of His greatness was above obedience. We may be tempted to think that our Superior, from some incapacity or other, has made a mistake; so we do as we think better, and question it, instead of accepting and submitting."

"We learn from the Gospel the merit and power of obedience. We see from it that the people were so thankful, overjoyed and elated that the Saviour had come, that they published it far and wide. His miracles were talked about, although our Lord expressly said: 'Tell no man,' yet they did not obey Him; to them, the thing seemed good and laudable, so that others would come and see the Saviour. Things bad in themselves would become good and harmless if sanctified by obedience, while on the other hand, the best things would cease to be good if done without obedience."

"Render to Cæsar the things that are Cæsar's, and to God the things that are God's." Matt. xxii. 21. "Let us pray that we may have the grace, promptly, thoroughly, always and everywhere to understand the

lesson held out to us in these words of our Lord: ' Render to Cæsar the things that are Cæsar's, and to God the things that are God's.' We are all liable to make a mistake down at the bottom, we want to give something great, so we add something of our own to render to God, instead of giving Him what is His own; for we never have, and never can have, anything of our own that is worthy to offer to God. We must offer Him ourselves just as we are from moment to moment, all our weakness, all our shortcomings, our very selves just as we find we are."

On Confidence in God. " After our Lord had ministered to the sad needs of the body of the paralytic, He turned to the soul, which was in a still greater need of cure. He said: ' Have confidence, My child,' and with these words He infused the required confidence. Without this confidence the cure of the body would be of little worth, but with this confidence all is ours. No matter how we have sinned, or how far we have strayed, if we have this confidence in God, all blessings will come to us with it. Judas would be now with St. Peter, if even at the last moment he had had confidence in the goodness and mercy of his Master. So we will try to increase daily in this confidence in God's mercy, and bear up cheerfully, steadfastly, and with a heart full of gratitude, ever remembering that He who requires this from us will carry us on, even to the light of eternal bliss."

" The gift to ask of our good Mother on her birthday is, that power and habit of confidence which our Lord is never weary of inculcating in such a variety of ways, as in the Gospel for the fourteenth Sunday after Pentecost. No one ever did, no one ever will, no one ever could, perish who trusts in our Lord. Judas would not have perished, even after his horrible crime, if only he had trusted in the goodness of God. Peter would not be where he is now, if he had not had, even in the time of his perfidy, in the depths of his soul, an unshaken, untouched confidence in the unutterable goodness of his Master. Let us ask the good Mother to help us, that wherever we are, whatever may be the state of our soul, just as we are, however great may be the sense of our misery, our perversity, our uselessness, we may have confidence in the unspeakable, inexhaustible, unchangeable goodness of God; that we may continually come back to Him, whatever may have come between us and our Lord, that He may take it away, even by main force, and that our soul may be reunited to Him ever more intimately, more powerfully and more perfectly."

" *Do not touch Me.*" *John xx. 17.* " Our Lord said to St. Mary Magdalen: ' Do not touch Me, for I am not yet ascended to My Father.' This implies that there is a closer, nearer, higher way in which we can touch our Lord than the way we know of here on earth through the senses."

" *Blessed are those servants whom the Lord when He cometh shall find watching.*" *Luke xii. 37.* " Pray for the grace to watch for our Lord's coming. He is coming always, wherever we are, at all times and places. If we are faithful in receiving Him in His hourly coming, we shall be sure to be on the watch at His last coming, and it will not matter to us when, if we have been on the watch up to that moment."

" *But one thing is necessary.*" *Luke x. 42.* " Well, we all know that there is nothing so troublesome and embarrassing as a multiplication and accumulation of duties. Nor is there anything so helpful as a simplification and unification of duties. This is the lesson taught by our Lord in these words of the Gospel. ' But one thing is necessary ' — that is, to love God."

Our Lord puts a question to us every day. " Our Lord asked Philip a question. Of course He knew, but

He did this to test Philip and to prove him. To you, to me, and to all our Lord puts a question every day, and all during the day, and this He does to prove us. He says: What do you think of Me? How much do you esteem Me? How much do you desire Me? Do you love Me? When the bell rings, He says: What do you think of My obedience? When a mortification or suffering comes to us, He says: What do you think of My suffering? My thorns, My nails? What do you think of My·sweetness, when they spat upon My face? What do you think of My humility and My silence? Let us ask Him to help us to hear this momentous question, and our lives will be more solemn and meritorious."

"There shall be joy before the Angels of God upon one sinner doing penance." Luke xv. 10. "When a soul does penance, our Lord takes her in His arms, and the Angels rejoice. Ah! it is in our power to give joy to the Angels, as well as sorrow; let us not neglect the only sure road to Heaven, which is also the only true road to peace on earth."

"Let us pray to understand the benefit of penance which we read about in the Gospel of Saint Luke. It is the only thing that our Lord said would give joy to the Blessed in Heaven. Ask that we may understand what it is to offend so good a God, whose sanctity makes the Angels tremble. We will endeavor to live in this spirit of penance, and if we keep this thought before our minds, all our actions will be flavored with this spirit, which gives joy to the Blessed in Heaven."

"Let us ask for the gift spoken of in the Gospel; charity for the poor sinner. The great God; Mary so sweet, gentle and tender; the great Archangel; all thrilling with joy over one sinner doing penance; this penance may not be lasting, either, still all Heaven is rejoicing over this one sinner, because he is penitent. This is charity, and if we have not this charity we are not fit for the Kingdom of Heaven. So we will pray for this spirit of charity."

"*Were not ten made clean, and where are the nine?*" *Luke xvii. 17.* "We learn from this Gospel the danger there is in being without a cross. The ten lepers were together, united in their sorrow; they helped one another, they prayed together while they bore the cross. But at their earnest solicitations the cross was removed from all ten; only one of these profited so much by the loving kindness of our Lord as to return to offer his thanks and show his gratitude; the remaining nine probably perished. So we will learn from this lesson not to be eager to rid ourselves of our little crosses, which are meant not only to keep us more closely united together, but to bind us more closely to our Lord, and to give us the life of the spirit, that true life which swallows up death."

There is nothing so dangerous as happiness. "Let us ask the Blessed Virgin, whose birthday we celebrate to-day, that we may learn the lesson given us in the Gospel, that there is nothing so dangerous as happiness. There were ten lepers healed, and of these ten there was only one who knew how to use his happiness. The others were made happy by being healed; if they had remained in their affliction, no doubt they would have been saved; as it was, they were probably lost. So let us ask for that permitted joy, joy in prayer, joy in constancy and in devout meditation, however hard, dry and stern the work — for success and happiness draw us from God. This is the lesson we will ask our Blessed Mother to teach us."

"*This Man receiveth sinners.*" *Luke xv. 2.* "Let us ask the grace to learn to know even at the last hour the full truth of these words. 'This Man receiveth sinners.' This is His rôle. He came expressly for this. He receiveth sinners at all times, in every place, just where we are; and the most sinful as well as those who are less so. Let us remember this, and not wait till some little wrong has grown up between us and Christ; we are so apt to wait for a Confession or Communion to ask Him to receive us. Oh no! let us go at once, and He will receive us."

On Forgiveness. "It is good to ask for the fulness of grace recommended to us in the Gospel, the grace of forgiveness; our Lord has recommended nothing so frequently and so solemnly as forgiveness. In great occasions where we are on our guard, this lesson is not so apt to be neglected as in the little daily occasions of slights, misunderstandings, thoughtlessness, which are always in our path; and it is here that we have to practise that forgiveness which our Lord recommends, so that each new demand made upon our virtue finds us equal to God's desire, not only outwardly forgiving, but forgiving inwardly."

"Can you drink the Chalice that I shall drink?" Matt. xx. 22. "Let us keep more and more personally fixed in our mind the great fact, that all that comes to us of pain or sorrow, from within or without, from others or from ourselves, is but a few drops of that chalice which Christ drained to the dregs for us; that He does us the honor to allow us to take the same chalice which He took before us. With this truth firmly fixed in our minds, all will be changed into joy, otherwise it would pass by uselessly, while Christ means us to share in His agony, that we may share in His glory."

What it is to take the lowest place. "To take the lowest place, as the Gospel directs is not to think ourselves the worst of all, for often the acknowledgment of our nothingness puffs up the heart, and comes from a secret pride. To take the lowest place is the knowledge of our ignorance, which makes us incapable of forming any judgment of ourselves or others. What we judge ourselves to be does not make us that, what others think us to be does not make us that; we cannot say this one is good, that one is better; we can form no true judgment of any one, we are only what we are in God's sight. Saint Paul says: ' Judge not before the time; until the Lord come.' 1 Cor. iv. 5. This knowledge of our ignorance, and that we must wait the coming of Christ, when He will make known the value and merit of each one, is to take the lowest place."

" The poor have the Gospel preached to them." Matt. xi. 5. " Let us ask the grace to learn what our Lord so often teaches us, and which He brings before us in this Gospel. He said to His disciples: ' Go tell John what you have seen; the lame walk, the dumb speak, the deaf hear, the lepers are cleansed and, above all, the poor have the Gospel preached to them.' This last point He wishes to impress upon them. Now, you are not preachers, you do not enter the pulpit, nevertheless you are preachers by your example, not merely once a week, or once a day, but every moment of the day."

" We ought always to pray." Luke xviii. 1. " Let us help each other by prayer. In trying to help others we may be only injuring them, but in praying for them we are sure of helping them, and it makes us more like the Son of God, who is always praying for us. Let us pray for every one, but especially for those who can do so much good — the Priests; it is our duty to pray for them."

" Many that are first, shall be last." Matt. xix. 30. ' " Let us take to heart the double word of our dear Lord in the Gospel: ' The first shall be last, and the last shall be first.' A word of warning to us! We have been first by the number of graces bestowed upon us up to this present moment; and first in spiritual advantages of every kind. How many of these have we

squandered, and how meanly have we corresponded to a few! Here were the Levites and Priests, first in vocation, position, honor, privileges, illuminations and grace, but they abused all these means, which were meant to help others as well as themselves. And the poor Samaritan woman, who was despised, shunned, abused and rejected, receives the grace which those who were called to be nearest to the Lord by prayer and meditation rejected."

"He that humbleth himself shall be exalted." *Luke xiv. 11.* " These words of the Gospel are fully exemplified in St. Francis of Assisi. Nowhere and to nothing is so much promised by our Divine Lord as to this abasement. We see this in St. Francis, for he abased himself, and not only was he exalted while he was on earth, so far as to be most like his Divine Master, but even at this moment he is exalted by Catholics and Protestants, and this exaltation will go on increasing to the end of the world; a prelude or forerunner of that greater exaltation which he has received from our Blessed Lord. So we will beg St. Francis to get light for us to see the hidden wisdom found in self-abasement."

" Let us ask our Lady of Ransom to obtain for us the grace to put in practice the lesson given to us in these words: They who humble themselves shall be exalted. Ah! that is what we have to learn, — to humble ourselves. No matter how we have spent the past years of our life, whatever good we may have done, or whatever bad we may have been guilty of, still, if we humble ourselves we shall be exalted. This lesson is for all, rich and poor alike; there is no exception, all must abase themselves. Then when God sees us in our nothingness, He will have pity on this nothingness, and in the end exalt it to His all-sufficiency."

" We have Christ's own words, that ' he who humbles himself shall be exalted,' without condition or

Rt. Rev. A. A. Curtis, D.D.

limitation, absolutely: he that humbleth himself shall be exalted, no matter what we are, or have been, no matter how guilty we may have been, we have only this one thing to do, humble and abase ourselves. We can always abase ourselves with God's help, and we can do nothing else. If we will only abase and yield ourselves up into God's hands, then our Lord will keep His promise, and we shall be exalted in due time."

The Wedding Garment. "We are referred in the Gospel to the Wedding Garment. You know that a garment is woven of many threads, sometimes so fine that they cannot be distinguished one from another; they are so close, and these little threads cross each other, making each time a little cross; if it were not so, there would be no garment. So it is with our wedding garment. Little pleasures which we should use with care, little disappointments, little pains and crosses borne sweetly and patiently, little annoyances received mildly, — all these are the little threads that go to make up our wedding garment, which we are to put on in the Kingdom of Heaven, towards which we are moving, moment by moment."

"Behold I am with you all days, even to the consummation of the world." Matt. xxviii. 20. "Let us ask for the grace to be with our Lord as He is with us, for there is a great difference. Christ is always with us, but are we always with Him? Christ is with us, He tells us He is with us all days, even to the consummation of the world. He is with us on dark days and on bright days, sweet days and bitter days; days of joy, days of sorrow, days of sickness, days of health; the days of life and the day of death — ' all days,' as He words it. What humiliations, and with what invincible patience He has suffered, still suffers, and will go on suffering to keep His promise: ' I am with you all days, even to the consummation of the world.' Let us be with Christ as He is with us, not at times and

264

places, here and there, on some occasions, but all days, at all times and in every place. Then all things will be alike to us, for all seasons, moments, places and things will be full of Christ, equally full of Christ, with His sweetness, His light and His blessedness."

Advent. "The lesson of Advent which we should learn is love for each other, love, love, love; that we may be patient, enduring, self-sacrificing for one another, as being of one and the same family. God shows Himself to us such a Father He took for Himself such a Mother, one that could not be touched by any flaw, the sweetest, gentlest, loveliest of beings. And this Father gave this Mother to us, to be as much our Mother as she is His Mother. He feeds us all with His own flesh and blood, using the very words of St. Paul: 'bone of His bone.' With such a Father and such a Mother, let us strive to do all we can to prove our love for them by loving one another."

"The grace for the Season of Advent is, I think, for greater watchfulness. It is so contrary to nature to do always the same thing incessantly, to be always on our guard. Without this watchfulness the other virtues would not thrive. It is the only command that our Lord explicitly says is for all: 'What I say to you I say to all: Watch.' Mark xiii. 37."

"Let us try to understand better the watchword of the Church at this season of the year: 'The Lord is near,' inconceivably near. He is nearer than the Angels, nearer than Mary, although she is very near and never forsakes us. He is nearer than any part of ourselves. Let us remember this, it will help us on our way to eternity."

Ash-Wednesday. "Ah! Dust and ashes! Dust and ashes brought into the Sanctuary. At first a little crackling noise, a little brightness; then darkness, all is dust and ashes! The Church wants to bring to our minds that we must return to dust and ashes, and to make it more forcible she puts the ashes on the head of each person, to show, no matter how wise or how ignorant, how rich or how poor, how strong or how feeble, how good or how bad, weak or powerful, all must return to dust and ashes. So we will beg our Lord to help us to profit by this lesson, which is to teach us that all must perish except what we do for Eternity."

The holy Season of Lent. "We cannot do better than to begin Lent by considering our Lord's agony in the Garden. Besides the torture of His blessed body, His soul was inundated with anguish and darkness; besides seeing clearly all the torments, scoffs and scorn prepared for Him, He saw He would fail in the very end for which He came, and that instead of making men better by His sufferings and death, they would be worse; He saw that most of them would be lost; but even in this He abandoned Himself to the will of His Father. Let us take to heart this lesson which He gives us; and let us abandon ourselves to Him, to the very core of our heart, so that we may come out of this Lent in the disposition to say truly: 'Father, not my will, but Thine be done.'"

"Ponder and brood over the sufferings of our Lord, one by one, but remember that what we contemplate separately He endured all at once. He knew all that He was to suffer; the effects of past suffering remained and ever increased. When we consider what He suffered, we will realize a little better the love that our Lord has for each one of us."

Lent — "Now is the acceptable time." 2 *Cor. vi.* 2. "Let us ask our Lord to teach us what He wishes us to learn, especially now, in this time of Lent; that we may realize that we are here to be tempted, and that no one is exempt from temptation; that we are always, in all places and in all conditions, being tempted and proved; and at no time is the temptation more dangerous, subtle and cunning than when we think we are not tempted, for then we show that we have lost sight of our enemy. There is nothing worth while but temptation, and we are losing time when we are not fighting, conquering and gaining the victory over ourselves. We are here for no other purpose, and when we cease to be tempted then we shall die. So, let us ask our Lord how to use each temptation, that we bear them sweetly and lovingly."

Holy Week. "The Church takes us this week into the very heart of the Passion. We came step by step; after considering all the horrors of the Passion, it may be summed up in these few words: ' He became obedient,' and to-morrow we make a step further — ' obedient unto death.' The moments as they slowly passed were used to the full, and now our Blessed Lord spends the last few seconds of His life in remitting His Spirit into the hands of His Eternal Father. Let us consider what He acquired by this absolute obedience: He acquired a name above all names. Let us take our obedience with all its deficiencies to the foot of the Cross, and we shall see how far we are from the example here set before us. He bears the effects of His obedience upon His sacred Person."

"You will do your best to occupy yourself with the Passion, for the time that is left to us of this holy season. There is in this mystery all that we need; it is an inexhaustible source of merit, of light and strength. We shall see how unlike His sufferings are to our little sufferings. In our suffering there is some relaxation; in His suffering there was none, no break in the entire course; it was always increasing, ever present until the last moment, when upon the Cross He cried out: ' It is consummated ' — it is finished. If we consider this we shall learn to be patient."

The Passion. "We should honor, praise and thank God for the holy and venerable Passion of Christ, and for the institution of the Blessed Sacrament the night before He suffered. It is not without a special meaning that it was just the very night before His Passion; it was because it was to be a prolongation and perpetuation of the Passion. Passion does not mean suffering of Christ, suffering was the effect of the Passion — the Passion was the cause of the suffering, therefore it is said, Passion and Cross; Cross is mentioned after the Passion. The Passion of Christ was His self-surrender, the yielding of Himself; the sufferings were the effect of the passiveness of Christ, of the absolute surrender which He made of Himself, so that men and devils could do with Him whatever they chose. Thus is the Passion continued and perpetuated in the Blessed Sacrament, in the self-surrender which He makes of Himself. He even makes a greater surrender in the Blessed Sacrament, for He spoke in His sufferings and on the Cross, but in the Blessed Sacrament, never — He is silent. Let us ask our Lord to help us to be mindful of this, that it may win our heart, and that we may be ever further from being of the number of those who outrage Him, and even from the neglect and thoughtlessness of those who call themselves His children."

Feast of the Seven Dolors. " Let us ask the Blessed Virgin to form in us that great truth, the compatibility in one person, of great suffering and great peace. Our Lord's suffering was continuous, yet He never lost His tranquillity of soul. His Holy Mother after Him had the greatest suffering, and the longest suffering, yet she preserved peace of soul. Let us therefore beg our Lord and His Blessed Mother for that wisdom which will enable us to combine these two great virtues in our soul."

The Scourging. " I have always thought it strange that the Church has no special feast for the Scourging, unless she thinks it so palpable that it cannot be lost out of sight. That cruel, merciless, shameful

Scourging! Each lash cutting deep, doing its destructive work. Imagine what that must have cost our Saviour's Sacred Heart. And this scourging was not only for all men in general, but each lash was for your sins, and for my sins; the Eternal Father did not lay this punishment on us, but upon His own Divine Son! Let us try, my children, to enter into the spirit of loving, thankful gratitude to our dear Lord."

"*Our Lord Hanging on the Cross* shows us what we cost Almighty God, and even after this, we have the shameful knowledge that if God did not force us by His Commandments to love Him, we would not, if left to ourselves, do it. This is the first Commandment, all the rest, if kept, would be nothing without this great one — to love God with all our heart — this is all — nothing else."

Vigil of Corpus Christi. "The Feast we will celebrate to-morrow is not named for the Divinity of Christ, nor for the soul of Christ, for these are not of this earth; but our Lord chose to name it for His Body, for It is of earth, to show us how closely He is united to us. He has abased and annihilated Himself in assuming this Body. So we in turn will strive to live continually in this annihilation of ourselves, that He may give life to all our actions."

Corpus Christi. "Let us ask for a truer and deeper knowledge of our Lord's presence in the Blessed Sacrament, as an end, to come to that closer, more real and better union within us, because it is more lasting. Let us ask that by means of this Most Blessed Sacrament He may take up His abode in us, heart within heart, spirit within spirit, person within person, until He has made of us another Himself, not for time only, but for eternity. If we keep this thought before us, we shall enjoy that union, which, commenced here below, is to continue forever afterwards."

Rt. Rev. A. A. Curtis, D.D.

Blessed Sacrament. "We will ask for light to get down to the littleness of the Crib, carried out and continued in the Blessed Sacrament; our Lord not only accepted this utter helplessness, but embraced it willingly, contentedly and sweetly until the present day. So we will ask Him to help us to imitate Him in this mystery, and to receive each little occasion as it presents itself to lead us to this helplessness; to know our littleness and to know that we are nothing without God; but all this must be in a spirit of sweetness and contentedness."

"We should even pay adoration to the helplessness of Almighty God, which manifests itself more and more every day, not only in the Crib, but also in the Blessed Sacrament. Man is having his day, and God remains silent; man denies and blasphemes God; and persecutes and puts to death his neighbor, but the time is not far off when God will have His day, then will He assert His justice."

Feast of the Sacred Heart. "Ask for grace to serve the Sacred Heart better within and without, through and through; to repair the outrages offered to this Sacred Heart, by ourselves in our neglect of His inspirations and His love; and still more by those of the world, who insult, despise and condemn Him, because He places Himself in their power, within their reach. All this He does for each one of us individually. If we keep this reparation before us, then all things will have a different aspect. We will do nothing new, but even the least things we will do better, with the view of making some return for so much love from the Sacred Heart — slighted love."

"Let us honor this Divine Heart, which is the center of all in Heaven and on earth; the source from which emanates all good, and to which all good returns. Let us consider the excess of His love, manifested in the sufferings of His Passion, and let us beseech Him to give us, not wisdom or power, or great things, or high things, but simply the interior desire, will and endeavor to love His Divine Heart."

" In the typical Holy of Holies it was permitted only to one man, and that the High Priest, to enter, and that but once a year, on a certain day, for a short time. And we can enter every day as often as we please, and stay as long as we choose, for the spear has made an opening in the Sacred Heart, and the veil of the Temple was rent, that we not only could, but that we must, we are bound to enter the Holy of Holies, which is the Sacred Heart; always open, ever waiting. There we can contemplate the dispositions which led our Lord to His Passion. The first and greatest of these dispositions is that of obedience. His Incarnation was an act of obedience to His Heavenly Father, so also was the Redemption; and another disposition is that of His unimaginable, unfathomable love."

Feast of the Ascension. " We must pray to get the grace of this season, which is one of detachment. Christ was detached from most things before His Ascension; from comforts, from consolations, from His reputation, from His friends, from His Apostles. But after His Ascension, He was detached from the best and most necessary things; from His Church and from His Blessed Mother. We must beg Him to give us this spirit of detachment. It is comparatively easy to be detached from exterior things, but we must go further, and also be detached from interior things, from lights in prayer, or what we thought were lights; from the Altar, from Jesus in the Tabernacle, from everything but Christ in the soul and His adorable will."

" In the sacred Humanity of Jesus Christ we see ourselves elevated far above all the powers, to the highest pinnacle of glory. But in considering this consoling thought, we are apt to forget that as He was exalted above all, to the uttermost heights of glory, so He descended lower, lower than He had ever been on earth — to remain silent, hidden, despised, rejected, abused, dishonored in the Blessed Sacrament, where He deigns to become our food. We forget that in proportion as God exalts us, we should humble ourselves. So we will ask our Blessed Lord to teach us this lesson, which He so well practised and which He loves so much."

Feast of Pentecost. "Pray to the Holy Spirit to understand the love of the Father for us; all that He is to us, each one individually, particularly; that He is more than a Father to us, who are so blind, poor, foolish, weak, senseless, miserable, cowardly and abject. It must be because of the Holy Spirit, who is in us, that He loves us, each of us particularly, as if there were no one else in the world. Then recognizing this, as we grow older, being more humble from the experience which age gives us of our nothingness, we shall love our neighbor as being the object of this Father's love, as well as ourselves."

"Let us pray that the Spirit, the only perfect Spirit, as we learn from the Psalms, may fill us with His charity, — love for God and man; that we may grow, grow more and more in this charity of Christ, that we may be permeated with it through and through. It is the only thing that lasts, — beginning here below and lasting through eternity. And with this charity come all good things; peace, joy, contentment, illumination, submission, devotion and humility."

"We may invoke the Holy Spirit under whatever title it may seem good; and perhaps we cannot do better than to invoke Him under the form of unity, for He alone makes things one, He alone can produce unity, — unity with those around us, and unity within us, for nowhere do we find so much strife as in ourselves. The war which St. Paul speaks of we, too, know well, the flesh warring against the spirit, and the spirit warring against the flesh. The good that we would, we do not, and the evil that we would not, that we do."

"Strive to obtain the Oneness which the Holy Ghost came to bring on earth. That oneness of mind, oneness of sympathy, oneness with our neighbor which would make of this earth, where there is so much pain, a kind of paradise. Oneness with self, not shifting and turning from side to side, oneness of will, choosing nothing but the All-sufficient Eternal Good, God Himself."

"Let us ask the Holy Spirit to come and take full possession of us, as He took possession of the Apostles, coming upon them in tongues of fire. St. James tells us that ' he who sins not with the tongue, the same is a perfect man.' There is an interior tongue, as well as an exterior tongue; an interior silence as well as an exterior silence. This interior tongue is dangerous and is almost unceasingly and persistently breaking this interior silence. St. James says, we have only to guard this interior tongue, and all good comes to us."

"The Feast of Pentecost is the apex, the culminating point, the completion of God's goodness and God's love. Our Lord was not content with coming among us, accompanying us, speaking to us, protecting us, providing for us: He was not content with laboring for us, suffering for us, dying for us, leaving us His word, His Sacraments, His Church, but He gave us His very Body, and even this did not satisfy His love. But what more could He give, having given us His very Flesh and Precious Blood? Ah!— He could give us His Spirit, and He would give us His one, only, eternal Spirit, and He gives His Spirit to each one of us, whole and entire, as if It were nowhere else, and no one else possessed It. This only, indivisible Spirit of God is in us to remain in us. We are the temples of the Holy Ghost, Who is in us to tranquillize, to enrich, beautify and transform our spirit, in order to prepare us for

Heaven. This should make us have confidence in God. Oh, how it should make us love Him! how it should fill our hearts with gratitude and make us cleave to Him, how it should teach us self-sacrifice, and make us venerate the neighbor, since the only Spirit of Christ is in the neighbor, and is to be there in time and in eternity."

"We should be filled with thanksgiving for the graces given us during this season, and principally for the gift of the Holy Ghost, which is not so much the completion of the Redemption as a continuance of it. We have received the indwelling of the Holy Ghost as a fund or source of grace, a forestallment, or a sample of what awaits us in the world to come; and as far as we mortify our senses, our inclinations and aversions, we are drawing into ourselves that future home, we are nearing the reward that is awaiting us; so we will try more earnestly to make good use of the time that is left to us, that with the aid of this Holy Spirit we may learn to control ourselves, and hold on to each grace as it is given to us."

"We must pray to learn how to wait for the coming of the Holy Spirit, to wait as the Apostles did. They waited without knowing how, or where, or when, or in what manner the Holy Spirit would come; but they waited in perfect submission, without doubt, in perfect contentment, without hurry. When we have learned to wait, we have learned everything, and if we have not learned this lesson, we have learned nothing. Let us learn to wait as Jesus and Mary waited, as the souls in Purgatory wait; as Jesus waits in the Blessed Sacrament. Waiting for God! When a soul waits in this manner, Heaven and God are sure to come to her."

The New Year. "Next Sunday we shall begin a New Year, and close the old one, and we ought to beg pardon for the faults and imperfections of the passing year in order to be able to begin anew. Our Lord said:

'Heaven and earth shall pass away, but My word shall never pass away.' All things will pass away; those around us, even the Church will pass away; all things will pass, and are passing away, and will soon be entirely gone, — but one thing will remain — Christ. Christ alone will always remain; so let us cleave to Christ, that we may live in Him, who never passeth away."

New Year's Day. "Well this new year is given to us as a reprieve, for how long we know not; it may be for a year, it may be for a month. The sentence: 'Dust thou art and unto dust thou shalt return' is continually hanging over our heads; when it drops, our time of meriting is over. So let us make good use of the respite, for we know not when our call will come."

Feast of the Epiphany. "God comes, not to show Himself as He is, but to show us what we are. He is little, and we are little. He is poor, and we are poor. He is in danger, and we are always in danger. He fled into Egypt from His enemies when He was a child. So we must do likewise; we must flee from every occasion which would lead us into temptation, where we are sure to find our enemies. Let us flee into the depths of our soul and remain hidden with our Lord, with no other desire than to be near Him. This is the grace of the Epiphany that we should beg our Lord to bestow upon us."

"Only a few days ago we celebrated the Feast of the Epiphany, the manifestation of God to His people. And what was this manifestation? It was weakness. Weakness in His birth; weakness in His Crib; weakness in His flight into Egypt; weakness in the Blessed Sacrament; weakness in our souls, to show us that we are to adore this weakness. To show us that we are to adore God for Himself, and not because of His might or power. And we will learn to know our own weakness, in proportion as we shall have learned to know that we are nothing else but weakness. When we have experienced this through and through, more and more, then we shall be glad of our weakness."

"This feast is only the exterior manifestation, the type and figure of that great interior manifestation of God in the soul. This first manifestation was made by obedience and poverty, living a hidden and annihilated life, — in the cloister, as it were. So that in the degree that we strip ourselves of our desires, our own will and judgment, even our thoughts, God will manifest Himself in our souls."

Feast of St. Agnes. "Although a child, St. Agnes had great wisdom. She cleaved to Christ, conversed with Him, and lived in and for Christ until the time came to die for Christ, and even then she saw only Christ and was occupied with Him, and not with her pains. We hear so much about prayer, etc., and yet we fall so short of what we ought to be; so let us ask St. Agnes to help us to simplify things, to teach us the secret which she knew so well — to simplify everything into the one view of Christ, that like her we may see only Christ. The best things are good only in as far as they lead us to Christ. St. Paul says: 'I judged not myself to know anything among you, but Jesus Christ, and Him crucified.' 1 Cor. ii. 2."

Feast of the Espousals. "This day brings us to the Feast of the Espousals, and we should ask Mary to help us to imitate her, as far as we can, in total abandonment to our Lord. He wished her to be a Virgin, and at the same time she was to be the real and true Spouse of St. Joseph, who had full power over her. But she trusted God entirely, even when He seemed to contradict Himself. And God commanded Abraham to slay his son before he had issue. Yet Abraham trusted God, knowing that in the long run God could and would bring all things right, even when all around was dark and seemed to convene to overthrow His intended plans or designs. And we know how fully God realized all their hopes. Let us, too, trust to the uttermost of our power, when we shall be called upon in our ordinary life to prove our loyalty to our Blessed Lord."

Feast of St. Paul. " Let us pray to St. Paul, who was solely intent upon one thing. When he was a Jew he was a Jew, and when he was a Christian he was a Christian. He loved God, and loved Him alone; he gave himself up entirely to this one thing, he loved his brethren so entirely that he was willing to be anathema that he might save them. This was the cause of his success; it was this that gave power to his words; it was this that made him so dear to God and to men. So we will ask St. Paul to obtain for us this singleness of purpose, that we may have God and God alone. Not self and God; but God alone."

Feast of the Purification. " On Candlemas day we bring candles to have them blessed, that they may burn and be consumed in the service of God, and shed their light around us; like Jesus and Mary, who were consumed in the service of God, while they were the light of the world. So it must be with us. We must burn with the love of God and the desire for the salvation of souls, and be consumed in His service. And as our Lord says, you do not light a candle and put it under a bushel, or under a bed, neither can we hide our light if it burns within us. We shall give light to those around us; we shall not know this here, because it would not be good for us, but hereafter we shall see that our light has saved many a one whom we knew nothing about; or that it has attracted, led or given light to many who were groping around in darkness."

" Let us ask Mary to help us to imitate her, in her almost astounding lowliness. To the public she appeared and lived as a poor, peasant woman, when in reality she was a royal Princess, and greater than all honors, she was the Mother of God. To all she appeared as a sinner and a penitent; her immaculate purity did not oblige her to subject herself to the law of purification, nevertheless in her humility she wished to appear as a sinner. Let us endeavor more and more, not only to admire and reverence her humility, but to imitate it in our daily life."

Month of St. Joseph. "Let us ask St. Joseph to obtain for us something of that constancy which he practised during his whole life; always doing the little things of which his life was made up, as faithfully, as promptly, as prayerfully the last time he performed them, as he did the first time. We are so inconstant, running here and there, leaving what is good for what is worse; never satisfied, always wanting change, no sooner here than we wish to be somewhere else. So we will ask St. Joseph to obtain for us that constancy which was so conspicuous in his life."

"He that is mighty hath done great things to me." Luke i. 49. "St. Joseph no doubt said the Magnificat, he might have said it at least, and no doubt he did say it: 'The Lord hath done great things for me.' What were these great things? Toil, labor, poverty and many crosses; and the people, then as now, could see no great thing in all this; and in the end to have to leave the two dearest objects in the world, Jesus and Mary; but all this contained the Will of God for St. Joseph. So he merged his will into the Will of his Maker, and had no will of his own. These are indeed great things for us, when we can so lose ourselves in the Will of God that we have no will outside of His Will."

Patronage of St. Joseph. "Let us pray to St. Joseph (the Feast of whose Patronage we celebrate today) that we may partake of his love for the hidden life. The world was then what it is now, clamoring loudly about the great things it was to do, effecting wonders, while St. Joseph remained hidden in his obscure life, drudging, drudging, drudging for a little pittance, scarcely sufficient for the necessaries of life, for those dependent upon him. He had no office to distract him; alone, obscure, hidden from others and from himself also. He lived this life because he was divinely illuminated. So we will ask him to instruct us, that we too may live this hidden, obscure life, hidden from ourselves, but still more hidden from others, that we may be accounted as nothing, and treated as nothing, and that like St. Joseph we may learn to love and seek this hidden life."

The Office of St. Joseph. "Let us ask grace to have the sight to see, and the wisdom to know and understand, how we are called to share in the office of St. Joseph, in guarding, caring and providing for the safety of Jesus; for He is in much more danger now than He was in the days of St. Joseph, for now all conspire to blot Him out of souls for time and eternity. Pride and sin of all kinds are striving to get the mastery, to put Jesus to death in souls, where He would have dwelt for all eternity."

Feast of the Annunciation. "Let us ask the Blessed Virgin to obtain for us the gift of wisdom, to know when to fear and when not to fear. If the Angel had come to her ugly, threatening, accusing and blaming, she would have been satisfied and happy, because she would have seen an opportunity to profit, but because the Angel came beautiful and praising her she was afraid. But we fear when there is no reason to fear. We fear in mortification, humiliation, correction and labor, and we do not fear when everything succeeds and goes well with us, when we are praised by men, when we are honored and elevated, or interiorly praise ourselves and feel safe."

The Month of May. "To spend this month of May in the best possible manner, our first intention will be to glorify God by a stricter application to our duties, and a further giving up of ourselves to God. Our second intention will be to thank God for having given us such a good Mother. The third intention will regard ourselves, that Mary and Joseph may help us to love Jesus Christ more, not in word and sentiment, but in deed and truth as they loved Him through and through, to the utter destruction of all self-interest."

" Let us ask the Blessed Virgin to obtain for us the blessedness spoken of in the Gospel; that blessedness which she enjoyed in a supereminent degree, and what this blessedness was we see from the words of our Lord: ' Blessed are they who hear the word of God and keep it.' Listening to Christ in the depths of the soul, waiting for Him there, remaining with Him, listening to His inspirations which He gives us, and speaking to Christ there. This is blessedness, so we will ask Mary to help us to be faithful to it."

The Blessed Virgin. " Honor *her* through whom the great, the divine, the incomprehensible love of God came into the world. And let us do what St. Paul exhorts us to do, in last Sunday's Epistle; namely, to be like God, to grow in His love always; to love all persons, good and bad, uninteresting, troublesome, offensive; there is no distinction, all are included in God's love. It is in this way we can imitate God. We have only this one end to accomplish, to be like God. And she who attracted this wonderful love, will help us to love, love, love."

Mary our Jewel! " If we were told that somewhere on earth a jewel of the greatest value was to be found, that it was to be seen but once, and that never again could anything be seen like it, how we would endeavor to possess it. Now, Mary is this Jewel; there never was one like her before, and there never will be one again, and as in Heaven all things are the opposite to what we find them here on earth, so Mary is whole and entire for each one of us, without lessening in the least what she has for others like us; it is her prerogative to bestow, without ever lessening or diminishing her gifts. We will ask Mary to help us to know her, to love her and to trust her with the care of ourselves, for she is wholly our own."

Mary our Mother. "We should be very thankful for that most necessary of blessings, namely, a Mother whose heart is always ready to receive her children, no matter how weak, poor, stupid or repulsive; and how much more must we be grateful for our Mother, Mary, who cannot err or make a mistake, for she is all wise and has all power with God, who has given her to us to be as much our Mother as she is His. She has a Mother's interest in each one of her children, following them in all their divers difficulties. And at what a cost, at what a time and place did He bestow her upon us! Remembering this, we will strive more earnestly to be less unworthy of her."

St. Monica. "Ask St. Monica to obtain for us the spirit of prayer that we may pray as she did. She prayed so long, so long for the conversion of her husband and her son, not recognizing that her prayer was answered immediately, for prayer, if it is true prayer, brings us to God; prayer brings its answer with it — prayer is always answered at once; if we do not get what we ask for, we get God, and this is, or ought to be, the end of all prayer. No prayer was ever uttered that did not bring its answer with it, that is, bring us to God. At every prayer there is a new creation in the soul, at least an increase of the virtue we are praying for, so we will ask St. Monica to help us to pray."

St. John the Baptist. "After Jesus, Mary and Joseph, St. John the Baptist was the most detached from everything. Without rule, without comforts of any kind, without bed or table. If he had a rule, he would have made better use of it than we do. He had nothing but his union with God; this made up to him for everything else. He sought God within his own soul; this close union was never interrupted. Let us ask St. John to help us to live in this close union with God in our own soul."

Feast of St. Peter. " As this is the Feast of St. Peter, we will ask him to help us to learn the lesson more and more, that God's prerogative is such that He not only forgives sin, but also the punishment due to sin, and such is His superabundant goodness that we enjoy a good, superior in degree, which would not have been ours if sin had not gone before. Where in our ignorance and weakness sin abounded, God caused grace to superabound. If there had been no sin, there would have been possibly no Incarnation, no Mary, no Joseph; so we will learn from all this to abandon ourselves more and more absolutely to this Divine Goodness, that He may bring us from the depths of our weakness. This lesson will teach us that far from discouragement and despondency we too may hope to be freed from our helplessness. St. Peter was greater by God's all-powerful grace, greater after God had forgiven him the denial of Christ, than he was before his sin. Such is the power of penance over the merciful Heart of God."

Saints Peter and Paul. " After Mary and Joseph the three highest places in the Kingdom of Heaven are filled by three of the greatest sinners, who were also the greatest penitents, — Mary Magdalen, first of women after Mary, and St. Peter and St. Paul first of men after St. Joseph. Their repentance was so sincere, that it does not lessen but rather increases their glory. We also can attain high perfection by accepting from moment to moment all the opportunities of suffering presented to us by our Lord, offering them to Him in satisfaction for our sins, and all during the day, within and without, we can practise penance at all times, which will increase our glory and our reward."

St. Mary Magdalen. "We find in this Saint all that is noble, precious, beautiful and admirable; her fortitude, courage, patience, generosity, contempt of creatures and contempt of self — and the root of all, her supreme and ultimate confidence in God. This unchanging confidence in God was founded on the knowledge of her misery and nothingness, which made her despise self. She knew our Lord, He had reproved her for her crimes, but she turned to Him with her whole heart, and sought Him at a time and place that men might call unseemly. Oh, what a gift to know and loathe one's self, and at the same time to believe that God does not loathe us! Let us ask St. Magdalen to get for us that confidence which she possessed in such a supreme degree."

Mary's Assumption into Heaven. "Her Assumption was the effect of her previous spiritual ascensions. We see it is in our power to attain this spiritual ascension, for the body is not so much, it is the spirit that is of importance. Let us ask for the grace to imitate Mary in one thing, which is first and foremost, that upon which all that follows depends — her true spiritual assumption — for the assumption of her body was only the exterior manifestation of what took place continually during her life — namely, the spiritual assumption of her soul, by an intimate union and conversation with her God in Heaven. We can share with her in this spiritual assumption, by keeping our will ever uplifted to the divine will of our Father and Creator."

Nativity of Our Lady. "As to-morrow will be the birthday of the best of Mothers, we wish to make her some present, and there is nothing she will appreciate more than that we should bear her in our minds, in our

Rt. Rev. A. A. Curtis, D.D.

hearts and in our actions, and more and more put into them the desire to help all her children who have strayed from her, who do not know her, or who do not think of her as Our Lord wishes them to think of her and feel for her. We will renew our resolution to do all we can by our earnestness and devotedness to bring back to Mary her stray children."

Feast of the Exaltation of the Cross. " Many persons in the world take the wrong cross which they bear without any merit, because they make it for themselves. But let us take the cross which our Lord gives us, which comes to us in great and little, high and low things, from ourselves, from within and from without, from those around us, from our duties, from our Rules and from our Superiors. This cross will be meritorious because it will be the true cross, because it is more like our Lord's cross. He never went in search of His cross, it was laid upon Him by His Heavenly Father. Let us ask of Him to give us the grace to bear His cross, the one He chooses for us; He knows the cross we need, and we will never make a mistake and get the wrong cross if we take the one which He gives to us from moment to moment, and which is not chosen by ourselves."

The Stigmata of Saint Francis. " This supreme mark of God's love for Saint Francis did not come to him without great pain and suffering. And afterwards, when it had been impressed upon him, the pain and suffering did not cease. We might think that it was sweet and delightful, consoling; but no, it was always a burden, an inconvenience, a suffering, a humiliation. And so it is ever, when God would give us a proof of His greater love. He does so by making us more like Himself; every new suffering, burden or humiliation is a proof of God's greater love for us. But, oh! the time to remember this is when the inconvenience, the burden, the suffering, the humiliation comes! Let us ask

St. Francis to help us to appreciate these proofs of the love of Jesus for us."

"The gift of the Stigmata which seems so great, must have been very painful at the moment, and ever after. We are apt to think of these favors as something happy, but in reality they are ugly and inconvenient, anything but pleasing to nature. This gift must have caused St. Francis an increased amount of suffering from others, for they could not understand it. And this gift was as all gifts which God bestows upon us, for He would not give us anything less than what would make us like Himself. Let us bear this in mind when the moment of pain and trial comes upon us."

Feast of St. Michael. "Well, next Sunday we will celebrate the feast of the great Archangel, St. Michael; that great spirit next to God and far above all the Angels, through whom He controls and directs the heavens and the earth, as He did for ages, before time commenced for us. And we see him bowing down in adoration, kneeling before the Man all bruised, torn and spit upon; adoring Him as his Master, his Lord and his God, and acknowledging Mary, poor, hidden and humble as his Queen. Let us learn from his example the great lesson of humility, that we like him may see God in all circumstances, however averse to our understanding, and that we may know that all things come to us from Him, who has the right to call Himself our Master, our Lord and our God. Let us beg the great St. Michael to plead for us, that we may imitate his humility."

Month of the Rosary. "This is the Season of meekness and simplicity when we must try to obtain the spirit of prayer. We must make use of that simple, universal prayer, the Our Father and the Rosary. Our Lord has said: 'Unless you become as a little child, you cannot enter the Kingdom of Heaven.' We know how little children run to their Mother, being sure of her heart and open arms to receive them, however ragged and dirty they may be. So like little children, we will run to our Lord for everything, playing around Him as it were by our dependence upon Him, always looking towards Him, and expecting all from Him."

" Let us beg our Blessed Mother to get us the light to see, and the grace to practise the sweet devotion of the Rosary, so simple, so easy and so powerful. And as we grow older we shall see that to pray for nothing set or expressed for ourselves, or for others, but to remain sweetly submissive to God's providence is the best of all prayers — keeping ourselves interiorly united to God, without thinking or doing anything, but satisfied in being near Him."

" *He hath given His Angels charge over thee: to keep thee in all thy ways.*" *Ps. xc. 11.* " Let us thank God for giving us the Angels for our protectors, and thank the Angels for the care they take of us. Let us thank God and the Angels for solving for us the problem of problems, namely, how to rest in God and at the same time serve creatures. The Angels render services to us continually; they save us from stumbling on the stones in our way, they serve us as no slave serves his master, and yet their eternal repose in God is uninterrupted. We do just the contrary. If we contemplate God, it is by withdrawing from the neighbor; if we are occupied in the service of the neighbor, we generally forget God. If we are occupied with temporal things, we forget the invisible and eternal things. So we will ask our Guardian Angel to help us as time goes on, to unite more and more our duty to God, and to the neighbor."

Guardian Angel. " Our Guardian Angel is the most devoted of friends, so peculiarly our own, and charged in a special manner with the care of our souls, never leaving us for a moment night or day, watching over us more tenderly than a Mother watches over her sick

child. We have Jesus and Mary in common, but our
Guardian Angel belongs to us in such a particular way
that if we were alienated from God, still this loving
protector would never leave us. Therefore we will
show him our gratitude by a greater trustfulness, and
fidelity to his inspirations."

" Our Angel is our oldest and best friend — an older
friend even than Mary, for she became our friend at
our baptism, while our Angel has been our friend from
our entrance into the world. Moreover, Mary is the
friend of all, whereas our Guardian Angel is peculiarly
our own, our special friend, who is constantly with us,
whether we are good or wicked, without ever abandon-
ing us. Our Angel is our best friend; he accompanies
us everywhere and cares for us as no friend on earth
could do; for our earthly friends sometimes leave us,
or we leave them. And at the hour of our death, that
hour when we shall so sorely need a friend, our Angel
is the only friend that can go with us; even if others
could go with us, they could not help us; at most they
can only follow us with their prayers, but our Angel
follows us in reality; he is there to sustain and guide
us in that unknown journey, where we shall most of all
need the assistance of our oldest, best and most lasting
friend. We should be thankful to God for giving us
such a friend, and be thankful to our Guardian Angel
for all his care; we must show our gratitude in the way
that will be most agreeable to him, which is to imitate
him, especially in his lowliness and charity."

St. Francis of Assisi. "We see in St. Francis of
Assisi such heights of virtue that we are startled at the
sight of them; we see no such prodigies nowadays.
The reason is, because we do not love poverty; our
starting point is not correct. St. Francis found in poverty a treasure we little dream of, but he knew, he
loved, he practised it, he lived in it — it was everything
to him. We see those who have taken the Vow of pov-

erty, but who are in want of nothing, for all their wants are supplied by those who have care of them. But to be in actual want is seldom seen. St. Francis was in actual want, and it was this actual want of the necessaries of life which constituted his riches; he called poverty his dear mistress. He learned this love of poverty from his Divine Master, Who said: 'Blessed are the poor in spirit.' Our Lord did not say: Blessed are the poor, oh, no! He was too wise for that, but He said: 'Blessed are the poor in spirit,' blessed, who love poverty, who desire it. We will ask St. Francis to teach us to love poverty as he did."

St. Bruno. "St. Bruno knew so well how to keep silence. He knew better than any other the value of silence, and practised so well that silence within. If our silence within does not produce the exterior silence we are losing time. Let us beg St. Bruno to obtain for us the virtue and spirit of interior silence; that silence which does not choose, does not complain, does not wish to see, or have other than God wishes for us; so that we look to Him, leaving all else, and letting Him decide for us, for He can only order or permit that which will be for our greatest good."

St. Teresa. "The gift to ask of St. Teresa is the spirit of prayer. To pray well does not mean to say a certain form of words, to be in a kneeling position, to have a book in hand, and to be in the choir. Prayer is an elevation of the heart and the mind to God, and this can be done at all times and in all places. We pray well if we do all our actions for God, so we will ask St. Teresa to help us to get the spirit of prayer."

St. Raphael. "The Church brings before us to-day the name of Raphael, which signifies healing. There is no doubt that we have wounds, and that it is God alone who can heal those wounds in such a way that from the scars themselves He may reap glory; healing them like the wounds of our Blessed Lord, which He holds even to this moment, and which will shine for all Eternity, so that they are His glory."

Feast of All Saints. "Let us honor all the Saints, and especially that numberless army of unknown Saints, of whom nothing is known. The canonized Saints, who are few compared with the former, have been capable of practising heroic virtue, virtue which is beyond our attainment. But we will consider the vast army of unknown Saints, who have no history, who lived the same common life that we do, who did common things uncommonly well, who toiled, waited, suffered; who believed, hoped, loved and repented. These we can imitate."

Hidden Saints. "We must honor the great army of unknown or hidden Saints, unknown to history, because there was nothing in their lives worthy of note or interest. They left the field, the workshop, and the kitchen, silently. They had done their little works, one by one, as Providence presented them, with submission, cheerfulness and constancy. So it is to this army we will join ourselves, until it may please the Lord to take us to Himself."

All Souls. "Let us pray to be able to understand the meaning of the Church in immediately joining 'All Souls' with the celebration of the Saints, which shows that they are united with them, and that they are now free from all the anxieties, pains, troubles, temptations and sins, and from the fear of ever being separated from God. They have chosen God, and now it is a settled thing for all eternity. They are God's, and nothing which gives us pain or distress will ever more touch them. We will learn from this what a good thing it is to die, and what death gives us; what nothing else can — namely, the surety of God, that is, never more to fall from Him. We too will learn not to fear death, but be glad that we are dying daily, until the total death comes to set us free."

Rt. Rev. A. A. Curtis, D.D.

"*It is therefore a holy and a wholesome thought to pray for the dead.*" *2 Mac. xii. 46.* "Let us pray for all the poor souls, especially for those who have no one to pray for them; for those who have dropped out of this world suddenly, perhaps died in some distant forest, or a shipwreck at sea; or many who unfortunately are forgotten by their friends and the world."

"There is no duty which demands greater attention than praying for the Dead. There are many reasons which prove this. The infinite wisdom of God orders it, the holy Church daily begs it and rewards it; charity demands it, the poor souls need it, since they cannot help themselves; our own necessity requires it, and in proportion as we pray for them, will they remember us, and by thinking of them frequently, we will not be so likely to forget that one day we shall be numbered among them, and we will have taken a fixed habit to keep them ever in our hearts and in our minds."

Feast of St. Gertrude. "This is the Feast of St. Gertrude, who so well understood prayer, that prayer which unites us to God in all things and in all places, not asking now and then, at stated times for something or some favor, but constant and uninterrupted union with God. But to possess such a favor, a price must be paid for it. St. Gertrude won it by her humility, by the annihilation and whole destruction of herself. So we will ask her to help us to get it too, that by self-abasement and effacement of self we may be able to pray always."

"St. Gertrude kept her mind on Christ and heavenly things, and became such a great Saint. In proportion as we keep our mind on Christ, we approach sanctity; to become a saint the way is simple but not easy — we must keep our mind on Christ; in as far as we have our minds on earth we are earthly."

Feast of the Presentation. "Let us ask our good Mother to help us to make the presentation of ourselves as she made her Presentation, and that the presentation of ourselves may be as acceptable as the presentation of Mary was acceptable; then we shall get God for our presentation. To give self is to get God, and to keep self is to lose God. We can never know whether we have made this presentation while God's will is suited to our will; but it is when we feel our will opposed to His Will, and we follow His will amid crosses and contradictions, repugnances, contempt and abandonment, then we shall know we have made this presentation, and for this we will beg our good Mother to help us."

" Our Lady did not know what was to be her honor when she gave herself to God day by day, hour by hour, but she was rewarded above all creatures for her abandonment. And so surely shall we be rewarded if we merge ourselves into the Divine Will though we may not see it now, and may be it would not be well for us to know what God will give us in return; but we may be sure that entire abandonment, no matter how long things may appear to the contrary, will bring us God, as certainly as the confiding abandonment of Mary brought God to her."

St. Cecilia. " The Church immediately after the Presentation of our Lady in the Temple shows us St. Cecilia, the patroness of music, not alone that earthly and lower music, but the higher and heavenly music caused by the presentation of herself to God; the infusion of that harmony which resounds in the celestial spheres. The presentation of ourselves to God and to God's Will is the true harmony, which vibrates in the heavenly spheres. So we will ask St. Cecilia to help us to understand the harmony of this presentation of ourselves to God, which should always be going on without ceasing."

Feast of St. Andrew. " St. Andrew comes at this moment to announce the approach of Advent; he opens the door; we see him standing there as a sentinel. He was the first to discover the Lord, and he brought his brother, St. Peter, to the Master. From St. Andrew above all others we learn watchfulness, the most necessary of all the virtues; even more necessary than charity, for it is only now and then that we are called upon to exercise charity, but watchfulness we need at all times, that we may be on the alert to prevent the least improper thought from entering the temple of God — the interior temple of our soul. We need this watchfulness, this vigilance, that we may see in advance even the shadow of evil before it reaches us, and we need our Lord to help us, for we very soon grow weary of this continual watchfulness, which is as necessary as it is difficult. Let us then pray to St. Andrew to help us."

"At the baptism of our Lord, St. Andrew heard the one word, and he took it. The others heard it too, but St. Andrew not only took the word, he kept it most faithfully; he lived by it, he acted by the faith he had in this word, until he became invincible, and he grew day by day, more and more in his Master's love. So will it be with us if we are faithful in sorrow, in joy, in darkness and in light, doing what we know we ought to do, whether we like it or not, having our gaze fixed always and ever on Him whom we follow. Faith will grow in us and transform us, rendering us in some measure invincible like St. Andrew."

Gift of Divine Love and Love of the Cross. "Let us ask St. Andrew to help us to love the cross, not to bear it, for bear it we must; not to bear it cheerfully, but to love it as he did. He loved it, because it united him to his Master, and we cannot love the cross, but in so far as we love Jesus Christ crucified. We must first get that something, that gift which will enable us to love it, and this will be given to us, when we ask for it humbly, daily and unremittingly. The gift of love — of love for this Divine Master! Oh, what an in-

comprehensible thing it is, that we should be permitted
to love Him, since He is what He is, and we are so far
beneath anything which could call forth love! Still
the Divine Master seeks our love; so we will beg this
gift day by day, humbly. We may have what seems to
us like love, for frauds are in many forms, but the true,
genuine love for Jesus Christ crucified can only come
from Jesus Himself."

The Feast of the Immaculate Conception. "There
is only one God; there never was one like Him throughout all centuries; there never will be one like Him.
He contains within Himself an infinite treasure of
riches; He is all wisdom, all powerful, all merciful.
So, in like manner, we may say there is only one Mary,
there never was one like her; there never will be one
like her. By the goodness of God she is the dispenser
of His riches, His wisdom, His power, His happiness.
There is then only one God, who is our Father, and
only one Mary, who is our Mother. Having then such
a Father and such a Mother, let us strive to be the
best of children."

Feast of the Expectation. "Our good Mother expected in truth, so she was peaceful and tranquil.
We expect all sorts of foolish things, which come and
go, and all that passes away is not worth possessing;
but while we are taken up with nothing, we neglect to
make use of our great all. We have Mary, the Saints,
grace and the Sacraments, and God Himself for our
portion, so we will ask our good Mother Mary to help
us to regulate our expectations."

Christmas. "Well, we see in this Feast of Christmas our Lord acting in opposition to the world. The
world depends upon wealth, reputation, position to
make one great, but we have it in our power to make
all things great by our use of them. We see our Lord
made all things great by His touch; poverty, labor, suffering, and in the end, death. So we can follow His

Rt. Rev. A. A. Curtis, D.D.

example, and make the most insignificant, repulsive, wearisome things great, by the proper use of them. Let us pray for the grace to use this gift of God as He intended."

" Beg for the grace to understand more and more the unselfishness of God in the great mystery of the Nativity. This unselfishness is beyond and above our imitation, but we can adore it. God in giving us Himself, gave us all for nothing. He took to Himself no reward, no recompense; He gave us all; He passed for less than nothing, and took upon Himself our weakness and misery, our pains and labors; He went so far as to take upon Himself the loathsomeness of our sins, and He did not stop here, but even took our death itself, as we learn from to-day's Epistle. God sent His only Son to redeem us, that we might receive the adoption of sons, whereby we are not only heirs of the things of God — but of God Himself."

Feast of St. Stephen. " St. Stephen was not only the first martyr, but also the only one of whom our Lord has written. He did not tell us of the death of Mary, or of the Apostles, but He does tell us of the death of St. Stephen, and the Church places his feast near the birth of our Saviour. St. Stephen accomplished the two ends for which our Lord became incarnate — that God might be loved, and after Him the neighbor. In his youth St. Stephen gave himself to God, to whom he offered his life and his blood. While he was in the torture of his cruel martyrdom, with all his strength he staggered to his knees to pray for his executioners, saying: ' Lord, lay not this sin to their charge.' So we can find no one better to pray to, to obtain the grace of this season, — love for God, and love for our neighbor, — than St. Stephen, to whom the Church gives such a place of honor."

St. John the Evangelist. " We will ask St. John to pray for us, he who leaned upon the Heart of Jesus

294

outwardly, but much more inwardly. Though naturally of a quick, impulsive, vindictive character, as the Scripture tells us, he became the disciple whom Jesus loved. Though not always with Him, nothing could touch or interrupt the interior union of his heart with the Divine Heart of Jesus. This gained for him all the superabundant graces which made him so God-like in forbearance and love. So will it be with us, if we strive for this interior union, for nothing can touch it. If anything is painful or difficult, then it will only bring us to a still closer union. Are we sinful? Well, the Heart of Jesus has been opened for us to enter in. So it matters not how or where we are situated, this union with the Heart of our good Master can never be disturbed or touched."

"After Mary, the Lord's Mother, St. John was privately and personally, first and foremost, nearest our Lord. He was called earlier in life and lived later than the others, hence he was separated for a longer time from the presence of our Lord in glory and also from our Lord's Mother, near whom he found so much consolation. He was a wreck physically, and was obliged to be carried to and fro — and a wreck mentally, only able to utter the same few words: ' Little children, love one another.' This may seem strange to us who do not understand the designs of God. Things pleasing to the senses are not good for the soul; but sufferings and things repugnant to the senses are good for the soul, and gain for us a happy eternity."

LITTLE RETREATS

BUT it was more especially during the private retreats of the community that this benevolent Father spent himself, giving his undivided attention and careful direction to the particular needs of all those who confided in him. Out of the abundance of his wise experience he counseled and consoled, and while following them closely in the pursuit of their attraction, he never went in advance of grace, but helped and encouraged them to coöperate with it. It was well known that whatever he advised he had already put in practice himself and in becoming all things to all, he gained all by his sweetness and discretion. He said: " Put more confidence in God, do not serve Him as though you thought all the time He wished to entrap you, but deal with Him confidently, calmly waiting His good pleasure and doing what He wills, and thus not serving Him with a sort of constraint. Do not multiply exterior practices, nor measure yourself by others, not wishing to be like them, nor to do what they do, but calmly, patiently resigning yourself to do God's holy Will."

" What our Lord wants of you is that complete interior surrendering of yourself, for the accomplishing of His Will in your soul. What we desire and frame to ourselves as the best, would be only for our ruin. God's goodness is infinite, and He will never permit us to lose ourselves or offend Him without warning or permitting us to see and know it. What He does is always for the best, therefore we have only to trust Him."

" Leave your sins, leave all that. Spend the rest of your time of retreat looking at our Lord. Give yourself to Him just as you are, with all your miseries, without desiring to be more holy — don't even try to be nothing. We are so blind, weak and ignorant, we know not what is best for us, and the very things we desire might be most prejudicial; but He does know and will give us what we ought to have, if we only go straight to Him, and leave ourselves in His hands, in His guidance. Say to Him: Here I am, Lord, and keep close to Him. . . . Cleave to Christ as the only object of your love, be attentive only to consider Him — this is best for you, and the only thing to do, and the only thing worth doing."

"Thank God for that which you call evil, and which is a good, and may become a very great good by being used aright. While many persons have not their attention fixed on anything, you may turn your attention to good by fastening it on God; on His goodness, His patience and His mercy, and so become tranquil and very still. The people in the Gospel of last Sunday were noisy and jostled against our Lord, and although they touched Him they did not feel Him, but the woman troubled with an issue of blood crept up silently behind Him saying: 'If I but touch the hem of His garment, etc.' "

"True Wisdom consists in accepting from the Hand of God, as happening by His divine Providence, and through the love He bears us, our present pains of any kind, whether of mind, soul or body, particularly sicknesses, aridities, drynesses and desolations; thanking God for them, and not struggling against them as many do, nor trying by vain and useless efforts to make oneself better, or imagining oneself to be in a very bad state of soul in having them; but only resting quietly, saying nothing, doing nothing, but trusting in God, and thanking Him, and waiting His divine good pleasure to be freed from them. This is true Wisdom and the true life of Faith."

"See only God, desire only His Will. Pray when

you get a chance, and when you can pray. If you cannot pray, do not be disturbed; be content with the Will of God in this, as in all other things. I know of no greater simplicity than to have our will one with God's Will, and not to think of the past, or of the future, but accept from His hand what He sends at this moment. To know only God is the greatest simplicity we are capable of."

"Oh, you and I, and none of us are grateful enough for what we have received from God! Let us try to be more thankful, the man who has a million does not appreciate it, because he is eager and anxious to make another million, and is too much taken up with that to think of or care for what he has. Let us ask the Blessed Virgin, the Mother of our Lord, to obtain for us the grace to be tranquil, to be very still. In our prayer we must listen to our Lord, for by that means He will give us good desires of serving Him."

"Can you not simply look at our Lord in prayer and not disturb or constrain yourself to make acts, nor to speak at all, simply giving yourself to Him just as you are, and being satisfied to look at Him without speaking; calmly and quietly brushing away the thoughts and distractions, as you would a number of flies or gnats lighting on your face."

"Spend the remainder of your time in looking at Christ, for He will flash more light into your soul for discovering your faults than all your examination and looking at self could ever produce."

"Give to God, my child, just one beat of your heart — yes, just one beat, from moment to moment."

"The more we are attentive to the presence of God in our soul, the more we will become invulnerable to the attacks of the enemy."

"A traveller, in ascending a high mountain and looking down from its heights, upon the different ramifications by which he came, would not stop at a stone wall to examine its details, but he would be employed in taking measures to improve his future course, he would look to taking new spirit. So it seems to me one would do in a Retreat: take a new spirit from its source — to push."

" Do not think of your past sins; think of the vastness of Eternity, the blessedness of God, the sweetness of Christ, the glory of Mary and the Angels. God knows where there is a good will and that satisfies Him. If you would think of the past for a thousand years, in the end you would have to leave it to the mercy of God, so you might as well do it in the beginning, and save your time and trouble."

" Instead of thinking of your sins during Retreat, see how you can study our Lord more clearly, how you can be fastened to Him, and have a deeper intercourse and communion with Him. Yes, see how to have our Lord's presence more real to you, His personal presence, the reality of His personal presence, and how you can be fastened to Him firmly and constantly."

At another time, " Well, my child, be very grateful to God for the gift of self-knowledge. It is one of the greatest favors that God can bestow upon us, and there is no progress without it. Ah! how many lights are given to us, but we do not make good use of them. If we find things difficult, our prayer unsatisfactory, let us thank God for showing us how poor and miserable we are. Be faithful to make your preparation for prayer, and when your mind strays away, bring it back gently, and then, when all is done that depends on you let God do the rest, and remain in peace in His presence."

FRAGMENTS

"Gather up the fragments that remain, lest they be lost."
JOHN vi. 12.

"THERE are many Saints unknown to the world. We know no more of their lives than we know of the leaves of the trees which have fallen a thousand years ago."

Speaking of the Wisdom of our Blessed Lady, he said: "All other wisdom is as far from true wisdom as our hills are from the eternal hills."

"When God forgives sin, not only does He forgive, but He gives that soul something that it never had before."

"The same exercises day after day should be made new by doing them with new love."

"Even a glance at the Crucifix will not go unrewarded."

"No prayer is ever lost; we may sometimes think it is when we see our misery, but God Who gives the dispositions for prayer also rewards the efforts we make."

"See no one, but only Jesus; yes, see only Jesus in your own soul; see Him in others; see only Jesus in all that happens, good or bad; always, in all things see Jesus alone."

"There is nothing too great for His power, nothing too little for His goodness."

"All that disturbs our peace, whether it comes from within or without, great or small, spiritual or temporal, good or bad, is wrong, useless, and we must use the first possible means to regain tranquillity."

"Rejoice that others are wiser, better, happier and holier than we are, or ever can be."

"'It is expedient for you that I go.' He goes in

300

this, and comes in that. He goes in life, to come in death in a better and more lasting way."

"Every good thing is purchased at a great cost."

"It would be a great temptation in a life like this to think you are doing nothing, for you are doing the work that God requires of you; this work is death to self."

"No prayer is unanswered; even if we do not get what we ask, God always gives us something better. He sees that what we ask would not be good for us, and He gives us what is best."

"The advantage in praying for the Departed is that it keeps our last end before us, and the Holy Scripture says: 'Remember thy last end, and thou shalt never sin.'"

"Our Lord took with Him all the hearts of His children when He ascended into Heaven, so that we are enthroned in that Sacred Heart, which gives not one single throb in which we do not share."

"If a person were paralyzed, perfectly helpless, blind, deaf and dumb, and still resigned to the Will of God, intimately united to Him, such a person would do more for the Church than all the activity of those who labor for the Church, but who are less united to God."

"Sweetly, quietly, lovingly look at God in the present moment, without fear or apprehension for the present, and still less for the future."

"The end of the Incarnation and of all the mysteries, even our Lord in the Blessed Sacrament — is Christ dwelling in us, elevating and identifying our life with His own — all we have to do is to remove the obstacles to enable us to say in very truth with St. Paul: 'It is not I who live, it is Jesus who lives in me.'"

"If we try to make use of all the opportunities for practising virtue, as, for instance, an occasion for practising patience, if we are patient, then God comes and effects a change in our soul, although we may not be conscious of it."

Rt. Rev. A. A. Curtis, D.D.

"If we live in union with God we know our failings at the very moment we commit them, and the examination is rather to gather what we already know than to search for others. If we live in God, for God and with God, He will show us our defects."

"Continually ask our Lord to give you His love, but do not look to see if you love Him more, for you will get yourself in trouble if you do. Oh, what you ask for, when you ask for His love! The Angels and the Saints, even the Blessed Virgin could not receive anything greater, and our Lord Himself could give nothing greater than His love, so ask for it humbly."

"All are beggars on this earth except those who have Christ in their souls, from Whom they draw revenues sufficient for every need."

"David said: 'It is better that I should fall into the hands of the Lord (for His mercies are many) than into the hands of men.' 2 Kings xxiv. 14. Yes, it is better to be in the hands of God's justice than in those of the tenderest mercy of creatures."

"Beg, dear children, beg for the grace of perseverance. Our failures through the infinite mercy of God tend more to our sanctification than our success would have done. The latter might inflate or puff us up, while the former show us our weakness, and that nature is full of folly and foolishness."

"When we feel our misery, and see our folly, and recognize our perversity, then it is we have a greater claim and a stronger call to absolute confidence in our Lord; for He has said: 'I am not come to call the just, but sinners.'"

"I have been taught from my youth that it is only Christian to fast."

"One act of submission of your will, will place you on a plane which you never knew before, and from which you will never depart."

"I know of but one thing whereby we may escape changes, and that is death."

Spiritual Counsels

" No work is small if done for God — it is the little things that count.".

" When my Master tells me plainly what to do, I am not afraid to do it."

" I have come to that point when I am certain as to few things, save what the Church propounds and guarantees."

II
EXHORTATIONS

EXHORTATIONS

THE following devout and useful extracts taken from the Exhortations given by this venerated Father in the Canonical Visits he made to the Community touch on the obligations of the Religious life and the strict observance of the Rule.

He threw himself into this duty as the constituted Superior of the House, and in virtue of his office as Bishop of the diocese, with that earnest piety which marked all the more serious actions of his life, faithfully fulfilling this sacred charge for about twenty years.

His inspired words on these occasions served to renew his hearers in the more faithful and exact observance of their religious obligations, but his example urged them more powerfully to attain at any cost that sanctity which appeared in his whole demeanor.

These extracts have been grouped according to the subjects rather than with regard to the number of years they embrace, and although not taken verbatim, must undoubtedly convey the impression produced on his hearers.

"*My dear children.* I think it well to say a few words of the Canonical Visit which I am about to make. I am going to make this visit, not because it is necessary, for I know it is not, God forbid that it should be necessary, nor does the Church expect or intend that it ever should be necessary; for the Community which needs the Visit is in a bad state.

" We may say of it, as of man and wife, if they have any troubles or difficulties, which they cannot settle between themselves, then they are in a bad state; and we may say the same of a Community that finds it necessary to call in some one from outside.

"I make this Visit under peculiar circumstances, holding as I do the three-fold office, or the three offices of Spiritual Father, Confessor of the Community, and according to the Order of the Visitation, as the Bishop of the diocese, I am the first Superior of the house.

"I am sure there is no necessity for this Visit, nor will I know any more about the Community after I have made it, than I do now; but the Church orders that the Bishop shall visit each cloistered Community in his diocese once every year, so that such a visit never may be necessary."

On Correction. "Of all the duties that can be imposed upon man by God, that of giving correction is the most difficult, and those who have not this duty to perform should thank God.

"There is always an absence of charity in a correction given by one who has not the authority to give it. It usually proceeds from passion, and does harm to the one who gives it, and to the one to whom it is given.

"As I have said before, there is no place where virtue is so much needed as in the office of giving correction, and there are very few who can do it, as it should be done, therefore when duty does not impose it upon you, thank God, for there is nothing more difficult than to give or take correction in the right way.

"And in taking correction from those who have a right to give it, after having received it well at the time, do not allow it to rankle in your heart, do not reflect upon it, turn your mind away from it, and accept it interiorly as well as exteriorly.

"One of the greatest advantages of your life is, that you are corrected, that you are told your faults, and be thankful for this. Why is it that so many go wrong in the world? That many priests go wrong? Because they have no one to tell them of their faults. Be thank-

ful that you are corrected, that you have somebody to
tell you of your faults; for every one of us needs correction, — the Pope, the Patriarch, the Archbishop, the
Bishop and the Priest, down to the lowest of his subjects, need correction, and if the priests are not what
they ought to be, it 's because they won't bear being
told of their faults. Try to understand the benefit of
correction. I do not say you must love it, or feel that
you love it, it is bitter to nature, but bring your faith
and reason to bear, and say to yourself, ' this is bitter
medicine, but I know it 's the very best thing for me,
it 's the very medicine I need.' Be thankful to God that
you are corrected, and don't speak of it to any one but
God. Take it as a grace that God sends, to prepare
you for a greater grace, and I know of no surer sign
that a soul is close to God, and in a good way of advancing in the spiritual life, than to take correction
well in the moment it is given. Pray, pray, children,
that you may have this grace, to receive correction
well, and for this you can never be sufficiently grateful,
but at the same time ask the grace to remember the
correction, and God Who gave the first, and greater
grace, will not withhold the second.

" It appears to me to be one of the greatest graces
to take correction well, and to profit by it. In the
world, if we dare to correct, it is seldom well received
at the moment. The one corrected flies up at once; he
may upon coming to his better self accept it, but to take
it sweetly on the spot, and profit by it at the same time,
is a great grace, which could come only from God.
Therefore thank Him for it, and beg the grace to remember the correction."

On Silence. In recommending Silence and Tranquillity, so necessary for the good order of a Religious
House, he remarked: " Many people find it difficult
to keep silence; this I never could understand, and for
my own part, I find it much easier to keep silence than

to talk, and I thank God that the benefit of silence was thoroughly impressed upon me, in my first essay in the Catholic Church.

" It is not an easy thing to know what to say, and how to say it, and to be able to stop in the full flow of one's feelings.

" I have told you, my children, that silence is most important in a Religious House, and if that is observed everything else will follow, for there is nothing which conduces so much to recollection and regularity."

" Try to observe that point of your Rule which requires you to speak at the recreation in the hearing of four or five, and avoid speaking *sola cum sola*. I remember a rule we had at the Seminary, which we heard so often, that we got tired of hearing it: ' Rarely one, never two, always three or four ' — and when the Director took us for our walk we were obliged to take the companion which Providence had sent us, and we were taught that to act the contrary was very much against perfection.

" I heard my fellow students say that the most difficult rule to keep was the rule of silence. Though just from Protestantism I could not understand it then, still less can I understand it now.

" To me it would be an intolerable burden to be in a house with one hundred, or a hundred and fifty persons, and to be obliged to give a word or mark of recognition to every one I met, so that if the rule of silence had not been instituted for any higher motive, it would have been established to avoid the trouble of having to speak; for me it is more difficult to speak than to keep silence, and the only time I want to speak is when I ought·not to speak, when I want to dispute or quarrel with somebody, then I can speak very easily. Now, as I don't want to quarrel with you I have very little to say."

On Obedience. " If you examine your obediences and obey with reluctance the merit is lessened, if not

lost. Father Abraham left his home at the word of
God, without knowing why, or where he was going.
If we understand the obedience, well and good, if not,
so much the better.

" You came to Religion to give up your will, and
every occasion which presents itself to enable you to
get rid of your own will is of great value. The more
difficult the obedience, the greater the merit.

" Try, my children, try to crush out the spirit of
independence, and thank God every day that you have
those over you who can teach you the religious virtues
of submission and dependence.

" Believe me this is a great privilege, a great blessing, and I say to you, make the best use of your time
and opportunities; imbibe all you can of that religious
spirit which will enable you to rise above that spirit of
independence which we see everywhere.

" If there is one thing we ought to be thankful for,
it is to have been called to a vocation which keeps us
beneath others, especially in our days, when no one is
satisfied to be equal to others, but wishes to be above
others. I have often thought if there is any position
that is enviable it is that of being a Lay Brother or
Sister in a community; there are many advantages in
that vocation, but the greatest among them is that we
are safe.

" A man will do anything to save his life, and how
grateful we ought to be for a state which makes our
spiritual life so safe; doing always the little that belongs to our vocation. This is what St. Joseph did;
we do not read that he ever did anything great, only
that he labored from day to day to support Jesus and
Mary. I recommend him to you as your model.

" Our Lord tells us that He came not to be served,
but to serve — and the Pope signs himself the Servant
of the Servants. The more we are placed above others,
the more we should humble ourselves.

" If in obeying there is not always that interior submission which does not stop to censure or question, then your obedience is imperfect; but if you obey the voice of the Superior, as the voice of God, then your obedience is perfect.

" If you do not obey the first sound of the bell, then you have not time to prepare yourself for the exercise. . . . You should set out at the first sound of the bell, or a little beforehand, so as to have time to gather yourself up, and if you sometimes complain of little distractions, inattentions or forgetfulness, they are perhaps the result of your not being faithful to the first sound of the bell. I think you would have been more recollected, if by obeying promptly you had taken the first grace held out to you. God does not want what you were doing before; drop it, whatever it may be; God does not want it, He wants you at the Office, or wherever the bell calls you.

" Our good old Master at the Seminary used to tell us that the sound of the bell was the voice of God, and God should not be kept waiting. He should not have to speak twice."

Exhortation on Humility. " When a father speaks to his children intimately he prefers being alone with them; not that I think speaking amounts to much anywhere.

" We read in the Gospel of people being possessed by devils, dumb devils, and the Lord help me! sometimes I think I must have one myself, for I don't care to talk to anybody, nor do I care much for anybody to talk to me; but if I do bring myself to speak to you, it must be of our Lord or of something connected with His life as told us in the Gospel.

" I say the same of reading as of speaking, it don't amount to much; for if all the spiritual books of the Saints were packed into one, they would not compare with one word of the Gospel. I do a little of these things; I talk a little, I read a little, I go on as a body once started keeps in motion for a certain distance; but I say to you, if you want to read, take the Gospels, read them, study them, and I 've got the Pope at my back for this.[1]

" If I do speak, I must speak of the truths of salvation; we all need this, from the Pope down, and if I were to preach before the Pope or the Patriarchs, Archbishops, Bishops or Priests, I would preach on the same truths, for they all need to be reminded of them, and even the nuns behind the grille need to be told of them, as well as the drayman or the market woman; we all need to know the truths of faith. What I find to say to you this morning must be a few reflections from the Gospel of last Sunday, a few suggestions which you may develop for yourselves.

" There are two women in the Gospel who are magnificent examples of Faith and Humility, and that of last Sunday taught us how beautifully a woman behaved herself. Then the other, who asked for the cure of her daughter, whose conduct was so sublime, so magnificent.

" It is the only place where the Master seems severe; for almost rudely, turning, He said to her sharply — never did our Blessed Lord seem so harsh: ' Is it fit to take the bread of the children, and throw it to the dogs?' as if He said: ' You are a dog, what have I to do with you?' What a rebuff! Does she lose confidence?

" She answered: ' Yea, Lord, I am a dog; I know I am a dog, but you are my Master, and You have still a crumb to throw to me, for even the little dogs eat of the crumbs that fall from their Master's table! Give me a crumb!' Oh, the sublimity of that act of humility!

" And that other woman who was afflicted with the infirmity, an issue of blood which had lasted twelve

[1] It was in this year that the Holy Father granted a Plenary Indulgence to each of the Faithful who would read the Scriptures for a quarter of an hour every day.

years — a figure of sin, and the Gospel tells us that she had spent all her living for her cure. In another Gospel it is related in a different manner, for St. Luke speaks rather ironically (he was a physician), and he says: 'she had bestowed all her substance on physicians, and could not be healed by any.' And St. Mark adds: 'and was nothing the better, but rather worse.'

" This woman having exhausted all human means despaired of her cure — this is the first characteristic; she had lost all faith in human means, but she thought within herself: ' If I can but touch the hem of His cloak, I shall be cured.' She had never spoken to our Blessed Lord, she had never caught a glance of His sacred eye, she only knew Him from what she had heard of Him, but she felt sure that He would cure her. This is the second characteristic: confidence in Jesus; distrust of creatures and confidence in God.

" As long as we put our confidence in human means, or in creatures, we have not perfect confidence in God, and He will not act in us. Humility — Faith and Confidence! In her humility she did not seek to touch our Lord Himself, nor even His garment, for our Lord wore, as all the ancients did, an inner garment called a tunic, and she said to herself, ' If I can only creep up behind Him ' — see her modesty; she dares not place herself before Him to arrest His steps, or even expect Him to look upon her once with His sacred eyes — ' if I can but creep up behind Him, and with the very tip of my finger touch the extremest edge, or the fringe of His outermost garment, I shall be healed.' When our Blessed Lord asked who had touched Him, His Apostles looked at Him with the greatest amazement and replied: ' Master, who touched You? What do You mean? Do You not see the crowd presses You on every side, jostling and pushing You before and behind, and yet You ask who touched You?' But our Lord paid no attention to them, but asked again, ' Who hath touched Me?'

Exhortations

" The poor woman, seeing that Jesus knew what she had done, threw herself trembling before Him, and our Lord said to her, ' Daughter, thy faith hath saved thee.'

" Our Lord saved her; He saved her body, the very least part, in order to save her soul; she was saved by her faith. Oh, I have always thought that it was the humility with which this woman approached Jesus that touched Him! We fail too often because we approach our Lord as the crowd did, pushing ourselves up to Him, jostling Him, knocking against Him.

" The world says: ' Away with your Church, away with your priests, away with your Sacraments, we want none of them; we will push up against Him ourselves.' If I were preaching to the Pope, to Patriarchs, Bishops or Priests, I would say the same to them as to the washerwoman: ' go with humility to our Lord.' I say the same to nuns: try to acquire humility, and you cannot acquire this or any other virtue without using the means.

" We must have the faith of these women of the Gospel, this saving faith. When all human help fails, when we have nothing to hope for from creatures, then we turn to God. Oh, this is the mistake we make, relying upon human means and devices! We must learn to distrust all human means, to detach ourselves from creatures, and then place all our confidence in God, and attach our hearts to Him alone.

" There is a great abyss between these two, — this despair of human means, and confidence in God, — this abyss is a deep pit, in which we must beware of falling. Some persons, in trying to avoid a particular friendship — the fear of loving one person too much — end in indifference, they love nobody; and our Lord says, we must love everybody; they despair of all creatures, and they despair of Christ — hence come sins and suicides.

" What is the matter with the world to-day? It

315

despairs — it despairs of Christ, it wants something new, a new Christ, as if the old Christ were worn out, as if He had lost His power. . . .

"Humility is the only thing that can unite us to God; detachment from earthly things is good in itself, but it is not all. The old Pagans knew how to contemn earthly possessions, for we read of one of the ancient philosophers who, having placed all his gold in a bag, put it on the back of his servant, but when the servant said, 'Master, this is heavy,' the pagan said, 'Well, throw some of it out in the street; throw it away and make the bag lighter.' That was detachment, but the pagans knew nothing of humility. Now the best means for acquiring humility is to accept corrections and humiliations; these bring us near to God. There are many persons who push against our Lord, even Religious, but how few there are who really touch Him, after the example of the woman in the Gospel, for we can only touch our Lord by humility."

Praise, Thanksgiving and Gratitude. "Rhetoricians and orators, in order to make their way into the hearts and minds of their hearers, and carry their audience with them, begin always with something pleasant; I have something pleasant to say, pleasant to hear, and pleasant to think of, and which I can say in all sincerity. Since the last visit the Community has made a decided step in advance, in the spirit of regular observance and of self-sacrifice, and I can say this safely, because I made the last Visit, and I know you all intimately, both your interior conscience and exterior lives. Though you may know this, still it is pleasant to hear a thing that we like. Some person has said: 'Happy is the nation that has no history,' and as well may it be said of a community which needs no advice or correction from outside, and happy am I when I think of all God has done for you. I feel that I cannot sufficiently praise and thank Him. I am emi-

Exhortations

nently satisfied with the community and I may now say to you, what I have often said outside; that there is not another community in the country where the work could have been better accomplished than it has been done here, where there has been no opposition, nothing to retard the good work. My dear children, I exhort you to praise God, to bless Him, to be grateful to Him, for He measures His graces in proportion to our gratitude. God does not need His creatures; He gives us His graces to make us happy, not for a return, for He only gives us one grace to prepare us for another."

In recommending openness and frankness with Superiors, he added the following: "God treats us as Kings, and we are Kings; each soul is a kingdom in itself, and no one can get into this kingdom unless you choose to let him in. God won't force you, and I can't, but I say to you, the more open and candid you are with your Superior, the better it will be for your soul. Be open, free, candid and sincere with your Superiors; the best Religious is the one who is the most open with her Superior, and in your Order of the Visitation I don't see how you can get along without it. Never allow any coldness to exist, — a wall, not even a film to come between you and her. This openness of heart is the most efficacious means to produce the spiritual growth which is expected of you. Oh! we are so weak, so blind, so insane, so crazy to want to govern ourselves; when we ought to be so thankful to God that somebody is willing to help us, to bear the responsibility.

"Any one who is conversant with history knows that ruin comes when we attempt to govern ourselves, or to cut off from those who are placed over us. Maybe you never allowed yourself to have this thought in reading history; that the meanest, vilest, most contemptible, craven set of men that ever lived have been bishops, whether of the East or of the West, who separated themselves from authority. Take, for instance,

317

Rt. Rev. A. A. Curtis, D.D.

the English bishops, if they had been in close union with the Holy See, and had given a clear and careful statement of their actions, receiving advice and instruction, then that brute, that blood-thirsty brute, Henry the Eighth, would never have had the power to make them the cowardly poltroons they were."

On Perseverance. "It is impossible for me, as I grow older, not to realize more and more the instability of the human mind. It is a miracle if one perseveres to the end, and this can be only by the power of the Omnipotent, Who never had a beginning, Who is unchanging and Who will never have an end. We have only to look into our own minds to see the proof of this mutability and fickleness. One moment we are raised to the heights of Heaven, where we have almost a glimpse of the glory of the Angels and Saints, catching the echo of their songs of bliss — the next moment in the depths beneath. So terrible is the mutability of our mind that we must continually pray for perseverance, not twice or three times a day, but at each moment.

"I wish you to write in your mind, in your heart, and keep before you the necessity of praying for perseverance; but we must remember while we pray that we have our own part to do. God wills to save us, but He will not do it without us, still less in spite of us. You all know the necessity of perseverance, for all the service gone before will be of no value if we do not persevere to the end.

"To attain to this perseverance the intention and the will must be renewed, as far as possible at every moment. We cannot bring back the past, though bad, — it is gone; there is no use in brooding over past sins, or contemplating our virtues; and the future is not ours. If we are anxious about something — that thing may never happen, or if it does happen, it will not be as our imagination has pictured it. So we have only the present moment, this one moment, and if we do our duty in this present moment, strength will be given us for the next moment.

" Never be discouraged; for discouragement is an enemy you have to fear. The Ancients used to say, ' Stand against your enemy in the beginning, or the end will become quite a different thing.' We should fear lest we lose confidence and trust in the inexhaustible, unspeakable, invariable goodness of God. If Judas had not lost his trust in his Master, notwithstanding his atrocious crime, he might be now where St. Peter is. We should never lessen our confidence in the goodness of God, but we must pray unceasingly to God, to the Mother of God and our Mother, to the Saints and to the Angels."

" It is the nature of all things in this world to change, never to remain the same, no matter how well established. In order to keep anything up, it must be constantly renewed, or begun again; all advancement consists in a series of beginnings. Happy are those who realize this, and are willing to believe it.

" The writer of Ecclesiasticus knowing the sun to rise in the East and go down in the West, to rise again in the East to repeat its course; the rivers to flow into the sea and to be drawn up again, the winds to blow from the North to the South, from the East to the West, and to begin again to blow from the North, and, considering all this, he sought for something in which he could rest, and found nothing.

" Even in the Religious life, in communities there is a constant need of a new beginning, a starting over again; so that each exercise is, as it were, a new beginning. Just as a traveller on a journey makes one step at a time, and that step is finished; but he would never reach the end of his journey, if that step were not followed by another, and then another, and so on, always making a new beginning until the end is reached.

" When a ship puts out to sea, the sailors keep their log so they will know where they are, but when the sun shines, or they can see the stars, they take their latitude and longitude, and make their reckoning from them, and thus see how far the little currents that they could not reckon have taken them from their course.

" So, in a Religious community, little currents, or relaxations, creep in, and it is necessary from time to time to make an extraordinary beginning. And that is what the Canonical Visit is intended for, to make an extraordinary beginning different from the constant beginnings of each day. No matter what the unworthiness of the instrument may be, and in this case it is very great, I assure you; but however mean the channel may be through which grace will come to you, it will come."

" Interior perseverance is not a relish and enthusiasm in the service of God. He may sometimes give us a foretaste of Heaven; it is a help He gives us, but it will not last; if it did last our life would not be worth much. Interior perseverance is the will cleaving to God, independent of our feelings and inclinations; the understanding recognizing God as the only Good, and cleaving to Him by virtue of the will. Nor do I speak of the perseverance of a year, or of twenty years, but perseverance of the present moment.

" Perseverance at one moment is so tremendous a thing that it takes the whole soul, Heaven and earth combined, even hell, and all that is visible and invisible, in this perseverance of one moment — one moment, — from the greatest to the least creature, all are factors moment by moment, as time comes to us, until we reach our end and our crown. Perseverance just at one moment is such a tremendous thing that it is infinitely impossible for human nature, without the aid of God, and God gives Himself to us with all He has every day, at least frequently for this end, that we may persevere one moment, the present moment.

" God is unchangeable — without beginning — from Eternity to Eternity; His unchangeableness is the least communicable of His attributes; but God could perform the miracle of having us go on with an ever increasing alacrity in union with Him, without ever failing, but it would be the greatest of miracles, and God does not wish to perform such a miracle, for good reasons.

" So perseverance does not mean never to fail, never to hesitate in our way, but it means to begin every day, and not only every day, but every moment of the day. My children, I told you before that success is not the way to humility, so if we were always interiorly successful in going straight to God, we would not have that consciousness of our misery and infirmity which is so necessary for humility; and without humility there is no union with God here or hereafter.

" If a person labored for years and failed in perseverance at the last moment, he would lose all reward; if at the last moment he changed his mind and his will, he would lose the reward of all his past labor.[1] How is this? I will give you one reason; he did not bring to God what God required of him. God does not want our work, our labor or our fasting. He wants only our interior perseverance, which is the recognition that God is the only good, and our will cleaving to Him. If I send a person for something, I want that one thing and nothing else; even if he should spend ten years in laboring for me, and then come to me without the thing I sent him for, I have no reward for him. I do not want his work, that was not our bargain. It is the same with God; we must bring Him what He requires of us, and what we have undertaken, which is interior perseverance, perseverance in the present moment."

---

[1] This, of course, must be interpreted conformably to the Church's teaching with regard to inequality of eternal punishment, as well as of eternal reward.

III
SERMONS

SERMONS TO RELIGIOUS

THE following beautiful thoughts drawn from a number of sermons given to his spiritual daughters, on the occasions of Clothing and Profession, of the Solemn Renewal of Vows, and special feasts, were written down by members of the community, as they recalled the imperishable words of their venerated Father.

These sermons were generally given in the way of a familiar talk, without any attempt at oratory, for this would have been foreign to the Bishop's sweet spirit of simplicity, which was so marked on these occasions.

Notwithstanding his multifarious duties as a Missionary Bishop, he would engage himself to say, or even sing a Mass for the community, perform the ceremonies of the feast, and turning towards his audience during the Mass, would pour forth his thoughts on the Gospel of the day, possibly developed in his morning meditation.

On one occasion, quoting from the Gospel of St. Luke vii. 13: "Weep not! Weep not!" he said: "in the Gospel of to-day Our Lord does not come to us—He does not wait for us to come to Him, but in passing He bestows His graces; and if we are not there, ready to receive them, as He is passing, then they are lost, and forever.

"It would be impossible for God to give us that same grace — we may receive something else, but the grace he had for us then we can never have, that one is lost forever. We may get another grace as good, but the special one — *never*. In the Mass of this morning He is passing, it may be as swiftly as lightning; if we lose the grace He has for us in this Mass we can never get it again. If you are drowsy and inattentive, and do not do all you can to rouse yourself, the grace is lost which He would have given you in passing, then that grace is gone forever. You may hear another Mass, but that one just passed — *never*. A grace bestowed upon us in childhood would not be proper for us in manhood; and if we have lost that grace which God had for us in childhood, we shall never be what we should have been, if we had received that grace.

"This is what gives to life its grandeur, its importance, its awful responsibility. It was in passing Our Lord bestowed His grace; what He did then, He does now. He is always passing. In this sickness there is a grace, if we lose it, it is lost forever; we may receive another grace, but not this one which God intended for us.

"But notice — He wishes His Lordship, His Mastership, His Judgeship to be recognized. He gives first a command, He commands obedience. 'Weep not!' The poor widow might have said, 'You command an impossibility; I cannot help weeping over my only son.' He commands, and the obedience seems impossible. He tells her nothing of the miracle He is about to perform; she must be obedient before He gives the grace. Sometimes He commands the most impossible things, the most contrary to reason, as in the case of the paralytic: 'Get up, take up thy bed and walk.' The paralytic might have said: 'You tell me to do a thing that is impossible; if I could walk I would not have been carried here.' But he had sense enough to know that He who told him to walk had at the same time the power to make him walk, and if he had not obeyed he would have lost the grace our Lord wished to bestow upon him.

"So it was with the Lepers: 'Go show yourselves to the priest.' He had not touched them, they had not quite come up to Him, only on the way to do so. If they had not obeyed and turned to go, they would have lost their grace, for it was on their way to show themselves to the priest that they were healed. Love and devotion are not enough, we must have a foundation, and there are some, it seems to me, who never will have a foundation. If we build a house we must be sure to have a foundation. We need not go out to look at the foundation every morning, but we must be sure it is there.

"You cannot treat our Lord as a friend, as a Saviour, and end there; you must recognize Him as the great God, the God of sanctity, whose right and dominion must be respected. Love comes after this acknowledgment. God showed this in the beginning with Adam and Eve. He demanded their obedience, their dependence on Him."

EXTRACT FROM A SERMON GIVEN AT A CEREMONY OF CLOTHING

January 3, 1891.

"The occasion which has united us here to-day is to witness the assumption of the habit and veil (which will be followed later, by the succeeding Vows), a sacrifice.

"It is a happy coincidence that it should occur at the very time when we celebrate the Mystery of the Nativity, for sacrifice was the object of the Incarnation. God could have saved us without becoming Man; He had in His Almighty wisdom and power other means to redeem us, but He could not have sacrificed Himself for us, had He not become man.

"It is to imitate Him that you are here to-day, my dear child. In what does the sacrifice which you are about to make consist? Is it in giving up money? No! [The Bishop here cited the philosophers of old, who had given up all.] Is it in the giving up of pleasure, the endurance of hardships and suffering, the separation from family and those who are dearest to us? No! There is no sacrifice of this kind, even among the martyrs, that cannot find its parallel in the man of science, the worldling, the lady of fashion.

"In what then does the sacrifice consist? In the giving up absolutely and forever of that which man clings to as to his very life — his will. In giving up your will, not in things bad, but in what seems to you good; your own ideas of holiness, your secret aspirations, in what appears to you to be the highest sanctity.

"This is horrible to nature, and would be impossible without the assistance of grace. But were this only for a time it would be easier; we can do anything when we know it will have an end; we could even crucify ourselves for a time. What makes the bitterness of the sacrifice is that it must always be. These words — 'This shall always be' — 'This shall never be.' Always to do the will of another — never to do your own will. And yet this, every one must do even in the world who would lead a perfect life.

"The Scripture tells us that every sacrifice must be salted with fire to be acceptable, and this absolute and irrevocable giving up of your will for the rest of your life is the salting of the sacrifice. Christ is your model.

"In coming into the world He said: 'In the head of the book it is written of Me, that I shall do Thy Will, O God.' Then said I, 'Behold, I come. Thy law is in the midst of My heart.'

"Let this be the spirit in which you make your sacrifice to-day. Remember that you do not make this sacrifice for yourself alone. Not even the solitary in the desert can say, 'My Father.' He is obliged by Christ Himself to say, 'Our Father.'

"Nor let it be thought that a life of good works in the world is better than the life of the cloister.

"Humanity has other needs than those of the body and mankind will ever exclaim: 'I want more than food for my body, I want life for my soul, I want light for my mind and my heart.'

"This is your work; to be accomplished more perfectly than the Sister of Charity can do it in the prison, or on the battlefield, by your prayer and sacrifice. I will speak now of only two principles which must be the foundation of your future religious life.

"First, God is enough. Second, What the world is worth, or rather that it is worth nothing.

"God is enough. Whatever your sufferings may be — and they will be great, — they must be so if you carry out your sacrifice, but God will pour His peace into your soul, and you will feel the sweetness of giving up all for Him.

"The world is nothing — nothing of what you give up to-day can fill your heart. Begin your religious life then with these two principles, and go through it to the end, in the same spirit, so that when your last moment comes, you can say with your Divine Model: 'All is consummated. Father, into Thy hands I commend My Spirit. I have sacrificed my life for Thee, receive me into Thy arms.' My dear child, may this be your lot, to have fulfilled to your last breath the work He has given you to do."

"It is better to do little Things always than a Great Thing now and then." St. Francis de Sales.

January 29, 1895.

"Although we may know this assertion to be true, still if we examine it, and study the reasons why it is true, we shall be enlightened and have a clearer knowledge of its truth.

"Neither will this be a want of submission or deference on our part; for although the Church in her doctrine commands obedience, she does not forbid our examining her reasons, but, on the contrary, advises it, that what she says may have an influence on our lives.

Rt. Rev. A. A. Curtis, D.D.

"Then much less would St. Francis de Sales have cause to doubt our allegiance, since, however saintly, he is not infallible. Therefore, we may readily examine the reasons why it is better to do little things always than a great thing now and then.

"In the first place, it makes us more like God, who from all eternity has ever been doing little things. He has never spent Himself and been fully occupied in doing one great thing. This world is made up of little things, and oh, that wonderful world within, which far surpasses the exterior world without!

"The marvellous world within a sanctified soul is made up of little things, *those little things* known only to God. A delicious morsel left untouched, an aching corn, or a crucifying bunion unheeded, a fly permitted to remain on the ear or the nose — these are the little things unseen that have gone to make up that wonderful world in a sanctified soul.

"The beauty of this world within, far surpasses all the combined beauties that can be conceived of our exterior world. But no one wants to do these little things. There are many who are willing to do great things. You will find many priests who are waiting to do great things, but the little things they care not to do.

"Nobody wants you to die for them; now is not the time for that; but what we do want is a kind word, a helping hand, a gentle forbearance, an encouraging smile — doing these little things all the day long, from sunrise till sunset — putting self out, to please another, without expecting or thinking of a return. While doing these little things makes us more like God, it at the same time makes us useful to our neighbor. I never see a gentleman now; there are none, and the reason is because the young men want to do great things — and they are not *equal* to great things, because they will not do little things.

"The gentleman of old was trained from his youth to restrain himself always, at all times, in all places;

330

Sermons

to restrain his passions, his feelings, his inclinations, his tongue, his appetite. The young man of to-day knows nothing of all these checks, he looks beyond and above all this, he aims at great things; and the young women follow the young men in wishing to do great things.

"Oh, for that dear old lady whose knowledge was little beyond pickles and preserves, and knowing how to keep her children fresh and clean, the sunshine of her home! She is nowhere to be found to-day. The trouble is, we won't be humble — neither the bishop, priest, nun nor secular.

"I was struck with the humility of that grand old Centurion in last Sunday's Gospel. Educated as he was, in the midst of all that was cruel, wicked and licentious in the Roman Legion, yet he manifested so much humility in addressing our Lord. 'I am not worthy to have you enter my house, but speak the word and my servant shall be healed; don't come down, I am too unworthy, say only the word.' God so loved this humility that by His inspiration the Church has ordained in consideration of it, that neither Pope, Cardinal, Bishop nor Priest should communicate before repeating these same words.[1]

"Even the laity repeat them three times before approaching to receive their Lord and Master: Humility! Humility! Humility! Oh, if we could fathom our misery! but we don't, we don't want to be humble; we are all mirrors, and reflect the sentiments and opinions of those around us!

"We are praised and flattered, and we then believe ourselves possessed of the accredited merit, while before God we are sorely wanting. God help *me*. I believe I am like those rascals who think the whole world like themselves.

"I was struck, as I was coming out here, by the

[1] "Lord, I am not worthy that Thou shouldst enter under my roof, say but the word and my soul shall be healed."

sight of one of those fine old oaks, the king of the forest. I don't wonder the Druids made choice of the oak with its wide spreading branches, under which to build their altars and offer their sacrifices. It is a fit emblem of an unresisting soul.

"This king of the forest was once an acorn, an atom, but from the continuous action of God upon this atom it has borne the storms and shocks of the elements for hundreds of years.

"So if our souls received the action of God's grace from moment to moment, they would grow strong, and have power to resist all the assaults of their enemies; they would expand."

Renewal of Vows

November 21, 1895.

"Just two points briefly stated, which you can revolve or develop at length and at your leisure. There is a great mistake in saying things are synonymous simply because they start from the same point; their divergence will cause them to become widely different.

For instance, there is a great difference between giving oneself to God and possessing God, although in giving oneself to God we shall possess God. If we start out with this end in view, *to possess God,* our lives will be widely different from what they would have been if we had in our mind to give ourselves to God.

"I say our lives would be entirely different, widely different; just as two drops of water falling close beside each other, upon examination, one will reach the Pacific and the other the Atlantic Ocean, or as two ships starting from the same port, sailing in different directions will have the world between them.

"We must give ourselves without reserve, and that is not what people generally do. We want to possess God, to have Him for ourselves, to make use of Him, to do what *we want* to reach a certain degree of sanctity, and perhaps God does not want us to be there.

"We conceive a sanctity for ourselves, or there is something in the life of a Saint we wish to make our own, or we set to work to reach something in St. Francis de Sales or St. Jane de Chantal, when God does not intend that for us; no two persons being called to exactly the same degree of holiness, and instead of being what He wants us to be, we aim at something else.

"A certain person sees something *he* thinks is *good, very good, it ought to be done, it must be done,* and he *flies off to do it,* without considering whether the commission is from God or not, or even with the thought that, *perhaps, he* was not the one whom God wished to do it.

"Let us give ourselves to Our Lord as *He* wishes; let us give Him our aspirations, our desires to be holy, and if we give ourselves to Him, we are His, to do with us just what He pleases. Then we will be as holy as He wishes, in the manner He wishes, and at the time He wishes, and not before.

"Let us keep our good will to do as He wishes, and then allow Him to act as He wills.

"There are some persons who are forever giving all the good they do to our Lord, but who never think of giving Him their faults and shortcomings. Let us give ourselves just as we are, with all our faults and miseries; then He will make us draw profit from these faults, which should serve to keep us humble."

ANOTHER CLOTHING CEREMONY

October 28, 1896.

"'Let not him who putteth on the armor boast as one that putteth it off.'

"Many people begin well and think in this the end is secure, but it is not so. The exterior may give satisfaction. We may go even to the door of heaven, and fall to the depths of hell.

Rt. Rev. A. A. Curtis, D.D.

"It is not in meditation, confession or Communion, neither is it contained in sanctifying or actual grace, nor merited by any prior grace. It is essentially in itself distinct, apart and beyond all these; it is in the gift of final perseverance, that is, interior perseverance.

"No one can be certain without a special revelation that he will persevere to the end; no Saint has ever known it, not even the Apostles. St. Paul, who had received so many communications from God, and believed by others to be confirmed in grace, was himself ignorant of the fact, otherwise, what did he mean by these words: 'I chastise my body and bring it under subjection, lest while I preach to others I myself become a castaway.'

"Therefore, pray for this postulant — pray for her perseverance — pray for perseverance for yourselves. Let us ask the Apostles who are our first Fathers, and after St. Joseph, the most powerful in Heaven, to pray for us, and obtain for us this perseverance.

But remember that when I speak of perseverance, I do not mean mere exterior perseverance, many may accomplish that; but I mean interior perseverance, which is to put into each succeeding action more will and more love, so that after a life of ten, twenty or thirty years spent in the monotonous routine of duties, you may yet put into each succeeding action more will and more love than in the preceding one, until the last repetition of the act shall contain more perfection than any of the former.

"Let us then beg this gift of interior perseverance with humility, and humility will aid us to get it.

"Of all the miracles God could perform on this earth, it would be the greatest to rid us of ourselves. But self-crucifixion is slow work. If we could be convinced of our misery, of our nothingness, and be willing that others should be convinced of it too, we would put our mouths in the dust, and keep them there."

Sermons

On the Vows

November 21, 1896.

" There is only one Being, only one immutable and immovable Being, God alone is the only real Being, — Being in its plenitude, Being itself. Every other being is a creation of His Omnipotence, and if He should withhold His sustaining power, all other beings would fall back into their original nothingness. God alone has the prerogative of immutability from age to age, from eternity to eternity, always the same, yet never growing old.

" Mary, the Angels and the Saints do not grow old, because God shares with them, in their union with Him, His immutability. Everything else changes, withers and grows old. The day dawns, grows old and dies, and is succeeded by another day. The years grow old and die. The trees grow old, and they may last a century, die and are replaced by other trees. In all nature there is this constant ebb and flow — passing away.

And we grow old and die; thanks be to God that we do, for were we to live on, our doom would be sealed. The soul grows old in proportion as it recedes from God, and would return to nothingness were God for one moment to withdraw His omnipotent hand.

" Surely you must know by this time that there is nothing better than to belong to God; by our Vows we belong to God; but as we have renewed them many times they have grown old, not the Vows themselves, but our dispositions, in regard to them, have changed and grown old, and we see that there is need to renew them.

" You cannot renew them yourselves, but you come to God to ask Him to renew these Vows in your soul, and to put you in such dispositions that your attitude before God may be as when you first made them.

335

Rt. Rev. A. A. Curtis, D.D.

" And oh, dear children, may you not only renew them to-day and then stop, but may you renew them all through the day, every day, every hour, a thousand times a day if possible! God could not have given you a greater grace than to have enabled you to make these Vows.

" *The Vow of Chastity.* I speak not here of negative Chastity, the removal of all that could defile the body or tarnish the soul, but of complete chastity, perfect purity of body and heart as Mary had it, of entire detachment from all creatures, from ourselves, from our way of thinking, acting, seeing, praying; even from an over desire of our sanctification, or of a thought, if it could come between us and God. Chastity is a perfect adhesion to God.

" The mysteries of religion are no mysteries at all, *no mysteries at all;* the Trinity, the Incarnation, the Divine Presence, the Blessed Eucharist; these do not trouble us, the Mystery of Mysteries is that God is, and that I am! that I can oppose my will to God's will. Our prerogative is that we have a will free — a frightful thought — that we have it in our power to use this free agency to our own destruction — to act against God!

" The Vow of Obedience takes this power out of our hands, and oh, how thankful we ought to be, to be freed from this frightful responsibility of the free use of our own will! Abandonment is the aim of this Feast of the Presentation.

" Abandonment, total and absolute, from top to bottom, through and through, within and without. As the men of the world, who take every means to increase their riches, we must take every means to increase the riches of our poverty.

" And *my children,* let us make acts of contrition, let us humble ourselves before God; let us come with our mouths in the dust to renew our Vows. Let us ask

336

Mary to help us, and I am sure she will; let us ask this through all the Mass which is to follow, and during the Holy Communion. We cannot renew our Vows of ourselves, but let us ask God to renew them in our souls."

"MAKE STRAIGHT THE WAY OF THE LORD." JOHN i. 23.

December 2, 1896.

" Now what I want to say, if God gives me anything to say, is this: There is a great difference between antique and modern Christianity. There is a softness, a flabbiness, if I may be allowed to use the expression, about our modern Christianity. We want to get to Heaven. We expect to get to Heaven, but by other means than the Cross. We multiply endeavors and means; we establish rules and regulations for the great day of conversion, and say it is near at hand. Now this is all foolishness.

" There is no other way to be saved than by a systematic, persevering self-denial, doing things we don't like to do, always opposing self. Now it seems to me that this lack comes from want of reflection upon, and of preparation for the visitation, the coming of our Lord. We do not keep Advent. We do not keep Advent as our Lord intended it to be kept.

When I speak to men, more learned and scientific than I am, of the end of the world, they laugh at me. Yet the Prophets lived with this thought constantly before them, they lived always in expectation and held themselves in readiness for the end. The early Christians were penetrated with this thought; it was their guiding principle; it was taught by our Lord and preached by His Apostles. St. Paul kept this thought always before his hearers. On one occasion our Lord said: ' The Father knows when the *end* will be, but the Son of Man does not know.' He did not mean that He was wanting in knowledge, for He shared all knowledge with His Father; but He did not know to tell it to others, just as we say in regard to the secrets of the confessional. When questioned, a priest can say he knows nothing — that is, he knows nothing to tell.

"Time is short; even if the world should last a thousand or a million years, it would be short when compared to eternity. For nothing is absolutely long or short, only relatively. A day is long when compared to a minute, but short when compared to a year. Time is simply nothing when compared to eternity. Ascend a great height, the highest mountain in the world, if you choose, and everything seems to fade away into nothingness. The houses appear like little specks, and the great cities seem no larger than a house when viewed from such a height.

"We know we shall die, but the thought of death does not take from us the thought of temporal things, as does the thought of the end of the world; for when we die we leave our relatives and friends, and our temporal possessions we leave to our children. God purposely conceals from us the time when the end shall come, in order that the thought of the great end shall be our abiding thought all day, and all through the day. It makes very little difference to the world whether we die or not. The Church will go on, the State will go on, the fact touches us only. But we cannot lie down even for one night, and say that we know that the heavens will not split over us. Scientific men agree that the end of the world is near at hand. Stars larger than the earth have existed, and burnt out. The heavens are filled with comets that are wandering about, and should any one of these deviate from its course and strike the earth, all would be burnt up, Church and State.

"It is a fact that the earth has changed its equilibrium, and that portions of it that were formerly covered with snow are now inhabited; and we know that there are worlds and worlds beneath our feet, there are fossil remains of birds and animals much greater in size and number than those which now exist, and they have left no traces but upon the rocks.

" Reason tells us that what has happened many times can, and probably will happen again. We know also that there are fires underneath the earth, but we do not know that they will not at any moment burst forth. We cannot say to ourselves that we shall not see the end of the world, and that the end will not come in our time; my life, precarious and frail as it is, may be long enough to witness that day. These thoughts meditated upon would give us a clearer view of the nothingness of earthly things than the mere thought of our own death."

A Few Words spoken over the Coffin of a Religious, professed on her Death-bed

December 21, 1896.

" Beloved, we are strange creatures; you have often heard this before. We are quick to assume to ourselves the prerogatives of God and want to finish things, and slow to see that it does not belong to us to finish things in this world. It is God alone Who can finish things. We may begin and stop anywhere, at any time or place.

" When God calls us to something else, what we were doing is finished to God, though unfinished to us. God does not want our work, or our labor; you may even sin in trying to finish. For instance, the bell calls you, you wish to finish your prayer, but the prayer is finished to God, when He calls you to something else.

" God does not want you to finish, even if it were to save a soul that is going astray; your work with that soul is finished to God, though perhaps not to you.

" These thoughts are suggested by her, who apparently did not finish the work she came to do, but was called away before the habit was fairly won. It was won though before God, for before Him her work was done."

Rt. Rev. A. A. Curtis, D.D.

This young Religious had become a Catholic three years previous to her entrance in the Convent, and after a fervent and edifying noviceship was received to her Clothing by the community; but in the designs of God she was to pass through a crucible of suffering before attaining her end. She was suddenly attacked with severe hemorrhages of the lungs, which followed each other in such quick succession that death seemed imminent. During fourteen weeks of the most intense suffering the Bishop visited and consoled her; then she made the holy Vows of Religion conditionally.

On the twenty-first of December, as the community stood around her open grave in the cold, piercing wind, the ground covered with snow, this benevolent Father turned to the Superioress, and in kind, gentle tones said: " Mother, can you not send the sisters in, it is too cold for them out here; we can do the rest." So the community was sent into the House, and the charitable, self-forgetting Servant of God helped to screw the lid on the coffin, and to put the earth in the grave; thus performing the last office of Christian charity for his departed child.[1]

" Blessed are the merciful: for they shall obtain mercy."

At the Clothing of a Widow advanced in Years

February 18, 1897.

" In the Gospel we read these words: 'The first shall be last, and the last shall be first'— and although Our Lord placed no limit to these words, it seems to me that He did not mean that all who are first shall be last, nor that all who are last shall be first, but it means that those who are first in opportunities, in talents, in grace, may fall and become the last, as they who have fewer

---

[1] It is a custom in the Visitation Order for the Sisters to carry the body of the deceased Religious to the place of burial leaving the coffin open until about to be lowered into the grave.

graces, by the good use they make of them, may become the first.

"The Angels were first by their creation, and the knowledge and graces which God gave them; they had not the power to choose and to unchoose, and to choose again as we have, by God's infinite Mercy to our poor weak nature: they could choose but once — God or themselves, and that choice was for eternity; and from the first they fell to be the lowest and the last.

"Others are the first by the wealth which God has given them to do good to others, and by a bad use of this wealth they may become the last, as in the case of the man who hires apartments in a New York hotel for his dog, hires servants to wait on it, has special meals served to it, or as those who spend their money on a ball — the papers recently have been filled with accounts of this ball, of which I hope *you, my dear children,* have not heard.

"In the history of nations we see the same; the first shall be last, and the last shall be first. And may not the same be said of our own American nation, which God has made first in opportunities, in wealth, in freedom from debt, and in so many ways that I have not time to enumerate. We see the causes, and the effects will not suspend themselves in our favor, and there are those who seem to be hurrying us on to our downfall — not intentionally, not voluntarily, but not the less surely.

"The serious and thoughtful observer may hear the seething and the rumbling of the volcano which is ready to burst under our feet; and though we, in our pride, stand shaking our fists in the face of other nations, the day may come when those we now look upon as the lowest, the most degraded, and despicable may rule over us.

"Look at the Jewish nation, called to be the *very first,* the most favored by God, among whom He was born, lived and died — the first among nations, now the last, no longer a nation — scattered as dry leaves before the wind, without home, without country, branded everywhere with a brand that cannot be effaced.

" Look at the early history of those who have caused most trouble in Church and State — wicked men who use dynamite, — were they not once Catholics, called by God to be the first by the gift of Faith, they are now the last, they have abused the graces God gave them, and have turned His very gifts against God Himself.

" The same may be said of many Catholics, even in this country, who have become the last by joining themselves to the Free masons, against the Church. What would we say of the doctor who used his medical skill only to poison his patients in a more subtle manner, or of the lawyer who used his talents only to betray his clients, or of the Bishop placed by God to be the first — the torch bearer — to go ahead to show others the dangers, the caverns and pitfalls — if he should be moved by ambition, by love of money, or by negligence, and instead of leading his people onward to salvation, lead them on to their own destruction?

" And the Religious, the cloistered nun, called by her vocation to be the first, may by ambition, whether it be for offices, or only for a button on her cap, by little spites, bickerings, by a love of the world, (for though her body is in the cloister, her heart may still be filled with the world) by the neglect of her Rule may fall to be the very last.

" And you, my dear daughter, God has called you to be the very first. He has called you from secular cares, distractions and anxieties, while thousands are left outside to struggle with the sorrows and trials of the world; He has called you not only into the house of the King, to the presence of the King, but into the innermost chamber of the King, where you can speak to Him at all times, you can plead with Him for others, for sinners, for all mankind.

Sermons

" When others wish to treat with the King they must employ a mediator to speak for them, but you are to be always in His presence. To whom much is given, of him much will be required. Be faithful, my dear daughter, and I pray to God that He may not only be your King, but your All — All."

During this instruction the venerable Bishop sat at the choir grate in his pontifical robes, his eyes closed, his mitred head bent low, like one of the grand old patriarchs speaking prophetically — for had not his lips been touched with coals of fire from the Altar of God?

FEAST OF ST. FRANCIS DE SALES

January 29, 1899.

" There are some people who have the happy facility of being able to speak at any time, in any place, on any subject, or on all subjects. I suppose such people are to be envied. I can't, I never could speak without preparation; I must know what I am to speak about.

" Formerly, I used to ask our Lord to tell me what I was to say, and generally He did tell me, at least I thought He told me, but it may have been my imagination.

" I don't know whether you know what it is to be bound up, sealed, without a thought. When this is so, it would be as easy to get water out of a stone, as to know what to say. I have asked the Lord to give me something to say to you; I waited till after the Gospel, I waited till after Mass, and still He gave me nothing. I went to Mary — I said the Rosary; she gave me not a word, as if she would say: ' I will have nothing at all to do with it.' I turned to Saint Francis, promising to wear my finest soutane with the longest train, if he would tell me what he wished me to say to you, but he, like the other celestial beings, was silent, as if he said,

343

Rt. Rev. A. A. Curtis, D.D.

' Don't talk about me, talk to me if you will — the more the better,' at least this was implied by his silence.

" We often find mention in Holy Writ of certain events which took place in the early morning. Why is it that such stress is laid on the time, *the early morning?* The adage says: ' A good beginning is half the work,' and often it is the whole work.

" The Gospel says that the householder, that is Our Lord, went out early in the morning to send laborers into His vineyard. The Greek version makes it still stronger, and says, He went out as soon as the daylight began to appear. God created man in the early morning, and some of the Fathers say, that He sent our first parents out of Paradise before the close of day; I don't know whether this is true or not.

" It was early in the morning when Moses went up to the mountain to receive the tables of the Law. He went up twice, and both times early in the morning. It was early in the morning when God parted the waters of the Red Sea for the Israelites to pass through, and it was early in the morning that the Israelites looked back upon the Egyptians swallowed up by the same sea.

" It was early in the morning when Abraham went up to the mountain to sacrifice his son. It was early in the morning that Our Lord was seized, scourged and condemned, and He passed through the greater part of His Passion in the morning.

" If God were to ask me what I wished in favor of the Church, I would answer, Restore to us the early morning. There is no more early morning in the world — it is all rush — far into the night, and the early morning finds them unable to rise until nearly the next night, thus turning things out of their true course.

" All things are in motion either by acting, or by being acted upon. Whether we know it or not the battle is constantly going on between grace and the devil. Sleep is a great battle-ground, where God almost always gains the victory, since the will being in repose does not resist Him. There is here something like a Sacramental, in a measure like baptism. Indeed if it were not for sleep I think it would be almost impossible for us to save our souls, because the soul would become so fatigued and weak from the struggle with the powers of darkness that she would be overcome.

"In baptism, whether we have lived forty, fifty or seventy years, all is blotted out. Our Lord says, ' Here is a clean, blank sheet; write upon it what you will.' So in sleep, God casts up the accounts and gives us a new day, saying as it were, ' Here is a new day, make what you can of it.' Each day we live our life. So, my children, we will endeavor to rise early in the morning, and at the signal given by the Rule, we will spring like the trigger; when *it* is *pulled*, it *shoots*." (Here the Bishop used his thumb and first finger, as if in the act of shooting.)

"A lifeless, dull thing of itself will have only a motion downwards, and if once it starts down, we must have an opposing force in proportion to its descent; it is easier to turn at the beginning. We must brace ourselves as well as we can, and turn at once in the right direction — towards God — a moment's hesitation and we lose our ground. Some people say, ' Oh, I am so *stupid* in the morning, I am good for nothing, I can do nothing!'

"But I tell you, my children, that if you do nothing else during the whole hour but make a good effort to keep awake, while way down in the soul there is a little flickering light of a good intention, and something akin to a few aspirations — I tell you, you are keeping the Rule. You have made a better meditation than six hours of ecstatic contemplation later in the day, for it gives you a better idea of your own nothingness, and of your utter, moral inability to do anything of yourselves, but you must do your part by placing yourselves before God, that He may do his divine work in your souls."

Rt. Rev. A. A. Curtis, D.D.

"STRIVE TO ENTER BY THE NARROW GATE."   LUKE xiii. 24.

"What is this narrow gate? The narrow gate is Christ, but is Christ narrow? In *one* sense He is, for only *one* thing can enter the narrow gate, and this one thing is *love;* unreserved adhesion to Christ, deep heart to heart value of Christ.

"'Strive to enter the narrow gate.' According to the Greek version, the meaning is, 'agonize to enter the narrow gate.' We would not be satisfied to appear before Christ as we are; not even the Pope would say that he is prepared.

"Well, then, we must prepare *now,* and how shall we do it? We must *agonize,* that is, we must have *one* thought, *one* desire, *one* purpose, which is to have *supreme* love for Christ — an inestimable value of Christ; and every *atom* of our powers should be employed in continually striving to cleave to Christ — to merge our soul in Christ."

"BEHOLD, I STAND AT THE GATE, AND KNOCK. IF ANY MAN SHALL HEAR MY VOICE AND OPEN TO ME THE DOOR, I WILL COME IN TO HIM, AND WILL SUP WITH HIM, AND HE WITH ME." APOC. iii. 20.

"Our Lord stands at the gate, or door of our heart and knocks; if we do not open the door to Him, He does not go away, but *remains* standing at the door of our heart *knocking.*

"If we open the door to Him by uniting our will to His, then, 'He comes in to us, and sups with us,' that is, He takes our good works and unites them to His merits, in order that we may afterwards 'sup with Him,' that is, partake of His glory in heaven."

PROFESSION OF A RELIGIOUS

December 28, 1899.

"Forty-three years ago last September I began to preach, and when I had to speak I never could find anything to say, unless it had reference to the time, or

346

some portion of Holy Scripture especially designated by the Church for that time.

"There was an ancient sect of Philosophers who passed seven years in silence, in order to learn to speak better, and with more profit. We might reverse the order and put silence at the end to atone for our faults in speaking. I had resolved never to speak in public; I have broken my resolution, and unfortunately I have sometimes spoken at too great length.

"When I was asked to preach to-day, I asked myself what connection can there be between the slaughter of the Holy Innocents and the profession of a nun. Outwardly there is none, but if you consider it, there is a connection, just as things which seem to differ on the surface, at the bottom coincide and resemble each other. We can understand what a terrible thing it is to commit murder, to take away life in hot blood, in the heat of passion, even in the most justifiable self-defence.

"With what horror the Church considers the crime of murder, when in the case of a duel, where both parties are previously prepared, equally matched, she punishes with excommunication the one who serves the challenge, or accompanies the parties to the field. But in the case of these little babies, where not only one, but many babies were sacrificed, babies who had committed no crime, were incapable of committing any, and were unconscious of the surrounding danger, it was an incomprehensible atrocity. And who was Herod? Was he a monster? Was he a man? A man — yes, a man, and nothing more or less. A Nero — a Diocletian. There was in Herod what was in St. Francis de Sales, and what was in all the Saints in Heaven, what you have and what I have and what these nuns have — human nature, and in the same condition, under the same circumstances we would have done what Herod did; but for the grace of God we are capable of committing all the crimes for which men fill our prisons and swing on the gallows to-day.

Rt. Rev. A. A. Curtis, D.D.

" What made Herod what he was? The world — and the world is just the same to-day. We may talk of its civilization and its progress, but the world has not advanced one whit. Like the ocean, which on the surface is ever changing with its glitter and sparkle, but down low, deep in its depths, are its under-currents unchanged from century to century.

" Selfishness is the Gospel of the world. Where do we see in practice: 'From him that would borrow from thee, turn not away. If a man take away thy coat, let go also thy cloak to him. And whosoever forces thee a mile, go with him other two. If he strike thee on one cheek, turn to him also the other.' This is the Gospel of Christ, and men will say: 'That's all very well to hear in Church on Sundays,' but ask them to bring it into their daily life, they laugh at you.

" Ambition is the Gospel of the world. Your great men of to-day — financiers, statesmen, distinguished and cultivated gentlemen, if you will, would smile and think you insane, if you spoke to them of the sanctification of their souls, or told them that their ambition was incompatible with the Gospel of Jesus Christ; and yet St. Paul tells us that whatsoever makes us forget God is fatal. The world does n't want God, it does all it can to make us forget God; it is the world that prefers Barabbas to Jesus Christ. It cries: 'Away with Him! crucify Him! crucify Him!' It is the same world that drove the nails into the hands and feet of Christ.

" St. Paul tells us that whole nations roll down into hell because they forget God. You may be good, devoted fathers, husbands, brothers and children without having God, for you may be all this naturally. Even in the cloister after having renounced all you loved so much, self may come to take the place of God. Even before the Altar something may take the place of God. The best and holiest things may take His place; even if it were zeal for the sanctification of souls, if we allow *that* to take the first place, it would prevent a personal

intimate union with God, either with His divinity or
His humanity.

"We can commit sin without murder, lying or cheating. You can't deny that the world is full of dangers.
If we were told that the road was full of reptiles and
asps, ready to rise up at any moment to strike us, would
we not be glad if we were told that our path lay in a
different direction, and that we would not have to pass
through those dangerous places, or if we knew that
there were lions and tigers in the way, would we not be
grateful if we knew there were secure walls to protect
us from these ferocious beasts?

"But if God commands us to go in the midst of these
dangers, go, go on; we must obey, God will protect us,
He has His grace for all. He will save us though we
were in the midst of the fiery furnace, as He saved the
three children from the roaring flames. I don't want to
give undue merit to nuns, for you can sanctify your
souls in the world. God has His graces for souls in
the world as well as in the cloister, nevertheless I say to
you, my dear sister, if our Lord says to you: 'Come
apart, My child, and serve My Person, I do not will
you to pass through these dangers,' should not gratitude fill your heart as well as the hearts of those who
have preceded you?

"You come to the cloister to imprison nature, to
shut it up, to confine it where you may receive admonition, remonstrances and corrections. Therefore be
thankful, or as St. Paul says: 'Giving thanks always
for all things' (Ephesians v. 20). He did not say feeling thanks, for these feelings of fervor may be the
mere spontaneity of nature, and soon pass away, to be
superseded by the weary, monotonous drag of the Religious life; but I mean that thankfulness which springs
from principle, from conviction of will, which will bear
you on, up or down, whithersoever it shall please God
to lead you.

"We should be grateful for all things, even our sins,

if we detest them, if they teach us humility, for this will put us on a plane, and give us a knowledge of our own weakness and nothingness, where perhaps but for them we never could have been.

INSTRUCTION GIVEN IN LENT

March 14, 1900.

" If man could reach such a state on earth that he was above temptation, not affected by it, then God would that very instant remove him from this earth, for he would be utterly useless, and God would not suffer a useless thing to remain. We are here to be tempted, and our future character will be such as we have made it by using our present temptations to our profit. We are always being tempted, and in those moments where we feel secure and, as it were, in no danger, then, oh then, is the temptation most real! It is this insidious temptation which is not suspected by us, which is the most dangerous. It is some good we expect to find, we aim at it; it is here we may look for temptations.

" Christ's life from the beginning to the end was a temptation. He was always being tempted. Mary was tempted. The successful issue of a temptation does not prove that there was no temptation before the victory.

" There were three things in Christ's temptation, and there are three ways in which satan tempts us, and which cause the greater number of our failures.

" The first, we are not where God wills us to be; we feel temptation, we wish to make a change, to get rid of an office, or to change places to get out of the way of temptation, and instead of that, we have all the temptation, and new difficulties added to our first ones. We will be tempted in our new place as much, or more than we were before, for we shall have our former temptation with new ones added. Go where you will, you will be tempted. As I said in the first place, you cannot escape temptation; if you had remained where you were, God would have given you grace and strength to be victorious; He is too merciful not to do so, and the reason why so many souls are wrecked is because they are not found where God wants them. They marry without consulting God; they marry at a time and in a place and whom God never intended them to marry. They are not where God wants them; they are themselves to blame, and it is a miracle if they are saved from shipwreck. They follow their inclinations and their passions, instead of consulting God. This, then, is the first point.

" The second you may say is far-fetched, paradoxical, if you will; Christ was victorious, because He was where God wanted Him to be, and there satan found Him, and tried to deceive Him by calling things by their wrong names. Satan knew who He was, though it is frequently said that he did not, but he knew that He was the Son of God. ' You are the Son of God, use the power which is rightly yours as the Son of God, turn these stones into bread, and do not remain hungry, like some miserable tramp.' Our Lord replied: ' It is true, I feel the pangs of hunger keenly, but I am not miserable, for I enjoy a delicious food, far above the food of the lower nature, which none can suspect, and it is by this suffering of the lower nature that the higher nature is fed.'

" Then the third is far-fetched, paradoxical, if you choose, but we will see its truth. There are some temptations which God has purposely allowed, where satan has a certain power over us. Our Lord wishes us to remain passive, under these temptations, and not try to overcome them, as He was passive under temptation. Satan took Him where he pleased. We would not allow this to ourselves, we are too good for that; but satan took our Lord whither and thither he would, and Christ was passive. ' Here you are on the top of the temple, see the immense concourse of people passing below, cast your eye down and manifest your power, and then your influence will gain all.' Our Lord was passive, so must we be in temptation of this kind, however sharp, putting our trust in God's protecting grace."

SERMON GIVEN ON ASH WEDNESDAY

1903.

" Through the sacred writings a great many names have been given to our blessed Lord to express what He is, and what He has done for us, and of these many names there is one that I have never heard applied to Him, and the one of which He seems to be the most deserving — that of Painter. He is the first of painters, a supreme painter, to whom none that have followed can be compared. He does not paint to please the eye, but to reproduce His image in the soul. He sometimes paints in words, sometimes in things, sometimes in both together; He paints principles and He paints the stimulus to act upon those principles.

" We see the story of last Sunday's Gospel etched with a few strokes of the pencil and very few words, but containing a great deal — the root disease which we all inherit, and which we bring with us into the world; its effects upon us; how it is cured, and the effect Christ has upon us in curing this disease.

" The story is that of a blind man, the root disease blindness. Some think the evil is pride, but I think it is blindness; pride is the effect of blindness. We are all blind in a certain degree: some are totally blind, others more or less so. We shall never see things clearly in this world; we shall never see things as God sees them, for who could see things as God sees them and be blind or proud?

" The man in the Gospel was a beggar. Because he was blind he could do nothing but sit by the wayside begging, and living on the chance alms given by those who had compassion for him.

" The world is the wayside, and every one is a beggar: he begs a little from his eyes, a little from his palate, a little from his bed, a morsel from each, that lasts but a moment, a passing satisfaction, and then he has to beg more. We beg from all creatures, and since we receive but a morsel it is soon consumed, for created things can never fully satisfy.

" And again, he is sitting by the wayside, for while we are being fed with these morsels we are not going on.

" The wise of this world beg not of this world; they have within themselves an estate which is Christ Himself. The revenue goes on all the time, and so far as we are united to Christ do we derive revenues from this estate, an all-sufficiency for every need. All things are passing and Jesus in them, in sickness and health, in peace and trouble; every opportunity for meriting grace once forfeited is forfeited for eternity. This is what makes life so solemn.

" I know St. Paul says: ' Redeem the time past,' and these words are generally misinterpreted, for there is no such thing as redeeming past time. St. Paul meant to redeem the future, that is, to be in such disposition of heart and mind as will enable us to get the graces that are meant for us in the future. For there is one thing which God does not do. He does not give us back time, or past time, if you choose. Time gone is gone forever.

" A Mass followed negligently does not bring fruit to our soul. Christ passes by, and we can never get those graces intended for us in that particular Mass. We may get fruit from another Mass, but none from the one that has passed.

" The one thing necessary to effect a cure is *to watch*. This is only said once in the Gospel, at least as far as I know: ' What I say to you, I say to all: Watch.'

Rt. Rev. A. A. Curtis, D.D.

"Our Lord was going to Jerusalem and would not return. It was an unusual event. Therefore, the blind man felt the necessity of watching, keeping himself awake that Jesus might not pass by unperceived, as He would not return that way ever again, and when he heard a noise he asked what it meant. He was told that it was Jesus of Nazareth passing by. The blind man knew what he wanted, it was clear in his soul, and when our Lord asked him what he wanted, he immediately answered: 'Lord, that I may see.' He merged his whole soul in that prayer. No doubt he was pushed aside with the words: 'Who are you, you blind beggar, interrupting the Master and Teacher,' but in spite of obstacles and opposition he continued his prayer and received his cure from the power of Christ. He did not then go home, he did not turn around to be felicitated on his cure, but he followed Christ, magnifying God, not only in word but in act.

"Thus we should follow Christ, magnifying the Lord as Mary did in her Magnificat: 'My soul doth magnify the Lord, and my spirit hath rejoiced in God my Saviour' — making little of everything else, of all created things, even making little of the Sacraments except as far as God intends them to be used. Depend only on Christ and not even on good things; it may sound rash, but it is true, we should make little of the Altar and of the Sacraments. We must not depend even on the best things *apart* from Christ. Of course, as long as we can receive the Sacraments it would be a sin not to do so, but we must use even the best things only as *means* to lead us to Christ, so that if the Altar were taken from us, if we could not receive the Sacraments or have Priests, if we were in the depths of the ocean or in the wilderness we would have Christ in our own soul — have Him present in us — the All-sufficient, Eternal Good. Let us rejoice in the Lord our Saviour! This will be the effect of the cure; it will withdraw us from everything, we shall depend upon nothing but Christ, who dwells in the soul. Let us ask grace to imitate the blind man of the Gospel, during this holy Season of Lent, watching to see Jesus go by for He will not return this way."

SERMON AT A REQUIEM MASS — ASH WEDNESDAY
March 8, 1905.

After having offered the Requiem Mass for the repose of the soul of the venerated Sister ———, the holy Bishop stood at the altar and said these words:

" The most fitting tribute to the dead is silence. The Church leaves no place in her Ceremonial for words during the Burial Service. Words are useless; they cannot help the dead, they cannot help the living. Praises cannot help the dead, they do not help the living. The hearts to which death does not speak will never be touched by human words. Silence, then, in the presence of the great Judge; this is His act, and words are impertinent. I don't mean in the ordinary sense of the word, but I mean that it is impertinent, unsuitable to speak in the face of death.

" If you were admiring a beautiful sunset, and some one would attempt to describe it to you, — or in the awful impressiveness of a storm at sea, would you not think it out of place and unfitting for anyone to undertake to give you a discourse, or lecture on it? Such a one would be considered a fool, and so is one who speaks in the face of death. I am old enough to know I am a fool, but since I have opened my mouth, I shall say but two things to you and then stop. The first is: Don't say Sister ——— is a loss; no, don't say Sister ——— is a loss. You may say you miss her, for we often miss a thing which is no loss. You may say you miss her as much as you please, but don't say Sister ——— is a loss. God is all goodness and never inflicts a loss upon anybody. He cannot do anything that would create a loss. It is a libel to say that anyone could suffer a loss at the hands of God. If God lends us a good thing, He is free to take it from us again. We cannot say that Sister —— has suffered loss, for she has passed from darkness into light. We are not to pronounce judgment: the judgments of God are so great that even the great St. Paul said: 'I dare not judge myself.'

"In some countries it is a criminal offence to canvas a cause before the cause has been decided by the judge; I do not say in our own country where the Press is a greater tyrant than the Czar, but I speak of other countries where they are not so free and have not gone so far to the bad as we have. But how dare we to speak in the presence of the Supreme Judge; He has decided this case, it is His act.

"The second point is: Don't say that Sister —— is too good to need prayers. I fear many a poor priest has remained a long time in Purgatory because he was not helped by prayers. Pray for Sister ——, keep her in your mind, take her with you to your work, keep her in your heart, take her to your meditations, remember her in all your Communions, and pray for all the poor souls in Purgatory. They will not do less for you than you do for them, and I believe that God would sooner be moved by their uplifted hands in the midst of burning flames, than by the prayers of the Saints, who are already enjoying the bliss of Heaven. I would rather commit my cause to them than to plead for myself; and we will all pray for Sister ——."

The unexpected demise of this beloved Sister was a source of great sorrow to the community which she had governed as superioress for several years, and the Bishop knowing and appreciating her worth entered into the feelings of his daughters, and wept with them, while encouraging them to be *strong* and *valiant* in the face of death. During her illness on hearing of the crisis, although sick himself, he took the first train from Baltimore, and reached the Monastery only in time to learn that his beloved daughter had passed to a better world, or, as he expressed it, " had passed from darkness into light."

After the funeral Bishop Curtis, on returning from the grave, went immediately to the confessional before breaking his fast. After he had heard all the confessions he dined, and then said to the superioress, " I will enter the enclosure and speak to the community." With eyes filled with tears he sat in the assembly room, and spoke these words of comfort:

" My children, I have just two things to say to you, and then I will give you my blessing. There is a passage in Saint Chrysostom that comes to me now, and which I often think of. There was a great palace, and there were many rooms in this palace, and all the doors were locked. People ran up and down looking for keys; one key was found, and with this key they tried to open door after door. It was found to open the last door, but to all the other doors this key was useless. So it is with sorrow — it is useless, and can be made pernicious. And yet it cannot be altogether useless, for God does not wish a useless thing. The only sorrow that is useful, is sorrow for sin. God must have made sorrow only for sin, for God is all goodness; He could not do a thing which would be a loss to us. I do not say we must not feel sorrow, but to foster it as a thing which is good and desirable — I say no, for this sorrow cannot help us, nor can it help her who has left us. If this sorrow helps no one, it is therefore useless, and God does not wish a useless thing.

" If God gives us a gift for thirty odd years, we ought to thank Him for the enjoyment of this gift for so long a time, and not grieve when He takes back what belongs to Him to place it in safety, for life is so full of responsibilities and dangers, that even with our greatest care and attention we stumble or fall. You see a height which you think you can reach, and when that is secured, up beyond is another, and still another; so that it is like walking on a tight rope across the Niagara river, bending beneath the weight of a heavy load, bending first to one side, then to the other, always in danger of falling into the abyss below.

"Now the second thing I have to say is about David. David showed himself very sensible in his conduct after the death of the child of his sin. When the child was living, David chastised himself, wept, abstained from food and drink, threw himself upon sack-cloth and ashes, prayed, and cried to the Lord to spare the life of the child. When the child died, the servants were afraid to tell him, and they said to each other: 'Who will tell him that the child is dead?' for they were afraid. David heard them whispering, and said: 'Is the child dead?' They answered: 'Yes, the child is dead.' Then David arose, washed himself and asked for food. His attendants said: 'What does this mean? When the child lived, you fasted, prayed and wept, and now that the child is dead, you cease to weep.' David answered: 'What more can I do? While the child lived I hoped to touch the Heart of God; but now that God has taken him, he cannot come back to me, but I can go to him.'

"Now this is the way we must do. Sister —— cannot come back to us, but we can go to her. 'Blessed are the dead who die in the Lord,' not happy, but *blessed* are the dead who die in the Lord. Death is God's greatest gift; it is the only entrance into peace and safety. I have often wondered at the manifestation of grief in the presence of death; and this manifestation of sorrow is often a scandal to others, not of our faith. They say, 'Where is your faith? you believe, and your actions are a contradiction to your belief.'" Here the venerable Bishop wiped the tears from his eyes as he said: "Now, my children, I will give you my blessing," and while the sisters were still kneeling, he passed out of the room. The effect of his words, so

Sermons

full of faith, can be likened only to oil poured upon the troubled waters, or as if a riven cloud revealed a rainbow from above, and it seemed that each heart heard within its depths a gentle voice saying: " What I do, thou knowest not now, but thou shalt know hereafter." St. John xiii. 7.

SERMON ON THE TWENTIETH SUNDAY AFTER PENTECOST

October 29, 1905.

" The last words of the Gospel of to-day are: ' And himself believed and his whole house.' And it must have been a large house, for he was a Centurion. And the whole house believed! And why did they believe? Ah! there 's the great secret; they believed because he believed.

" If you know anything about scholastic theology you will know that there are two parts in Faith: potency and action. The potency comes from God; action from our coöperation. Scientists make many mistakes, but they teach this truth, that no atom of life can be produced without prior life, and so the Centurion could not have imparted this Faith, unless he, himself, believed.

" If the Apostles had not had their tremendous faith their miracles would have availed them little. The world saw that those men had something which they themselves lacked. The Apostles accomplished what they did by the all-sufficiency of their faith in Jesus Christ; not by what was found in books.

" I hope, my children, that none of you will ever take it into your heads that you have a vocation to write or publish books! The world is suffocated with books! The printing press thinks it possesses all power and is doing everything. Where then was the power of the Apostles? Was it from discourses and reasoning? Saint Paul says that ' Faith cometh by hearing.'

Rt. Rev. A. A. Curtis, D.D.

In holy Scripture the word 'hearing' signifies all the senses, seeing, or coming in contact with.

"You have a mission, for no one lives for himself alone; your mission is not for exterior works, but your lives should be such that as a good odor, you should manifest the all-sufficiency of faith in Jesus Christ. This faith should be in your eyes, on your lips, in your hands; your whole life should be as a good odor to manifest the all-sufficiency of faith in Jesus Christ."

SERMONS GIVEN TO THE LAITY

THE plain, practical exposition of the Gospels which the holy Bishop took so much pleasure in developing for the use of his Spiritual daughters is followed by a few select Sermons given to the faithful.

In admiring the originality of their style and deducing the practical lessons contained therein, it is to be regretted that they are so few in number.

The Bishop, when speaking on topics into which theology entered, often employed his own characteristic style, rather than the scientific expressions with which those trained from youth in the Catholic schools and colleges are familiar. It is not, therefore, surprising that the lack of early training in formal terms sometimes appeared, and was criticised; although in essence his philosophy and theology were never at fault.

THE NARROW GATE

THE ONE CONDITION NECESSARY FOR ENTERING IT

Preached in the Cathedral, Baltimore, 1900

"Strive to enter by the narrow gate, for many, I say to you, shall seek to enter and shall not be able." LUKE xiii. 24.

"One who is not able to do anything, does not, on account of failure, deserve even the mildest kind of censure. Our Lord presumes, takes it for granted that every one without exception has the power, the ability to make his way through the narrow gate. We are given to understand what is meant by the narrow gate, and there can be no room for misunderstanding it.

"Our Lord Himself is the One Only Door, but the question may occur: 'Is it anything less than blasphemy to call our Lord narrow?' Yes, so it would be undoubtedly, but for His own word: if He had not Himself often and thoroughly affirmed that the way is narrow. Is He narrow? Yes and no. As to His power to save and to receive all into the Heavenly Kingdom? *No,* a thousand times no. Is He narrow as to the sole condition upon which He will use His power? *Yes,* a thousand times, yes; terrifically narrow. If we brought Him a whole world full of things beautiful, ornate, splendid, necessary and should not bring Him the one thing necessary, He would reject us as absolutely, as entirely as if we brought Him nothing.

" A public life; a public life, if you please, ingenious in devising, persevering in executing, filled with schemes for the good of the people, plans for the purification of politics, for the betterment of education, as to morals, for the comfort of the Community; in all this there is nothing which can with success challenge Christ, ' the Narrow Gate.'

" A private life; a private life, indeed, pure and undefiled, cannot, on account of its own value, claim to possess a right and just and sufficient title, to enter by the narrow door.

" Parishes founded, dioceses governed and increased, food given to the poor, in all this, nothing which by itself, of itself and for itself, gives right and title to pass the narrow gate. The one thing needed, the one thing necessary, is not purity, truth, honesty, self-denial nor any other virtue public or private. All these exist, and prominently exist, at times, apart from the one thing in question. The supreme, important thing, the vitally necessary thing is that we must love Christ, we must center all our being in Him, we must adhere to Him in all things. We must have a supreme esteem for the person of Jesus. He is all, the Beginning and the End of everything.

" Let one come before that gate with riches heaped up on earth, with a great and useful life behind him, but without that great value for Christ, and he will knock and knock for all eternity in vain. Never for him will that gate open.

" Our Lord pictures the striving by which alone we attain to that condition. ' Agonize; agonize, enter the narrow gate.' The ancient athletes who contested in the great Grecian games were called agonistes. The ancient athlete did not prepare at stated times, but, says Saint Paul, ' he governed himself at all times, as to all things.'

" We know what we must do during this season. Before another Lent shall come that tremendous trumpet may sound, encompassing the whole earth; that trumpet, under whose pealing nations shall tremble. It will signify the close of the contest.

" But if that trumpet be not sounded, there is something else. The Angel of death may visit any one of us. The particular judgment will decide as thoroughly as to the individual, as the last judgment as to all.

" We know not how soon we shall be called upon to prove ourselves able or unable to pass the narrow gate. Let us put away all sloth and indifference, and urge ourselves once and for all to produce, to maintain and to increase in our souls, not only piety and devotion and the use of the Sacraments, but the adhesion to Christ and attachment to Him and His Will for time and eternity, which alone shall suffice."

*Preached in St. Peter's Cathedral, Wilmington,
February 27, 1901*

" The Leper coming, adored Him, saying: Lord, if Thou wilt, Thou canst make me clean." MATT. viii. 2.

" There is a vast difference between a science and an art, although they are generally confounded. One may be versed in the science of theology, and yet be totally ignorant of the *art*. One may be master of the science of music, and yet be entirely lacking in its art.

Rt. Rev. A. A. Curtis, D.D.

" An art can be learned in two ways. One must be under the constant influence of a teacher, skilled in the art. He must associate with that teacher, he must practise under his guidance, he must absorb the art from the teacher, who is its very embodiment.

" Another way to acquire an art is the slow, painful process of plodding, profiting by one's mistakes, stumbling at times, yet all the while endeavoring to acquire the art by constant efforts. Now, I am going to speak to you of an art that is the most difficult of all arts to acquire. And what is that art, dear children? It is the art of prayer, the art on which so much depends, both in this life and in eternity. The art of prayer, the art above all arts. The art of prayer, the art which if mastered will decide our destiny, no matter who we are, or where we are.

" He who has learned the art of prayer has all that he needs for time and for eternity; he may be in a solitary desert, deprived of the Sacraments and of all other spiritual helps, yet, if he has the art of prayer, he has that which will make his eternity one of super-excellent sanctity, provided, of course, that he is deprived of Sacramental graces through no fault of his.

" Another may confess and communicate often, may spend most of his time in the church, and yet be very far from pleasing God, in fact, be in great danger of eternal damnation, and why? He has not learned the art of prayer.

" Well, as I remarked before, there are two ways of learning an art, or two ways in which we can learn an art. First from a teacher, who is its perfect embodiment, now who is such a teacher of the art of prayer? It is the Leper, who, coming, adored Him, saying: ' Lord, if Thou wilt, Thou canst make me clean.' Let us contemplate the Leper and learn from him this art, so important and so necessary for us.

" The first thing he did was to renounce all. He separated himself from his wife and children, if he had

364

any; he cut himself away from his associates; he
stopped his occupation; he banished all distracting
thoughts; his whole mind was directed towards Jesus,
and Jesus alone.

" Ah! even in this, the beginning of the art of prayer,
we fail. We do not detach ourselves from everything,
and let our mind dwell on Jesus alone. Like the Leper
we should realize that everything in the world is nothing: Christ is *all*. The art of prayer cannot be mastered until we learn to leave everything, to annihilate
the world from our thoughts, to have our thoughts
intent on nought but Jesus, to think of Him and Him
only.

" Do you think that is an easy thing to do? Can
one in a few moments, as some persons really think,
easily prepare oneself as the Leper did, by renunciation of all that would distract him from the art of
prayer? Ah! no, this art is not learned in a moment,
but is mastered only by constant vigilance at all times,
and in all places; in the street, in bed, at work, wherever we are, we must learn to separate ourselves from
the persons, places or things that surround us; we
must train ourselves to be deaf to them, that we may
think of Jesus.

" The next thought that strikes us when we contemplate the Leper is, that he adored Jesus. 'The Leper
coming adored Him.' Do you realize what these
words mean? Ah! we fail here too. Do we adore
Him? Lord, Thou art my God and my All! Thou
art the King of kings and I am nothing. Thou art
all-powerful, and I am but a worm of the earth; Thou
art worthy of all love and praise; I adore Thee!

" Such words as these were poured forth by the leper,
in adoration. Do we ever think of adoring Jesus?
Beyond a slight recognition of His patience, His mercy
and forbearance, does the thought of adoring Jesus
often enter our minds at prayer? Rather do not our
prayers consist of favors and petitions we wish Him

Rt. Rev. A. A. Curtis, D.D.

to grant? Do we not ask for this and that and the other favor, instead of offering Him the Adoration which should be offered to Him? Would you value the friendship of one who never spoke to you, except to ask of you a favor, who only recognized you when he wished you to confer some benefit upon himself, or upon some one in whom he was interested?

"Let us learn, then, that after endeavoring to free our mind from distractions, our next duty in the art of prayer is to adore Jesus. Another point that strikes us in the Leper's prayer is his perfect conformity to the will of God, his utter dependence upon Him. He did not tell Jesus what he thought He ought to do; he did not say: Lord, I am very sick, cure me. Ah! no, his was a different prayer. 'Lord, Thou knowest all things; Thou knowest me; Thou knowest how blind I am; Thou knowest whether it is best for me to remain sick, or to be cured. I know Thou canst cure me if Thou wilt; do with me as Thou wilt, let me remain a leper, or let me be cured; as Thou wilt let it be done to me.'

"Ah, how few of us pray as this Leper prayed! He knew he was best cared for when he was in the hands of Jesus. Do we not, in our folly, dictate to Jesus, instead of placing ourselves without reserve into His hands to do with us according to His holy Will?

"We shall not understand the art of prayer until we learn to detach ourselves from outside distractions, to adore Jesus, and to commit ourselves to His guidance. Then our prayer will be heard; Jesus will never turn a deaf ear to the soul that prays like the leper, with full confidence that whatever Jesus wills is always best.

"We often hear people say: 'My prayers are not answered; I may as well give up praying.' This is simply foolishness. No prayer rightly made remains unanswered; but remember we should pray that God's will and not ours may be accomplished. Then rest assured that all our prayers, whether they be for the Church or for our own spiritual or temporal needs, will be answered in God's way, by giving us what He sees best for us.

" We make grave mistakes with regard to spiritual as well as temporal necessities. We ask for more faith, more charity and for other graces, and we think that our prayer is unanswered, because we do not see its effect. God knows that if we saw we had more faith, we might have more pride; if we saw we had more charity, it might mean the loss of some other virtue.

" God gives us the graces He sees most necessary for us, when we leave ourselves to His care, to be dealt with as He wills. Prayer need not be accompanied by petitions for favors or graces. The best of all prayers is the adoration of the soul, the homage rendered by the creature to his Creator, the acknowledgment of the power, majesty, wisdom and perfection of God, and our utter dependence on Him.

" Let us try to learn the art of prayer; let us with the disciple say again and again: 'Lord, teach us how to pray.' Having learned this art, we need have no fear. Detached in spirit from worldly distractions, with a soul adoring the God of Heaven and earth, with full confidence in Him, we cannot fail to reach the state of perfection He requires of each one of us, and thus win for ourselves a blessed Eternity."

" What think you of Christ? " MATT. xxii. 42.

" Of all questions this is without doubt the most momentous. Answer other queries mistakenly, and you will suffer little, if at all, provided you know, and are prepared and determined to act upon what ought to be thought of Christ. You may err as to, or be ignorant of biology, psychology, geology, sociology and all other ologies discovered, or going to be discovered, theology itself included, and notwithstanding live a hero, die a saint, and then flash quicker than thought straight up from the rocking, raging, restless, treacherous, bitter sea of this life, to an eternal home in the bosom of God, provided you clearly know, fully remember, and as the one sufficient, sovereign aim of life, study to render what is due to the one, single Person of Christ. And 'What think you of Christ?' is as comprehensive as momentous. It addresses itself to every individual, and is propounded to, and must be answered by, every nation, and in either case the answer will be decisive as to the value of the present and the character of what is to come. For all questions whether concerning the nation or individual are comprehended in the single demand, what think you of Christ? and are virtually answered when we fully and rightly reply to that single demand. State-craft must kneel before Him, and with full submission and loyalty hear and record for invariable use His sacred instructions, and then address itself to the solution of its problems, or else every statesman will be simply Pontius Pilate over again; that is, one parrying present threats at the price of his own downfall, and the utter destruction in the future of the people he for the moment contents. And the sciences too must group themselves in adoration around the august Person of Christ, and thence each following some ray emanating from Him, make their excursions into the darkness, to return incessantly whence they started, — otherwise they will lose themselves totally in that darkness, uselessly wandering to and fro, and accomplishing nothing save to mislead one another in spouting out lies as to clues, which end in nothing, and paths that tangle themselves more and more, and never bring any one nearer to an issue into light or an arrival at a worthy destination. And this supreme question is not only so momentous, so comprehensive, so aimed at each individual and at each agglomeration of individuals, but it is imperishable!"

Sermons

" When thou art invited to a wedding, sit not down in the
first place. . . . But . . . go, sit down in the lowest place."
                                        LUKE xiv. 8–10.

" A. The Church and what we possess and enjoy
in the Church are signified by this wedding feast. And
the Church is likened unto a wedding, as growing out
of and depending upon the perpetual union, in the one
Person of Christ, of two things in themselves so wide
apart as the nature of man, and the nature of God.
Again, the Church is a wedding, because the final intent and effect of the Church, if not thwarted, are to
unite each of us wholly and forever with God, without
loss, of course, to our personal identity. Furthermore,
the Church is represented under the wedding feast, as
implying that in the Church alone we find not merely
what our strict needs require, but if we will, a rich,
rare, costly, sufficient, lavish provision for all our
proper desires and tastes. Yet once more, the Church
is typified under a wedding feast as signifying the
unity, amenity, sharing with one another, and service
of one another, which ought to exist, and conspicuously
exist, too, among Catholics. Finally, the Church finds
its symbol in a wedding feast as teaching us that to
be fit for a place in the Church, we need to be specially
and nicely clothed with grace, and the effects of grace.
And unless so clothed, we are warned as to what will
be said to us and done with us, when the King enters
to inspect His guests. ' Friend, how camest thou in
hither, not having on a wedding garment? Bind him
hand and foot, take him away, and cast him into the
exterior darkness.' We may then well question ourselves as to whether we possess such a garment as will
stand the scrutiny of the King. And whether, too, we
are finding in the Church, a rich and perpetual feast of
the soul; or whether on the contrary, while in the
midst of such a superabundance, not merely of necessary food, but of dainties, many and delicious, we
are notwithstanding, from the simple failure to appre-

369

ciate and use what is always before us and within our
reach, more empty, hungry and restless than are many
for the time, by virtue of feeding to the full upon the
poisonous, fever and delirium-producing things, set
before them by the world.

" B. We, then, are called in the Church to the
rich and only fully satisfying Table of the Lord. And
next note well something which to one having as yet
never looked very deeply and closely into himself may
seem strange and even false. Namely, our Lord implies that each of the guests at His wonderful feast
is disposed to claim for himself the very highest of all
the many seats provided, which is another way of saying that every man is by nature prone to assume that
he is immeasurably better than anybody else, and entitled to gratify even his mere whims, at any cost whatever to any number of other men. And would this
were all, but naturally the folly and malice of each
human soul goes infinitely further, for until re-begotten,
enlightened, subdued and transformed by Christ, each
is not only disposed to take for granted that he is of
more worth than the rest of mankind, but each just
escapes being incurably impregnated with the mon-
strous delusion that he is a great deal better than
God Himself. I can't take the time to demonstrate
the truth of this tremendous assertion. And I feel
quite sure that to some — perhaps to all of you —
this assertion will seem to be hideously, enormously
false. But charge your memories with what I assert,
and if you go on thinking, praying and studying yourselves, and if ten or twenty years hence, you still remember the preacher and his hideous accusation of
human nature, you will say to yourself, whatever may
be the case of others, yet as regards myself, the Bishop
of Wilmington said simply the truth, when he affirmed
that until of Christ re-created, every man assumes, not
only that he is entitled to trample down all other men,
in order to get anything he chances much to desire,

but entitled also to make nothing at all of God Himself, in behalf of the fulfilment of any one of his caprices.

"C. Note next, how our Lord intimates that the only way of curing our innate propensity to arrogate to oneself the highest seat, is to make oneself take the lowest seat of all. The seat, it is plain, is not any exterior position. Because exteriorly there is but one lowest seat and one only can occupy that. But our Lord recommends each and every one to take the lowest seat. This seat then is to be found in the heart of each. Exterior prominence and superiority have nothing to do with it. The Pope not only may occupy, but ought to occupy, — and he will not be enviable hereafter unless he does at once occupy, — the highest exterior and the lowest interior seat; that is to say, every Christian, from the Pope down to the collector of garbage, ought to study to impress himself more and more with the ever present, ever effective conviction that he is the very least and lowest of the children of Adam. Half measures will not succeed. If we do not incessantly and vigorously depress ourselves down to the very bottom in our own esteem, we shall be eternally climbing to the very apex, not only above men and angels, but over God Himself.

"How well Mary had learned this secret, and hence at the very moment when assured that she was to be above all creatures and next to God Himself — she said not 'happy Mary,' but 'my soul doth magnify the Lord' — because He hath vouchsafed to cast a glance upon the baseness and abjection of His slave. So, then, we must genuinely aim to make ourselves last, or we shall not cure thoroughly even if we begin to cure ourselves, of the hideous insanity of tacitly taking it for granted that we are the very first of all. But, one says, this is too much. There ought to be reason in all things. And, then, can any good come of thinking and acting a lie, even in behalf of the acquisition of a thing so beautiful and restful as lowliness? I am not the lowest of all, and why should I pretend that I am? I know that I have more sense than some possess, and I know, too, that I am not as bad as many others. But listen: what do you really and truly know of others? A good deal less than just nothing at all. You are full of imaginations about others, and nearly all utterly false, and the rest having a little truth mixed with and nullified by a great deal more of falsehood. And ignorance is better than delusion. You, then, genuinely know nothing of any one save yourself. And of your own self you know little fully and indefeasibly save that you have always been an immense fool, and have been over and over again guilty of sins, the length, breadth, height and depth of which God alone can adequately appreciate. You, then, really know — nor can ever come thus to know — of your neighbor anything justifying you in making little of him, while on the other hand, of yourself, and as really belonging to yourself, you know nothing at all save that you are, and always have been, an inexhaustible mine and magazine of folly and sin. But upon which should we act, ignorance or knowledge? Knowledge, of course. Of my neighbor, then, I know almost nothing, and what I really do know, not what I imagine of him, all tends to entitle him to my veneration. For I do know that he is the child of God, and is redeemed of Christ, is dear to Mary and wonderfully valued of the Angels. But whether he has much or little sense I cannot tell. For most real sense is most to love and serve God and man, according to one's place, abilities and graces. And I am far from being able to determine with certainty, that the murderer going to be hanged to-morrow, would not have loved and served God more than I have done, had he had my graces, abilities and opportunities. Able, then, to be absolutely certain of nothing to my neighbor's discredit, I am absolutely certain of a host of things proving me

filled with hideous malice and boundless folly. And
being certain of so much more to my discredit than
I can ever become certain of with respect to any one
else; reason, as well as the word of the Lord, affirms,
that instead of putting any one below myself on account of the imagination of infirmity on his part, I
ought rather to esteem myself least of all on account
of certainly knowing of myself such foolishness and
guiltiness, as I can never with certainty and safety
ascribe to anybody else. But, be it that you know
that you have more sense and goodness than some
others whom you have seen, or of whom you have
heard, are that sense and goodness really your own?
If not, be they as great as they may, how do they
furnish any reason for putting yourself before others?
My neighbor and myself are going along together to
the same bank, each with nothing at all of his own in
his pocket, but I carrying a larger sum than he to
be deposited, in either case to the credit of neither.
Have I any right to regard myself as richer than he
because I am entrusted with a larger sum than he
transports? If not, how am I better than my neighbor because I am carrying towards judgment and the
day of accounting for all, more of God's goods than
God has been pleased to entrust to some of my neighbors? God's gifts then are God's glory, and ought
not to be falsely and wrongly perverted as to foster
man's self-esteem. What is truly and altogether my
own is, then, not sense or goodness; but the immense
and incessant frustration in myself and in others of
God's gifts, graces and operations — I know how great
and obstinate this frustration has been, and still is,
on my own part. But never can I come to know with
certainty that such frustration has been greater in
any one else whomsoever than in my own self. And
again, what I indefeasibly know of myself ought to
triumph over what I can at best but suspect as to
others; hence reason puts truth and certainty before

the most uncertain of suspicious reckoning. Christ says: Put your known frustration of God — your only real piece of true property — before an imagined deficiency on the part of your neighbor, draw thence your conclusions, and do your utmost to get and keep below him."

SHORT SAYINGS FROM VARIOUS
SERMONS

"WE must pray for Faith. We think we have it, but if on occasions we sift things to the bottom we will find that we have more faith in our own judgment, our wisdom, even our senses and inclinations, than we have in the wisdom and goodness of God. If this were not so, we would not be constantly choosing one thing and rejecting another."

"What a terrible thing it is to communicate hasty impressions! Remember this one thing — it is terrible, but it is a fact, that when an accusation is once made (O when you come to think of it, it is terrible!) that person is never just the same as he was before the accusation was made, even if he is not in fault, still he is not the same. When this is done, you injure yourself, the one who listens, and the one of whom it is spoken."

"There is one thing that gives a charm to life in the world, and that is mutual, respectful intercourse, cordial politeness and courtesy. It adds so much to peace and happiness to see and feel the mutual respect which comes from the recognition of God's image."

"And the Angel departed from her."

"Had the messenger been other than an Angel, a man, even a good, holy man, he would have waited to ask some questions; but the Angel having fulfilled the mission of God departed."

Feast of the Annunciation.

375

Rt. Rev. A. A. Curtis, D.D.

" Ridicule, even if not meant, shows clearly that at bottom we have no respect for the person, — for where there is respect there cannot be ridicule. Of all dangers, scorn is the most to be feared.

" Tennyson, who was not a spiritual man, said:

' For in those days no knight of Arthur's noblest dealt in scorn;
But if a man were halt or hunched, in him
By those whom God had made full-limbed and tall,
Scorn was allowed as part of his defect,
And he was answered softly by the King
And all his table ' —

" The poets sometimes have very clear spiritual insight. A noble soul could have but a noble thought, a mind that could entertain, or give birth to thoughts of scorn, must indeed be a mind mis-shapen and deformed.

" There are some who by nature see the ridiculous first. They are struck by it, and it is a dangerous disposition. It can bring them no good to prove that others are in fault. It is so foolish; they can be no better for showing up the faults of others; it adds nothing to their merit to prove that others are in fault. The person who is censured does not hear it, cannot correct the fault; and the one to whom they speak is injured by the conversation."

IV
NOTES FOR RETREATS

GIVEN ON FOUR DIFFERENT OCCASIONS TO PRIESTS

*Found in Note-books in Bishop Curtis' own
Handwriting*

INTRODUCTION

THE complete and perfect arrangement of Notes for retreats, the " Three Hours' Prayer " and the selected quotations from the early Fathers, give a better idea of the Bishop's depth of intellect and sublimity of thought than anything that has preceded; these are invaluable in portraying the greatness of his ascetic soul. The care and precision in collecting these notes, traced by his own hand, testify to the admirable order which reigned in him, and which was conspicuous throughout his whole career.

The first of these retreats was given in Baltimore at Saint Mary's Seminary in the year 1896 to the Clergy of the Diocese of Wilmington, and of the Archdiocese. Although he had preached a good number of retreats to Religious and seculars as a priest and afterwards as Bishop, this was the beginning of a series of retreats to the Clergy, Seminarians and Students of the Universities and Colleges.

For years the Bishop had a burning desire to deliver his soul to the Clergy in a retreat, and now as he neared the time of his resignation of the See of Wilmington, the Will of God was made manifest by a sort of command on the part of Cardinal Gibbons. Hitherto His Eminence had requested it as a favor, but on this occasion the Bishop felt that it was no longer allowed him to refuse.

The Cardinal declared at the close of this retreat that it was the best he had ever attended, " although Father Curtis," as he fondly called his Vicar-General, " did not spare our feelings." Many of the Priests were of the same opinion; and some were heard to say, that it was the first retreat they had ever *really* made. When the Bishop was congratulated on his success and told what a good retreat it had been, " Yes," he replied, " so good, that I had to do penance for it." He actually humbled himself at the close of that retreat by asking pardon of all who participated.

The notes of the retreat are very meager and hardly give more than the substance of the Bishop's deliverances, which consumed more than an hour at each exercise, and it may readily be understood that the preacher, who was a living embodiment of the ideal man of God, must have held his hearers captive by the vigorous intensity of his language and the earnestness of his manner.

" The Three Hours' Prayer," prepared and preached by the Bishop on Good Friday of every year but one during the administration of his Diocese, gives some idea of the knowledge he possessed of Scriptural Church History. The tableaux will no doubt furnish a good object lesson to those Religious and seculars, who can understand and appreciate his rare abilities, while the quotations from the works of the early Fathers and the Pagan Authors display the depth of his ascetical studies.

The Prodigal Son seems to be his favorite subject, for there are no less than three different versions of this old, but oft repeated Story of the Gospel.

In publishing these fragments of the Bishop's Spiritual Doctrine, his saintly influence must be felt and extended, and thus " prolong the sanctifying action of his direction, which was strong and sweet like the Gospel," from whence he drew all his supernatural force.

ST. MARY'S SEMINARY

INTRODUCTORY

A. What am I going to do? Why am I going to do it? How is it to be done?

First. We are going to make a retreat, and what precisely is a retreat? It does not consist in producing in ourselves a present interior glow, this is an accident merely. It may come, and yet rather as an occasion of vitiating than of fructifying our retreat. For resolutions made under sensible fervor very commonly fade away, as that fervor itself exhales. I am far from forbidding anyone from heating his soul till it, so to speak, melts, becomes fluid, and is thus rendered capable of being moulded over into another and better form. I merely wish to assert that the retreat is not primarily for the time of the retreat itself, as a good many I think tacitly at least imagine.

Second. Not principally as a preparation for an extraordinary confession.

Third. Least of all as an act of mere exterior obedience to the Bishop. The thing itself to be distinguished from its appendages — from the means to it, and from all that which is of its integrity, but not of its essence. The thing itself then, or the essence of the retreat — attention.

B. Why do we make the retreat? Because we all imperatively need to make it; if in mortal sin, if in venial sin, if having done well since the last retreat. Some will never make another, dying before the time comes. Worse still, some may live a good while, and never really make another retreat.

Rt. Rev. A. A. Curtis, D.D.

C. How shall we make the retreat? First, we must have the will, genuine will to make it. Second. We must go to bed in due time, and keep out of one another's rooms. Third. We must keep silence. Fourth. Give right attention to preacher, and pray for him.

MEDITATION. TUESDAY MORNING. "THE FEAR OF THE LORD IS THE BEGINNING OF WISDOM"

First Point. What precisely do we mean by the fear of the Lord, *i. e.*, the reason why we fear Him. God's divine attributes of greatness, truth, justice, goodness, love, and particularly the latter. The same God who is infinite love will say to the damned: "Depart from Me, ye accursed!"

Second. Common grounds of this fear. A. May misuse all. B. Propensity to misuse. C. Temptations to misuse. Blindness, coming of misuse; mutability in the good.

Third. Reasons for fear peculiar to the priest: tremendous duties, responsibilities and heinousness of sin in him; so many more ways in which he can sin. His freedom practically from restraint or admonition even. His autocracy, and the veneration and deference of the faithful. His secure position tempting him to take things easily. Formality: professionalism, coming to regard truth, right, humility, penance and all the things he inculcates, as rather for the people than for himself. Becoming taken up with the sense of his immunities and emoluments, to the forgetfulness of his duties and dangers.

Difficulty of converting to a better life. Priests often have only the rule of conscience and the unseen eye of God; and the world, flesh, and the devil laying snares for the abuse of their liberties.

Notes for Retreats

1. Maxims, the good of them if true.

2. Mischief arising when maxims are false, such as a man must look out for himself first. Business is business; this justifies all forms and methods concerning stocks, etc.

3. Greater mischief perhaps when the maxim is ambiguous.

4. Maxim in question very ambiguous. Many kinds of gentlemen.

5. Define a true gentleman, in the only sense in which a priest is permitted to aim at gentlemanliness. Truth, justice, temperance, fortitude, reverence for all things, specially for the weak, lowly and despised; wider, nicer and more intelligent consideration of others as to all things, and very specially as to personal eccentricities and peculiarities. Christ is the model, illustrated in manifold ways; not the least when dying upon the Cross in indescribable agony, He puts His lips to the soporific balm offered Him by a sympathetic soldier, as a courteous recognition, though He would not take the relief. Only a true disciple of Christ can be a true gentleman.

Acting on Principle. A few right principles: Do not do what you cannot do rightly. Do not build or improve churches if you have to contract debt. Do not act when you are in doubt, wait until you get further light.

Principles or maxims to be valuable must be universally applicable. Nothing so dangerous as principles or maxims half truths and half lies; whole lies are not nearly so pernicious.

Rt. Rev. A. A. Curtis, D.D.

CONFERENCE. TUESDAY P. M. EXAMPLE

Example is a great power for good or evil, possessed and exercised by all, at all times, and its effects are for all time. It may be compared to the rings made by casting a stone in the river.

Every man has more or less power of influencing others, and each is responsible for the effect of his example.

Christ an example principally by virtue, not of His official acts, but by means of His private conduct as Son of Man.

A function of the priest is to prolong and perpetuate Christ's example.

Some ways in which we generally disedify by our examples: Want of economy. Restlessness, roving and idleness. Most of all prayerlessness. Priests ought not to be ashamed to be pious; it is their business to be so. Doctors and lawyers are not ashamed to appear what they are; why should priests be otherwise?

MEDITATION. TUESDAY P. M. EARNESTNESS

First Point. What is earnestness? It is not great oratory, great power, emotional feeling. It is not doing anything out of the common. It is constantly, consistently, monotonously accomplishing the duties assigned us by God's authority at every sacrifice. Religious monks and nuns are the highest types. Their lives are the highest sort of martyrdom.

Second Point. Opposed to it is tepidity. It was not a layman, but the highest prelate that the Lord spewed out of His mouth. Indifference, the curse of our age. Indifference, the great enemy everywhere. The liability of the priest to fall into the worst kind of indifference. Fear expels indifference more thoroughly and quickly than anything else.

Notes for Retreats

Third Point. Distinguish earnestness genuine and sustained, from earnestness fitful and rather matter of passing emotion than the effect of principle. Test of genuine earnestness: superiority to monotony and sameness. Power of earnestness as seen in men of the world. The power it too will give the priest, and not only so, but the greater happiness it will bring himself. Grounds of earnestness. God deserves the best service we can give. Priests should not be outdone by laity in loyalty and piety, we become priests of our own volition, none forced us to be such; all we have and are, all intellectual, spiritual and natural gifts ought to be given to the duties of the priesthood.

MEDITATION. WEDNESDAY A. M. REFLECTION

First Point. The fear of the Lord taking hold of us produces earnestness, which in turn begets reflection. What is reflection? Not finding out something new; not proving to others or to one's own self anything. But for one's self alone trying to see more and more the value of truth, once for all previously recognized. It is, as the word signifies in its old meaning, a " bending back," on and into ourselves. Gazing at God while contemplating and dwelling upon any truth applicable to, or applied to our soul. To do this properly it is necessary to drop every other thought and surrounding, and all other consciousness. Distinguish from contemplation, distinguish from discursive thought. Books are not necessary. This form of reflection leads to sanctity, nothing can take its place. Reflection is the nearest, easiest, most ready and most powerful means of sanctification. This is the great work for which everything in the heavens and on earth is created.

Second Point. Necessity of reflection: not reading, not study, not discoursing, not culture nor vocal prayer nor work. In no other possible way can one sufficiently appreciate, assimilate and appropriate the truth. No

Rt. Rev. A. A. Curtis, D.D.

one can sanctify us but ourselves. We must grow, grow, grow in it like the oak. Not God Himself can help us without our coöperation. We ourselves must do the work. We are created alone, one by one. We shall be judged one by one, rewarded or punished one by one. Without reflection there can be no sanctification, and according to reflection will it be proportioned; away then with all theories and formulas. Face to face with God and our own soul, must we reflect.

Third Point. Hints as helps to reflection. Few subjects, and they the principal things, — assign different days of the week for different truths to be reflected upon; for instance, Monday, Sin; Tuesday, Hell; Wednesday, Judgment; Thursday, Real Presence or the Blessed Eucharist; Friday, the Passion; Saturday, Death; and Sunday, Heaven. These are subjects always ready and inexhaustible.

A time every day for reflection — Beads, Office, Mass.

CONFERENCE. WEDNESDAY A. M. "IT IS NOT A MORTAL SIN"

Hypocrites give utterance to such language.

1. What is mortal sin in any one? It is the very effacement of God. The most stupendous mystery is our power to frustrate, aye, to annihilate God's will. This we do by one mortal sin. Examples: A doctor poisoning his patients. A lawyer selling his clients. A general betraying his troops and his country. A watchman burning down the city. Banker investing and stealing deposits. Master scuttling the ship, and drowning the passengers and crew. Mother murdering her children. Wife Clytemnestra slaying Agamemnon. Pilate. Magnates. Judas.

2. What in a Priest? Mortal sin in a priest makes him worse than Judas. A priest ought to be another Joseph, spouse of the Blessed Virgin Mary, and how

is it conceivable that he could live only to avoid mortal sin? Take the priest with his Office. It ought to be his greatest solace to turn to its holy, sweet inspirations after hours spent in listening to the sickening details of poor, sinful humanity. How is it possible that a priest could neglect it, could wish to curtail it?

3. Impossibility of determining even in the case of others what is or is not a mortal sin. Who is the theologian that can always draw the line of demarcation?

4. Dreadfulness of deliberate, venial sin. Venial sins lead to mortal sins. Moral theology was not for one to apply personally to one's self, but officially to others; no man can judge rightly, for when he has judged, when his confessor has judged, it will still be Christ's privilege to judge. Hence St. Paul could say: I do no wrong, yet in this I am not justified, for it is not I, but Christ who judgeth me.

5. All Christians are meant not merely to keep from sin, but to grow in grace and virtue, most of all priests.

CONFERENCE. WEDNESDAY P. M. PREACHING

What is preaching? Not oratorical display; not scolding as to matters personal or parochial, nor even necessary rebuke or instruction on these matters; not putting in so much time; not discussing questions and fads of the day. But the inculcation of something of concern to all, and asserted, or evidently contained, in the everlasting Gospel of Christ, and itself, therefore everlasting. The real ideal orator is the sanctified man. We can all be and we are appointed to be preachers. What is a preacher? The Scripture and our Blessed Lord define him to be a herald — a herald is one who delivers a distinct, definite message of another. Priests have received this definite message, and when they confine themselves to this they are preachers, no matter what their learning or eloquence or defi-

Rt. Rev. A. A. Curtis, D.D.

ciency may be. The message they have received is to preach Christ and Him crucified. This is all, and this is enough to occupy them. What is the use of going hither and thither, boasting and bragging of what one knows nothing about: the future of this nation or of that nation. A preacher must see clearly his message, recognize its worth if he really wants to bring it home to the hearts of his hearers. Never must personal pique find place in him, and never must he mean to reflect upon individuals.

Methods, doctrine and practice always together; brevity; have a distinct proposition; define it; give the cause or grounds of it, and then add the result.

Helps, study of Holy Writ. Select theme, one week ahead — so many things during the week will come up as data and suggestions. Do not keep the people waiting more than one half hour when there is Mass or Vespers; you may be longer without these.

MEDITATION. WEDNESDAY P. M. PRAYER

What is prayer? We can pray without moving our lips. Prayer is a gazing at God. It is an elevation of the soul. It is properly a cry — the cry of weakness, of helplessness — the babbling cry of babes in the dark. A parent loves the babbling of children, and so our Father who is in Heaven loves the babbling of His children. We must pray in submission to, and in union with God's will — as slaves, and not as masters.

Necessity of prayer. Without it no possible sanctification; with it, holiness and true wisdom. St. Thomas got all his science and wisdom at the foot of the Cross. One hour of prayer is worth years of study.

Necessity of prayer for the priest. He is the chief of prayer. He must pray himself, and for himself. He must pray to make up for the deficiencies of his people. The people must learn to pray from his example, and he must pray for his people.

Notes for Retreats

Special danger of prayerlessness. We should make everything a prayer, and pray for the minutest thing, and not be afraid to have familiar intercourse with God.

Prayer most necessary to the priest: officially intercessor; necessary for his own instruction; necessary for his own consolation and support; necessary for his own sanctification.

Breviary — beads.

MEDITATION. THURSDAY A. M. HUMILITY

First Point. Humility is not brooding over, lamenting and dissecting one's sins. It is the contrasting ourselves with God, and thereby concluding our own nothingness, and the doing it unconsciously. The greatest sinners are the proudest; the holiest people are the humblest individuals. Humility of our Lord and Mary. Of David. St. Elizabeth. Saints generally.

Second Point. *Necessity to all;* eminently necessary to a Priest. To save him from becoming specially odious to God. To give him weight and efficiency with the people. To save himself from everlasting discontent, unrest and conflict. Humility is a virtue which demands a life-long struggle to obtain.

Third Point. *Means of humility* — reflection, prayer of course. But even more, fear and avoidance of praise, publicity, appreciation and success. Acceptance of failure, contradiction, opposition. Forgive and forget.

Grounds of it. Otherwise our life is a lie; whereas we are nothing, we think ourselves something. The most odious to God is the proud priest. Humility is our greatest possible comfort in life and death.

CONFERENCE. THURSDAY P. M. " CONFESSIONAL "

Peculiar power and glory of the Church. Preaching, science; confession, art; science deals with generals;

art with individuals. The apex of the priest's power is in the Confessional, where he represents God's purely divine power. In the Mass he is Christ's representative, who Himself is there present, human and divine, priest and victim. In the confessional, it is Christ's divinity alone that he represents exclusively. What a mighty power; what a dangerous one; also what a hard task for the city priest. *How ought a priest go into the confessional?* With preparation and prayer. Assiduity in confessing. Willingness. No undue attempt to classify the people. No rigid insisting upon particular times. No bidding for confessions of those of the reputedly better classes, or those of devotees.

In the confessional neither all sugar, nor still less pure vinegar.

Get children into the confessional as soon as practicable, and as often as practicable. Almost invariably a word or two to each penitent, suggested usually by confession itself, if not by the time or occasion. Practise patience with the ignorant, rude, bad, garrulous.

Sigillum. Never refer privately or publicly to what is told in the sacred tribunal. In the confessional it is the priest's paramount duty to be above and beyond all suspicion. How any priest living in the open evidence of God's work in a country mission could sacrifice these enviable advantages, to be a lackey in the city which witnesses chiefly man's destruction of God's work, is one of the mysteries of blind, fallen humanity.

MEDITATION. THURSDAY P. M. CHARITY

First Point. *Distinguish from counterfeits.* Charity is not liking this and disliking that other. It is not mere sympathy for misery and distress, good nature, family affection, patriotism, indifference. It is not zeal alone.

Second Point. *"Bond of perfection."* When we fear God we drive out indifference and overcome tepidity. Then we grow in reflection by gazing on God and finding Him the only Truth, the only Good, the only Happiness, the only Beauty, the only Life. Finding Him we become earnest, setting our mind and will upon God and the things of God — little and great — and always, and with our whole being; we are in consequence naturally led to an apt appreciation of God's greatness and our own littleness. We are nothing, can do nothing without God. When we arrive at this sincere acknowledgment and carry it out in our lives, we come to God as our only Truth, Beauty, Goodness, Happiness, our only Life — the only One worthy of all our love — and we get to love Him for Himself without any thought of self, and love Him in all creatures as His images, this is charity. Charity is thirsting and hungering for God as the supreme Good in Himself, and for Himself alone, and loving our neighbor as ourselves for God's sake. Could we love our mother and then spit upon her portrait? How, then, could we refuse to love our neighbor who is God's image? Charity includes rejoicing in another's good, as well as taking to heart another's evil. We cannot love God unless we love our neighbor; vice versa.

Third Point. Uncharitableness towards one another, special danger of priests.

MEDITATION. FRIDAY A. M. SACRIFICE

First Point. What is it, what does it imply? Sacrifice is salvation. Christ was salvation, entire salvation, and therefore was He entire sacrifice. He became sacrifice when in obedience to His Father He said: " Behold, I come." I come, therefore, a willing sacrifice, a complete sacrifice. He gave Himself up utterly to take on the nothingness of man, in the womb of the Virgin Mary. This was sacrifice.

Second Point. Christ was in sacrifice, body and soul, and all His life long, until He consummated it on Calvary, by death. For death is its completion. All that

Rt. Rev. A. A. Curtis, D.D.

stops short of death is incomplete, all may be made perfect in death. We must give up ourselves, not a part of ourselves, but ourselves; not our possessions, not what is external to us, not our bodies alone, but our entire selves, and not for awhile, but always. We must make our sacrifice complete by accepting death, not in the way we would, but in God's way. To God alone must we give ourselves. We must have no will of our own, but only God's will.

Third Point. We must use all things, all we have and all we are for God. The priest is made for sacrifice. Every day he plunges himself in sacrifice, in order to become a sacrifice. Like the iron plunged into the fire, and which becomes fire, the priest is plunged daily into the Sacred Heart of Jesus, that he may become divine fire.

Necessity of sacrifice. Either for weal or woe eternal, we must sacrifice ourselves either for Christ or satan, either for God or self. Hell means essentially to have sacrificed ourselves for no better end, and to have no other reward than our miserable selves eternally. Heaven here on earth means the sacrifice of all for God. Then only can we say at the last day in the words of St. Paul: I have lived; no, Jesus, Thou hast lived in me. Take me now — rather take Thyself now, for eternity. We must never forget that the sacrifices made for God are far less than those the devil requires, and infinitely less than those Christ made for us. Sacrifice may become easy by habit, none the less sacrifice. We are priests not merely to offer Another as sacrificed, but to become more and more sacrificed ourselves, perpetually, totally, irreversibly, in detail.

CONFERENCE. FRIDAY A. M. " A PRIEST HAS ALL THE RIGHTS AND DUTIES OF AN AMERICAN CITIZEN "

A. Priest gone down far when he begins to think much, talk much of, and insist much upon his rights.

Notes for Retreats

The only rights worth insisting upon are also one's duties. Again, the only rights worth while are such that we can never be deprived of them or even become maimed in the use of them, by any creature or any combinations of creatures. God alone, absolutely speaking, has rights; men, priests, have only duties.

B. Each calling prescribes duties, and these duties limit rights everywhere. A priest, then, has the right to live, and to be fully and freely a priest, doing his work within his own limits, and finding, as far as he may wish it, such pleasures or gains as may be compatible with his character and duties.

CONFERENCE. FRIDAY P. M. PRIEST AS PASTOR

Society priest as bad as newspaper priest, or political priest, or priest making himself the apostle of fads.

1. Duty of pastor to stay at home.

2. As far as possible to know his people, therefore to visit them — no favorites.

3. Special visiting of the sick. A list of sick and disabled kept and visited regularly, sometimes daily, or even oftener.

4. Constant and kindly remonstrances with the wicked and scandalous or indifferent.

5. Get access to the Protestants when you fairly can. Try to make them sure of welcome when they come to your churches.

6. The children — the children — visit the schools.

7. Some means of gathering people in Church on week days. Societies or Evening Prayers or both. Hard work, surely.

Pastors and Assistants should never be absent together.

Rt. Rev. A. A. Curtis, D.D.

MEDITATION. FRIDAY P. M. EFFECTS OF LIFE BEGIN-
NING IN THE FEAR OF GOD, AND CULMINATING IN
SACRIFICE OF SELF

First Point. Sacrifice makes us dear to God. Witness the power of Moses, Elias, David, St. Paul, as
the result of sacrifice.

Second Point. Sacrifice renders us more useful to
the people. Weight with the people, even with non-
Catholics. Difference between popular priest and
priest weighty by virtue of sanctity. Who is the priest
whose word is most valued, who draws most respect?
Not the orator; it is the priest who proves that he is
not fond of money, who attends to every duty faithfully, at every personal cost and sacrifice and self-
denial.

Third Point. Peace in one's self. Peace, only
earthly thing worth while, not to be directly sought for
its own sake. Priest worldly and selfish, can never
know peace.

Sacrifice produces what is most valuable on earth —
peace.

RETREAT AT THE CATHOLIC UNI-VERSITY OF AMERICA

WASHINGTON, D. C.

INTRODUCTORY

1. A reason for whatever we deliberately do, — Dogma, reason for morals. Retreat being costly, we must be impelled to it, and supported during it by sufficient reasons.

2. The grace of God presupposed, afterwards all in us is the result of the faculty we call attention. Rocks, lasting — precipitated from one of the most mutable of all things, water.

Intention, habit, character precipitated from oscillating attention.

3. All things conspire against our making due and sufficient use of our attention. All have failed more or less to make this use. All therefore have need of a retreat, and reason enough for making it. Those who have fallen into grievous sin clearly need it. Those also who have been guilty of nothing worse than venial sin. And those, finally, if any, who have not fallen into any kind of sin.

4. How shall we make the retreat? First and principally, by virtue of a good and strong will. And this *will*, each one if he has it not, must produce in himself by the help of God. These two considerations may help: I must come back to God. A retreat alone will return me thoroughly to Him. A retreat then must be made, and I can never make it more cheaply than now. Second, it may be with me now, or never at all. After the good will, I regard strict silence as the most

395

Rt. Rev. A. A. Curtis, D.D.

necessary means to a fruitful retreat. It will also help if we impress our minds with the fact that we are making the retreat not so much for the sake of producing in ourselves a present glow of soul, as dispose ourselves to live better day by day in the future.

Finally the retreat may perhaps be a little furthered, if we pray for the preacher.

MORNING MEDITATION. FIRST DAY. DEATH

First Point. I must die. But what is it to die? To quit the body and thereby to quit this world. And how much does this imply? No seeing, no hearing, no eating or drinking, no sleeping, no reading, no talking, no moving from place to place; no novelty, no change or variety of any kind, no study, no learning, no human affection, esteem or opinion, no industry, activity, pursuit or enjoyment of any kind.

Picture a man on a small rock alone in mid-ocean — blind, deaf, dumb, paralyzed, insensible. Death then divides from all, and leaves us merely our thought, and what we can derive from our thought. And to death I must come. It is the effect of nature. The immutable decree of God.

Second Point. I can die no more than once. In oneness are value, sublimity, awfulness — oneness gives dignity, worth, solemnity to the smallest thing.

Third Point. All life ought to be, and if right, life must be a preparation for our one, inevitable death.

Resolution. Besides the reminders of death, through the wisdom and mercy of God, meeting more or less always and everywhere, and besides such recognition of death as I shall try to make all along the day, I shall find somewhere in the day's routine a few minutes to be given solely to the endeavor to make death ever more and more to myself the awful all-determining fact it in itself is.

Notes for Retreats

FIRST DAY. MORNING CONFERENCE. DANGER OF THE
PRIEST

Formalism. Danger everywhere. Danger from everything, and danger all the time. The Priest subject to peculiar dangers. The glow and fervor of the young Priest just ordained. How he falls into official-ism. Cause, familiarity with the small outer signs and exponents of divine things, without consideration of the things themselves.

Defense. — Regularity, meditation, preparation for all greater functions. Avoidance of those practising and inculcating formalism.

FIRST DAY. AFTERNOON MEDITATION. FIRST DUTY OF
A PRIEST

Prayer, — what it means.
First Point. Of prayer to the individual; to the Church in general; why necessary; always in our power; to impregnate us more and more with the first truth of all our existence in God and absolute dependence upon God. It transforms and strengthens us more than anything else we do or can do.
Second Point. The sublimity of prayer.
Third Point. The comfort of prayer. In it alone we find the first and most imperative need of our nature, companionship.

Resolutions. My Breviary. My beads. My preparation for and thanksgiving after Mass shall be made genuine prayer. Besides I will aim at the habit of uniting exterior work with interior recollection and prayer.

SECOND DAY. MORNING MEDITATION. JUDGMENT

First Point. Parties to the judgment. God and I. God's eternity, my short span. God's vastness and im-

397

Rt. Rev. A. A. Curtis, D.D.

mensity, my littleness and narrowness. God's infinite knowledge and wisdom, my ignorance and folly. God's splendor and beauty, myself scarred, marred, polluted. God's sovereignty and sufficiency. My dependence and nothingness. God's infinite power, my absolute helplessness in His hands. God's justice. His unbounded infinite hatred of sin, myself saturated with evil. From top to bottom, from circumference to inmost center, defiled, leprous, loathsome even to myself. God's awful immutability, not to be cozened, flattered, bribed, intimidated or evaded; myself with such multiplex and overwhelming need of a judge in some way to be propitiated or deluded. God's goodness, speaking from the wounds of Christ and from the Tabernacle, and is seen in so many Absolutions and Communions; my own indomitable perversity, my incurable ingratitude, endless insult and outrage. I alone under the eyes, in the face of, in immediate contact with such a God. No friends, no witnesses, no counsel to plead, no forgetfulness, no excuses left, though once so endless; no false conscience remaining, no worse examples of others to keep me in countenance, no maxims and sentiments, customs and uses of the world to justify; myself in all nakedness and just as in myself I am, and have been before God, to hear and know what He thinks of me, and means to do with me.

Second Point. Matter of the judgment: sins I remember, sins I have forgotten, sins I recognized as such, sins I would excuse and justify, against the suppressed, smothered sense that I was cheating myself; sins that I knew, sins that I ought to have known and might have known, but criminally failed to detect. Sins abandoned, yet never really repented of. Sins I actually committed and sins I had the disposition to commit, and under temptation and with opportunity would have committed. Sins of omission and sins of commission. Sins into which I led others. Positive acts and standing deficiencies. Finally, I shall be judged not

398

merely for sins done, but for good spoiled in the doing.

Third Point. I shall be judged, not only fully, but finally, irreversibly, forever.

Resolutions. 1. To try to know myself better as the only way of lessening my confusion under the judgment of God, and of mitigating the immutable sentence then to issue.

2. I determine that henceforth I shall make as little as I can of man's judgment.

SECOND DAY. MORNING CONFERENCE. SECOND DAN-
GER OF THE PRIEST. SELF-SUFFICIENCY

Pride the primal sin and presupposed more or less by every other sin. Many forms, under many disguises and bearing many names; one of these names, self-sufficiency. And self-sufficiency a vice of Priests and very specially of young Priests. Methodist preachers and young Priests.

Describe what is meant by self-sufficiency.

Maxim much in the mouth of the self-sufficient Priest: "A Priest is entitled to live as a gentleman." Show absurdity of maxim as meaning just whatever one pleases, and in a Priest's mouth almost never meaning anything true or good.

Causes of sacerdotal self-sufficiency.

1. Contrast between long and almost total repression and almost absolute liberty to do as one pleases — in connection with the puppy devotion heretofore mentioned.

2. Avoidance of one's elders and superiors, and association almost exclusively with inferiors and toadies, and specially with women pious or otherwise.

3. Veneration and obedience of the faithful, and being without conflict and contest most of the time with one's equals or superiors.

4. Failure to contemplate assiduously one's tremen-

dous responsibilities, and the awful judgment awaiting him and to overtake him, no one knoweth how soon, and certainly much sooner than one will be sufficiently prepared for.

Care. 1. Clear sense of danger, and acceptance if not quest of failures, mortifications and humiliations.

2. Much converse with living superiors, and continual intercourse with the gigantic dead.

3. Much meditation.

SECOND DAY. EVENING MEDITATION. SECOND DUTY OF THE PRIEST. EDIFICATION

First Point. Priest more than secundus Christus. Christus Ipse.

Second Point. Like Christ, then, the Priest must in the main edify by his private life more than by his public functions.

Third Point. Virtues of Christ which reproduced in the Priest most specially edify.

A. Love of retirement and obscurity.

B. Love and practice of private prayer.

C. Meekness under provocation, and thorough forgiveness of injuries, real or imagined.

D. Simplicity and poverty.

E. Tenderness towards the poor and ignorant, and no undue complaisance towards, or fondness for the rich. Politeness.

F. An evident preference of duty, and the welfare of souls.

Resolutions. 1. To contemplate often the awfulness of my character and position as the vehicle of Christ, and Christ in a true sense Himself.

2. To consider much the dreadful hypocrisy of always holding up to the people the example of Christ, while never really trying to copy it myself.

Notes for Retreats

Short answer to objections. I imperatively need it, and without it certainly should never qualify myself for Heaven, as a Catholic understands Heaven. And the world in general needs it, for it is being proven that nothing less will restrain men from crimes — in the outcome destructive of all society.

Elements of Hell already existing and operating.
First Point. The capability of pain residing in the body almost infinite in multiplicity and intensity.

Second Point. The mind's capabilities: reconstructed memory, fully illuminated intelligence and thoroughly rectified conscience. Being eternally cut in two — will, irrevocably at war with intellect and conscience.

Third Point. Anticipation. Hopelessness. Pœna damni.

Resolutions. A. Not to be high minded but to fear.

B. To make meditation at least once a month, and if once a week so much the better, upon Hell.

C. To preach Hell faithfully but with the greatest lowliness, and making it evident to the people that to the core, I feel and fear what I preach.

D. Hell being so awful, intolerable, to keep always as far as I can from it.

THIRD DAY. MORNING CONFERENCE. THIRD DANGER
OF THE PRIEST. ENVY AND JEALOUSY AND WHAT
COME OF THEM

Beauty and ferocity and pitilessness of nature.

Beauty and ugliness of human nature. The ugliest and most absurd thing in it is envy and jealousy.

Describe fact and consequences. Assign cause.

A. " Two of a trade, etc."

B. Sometimes because jealousy cloaks itself under the name and pretence of zeal.

Rt. Rev. A. A. Curtis, D.D.

C. Because he is so little in contact with superiors or equals.

D. Primal cause, want of love to Christ and to souls.

Care. Much consideration of the folly, misery and maliciousness of envy.

Custody of one's own tongue and discouragement of the careless or evil tongues of other people.

Assiduous contemplation of the fact that all is of God, and for God.

THIRD DAY. AFTERNOON MEDITATION. THIRD GREAT DUTY OF THE PRIEST. INSTRUCTION

First Point. Dire need of instruction on the part of Catholics and Protestants, young and old, rich and poor, learned and unlearned.

Second Point. How shall I render myself competent to instruct with effect?

Third Point. Manner of instruction in the pulpit. In the Confessional. In the school. Why not also in pastoral visiting?

Resolutions. A. I will carefully prepare all instructions, public or private.

B. I will never speak save with distinct intention, before earnestly commended to God, of fixing in the hearts of the people some truth or truths to myself applied, and of myself recognized as of the highest moment. I will preach the Gospel of Christ and not patriotism, political economy or sociology, or burning questions. All really important questions are no more burning now than they were on the day Adam was expelled from Eden.

FOURTH DAY. MORNING MEDITATION. HEAVEN

First Point. What is Heaven? The full, final, irreversible rest of the whole man.

Notes for Retreats

1. Condition of rest, extinguishment forever of all ignorances, perplexities, uncertainties, fears, regrets. The being eternally raised above toil, pain, responsibility. The removal once for all of need, deficiency, disability of every kind. The being made superior to oscillation, temptation and possibility of sin. Finally the being forever done with most of what we now call pleasure.

Second Point. Second element of rest. The satisfaction fully of the intellect in knowing absolutely all to be known. In knowing it, too, not by inference, not by signs and effects, not according to its surface and its exterior aspects, not intermittently, remembering and forgetting. But knowing it in itself to the core through and through, and knowing it always in the same way, without excursion or succession of mind, knowing it even better than we now know the primal and most self-evident axioms, such as a thing cannot at once be, and not be. A square remaining a square cannot become a circle, nor the part ever equal the whole. This being the knowledge of Heaven we see that even our present knowledge of God is really scarcely worthy of the name. It is rather ignorance of God patiently borne, and as thus endured rewarded hereafter with real knowledge. For what know we or what can we know of even the very first thing we ascribe to God, to wit, His absolute oneness? And so with everything else we ascribe to God. It is at bottom merely the saying in one or another way that while we know He is, yet we know not and now cannot know what or how He is. And even His " is," is so infinitely above and apart from all other " ises," that we are far from understanding fully what is meant when we ascribe to Him simple being and nothing more.

Third Point. The satisfaction of the will. The perfect and indefeasible love of God and all His creatures (aye, the love of the lost Angels and of eternally shipwrecked men). Love not as now coming and going,

Rt. Rev. A. A. Curtis, D.D.

active or inactive; but no more at all habit or potentia, forever wholly act, and act fully perfect.

Resolutions. A. To render myself more and more profoundly and ineffaceably convinced that but two things are worth while, or rather two aspects of the same thing, to wit, safety and rest, and that these two are on earth, absolutely — essentially impossible.

B. To subdue more and more my pride in keeping myself ever clearly reminded that my highest wisdom on earth consists not so much in knowing as in freeing myself further and ever further of the imagination, that I know or can know; and thus making room in myself for the knowledge to come hereafter.

C. To remember that as on the one hand my work is rather to vacate my mind of the delusion that I know, so on the other, my task is to free my will from all preoccupations, preferences, biases, entanglements, that being empty I may not so much love God now, as be able to hunger and thirst for the love to come hereafter.

FOURTH DAY. MORNING CONFERENCE. FOURTH DANGER OF THE PRIEST. SENSUALITY

Extremes meet. The reaction and recoil from the sublimity of the supernatural is apt to be towards the lowest and basest phase of the natural. Various forms of sensuality. Describe some of them; of the table, of dress, of furniture, of curiosity, of idleness, gadding and gossiping, of games and amusements, of reading, fast horses, horse racing and theater going.

Causes. A. The trend itself of the times, which dignifies or more and more elaborates sensuality with the name progress, civilization and makes it rather virtue and grace, than ugliness, weakness and vice.

B. Confounding orthodoxy with faith.

Care. Mortification, not so much voluntarily procured as voluntarily accepted and embraced, when divinely provided.

Notes for Retreats

Offers and receives Christ as a sacrifice so often —
to be himself in and with Christ rendered a sacrifice.

First Point. Necessity of self-sacrifice; we may determine what shall be our good, but not the price to be
paid for this good. We may choose the end and effect
unto and for which we shall be crucified, but crucified
we must be.

Second Point. Details of the sacrifice. Time. Lib-
erty, ease and leisure. Society. Publicity. Study.
Devotion itself occasionally. Novelty and variety.
Regularity, sometimes. Health. Life.

Third Point. Reward of sacrifice. Peace, if the
sacrifice be willing and thorough.

Resolutions. A. Never to say Mass save with the
clear and prominent intention, that I may thereby more
come to know, and reflect, Christ as sacrificed.

B. To keep ever on the watch to make enough of
the truth that I must for Christ, and His people, sacrifice even the true, the good and the beautiful, as well
as the false, the evil and the ugly.

C. To make my sacrifice of self in one or another
way and degree, not intermittent but incessant.

FIFTH DAY. MORNING MEDITATION.
PERSEVERANCE

It alone proves and crowns all. True nature of perseverance. Reason why perseverance alone is crowned.

First Point. I must persevere, or as well, or better,
not begin.

Second Point. Everything against perseverance
within and without.

Third Point. Hence great, multiplex and irremov-
able danger of not persevering.

Rt. Rev. A. A. Curtis, D.D.

Resolutions. A. To try to produce in myself more and more of that rational, godly fear which is beginning in the sense of the ever remaining foundation upon which rests all the structure of wisdom, and without which the whole building collapses.

B. To pray at least in short interior aspirations many times a day for perseverance.

C. Never to permit myself to be discouraged, nor to hide myself from God, no matter what my falls.

RETREAT AT ST. CHARLES' COLLEGE

FIRST Point. In contact with the majesty and power of God.

Second Point. In contact with the truth and justice of God.

Third Point. In contact with the beauty and goodness of God.

Resolution. To be more faithful in trying to be habitually in the presence and company of God.

Instruction, A. M. First duty of youth: obedience, docility.

Nature of obedience includes judgment and will.

Advantages: safety, merit, peace.

Instruction, P. M. First danger of youth: self-confidence. Why? Ignorance, imagination in place of experience. Effects: censoriousness. Remedy: much consideration of the littleness of the creature, and our inability to initiate or complete anything of ourselves.

THURSDAY, SEPTEMBER 26. MEDITATION, A. M. MATTER OF JUDGMENT

First Point. Sins forgotten. Second Point. Sins remembered, but not duly estimated, specially sins of omission. Third Point. Good things spoiled.

Resolution. More earnestness and diligence in examination of conscience.

Instruction, A. M. Second duty: to discover and correct evil propensities, specially those most predominating; (1) to discover them; (2) to oppose them. Advantages of undertaking this work now: (1) evil propensities will not be acquired; (2) present ones, now much more easily rooted out.

Instruction, P. M. Second danger: illusion. 1. What is it? With at least the capability of recognizing our error regarding as fact and truth some picture of what we wish to be the case. 2. All more or less under illusion. 3. Difference between illusions of the old and the young. 4. Particular illusions of the young as to length and certainty of life. As to the value of the individual. As to exemption from inevitable penalty. As to quick, easy, thorough success. Remedy: think, and refuse to dream instead.

SEPTEMBER 27. MEDITATION, A. M. MANNER OF
JUDGMENT

First Point. Each single soul all alone with God. Second Point. Memory fully reconstructed. Third Point. With intellect disabused and conscience thoroughly rectified. Resolution: to set myself against my innate propensity to excuse and justify myself.

Instruction, A. M. Third duty of the young to acquire right habits. What is habit? Strangeness of habit — implies a substance prior to intellect and will and comprehending both; it implies, too, on one hand, Heaven; on the other, Hell. Necessity therefore of beginning early to acquire good habits. Habits in particular to be acquired: regularity, thoughtfulness, silence, prayerfulness.

Instruction, P. M. Third danger of the young. Procrastination. All are prone to procrastination. The young specially thus disposed. Why? Because they promise themselves so much as to the future. Because their defects are not yet so ugly, so obstinate or so gravely and immediately threatening. Reasons against procrastination: work must be done, most cheaply done now. If postponed more hardly done, probably never done at all.

SEPTEMBER 28.   MEDITATION, A. M.

First Point. Last Judgment. Second Point. Perfect judgment. Third Point. Irreversible, eternal judgment.

Resolution. To distrust myself and to make little of what others seem to think of me.

Instruction, A. M. Fourth duty of the young. To discover and choose each his proper vocation. Each thing no matter how small, individual, with its own peculiar office. This follows from God's knowledge of each; nothing therefore can be perfectly lost. It can merely descend to a lower place and use. All mischief, something out of place; worst mischief of all, man out of place in the priesthood. But must not suppose vocation to priesthood a thing ready made. How to discover whether we are capable of this vocation.

Instruction, P. M. Fourth danger of youth. Substituting fancy for fact. Difference between fancy and imagination. Never too much use of imagination, always too much of fancy. How and why we deceive ourselves with fancies instead of fact. All do it more or less, especially the young; some encourage them to do it. Certain reading tends to this end. Certain company has the same effect. But mostly the habit of day dreaming. Let us be men, not cowards, shirking the truth at such bitter cost in the end.

WEDNESDAY, SEPTEMBER 25.   SACRAMENT OF PENANCE

Ratio sacramentorum in genere. 1. Gratia. Presence, action and effect of God immediately and solely. 2. This presence, action and effect necessarily incognizable by us. Hence necessity of sign visible. 3. God's action in itself always one and the same, but producing many and different effects, according to the dispositions and needs of the creature. Our needs many, hence many Sacraments. Besides, we forget. Hence Sacraments many and some of them many times given. One standing need: healing of the soul. Answering to this Sacrament of Penance, only Sacrament with seemingly ugly name — not really ugly, however. (1) Because penance voluntary. (2) Because of God. (3) Because so blessed in its effects.

THURSDAY, 26. BEFORE CONFESSION

What ought to move us to confession? Not human respect, not mere compliance with established routine. Not the wish for purely temporary relief and comfort. Not merely and solely the desire to be forgiven our past sins, but with this even more, the will to cure our defects.

How to prepare. First defect, insufficient examination, making more of things extraordinary than of things habitual. Second defect, too little time to contrition — mistakes as to contrition itself. Motives to it, supernatural. Test of it, the genuine will to try to do better.

FRIDAY, 27. IN CONFESSION

Why must we confess? 1. As fitting penance and sometimes grievous penance. 2. As easiest, quickest and most certain way of ridding ourselves of sin. 3. That judge may determine, and doctor apply remedies. 4. That we may thereby the better see and know ourselves. The confession itself must be: 1. Humble. 2. Sincere. 3. Full, but not scrupulous, nor going into unnecessary detail.

SATURDAY, 28. AFTER CONFESSION

First of all, Thanksgiving. 2. Saying or doing of penance. 3. Renewal of resolutions particularly as to voluntary occasions of sin. 4. When resolutions have been forgotten or contradicted.

Notes for Retreats

First Point. What it is to relapse. Second Point. The folly and crime of thus relapsing. Third Point. The mischief and danger of same.

Resolution. I will try to keep my confidence in God's power and mercy, and will return always to Him.

INSTRUCTION AT HIGH MASS. SORROWS OF MARY

First, Perpetual. 2. Singularly intense, as for the best of sons. As for her God in this Son outraged. These sorrows upon her Son and her God occasioned by the very children for whom she sacrifices her Son. The core of the sorrow; the worse than uselessness as regards so many of Christ's sufferings and her own sorrows. 3. Children of such a Father and Mother, what should we expect, what should we desire?

RETREAT AT ST. MATTHEWS

WASHINGTON, D. C.

March 10. Afternoon

INTRODUCTORY

IF one be quite certain that all by himself and solely
of himself he can execute the purpose he enter-
tains, he need not make known that purpose to others.
Indeed in many cases the manifestation of a purpose
such as I have mentioned would be more than merely
unnecessary, *i. e.*, it might occasion opposition and pro-
voke obstacle. But when the end in view is such that it
cannot be reached save through the intelligent and willing coöperation of others, then of necessity it must be to
them more or less distinctly revealed. And the more
fully and clearly must they know what is contemplated
when all proposed is to be done by them and for them,
and when the part of the leader in the transaction afoot
is not and cannot be more than simply to point out
to his followers something with which each of them
is most momentously concerned, and something, too,
which one cannot do for another, but which each must
for himself undertake and execute or else eternally
groan and wail under intolerable and irreversible pen-
alties. And this is precisely our case. Were I going
to make a retreat for myself I need not reveal to any
one my purpose itself, and still less the particular means
and methods whereby I meant and hoped to execute
that purpose. But the retreat now to be made is to be
made through as well as for you, and each of you must
make it of himself, as well as for himself. I cannot
directly and immediately do anything whatever in be-

half of the retreat. I am here simply to stimulate each of you if I can, to undertake and fulfil what a genuine retreat implies and demands. It is necessary, then, that I state the one proximate principal end towards which the whole retreat should be directed. I say proximate end, observe.

Ultimate end of retreat as of everything else, salvation. Proximate, distinctive end of retreat. To obviate that which is most universally and necessarily fatal to the soul, it is not sin proper, not ignorance, not temptation, nor obstacle or hardship, but simply indifference, want of earnestness, singleness, wholeheartedness as to procuring our salvation. Really, if not nominally, valuing some other things more than we value our salvation.

This retreat then will throughout aim to extinguish indifference and produce in us due concern as to the salvation of our souls. Each must make his own rule for the retreat. Above all each must pray for a thoroughly good will to make the most of this grace and this opportunity.

MARCH 11, A. M.

We shall become full, earnest, ardent, steadfast as to our salvation if we duly recognize the value of the soul. And that we may see the worth of the soul we shall begin with considering it in itself.

A. Its singleness, uniqueness, individuality. And all things valuable as they possess or approach singleness. God, the truth, the Church, life, death, office, position, wealth.

B. Sovereignty of the soul, actually owning and capable of controlling all things even of thwarting its Creator and Redeemer. And its exhaustless power of knowing and of loving.

C. Immortality of the soul.

D. How God values each human soul, — the good Angels, Martyrs and Saints generally.

Rt. Rev. A. A. Curtis, D.D.

E. How satan esteems the soul. What the crime of even gratuitously risking the soul?

MARCH 11, P. M.

A. From the singleness, individuality of the soul it follows of necessity that each soul must, under God and with the help of God, work out its own salvation. No delegation of the work is possible. It cannot be so committed even to God that we leave all to Him, while ourselves making no genuine or sustained effort.

a. The greatness of the work in itself and on account of arrearages.

B. Not only must each particular soul work out its own salvation, but it cannot effect this salvation save as pursuing it at all costs, and as the one sovereign end to which all other ends are subject and subsidiary. — The soul not divisible, wholly saved or entirely lost.

C. Such a pursuit of salvation must be maintained to the end.

D. And with the genuine, ever present, ever influential fear of sooner or later faltering and falling, somewhere short of the line beyond which only is safety assured.

MARCH 12, A. M.

A. One soul; under God this one soul, the one only savior of itself. One time and opportunity of salvation, — the present life.

B. This no more than sufficient when longest and best used.

C. This time and opportunity going incessantly.

D. So much of it already gone and perhaps rather to our guilt and danger than to our benefit.

E. What is left may be so much less than we expect. Surely time to end our procrastination.

MARCH 12, P. M.

The place, etc., in which and the conditions under which each must effect his own salvation.

414

Notes for Retreats

A. We being what we are, in the world without us, all things, without exception, will oppose our salvation and combine to effect our ruin. Not that there is any exterior thing in and of itself at all amiss. But we are interiorly fools and sinners, and it is the dire curse of sin, that it perverts and misapplies everything — the best as well as the worst.

Under a heaven smiling, wooing, caressing or frowning, threatening, pinching. In plenty or under poverty. In leisure or under toil. In public or private, esteemed, and in honor, or despised and disliked, known to many or few. From the example of the good and that of the evil.

B. The world within is greater and more dangerous than the world without. 1. From our evil propensities. 2. Our delusions and self-deceivings. 3. Our fickleness and inconstancy. 4. From the very truth itself, and from our own virtues. Envy and censoriousness. What safety for us? None on earth anywhere or anything. And none will be found elsewhere, save at the cost here and now of ceaseless fear and never-failing watchfulness.

MARCH 13, A. M. HELL

If in spite of all the reasons to the contrary we neglect to render ourselves sovereignly earnest and single-hearted as to our salvation; if therefore we run into great excesses and fall into gross vices; if on the contrary, something counting for less than nothing with God keep us from such vices and excesses, but leave us accustomed to value all sorts of things more than God, and to live rather for any and every end than for our own salvation, — then, what? Hell. Is there a hell? Most do not now believe that there is. But neither do they recognize death or many other facts, which, nevertheless, exist and in due time assert and revenge themselves.

Two ways of contemplating Hell: 1. As a purely

positive and supernaturally revealed penalty. This no doubt the better way. 2. As the necessary consequence causes, forces and tendencies now in operation under our eyes — one thing only presupposed and derived from revelation, *i. e.,* the irreversibleness after death of our moral status. And even this reason alone many suspect as probable, if not able to demonstrate as certain.

A. Leave out all coming of a body thoroughly, incurably and eternally disordered in every part, and as to every function.

B. The companionship of all lost souls and worse devils.

C. Severance from all present enjoyments, pursuits, distractions.

D. Severance from God and the good.

E. Illumination of the mind, restoration of memory.

F. Anticipation, hopelessness, eternity.

MARCH 13, P. M. HEAVEN

If by the help of God and the aid of Mary and the Saints we become, and till the end remain thoroughly in earnest as to the salvation of the soul; if falling, we rise, if failing, we begin afresh, if erring, we turn back to the right way; if sinning, as sometimes we shall sin, we repent, confess, renew our resolutions, resume our efforts, and maintain a sometimes temporarily impaired, but never lost, trust in God, and determination to hold fast to Him as our only sufficient end — what? Heaven. Purgatory before, no doubt, but Heaven afterwards. And Purgatory itself far better than what now is — why? And what is Heaven? Rest. And Rest what?

A. Freedom from pain, toil, responsibility, danger, conflict, temptation, fear, desire, sin.

B. But this is negative rest. What is rest positively?

1. Satisfaction of the body, everything fully answering

to it as it then will be. 2. Indefeasible contentment and filling up to the utmost of the soul. 3. As to knowing and the will to be known. 4. As to loving and the hungering and thirsting to be loved.

MARCH 14. FINAL

Whatever our earnestness and concern now, they will not last unless we foresee and provide the means whereby they are to be maintained and increased. And I may put these means in one word: stop drifting, stop living at random; and doing well, if doing it at all, rather by accident than upon principle and according to system.

A. Each therefore must make for himself a rule: as to prayer in private; meditation; self-examination. Good reading and the reverse. As to retiring and rising. Then as to occasions of sin. As to keeping Sundays, hearing Mass, making confession, communicating.

V

NOTES FOR THE THREE HOURS' AGONY

FOUND IN THE BISHOP'S OWN HANDWRITING

Given on Good Friday of various years in St. Peter's Cathedral, Wilmington, Del.

THREE HOURS' PRAYER

GOOD FRIDAY, MARCH 23, 1894

Preached at St. Peter's Cathedral.

PASSION TYPIFIED AND PREDICTED IN TABLEAUX FROM OLD TESTAMENT

FIRST TABLEAU

Cain and Abel

COMPOSITION *of place.* Gates of garden of Eden.

1. Two brothers; the elder the murderer.

2. Motive to the murder: simple hatred of the greater wisdom and goodness of the younger brother.

3. Cain's sacrifice, a denial virtually of the fall and guilt of the human race; so the Jews. Abel's confession of fall and of the need of a sufficient sacrifice and atonement; the quarrel between the Jews and Christ, the same.

4. The instrument of the murder — wood, according to tradition.

5. Conduct of Cain when accused, that of the Jews.

6. Punishment of Cain and that of the Jews the same.

In this tableau the thing most prominently presented is the extreme wickedness of the human heart, slaying God merely as God and simply for His goodness. And properly in the beginning the dreadfulness of the disease is shown, that thereby we may see the need of and sufficiently desire and seek the only remedy. Meditate on the extreme malice and dreadfulness of sin as hating God merely as God and for the very things supremely entitling Him to our adoration.

Rt. Rev. A. A. Curtis, D.D.

Abraham and Isaac

Composition of place. A wide plain. In the far distance a mountain dimly defined against the sky; crossing the plain towards the mountain a small caravan of four. In front an old man with head drooping, eyes on the ground and filled with unutterable sadness. The whole mien and countenance expressive of the deepest grief. At his side not a child but another man, unworn by toil, untarnished by sorrow, with all the vigor, alertness, brightness, smoothness and beauty of youth, as yet a stranger to deep-lasting grief or long and severe conflict. In the rear, following, two servants carrying wood and fire, bonds and the sacrificial knife.

1. Contrast this tableau with the first. There, all darkness and wickedness and its punishment. Here, only faith, obedience, sacrifice and their reward; three days going to the mountain — three periods before Christ.

2. Abraham typifies the Eternal Father, willingly for us yielding up His Son; stands also for the enlightened of the Jewish nation, — Joseph, Mary, Zacharias, Elizabeth, Simeon and Anna and such, all along the ages.

3. The willingness of Isaac typifying Christ's laying down His Life of Himself.

4. Willingness to die but not actually dying, as representing the divinity of Christ, which could not be slain. Isaac returned home unharmed from Mt. Moriah. So the divinity of Christ returned untouched to Heaven.

5. The ram sacrificed; first caught by his horns, in brambles. Horns, dignity, power; brambles, sin. Christ taken through His very beauties and perfections and according to His flesh slain.

Notes for the Three Hours' Agony

6. The mother Sara apparently ignorant; the Jewish church ignorant.

7. Promise of universal salvation.

Meditate on the infinite goodness of God, and the necessity of blind trust in and obedience to Him.

THIRD TABLEAU

Joseph and his Brethren

Composition of place. Again a wide plain on every side, losing itself in the distance. In the center and foreground a grove of large trees, under these trees the great tent of the Master; near it smaller tents of the servants. An old man wrinkled and worn, with a long white beard far down his breast, sitting in the open door of the great tent. He gazes, shading his eyes, into the distance, and smiles with gladness as he discovers far-off men approaching; they arrive downcast with every simulation of great sorrow. They hold up before the old man, Jacob, a torn and bloody garment, saying, " this we have found," etc., etc.

1. Again two brothers: Joseph and Benjamin, — Joseph the elder, the remnant of the Jews adhering to Christ and identified with Christ. Benjamin the younger — the Gentiles — other ten only half brothers to Joseph, as of another mother, so the body of the Jewish nation, half brothers of Christ, only akin to Him according to the flesh indeed, but totally estranged from Him according to the spirit.

2. Motive to the crime: envy of the greater wisdom and greater dearness to his father on the part of Joseph.

3. Immediate occasion of the outbreak of this envy; revelations of Joseph as to his future dignity.

4. Casting into the pit and the drawing; burial and resurrection of Christ.

5. Selling to Madianites for a little silver. For the sake of small temporal interests the Jews gave up

Rt. Rev. A. A. Curtis, D.D.

Christ to the Gentiles. The Madianites sold him to Putiphar; first kind; then unjust; the Roman Emperors as Pagans. Pharaoh the same. Christians.

6. Joseph comes to rule; feeds the world; wins again his brethren.

Meditate on the universality and dreadfulness of the particular sin of envy, as alienating from one another, those who ought to be to each other nearest and dearest.

Fourth Tableau

Brazen Serpent in Wilderness

Composition of place. A desert, treeless, waterless; long sweeps of bare sand, here smooth, there rising into rounded swells, broken in places by ledges and protuberances of bald rock, crossed by dry winds; on one hand in the distance, the purple mountains of Arabia; on the other the red hills of Edom and Moab, and showing above them in their rear the blue ridges of Lebanon; on the sand the tabernacle, about it on its four sides, stretching away the many tents of the twelve tribes; three tribes encamped on each side of the tabernacle, — the many people: men, women and children massed together here and there, all talking, gesticulating, angrily blaspheming God and Moses. But these mobs suddenly begin to scatter, their anger becomes fear and their blasphemies are turned into shrieks of pain. The serpents are among them on all hands, darting to and fro, hissing, striking and producing in whomsoever they strike burning fever and speedy death. The serpents found in every place, and many people already dead; more dying, and all in danger; the multitudes terrified and repentant resort to Moses for rescue, and he in obedience to God erects upon a high staff, standing also upon an eminence so as to be visible to every part of the camp, an image in brass of a serpent; that all bitten, in faith and obedience, gazing upon this brazen serpent may find healing.

424

Notes for the Three Hours' Agony

1. The serpent, sin. The brazen serpent, likeness of sin.

2. The serpent dead, Christ as crucified and dead heals.

3. Lifted high by the wood. The cross, highest thing in the world.

4. Mere gazing at the dead serpent produced healing. Gazing enough at Christ crucified, the means to all wisdom and sanctity.

Meditate on our ingratitude towards, and distrust of God and rebellion out and out, so often against Him.

FIFTH TABLEAU

Samson

Composition of place. An immense circular building. The roof runs to a point in the center and there rests upon and is upheld by two great columns extending from the floor to the apex of the roof. All round the building, even up to the starting place of the roof is tier above tier of seats. And these seats are all filled with the men, women and children, the noble and the wealthy of the Philistine. In the vacant space in the center and round about the columns are densely packed, many of the populace of the same nation. Even from the roof in which there are openings, many heads are pressed close together, and are looking down into the temple. Throughout all the vast assembly there is the hush of expectation. All eyes are turned towards a door from which a narrow path, kept clear, runs to a platform raised high between the two great columns. The door opens. Soldiers in armor and with weapons issue therefrom. Among them and towering above them, with hair hanging far down his back, comes the strong man, so long and in so many ways the scourge of the Philistines. His eyes turn hither and thither but see nothing, for he has been blinded. The very sight of him, blind, and in custody, causes many to shrink with fear. Others mock and demand an exhibition of his strength. This is given at length and in many ways, till he is permitted to rest for a while between the columns. He winds one of his long arms around each of the pillars; he bends forward and puts forth all his strength, when lo! he and the columns go down together and the roof falls in upon the multitude, slaying, wounding or suffocating the vast assembly.

1. Many pictures of the Passion, in Samson and not one only. Slaying thousands with the jawbone of a dead ass. Ass our Lord, the jawbone His word. Fountain issuing from the jawbone. Life and refreshment coming of His word.

2. Carrying away the gates of Gaza. Our Lord's carrying away the gates of Limbo.

3. Catching foxes, fastening them two and two with a firebrand between. Our Lord winning His disciples, making them wise and sending them out two and two with the fire of the Spirit, to burn up the harvest of this world.

4. Dalila legally his wife; stands for Jewish church. Her wiles to discover Samson's secret. The artifices of the Jews to entrap our Lord and to make Him confess His divinity. The cutting of the hair, meaning, blinding Samson. Blindfolding Christ.

5. Two columns pulled down in our Lord's death. A desire of temporal things. Fear of God and of the cost of subduing ourselves and conforming ourselves to God.

6. More slain by death than by life.

Meditate on. To become strong we must know ourselves to be helpless.

SIXTH TABLEAU

The Passover

Composition of place. A large upper room scantily furnished. In the center a table. Six on each side of the table; eleven downcast, sad, evidently in the shadow of some great grief impending; one worse than sad, — ill at ease, at war with himself, and in his roving eyes and general restlessness showing that he feels himself entirely out of place. On the table is the lamb roasted and whole. On the table also dishes of round, thin unleavened bread. At the head of the table stands one acting as Father and Host and showing in His Face and mien more of dignity and tenderness than any other ever displayed; under His hand are a flagon of wine and a large chalice, and a vessel of water. He pours wine into the chalice and mingles with it a little water. Then He says: " With desire I have desired to eat this pasch with you before I suffer." Luke xxii. 15. " Take, and divide it among you: for I say to you, that I will not drink of the fruit of the vine, till the kingdom of God come." Luke xxii. 18.

1. The lamb of the Passover was to be without blemish of any kind. The perfections of Christ.

2. It was to be of the first year; the eternal youth, the undying Life of Christ.

3. It might be taken from among kids or lambs proper: kids, sinners; lambs, the just.

This signifies Christ genuinely offering Himself and undergoing His passion and death for the lost as well as the saved.

4. Slain in the evening and in Jerusalem. And then in the evening of both Jews and Gentiles, Christ slain.

5. It was to be roasted whole with head and feet and interior appurtenances. The completeness of Christ's sacrifice of Himself. Altogether devoured by the fire of His love for us.

6. No bone was to be broken. Literally fulfilled in Christ. Morally also, as implying that all His purposes were and are fulfilled, even when apparently most thwarted.

7. Nothing to be left over till the next morning.

Rt. Rev. A. A. Curtis, D.D.

No use and appropriation of the sacrifice when the morning of another life shall have arrived.

Meditate upon — " He that loveth his life shall lose it: and he that hateth his life in this world, keepeth it unto life eternal." John xii. 25.

NOTES FOR LENTEN SERMONS

St. Peter's, Wilmington

WEDNESDAY, FEBRUARY 19

A. WHY our Lord made so much use of parables.
B. Mysteriousness of Holy Writ seen in the fact that St. Luke alone gives the parable of the Prodigal son.

C. Why two sons only? Jew and Gentile.

D. Why the younger is the apostate?

E. Why no mother is mentioned or implied?

F. Contradiction of prevalent errors as to the determinativeness of heredity and environment.

G. Comfort for parents. When they have done all, some of the children will go astray. But to return in the end.

WEDNESDAY, FEBRUARY 26

" Father, give me the portion of substance that falleth to me. And he divided unto them his substance." Luke xv. 12.

A. Holy Writ deserves minute consideration; one asks, and to both division is made. What is meant by this? Greater liberty granted to some becomes inevitably a grant to all. The some Gentiles asked, all received. Thus in the Church Catholic also. He did therefore divide to the Gentiles. Hence things in Holy Writ and in antiquity elsewhere. But how does the Father, God Himself, divide to His children? He literally gives all to each, yet He divides also. But how does He divide at the request of the disloyal in heart? He does not actively, but He does in effect. He wills that all should be one but He lets those separate who

429

Rt. Rev. A. A. Curtis, D.D.

will separate and take away with them from His household as much of the truth as they may choose to keep and as much of grace as they are competent to retain.

B. So much as to men in general; now as to the individual soul. The younger son says in effect: I want more liberty, more independence. In how many families is the younger son literally reproduced! And in the great family, the Church, how many younger sons craving more liberty are found all the time.

C. The younger son's request not suddenly reached. An approach to it for some time previous; so always.

D. Take care as to small infidelities and withstand the beginnings of evil tendencies.

LENT

Downfall and Restoration of the Soul as Painted in Parable of the Prodigal Son

Wednesday, February 19. Before downfall.

Wednesday, February 26. Beginning of downfall. " Give me the portion falling to me," — interior separation from the Father.

Wednesday, March 4. Downfall completed in exterior separation. " He gathered together all and went into a far country."

Wednesday, March 11. First consequence of downfall. " He spent all."

Wednesday, March 18. Second consequence. In dire want and forced to hire himself to feed swine.

Wednesday, March 25. Repentance and return.

WEDNESDAY IN HOLY WEEK, APRIL 1, 1896

The crown of thorns — no real crown ever made of anything else save thorns.

THURSDAY IN HOLY WEEK, APRIL 2, 1896

Five wounds — few among many. Five selected to teach us that we must be wounded and weakened as to the use of the five senses.

GOOD FRIDAY, APRIL 3, 1896

First our Lord carries and controls the cross. At last the cross carries and controls Him.

THREE HOURS' PRAYER. GOOD FRIDAY, APRIL 3

A. What is death in itself? B. Whence caused and produced? C. Effects palpable. Destruction of

431

sense and we reduced to intellect and will, and what we can make of them. D. Effects invisible in soul. Determining and fixing once for all one's value and one's destiny. E. Death inevitable and why? F. Always before our eyes, but time, place and manner thereof hidden and why? G. Takes place once and once only. H. Supreme act of sacrifice and penance. I. Unconsidered, cause of all sin. Duly recognized, cause of all goodness and wisdom.

This probably was the last occasion Bishop Curtis preached the Three Hours' Prayer. He had prepared to preach on the foregoing notes, but suddenly changed his mind, owing, as he believed, to an inspiration that came to him in his morning meditation to take instead the Five Sorrowful Mysteries of the Rosary. These were the most touching discourses he ever preached, capable of melting a heart of adamant and of producing intensest horror of sin in the soul of any but a reprobate, and yet these masterful discourses were, as to all human artifice, utterly spontaneous and impromptu, but none the less to all who heard them divinely inspired.

VI
EXTRACTS FROM THE EARLY FATHERS

FOUND IN A NOTE-BOOK IN THE BISHOP'S HANDWRITING

DOCTRINAL EXTRACTS FROM THE GREEK FATHERS [1]

AND SOME OTHERS FROM PAGAN AUTHORS

ORIGEN

CONTRA CELSUM, Lib. I. p. 644: The Lord was silent before His accusers because He held that His life and deeds among the Jews were a better refutation of the calumnies than could be given in mere words.

P. 756: Mention made of the grotto of Bethlehem and of the stall therein and the identity then acknowledged even by the unbelievers.

P. 775: Origen makes Levi and Matthew different persons and says that the former was not among the Apostles.

Ib., Lib. II. p. 797: According to Origen the many things the Lord had to say which were reserved because the disciples were not then able to bear them, related, some of them at least, to the abrogation of Judaism and the call of the Gentiles.

P. 845: The Lord said, " Let this cup pass from Me," not on His own account, but as foreseeing and deprecating the total ruin which His murder would bring upon the Jews.

P. 872: " The lame man shall leap as a hart " (Isaiah). He refers to the leaping of the hart *to*[2] his hostility to serpents and his leaping upon them to kill them.

[1] Edit. Maurinorum (Migne).
[2] This *to* was inadvertently written by the Bishop instead of *in*, as we suppose. — EDITORS.

Rt. Rev. A. A. Curtis, D.D.

Ib., Lib. IV. p. 1096: Origen understands the ark to have had its roof ascending with four planes from each side and end and these four planes to have met in the middle and there terminated in a square of one cubit.

P. 1145: He denies the assertion of Celsus that Providence has as much respect to irrational as to rational creatures and maintains that the irrational are provided for only as a condition of the end which is to take care of man.

Ib., Lib. V. p. 1256: Names the son of Moses, whom Zipporah circumcised, Eleazar, and understands the Angel as an evil angel and hence restrained by the circumcision; says, too, that the Jews counted circumcision not made on the eighth day as not afterwards of obligation or value. In the same place notes the difference between the Septuagint and the Hebrew, the latter saying, " A husband of blood thou to me." The former, " the blood of the circumcision of my child has stayed or stood."

Ib., Lib. VI. p. 1269: Celsus says that the Christians supposed the warm springs to be the tears of the angels condemned and imprisoned under the earth.

P. 1313: Plato says that it is impossible that one should be at the same time very rich and very good. Celsus accuses Christ of having made use of Plato. Origen laughs at the notion that the reputed son of a Jewish carpenter not versed even in the literature of the Jews had read and admired Plato.

P. 1317: Origen like St. Bernard understands that the seraphim seen by Isaiah cover with their wings not each his own face and feet, but the Feet and Face of God.

P. 1332: Origen seems to hint at rather than state his belief in Purgatory.

P. 1351: Note — quotation from Justin Martyr — also says that Christ was a carpenter making ploughs and yokes.

436

Extracts from the Early Fathers

P. 1365: Origen considers, it seems, the Book of Job older than those of Moses.

Pp. 1368–69–71–72: Antichrist. As in the man Jesus the apex of the good, so in Antichrist the apex of evil — and evil all the worse as counterfeiting the good. Antichrist, foretold in Daniel by the King, "understanding riddles, etc.," "abomination making desolate in the Temple," answers best Paul's "seating himself in the Temple of God and showing himself as God."

P. 1393: Origen faults Celsus for not distinguishing between the "Image of God" and "according to the Image of God." The first proper to Christ alone, the second said of man.

P. 1401: Something worth seeing as to the Incarnation in general and the transfiguration in particular. Christ dwelling in us carries us up into the high spiritual mountain and there shows us His own Glory — the glory of the Law spiritually understood symbolized by Moses and of prophecy represented by Elias.

Ib., Lib. VII.: In the beginning, strictures upon Apollo and the Pythones. Heathen μαντεῖαι compared with prophecy.

P. 1440: The vinegar and gall stand for the malice of men of which Christ is continually made to taste and which He always refuses to drink.

P. 1448: Celsus objects that Christ, who had recommended poverty and threatened riches, also had disallowed force and commanded ταπεινοσύνην, could not be either the God or the ambassador of the God who had promised the Jews wealth — had required them to expunge their enemies and had in all ways shown great severity and jealousy of His dominion. Origen answers 1448–9–52–53 mainly that the law had two senses and that the spiritual sense was the better and the one chiefly intended.

Rt. Rev. A. A. Curtis, D.D.

Dialogus Adamantis.

P. 1757: John the Baptist — the precursor of Christ in Hades as well as on earth.

In Exodum.

P. 277: As one having been very kind to his servants and they having abused to their ruin his kindness is accustomed to say: "I have ruined you; I have made you wicked," though in very deed he has not been either the cause or the necessary occasion of their ruin since his kindness ought to have made them more loving and faithful. So God says to Pharaoh, or of Pharaoh, I have hardened his heart, that is, my forbearance against my intention has simply made him more stiffnecked and presumptuous.

P. 285: The Paschal Lamb to be eaten in one house only, that is, we cannot at the same time partake of Christ in the Church and in a heretical or schismatical communion.

P. 994: David's eating the shewbread prefigured that his descendant, the Messiah, was to discharge at the same time the functions of King and Priest.

P. 1089: Origen's Jew told him that the Scriptures are like many homes contained in one house, while to each home is affixed a key not opening the house to which it is assigned. Hence the labor is to find here and there the key pertaining to each particular door. That is, if we would understand one place of Scripture we shall find its solution in itself, but by resorting to other places for the clues by which it is to be understood. Hence St. Paul says "comparing spiritual things with spiritual."

In Psalmos. Ps. xxi.

P. 1253–56: Passage implying it seems Catholic doctrine as to our Lord's birth and as to His having been even in infancy perfect in wisdom and knowledge.

438

Extracts from the Early Fathers

P. 1257: The bones of the Pasch not to be broken are the Dogmas of the Church.

In Jeremiam.

P. 356: The perpetual generation of the Son by the Father. Illustrated by the perpetual production of light on the part of a luminary and of wisdom in the mind of the wise.

Commentary on St. Matthew.

P. 989: Leaven stands always for teaching. Hence leaven was never to be offered with the Sacrifices as signifying that prayers must never teach but simply ask or render glory to God.

P. 1073.: He supposes St. Peter to have said, " Lord, it is good for us to be here," under the instigation of the same evil spirit which had tempted him to oppose the Lord's passion some days before, on account of which evil spirit the Lord had then styled him " Satan and a scandal."

P. 1556–7: Recognizes and states the difference between the " visio abstractiva et visio intuitiva " of God and clearly asserts the Beatific Vision.

Commentary on St. John's Gospel.

Tom. I. p. 52: Every true Christian the son of Mary.

Tom. II. p. 129: Ascribes the procession of the Holy Spirit to the Son.

Tom. II. p. 145: He implies that the sanctification and immortality are essentially " indebita."

In Matthæum, Tom. XI.

P. 548: Something as to the Eucharist, which implies more or less clearly the Real Presence.

P. 1128–29: The question " Who is the greater? " suggested by our Lord's having paid tribute for Himself and Peter alone.

Rt. Rev. A. A. Curtis, D.D.

Libellus de Oratione, Tom. I.

P. 448 : Invocation of Angels and Saints. In this same treatise are many quotations from the deutero-canonical books.

P. 540–4 : seems to teach purgatory very plainly.

ST. CHRYSOSTOM

Epistola 1ᵃ ad Olympiadem.

P. 554 : Christ scourged ἐν μεσημβρίᾳ μέσῃ.

Epistola 2ᵃ ad eandem.

P. 565 : Job knew nothing of the resurrection.

Epistola 4ᵃ ad eandem.

P. 592 : Job was older than Moses.

Vol. III. p. 20 : Peter the coryphæus of the Apostles — the mouth of the disciples, the pillar of the Church, the fundament of the faith, the basis of the confession, the fisher of the world. He bringing up our race from the deeps of error unto Heaven.

P. 174–5 : Πέτραν γὰρ κοιλαίνει ῥανὶς ὑδάτων ἐνδελεχοῦσα.

P. 197–8 : the distinction between counsel and pre-cept.

Adversus Judæos.

P. 951 : " Peter first of the Apostles and entrusted with the whole world."

Hom. VIII. in Epistolam ad Philippenses.

P. 246 : " If he had lived perhaps he would have changed, one says. But God would not have taken him if he had been going to be changed. For He that is doing everything for our salvation, why would not He suffer him to do better? If He spares those who do not change, much rather would He spare those going to amend."

(Confirmed by Cyrill Alex. Vol. V. Comment. in St. Matt. p. 393.)

Extracts from the Early Fathers

Vol. XIII. p. 279: Some thought the term "genuine yokefellow" an address to St. Paul's wife. But St. Chrysostom denies it.

Vol. II. p. 506: Questioning and seeking, incompatible with faith.

P. 554: Bishops excel presbyters in the power only of ordination.

P. 555: Angels did not see the Son of God till after the Incarnation.

ST. GREGORY NYSSEN

Vita Moysis.

P. 95: Transubstantiation. Perpetual Virginity of Mary.

P. 338: Two angels according to tradition to each man.

P. 357: Another reason for not breaking the bones of the Paschal Lamb: Bones are broken in order to get at the marrow, the innermost part of the animal. In our dogmas for which bones stand, there is an innermost something which is not for man at present. And we must break the dogmas only in the attempt to get at their marrow or their deepest and most hidden meaning.

P. 421: Ascribes the speaking of the ass of Balaam not to the power of God, but to that of the demon and throughout he considers Balaam not as in any wise a prophet of God, but that of the Devil. Illustrates his speaking the truth by reference to the demons of the New Testament who gave testimony to the Lord against their own will.

P. 1053: "For this Birth was without travail as without marriage. But as a Son was given to us without a father so also the child without travail was born. For as the Virgin did not know how the divinely received Body was composed, so neither was she sensible of the birth, the prophecy indeed bearing witness to the painlessness of this Birth. For, saith Isaias: 'Be-

441

Rt. Rev. A. A. Curtis, D.D.

fore the coming of the pangs of delivery she produced and brought forth a Male.'"

Vol. III. p. 524: "That then, power of choice might remain with our nature and yet that evil might be at the same time obliterated, the wisdom of God contrived this method, to wit, to leave man in that state which he had himself chosen, that having tasted evil and having learned by trial what an exchange he had made, he might return through his own desire willingly to the first blessedness. Having purged his nature from everything irrational and concupiscent as being a mere burden either during the present life by prayer and philosophy or after his departure hence by the purgation of the smelting fire." A clear testimony in favor of purgatory.

P. 312: "Through Peter He (Christ) gave to the Bishops the keys of the celestial honors."

ST. CYRIL OF ALEXANDRIA

Vol. I. p. 513: "Corban as it is a gift," explained.

Vol. II. p. 285: "The divinely illuminated Peter, he having precedence among the disciples and overstepping the others."

P. 308: The scope of the divinely inspired Scripture is to signify the mystery of Christ through as many things as possible. One might liken the Scripture to a splendid and distinguished city, having not one image only of the king but a great many and these in every place conspicuously set up.

Vol. IV. p. 377. Commentary upon Joel — ἴδιον αὐτοῦ τε, (υἱοῦ) καὶ ἐν αὐτῷ, καὶ ἐξ αὐτοῦ τὸ Πνεῦμά ἐστιν.

Vol. V. p. 432. Comment upon St. Matthew: Transubstantiation.

Vol. VI. p. 420: St. John's Gospel.

"Search the Scriptures," indicative, not imperative.

P. 456: Item.

Five loaves of barley, five books of Moses. Two

Extracts from the Early Fathers

fishes, the truth through the Apostles, fishermen.

P. 722: But she (Mary) as yet exercising authority over her son on account of the exceedingly great subjection of the Saviour and as at the same time knowing through much experience this subjection even in the midst of His divine power, says " they have no wine."

Vol. IX. p. 269: Perpetual virginity of Mary asserted.

ST. GREGORY NAZIANZEN

Vol. II. p. 195: Dost thou not see that of the disciples of Christ, all of whom are high and all worthy of the election, one was called the rock (ἡ πέτρα) and was entrusted with the foundation of the Church?

P. 352: "Since one swallow does not make a spring."

P. 369: " Who will be surety that the end will tarry for our cure and that the judgment shall not receive us still in debt and needing the burning there."

Oratio I. *contra Julianum.*

Cap. 62: For it is not according to nature that the leopard should rub away his spots or an Ethiopian his blackness.

Cap. 59: " Of whom (the martyrs) are the great honors and assemblies, by whom Devils are chased away and diseases cured, of whom the bodies alone have power equal to that possessed by their souls, when touched or venerated. Some drops of the blood of whom or some small signs of their sufferings produce the same effects as their bodies."

Cap. 99: " Of our legislation some points are imposed under necessity so that to those not observing there is danger. But other provisions are not of necessity but are left to our choice, and such that if not observed, no peril results to the non-observance."

Oratio 37, P. VIII. p. 292: *Separation merely* granted in the case of adultery on the part of the wife, — nothing else conceded, and this because of the vitiation of progeny.

Rt. Rev. A. A. Curtis, D.D.

Oratio 39, P. XIX. p. 357 end: Seems a clear insinuation of the fire of Purgatory.

CLEMENS ALEXANDRINUS

Vol. I., *Pædagoge*, L. I. p. 365: " Honey the sweetest of things is productive of bile; as the good is of contempt. But mustard diminishes bile, that is, wrath. It is also destructive of phlegm, that is, pride."

Vol. I., *Stromata*, L. III. p. 1109: Epiphanes, son of Carpocrates, teaches exact and full blown communism.

P. 1128: The Pythagorean prohibition of beans referred to the fact that the use of beans was supposed to produce sterility in women.

L. II. cap. 23: All marriage, adultery if made after divorce.

EPIPHANIUS

Vol. I. L. II. p. 1024: Mention of subdeacon as obliged to continence.

JUSTIN MARTYR

Dialogue with Trypho:

P. 657: Mentions the cave of Bethlehem as the birthplace of Christ.

P. 712: Item.

Analogy between Eve and the Blessed Virgin Mary.

ST. BASIL

Vol. I., *Hexaemeron,* Hom. 5, p. 109: At this time and in these parts a pine wood when cut down grows up in oak. And the same was true in St. Basil's time and country.

Vol. II., *Comment. in Isaiam,* p. 548: Auricular Confession.

Extracts from the Early Fathers

Epistle 69: " It appeared to us requisite to send to the Bishop of Rome to take cognizance of matters here, and to give sentence that since it would be difficult to send thence any to us by common decree, he himself may exercise full authority as to the matter, and having chosen men able to bear the fatigues of the journey and sufficient by virtue of combined meekness and rigor of conduct to admonish the perverse among us discreetly and with due consideration of the time making use of their word."

Epistle 93: Communion in one kind and at home.

ARISTOTLE

Nikomachean Ethics: One swallow does not make spring.

P. 1118: A man gluttonous wished his neck as long as that of a crane.

EURIPIDES

Electra, 294–297: Grief never comes to the stupid but to the wise. And it is not without cost that the wise are so wise in their sentiments.

Rt. Rev. A. A. Curtis D.D.

TACITUS

Annales VI., cap. 28, A. C. 34 : Phenix appeared in Egypt.

ÆSCHYLUS

Agamemnon, 251–252 : Τὸ προκλύειν δ' ἤλυσιν προχαιρέτω· ἴσου δε τῷ προστένειν.

(*The following extracts from St. Bernard were found written on the cover of the Bishop's note-book.*)

St. Bernard. *Lætatus. De Passione.*

P. 1596 : " Circumcisio delebat in patribus originale peccatum sicut Baptismus in nobis." [1]

P. 1598 : " Quæ sola (id est, virgo) per illud triste sabbatum stetit in fide et salvata fuit Ecclesia in ipsa sola. Propter quod aptissime tota Ecclesia in laudem et gloriam ejusdem virginis diem sabbati per totius anni circulum celebrare consuevit." [2]

---

[1] "Circumcision blotted out original sin in the [Old Testament] fathers as Baptism does in us."—EDITOR, 1991.

[2] "In her alone (that is, the Virgin) the Church stood fast in faith and was saved throughout that sorrowful Saturday. Wherefore is it most fitting that the whole Church has been accustomed, throughout the course of the entire year, to celebrate Saturday in praise and honor of this same Virgin."—EDITOR, 1991.

If you have enjoyed this book, consider making your next selection from among the following . . .

Prices guaranteed through June 30, 1993.

Autobiography of St. Margaret Mary.................... 4.00
Thoughts and Sayings of St. Margaret Mary.............. 3.00
Life of St. Margaret Mary. Bougaud....................12.00
Little Bk./Work/Infinite Love. de la Touche.............. 1.50
Voice of the Saints. Comp. by Johnston................. 5.00
St. Teresa of Ávila. William Thomas Walsh..............18.00
Isabella of Spain—The Last Crusader. Wm. T. Walsh......16.50
Characters of the Inquisition. Wm. T. Walsh.............12.00
Philip II. William Thomas Walsh. H.B..................37.50
Blood-Drenched Altars—Cath. Comment. Hist. Mexico.....16.50
Self-Abandonment to Divine Providence. de Caussade......15.00
Way of the Cross. Liguorian........................... .75
Way of the Cross. Franciscan.......................... .75
Modern Saints—Their Lives & Faces. Bk. 1. Ann Ball.....15.00
Saint Michael and the Angels. Approved Sources......... 5.50
Dolorous Passion of Our Lord. Anne C. Emmerich.......13.50
Our Lady of Fatima's Peace Plan from Heaven. Booklet.... .75
Divine Favors Granted to St. Joseph. Pere Binet......... 4.00
St. Joseph Cafasso—Priest of the Gallows. St. J. Bosco.... 3.00
Catechism of the Council of Trent. McHugh/Callan.......20.00
Padre Pio—The Stigmatist. Fr. Charles Carty.............12.50
Why Squander Illness? Frs. Rumble & Carty.............. 2.00
Fatima—The Great Sign. Francis Johnston............... 7.00
Heliotropium—Conformity of Human Will to Divine.......11.00
Charity for the Suffering Souls. Fr. John Nageleisen.......13.50
Devotion to the Sacred Heart of Jesus. Verheylezoon.......12.50
Sermons on Prayer. St. Francis de Sales................. 3.50
Sermons on Our Lady. St. Francis de Sales.............. 9.00
Sermons for Lent. St. Francis de Sales.................10.00
Sermons for Advent & Christmas. St. Francis de Sales..... 7.00
Fundamentals of Catholic Dogma. Ott..................16.50
Litany of the Blessed Virgin Mary. (100 cards)............ 5.00
Who Is Padre Pio? Radio Replies Press................. 1.00
Child's Bible History. Knecht.......................... 4.00
The Life of Christ. 4 Vols. H.B. Anne C. Emmerich......55.00
St. Anthony—The Wonder Worker of Padua. Stoddard...... 3.50
The Precious Blood. Fr. Faber........................11.00
The Holy Shroud & Four Visions. Fr. O'Connell......... 1.50
Clean Love in Courtship. Fr. Lawrence Lovasik........... 2.00
The Prophecies of St. Malachy. Peter Bander............. 4.00
The Secret of the Rosary. St. Louis De Montfort......... 3.00
The History of Antichrist. Rev. P. Huchede.............. 2.50
Where We Got the Bible. Fr. Henry Graham............. 5.00
Hidden Treasure—Holy Mass. St. Leonard............... 4.00
Imitation of the Sacred Heart of Jesus. Fr. Arnoudt........13.50
The Life & Glories of St. Joseph. Edward Thompson......12.50

At your bookdealer or direct from the publisher.

Prices guaranteed through June 30, 1993.